D0850463

*Elite Activism and
Political Transformation in China*

MARY BACKUS RANKIN

Elite Activism and
Political Transformation in China
Zhejiang Province, 1865-1911

Stanford University Press, Stanford, California

1986

Stanford University Press
Stanford, California
© 1986 by the Board of Trustees of the
Leland Stanford Junior University
Printed in the United States of America

CIP data appear at the end of the book

Published with the assistance of
China Publication Subventions

For Louise Laidlaw Backus and Dana Converse Backus

PREFACE

This book began long ago as a quick paper on
the early twentieth-century railway movement in the Chinese
coastal provinces of Zhejiang and Jiangsu. While reading materials on the 1907 demonstrations against a British loan, I realized that neither the people involved nor their organizations
nor their writings fitted easily into the historical categories
conventionally applied to the early twentieth century. Looking
for explanations led backward in time. Eventually I settled on
the half-century between the end of the Taiping Rebellion and
the 1911 Revolution as a useful period for examining changes
in political relationships at the end of the imperial period in
China.

Historians are now turning their attention to two great interlocking themes in nineteenth- and twentieth-century Chinese
history: state-building and social mobilization. This book is
the obverse of studies that focus on governmental structure and
state capacity to intervene in society and control it. Its topic,
broadly speaking, is the rise of political opposition within the
late imperial system. My emphasis on the societal side of the
state-societal nexus arises from an observation that, although
both the Qing and the major republican governments initiated

changes that contributed in the long run to transforming the
Chinese polity, they did not succeed in doing so themselves.
The most dramatic changes in politics and state structure came
through a societal mobilization that governments could not
control, co-opt, or suppress. The route to change led through
revolutions.

In looking at the social mobilization that led to the 1911
Revolution, I have moved away from established patterns of
analysis in terms of the reform and revolutionary movements
from the mid-1890's onward to consider a longer process of organization, politicization, and mobilization, beginning with
subtle shifts in the interaction between government and societal leaders and ending in revolution. Doing so calls attention
not only to the changing character of Chinese elites but also to
reasons why some members of the social groups that had benefited most from the imperial state also had reason to oppose it.
This approach, moreover, suggests that there were complex in-
teractions between nineteenth-century foreign and domestic
crises, which eventually stimulated competitive state and societal initiatives.

Local records are the major sources for this study, but, even
though I concentrate upon one province, the territory is too
large for the kind of detailed socioeconomic analysis that can
be undertaken for still smaller areas. In any case, the issues of
social mobilization and state-societal relations do not belong
solely to local history. Nor am I chronicling a devolution of political power from the center to localities. Instead, I am looking
for intersections between activities of local elites and national
political trends; I am trying to discover how, under the conditions set by the late imperial state structure, these intersections affected the national, more than the local, sphere. Events
in Zhejiang province illustrate the outward thrust of locally
based social initiative from the most commercially developed
parts of China during the late Qing. New conditions and new
political dynamics were introduced during the republican period, but a fuller understanding of what was happening to the
imperial political structure is essential to interpret the events
that followed.

The insights of Europeanist historians of state-making and

social protest, the approaches of anthropologists working on Chinese society, and the frameworks suggested by core-peripheral regional analysis have all contributed to this study. Nevertheless, it does not strictly follow the methods of, or pursue the same questions as, any one part of this rather diverse col lection of scholarship. Incomplete historical records and variable data are familiar problems to social historians of China. Extrapolating such data to national political issues creates still greater methodological problems. Difficulties in finding satisfactory solutions should not, however, discourage all efforts at sociopolitical research. To transcend the anecdotal level of historical writing, I have illustrated my main points with detailed examples showing how structures fitted together in a few relatively well-documented localities, in combination with more fragmentary evidence drawn from a variety of places. Where there is enough meaningful data, I have used tables. Much of the material is, however, sub-statistical. Tables are helpful in gaining a perspective on individual examples and core-peripheral differences, but the reader should always keep in mind the familiar warnings about the reliability of statistics in Chinese history.

The available material offers little basis for quantifying the inherently nebulous intersection of social initiative and national politics. The general frameworks presented in the introduction are my attempt to make sense out of the evidence found in Zhejiang. The possibility of writing several monographs on each of the general points underlines the gaps in our knowledge of Chinese socioeconomic and political history as well as the probability of different lines of development in different parts of the country. I hope that other scholars will investigate the extent that the processes described in this work fit events in other regions of China and that they will examine more fully the beginnings of these processes in the eighteenth and early nineteenth centuries. The further reevaluation of state-societal relationships in China and the exploration of different manifestations of analogous problems in Chinese and European history are among the many other exciting possibilities for future research.

This study would never have been completed without the

splendid collection of local gazetteers at the Orientalia Division of the Library of Congress, and my respect for the disciplines of both history and Chinese studies owes much to the standards inculcated by John K. Fairbank. Among the many people who have helped shape my views through discussion and writing are, in order only alphabetical, Marianne Bastid, Helen Chauncey, Paul Cohen, James Cole, Arif Dirlik, Jerry Dennerline, Prasenjit Duara, Philip Kuhn, Susan Mann, Jonathan Ocko, Elizabeth Perry, James Polachek, William Rowe, Keith Schoppa, John Schrecker, G. William Skinner, Judith Whitbeck, and Madeline Zelin. If any of them thinks this a strange bunch of bedfellows, comfort may be found in the thought that I must bear even more than the usual share of responsibility for the final product. On a more personal level, this book is dedicated to my parents, Louise Laidlaw Backus and Dana Converse Backus, both of whom set high standards of achievement. My husband, Douglas Rankin, and our daughters, Katharine and Andrea Rankin, constantly provided balance by energetically pursuing their own goals, thereby proving that life need not be bounded by Chinese gazetteers even while having to maneuver among them.

M.B.R.

CONTENTS

APPENDIXES

REFERENCE MATTER

MAPS AND TABLES

Maps

Tables

NOTE ON ROMANIZATION

With very few exceptions this book uses the *pinyin* romanization system. To avoid excessive consistency, I use the long-established postal system spelling of Yangtze. To avoid charges of greater Mandarin chauvinism, I use well-known Cantonese place names like Canton and Hong Kong. The names of all Chinese authors of Chinese works are listed in *pinyin* in the Bibliography. Names of Chinese authors of works written in English are spelled as they appear on the book or article. If a person's name is spelled in two different ways, it is cross-referenced.

Elite Activism and
Political Transformation in China

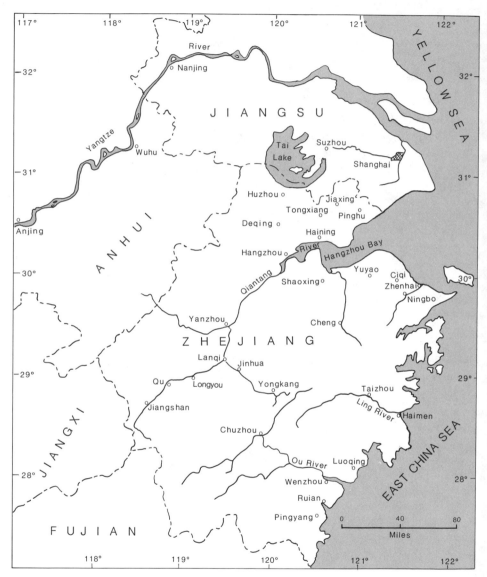

Map 1. Zhejiang and Vicinity

ONE

Introduction

At the beginning of the twentieth century, the governmental structure in China began to change, and oppositionist political movements arose with remarkable rapidity. These developments led to the 1911 Revolution against the Qing dynasty (1644–1911), an uprising that ended the imperial state in China and set in motion processes that would continue to shape politics well into the following republican period. It is not surprising therefore that historians have studied this decade intensively. Nor is it surprising that the heirs to the 1911 Revolution in China have devoted most of their attention to the revolutionaries and the other men who introduced strikingly new ideas and practices from Western countries. In the resulting literature, brief episodes of reform or revolution from the mid-1890's to 1911 appear as new phenomena, antithetical to the social and political organization of the past. Unable to control these movements, the Qing dynasty appears as weak and corrupt, too far along in a familiar process of cyclical decay to save itself from internal rebellion or the country from foreign invasion.

A closer look at these political movements suggests that broad processes of long duration were at work and that events can not be explained by the rise of new classes or heightened foreign intrusion alone. Considerable segments of the mobilized populace were neither members of new social groups nor strong advocates of Western theories. The rapidity with which elite organizations grew during the last fifteen years of the dynasty suggests that there was already a social basis for new institutions and new political demands. The vigor with which officials promoted change from within the government, moreover, suggests that even though the Manchu rulers themselves had certainly weakened, the government as a whole was not hopelessly decayed.

It is plausible to argue that both Chinese elites and the Chinese state had begun to change before the late nineteenth century. Western imperialism then accelerated these changes and brought them to a critical point by introducing new industrial technology and organization, tying parts of the Chinese economy to Western-dominated international markets, stimulating social change, threatening Chinese territorial and economic sovereignty, and providing examples of new kinds of political institutions and relationships. Despite this crucial foreign role, it is still possible to trace indigenous social trends, dating back to the early nineteenth century and before, into the 1890's and 1900's, when they became part of a new political impetus under different structural conditions.

In this study I stress the changing relationships between the late imperial state and its officials and the elites at the top of social structures outside the bureaucracy. The activists upon whom I focus included people prominent in provincial or regional networks as well as those in the top layers of district or market town societies. Within a state-societal framework, a salient characteristic of these elites is that, even if they had been or would later become officials, they undertook the activities described in subsequent chapters in their capacities as social leaders.

Behind the changes in state-societal relationships of the nineteenth century were gradual changes in the character of social elites that reflected progressive commercialization and urbanization from about the sixteenth century. One manifestation of the changes was the emergence of an organizational capacity within existing elite society that altered relationships between elites and the state. Just as the social changes produced by foreign trade and industry followed a longer evolution caused by indigenous commercialization, so the rapid political changes at the beginning of the twentieth century rested on long-term shifts in relations between the bureaucratic state and social leaders. Under these circumstances, de facto changes that redefined political relationships often occurred well before conscious demands for structural change. Such changes did not occur uniformly throughout China. They were most marked in the economically advanced areas of the Lower Yangtze, and also of the Middle Yangtze and the Canton Delta.

The Taiping Rebellion marked a decisive shift in the balance between the state and elite society, in part because it brought about widespread and sometimes persisting local militarization. More important, post-rebellion reconstruction fostered a rapid and permanent expansion of elite-managed, quasi-governmental local activities. In economically advanced areas this expansion was reinforced by the growth of other public and private activities as a result of foreign trade. Career opportunities opened up, and activist gentry and merchants reached out for more power and broadened their conceptions of their roles in public affairs. In the process they expanded public activities across administrative boundaries. Lines between local and national concerns began to blur, and assertive elites began to engage in new kinds of competition with official representatives of the state.

Heightened foreign intrusion, beginning in the 1870's, played a large part in accelerating and politicizing these embryonic changes in state-societal relationships. When the state failed to repulse the Western invaders, members of the old-regime elite began to lose confidence in the very legitimacy of the political system; they became more assertive in demanding an influence on national policy. From the mid-1890's until the end of the dynasty, a series of nationalistically infused elite mobilizations involved both the old-regime elite and new social groups. The elites organized across what have often been treated as separate local, provincial, and metropolitan levels. The mobilizations became progressively politicized and ended in irreconcilable conflict with the Qing state.

In examining these processes, I have sought ways to explain situations in which events seemed to burst through the common distinctions made in Chinese social history. One such distinction is the division between the local elites in district cities and towns, provincial elites, and national elites. In the late Qing these levels were becoming mixed up, and I have looked for explanations in core-peripheral distinctions, the involvement of cosmopolitan elites in district and sub-district management, trade and population mobility, the networks connecting elites at different urban levels, the growth of public activity outside the bureaucratic structure, and the impingement of national problems on local societies.

A distinction is also made between the long-range changes that were slowly altering institutions and relationships and the rapid, discontinuous changes that ultimately produced revolution. Crises of rebellion and war frequently linked the two, revealing the political implications of de facto change within the rather elastic, existing structures. The problem has been to locate the centers of power and define the changes within the theoretically unified structures characteristic of the late imperial polity. My solution has been to look for the sources of initiative in action or decision-making. During the nineteenth century, changes in the loci of initiative shifted power away from the bureaucracy toward the social elites. The concept of initiative also provides a key to the origin of demands for participation and representation; it suggests how shifts in state and social power on the local level might not simply imply devolution and disintegration but relate back up to the distribution of power at the center of government. Views of national policy-making that assumed an upward flow of initiative and opinion from social leaders or lower-level officials differed fundamentally from those that assumed a downward flow of authority or sought to control social activism for the purposes of the state.

Questions of how Chinese outside the government organized, developed political demands, mobilized a following, and finally took action against the Qing state lead into broad explanations that include the effects of the existing governmental structure, indigenous social and economic conditions, and international factors. Sweeping questions of state-societal relations can be reduced to more manageable proportions by focusing on a specific geographical area, certain spheres of activity, and particular segments of the elite. I will approach them here by studying elite public management within Zhejiang province from 1865 to 1911. This period, from the end of the Taiping Rebellion to the 1911 Revolution, was seminal in the change from an apolitical social activism to a politicized challenge to the government. Zhejiang, on the south-central China coast, was mainly within the commercially and culturally advanced Lower Yangtze region, and the economies of parts of the province were connected to Shanghai. It is therefore a good example of those parts of the country where wealth, involvement in government, and exposure to foreign pressures fostered social activity and an awareness of current affairs. Although Zhejiang was no more typical than any other Chinese province, the processes identified there may serve as bases for comparative investigations in other regions during this period.

Elite public managerial activities were an important arena of state-societal interaction that could reflect broader sociopolitical trends. I will concentrate on the societal and managerial side of the interaction out of a conviction that it did the most to upset old political relationships. The 1911 Revolution was a broad political uprising of the elites in the economically advanced areas of south and central China; it had a different background from the subsequent twentieth-century social revolution. Although the processes can be traced throughout both periods, the revolution itself was not continuous. The great rebellions of the mid-nineteenth century, involving large numbers of peasants, failed to bring down the dynasty. Although rural discontent did not disappear, it was the elites that had the organizational capacity first to erode Qing rule and later to challenge it politically. The inability of these elites to establish

a strong, new government then opened the way for the violent
social and political redefinitions that eventually culminated in
another kind of revolution.

The Social Effects of Chinese Commercialization
and Foreign Capitalist Intrusion

Historians of revolution in modern Europe generally start
with the rise of capitalism, and Marxist historians have looked
for similar Chinese antecedents to a bourgeois revolution in
1911. Increasingly extensive research has unearthed many examples of capitalist relationships during the late imperial period,[1] but it has not demonstrated that these "sprouts" coalesced
into an indigenous capitalism. On the contrary, it appears that
China remained a predominantly agrarian, peasant society.
Even the capitalism that unquestionably existed by the twentieth century did not fundamentally change this characteristic
of much of the country although the economy did become increasingly commercialized. The commercial expansion that began during the Ming dynasty (1368–1644) continued during
the Qing after a relatively short hiatus during the seventeenth
century.[2] This expansion was in part caused by, and then interacted with, demographic growth, increasing the Chinese population from about 200 million in 1750 to about 410 million in
1850.[3] The quantitative increase in trade was not accompanied
by substantial technological changes in agriculture or industry,
such as might have led to a marked increase in productivity per
unit of labor, or by widespread changes in relations of production. However, the rising population pressure did elicit increases in the food supply; more land was brought under cultivation, seed strains were improved, and more labor-intensive
methods were adopted.[4] Agriculture also became more oriented
to the market, and handicraft production rose as growing numbers of people in towns and cities increased the demand for
grain, agricultural specialties, and household goods.

Even though per capita expansion slowed or stagnated in the
late eighteenth and early nineteenth centuries, the total volume
of commerce continued to rise.[5] This commercialization did not

have as fundamental an impact on class structure as European capitalism did, but it was a dynamic factor in the late Qing that had important social and organizational consequences within the existing boundaries of late imperial society.

Commercialization encouraged the fusion of merchants and gentry into a vigorous, numerically expanding elite whose power rested on varying combinations of landownership, trade, usury, and degree holding. The fusion, which was never complete, can be most easily documented in the wealthier upper layers of elite society. Despite numerous local variations, merchants and gentry can no longer be considered two separate classes in the nineteenth century—particularly if one looks at the career patterns of entire families as opposed to isolated individuals.[6] Historians have acknowledged that the economic and social status of merchants rose during the late imperial period,[7] but they have been slower to see that these changes affected gentry as well. Major interpretations of gentry society recognize that gentry received income and power from various sources, and some authors have argued that considerable social mobility existed. Nevertheless, the picture of the class as a whole has been static, especially in analyses of lower-degree holders.[8] My own view is that commercialization and demographic growth produced changes in the character and interests of gentry as well as merchants. Although these social changes were initially less unsettling than those caused by the Industrial Revolution in Europe, gentry ties to the bureaucratic state began to fray as the size of the elite population increased and the range of available careers expanded.

Commercialization and population growth also stimulated social organization outside the existing bureaucracy. One obvious example was the proliferation of trade guilds and native place associations during the nineteenth century. Private banking and other commercial support facilities also gradually developed, as did local institutions for such matters as water control.[9] Lineage institutions, which had a long history in parts of central and south China, represented another form of social organization that expanded during the Qing. Such examples in the respectable, settled sectors of society were matched by il-

legal or quasi-legal organizations of socially peripheral or in-
secure elements. All these associations were likely to encourage collective demands and collective action and to contribute
to conflicts between different components of society, between
different communities, and between social groups and the state.

Demographic growth, commercialization, and urbanization
fostered population mobility. As barren lands and border areas
filled up, permanent migration was rivaled by temporary, occupational or livelihood-related movements of sojourners from
all levels of society who returned home annually or at greater
and more irregular intervals.[10] Two consequences of this mobility were a weakening of governmental control over the populace and a constant interchange between lower- and high-order
urban areas. Direct movements between villages and large cities,
or from town to town cut across marketing systems and did not
follow an orderly progression from lower- to next-higher-level
cities in the urban hierarchies.

The economic gap between the core and the peripheral regions grew because urbanization proceeded more rapidly in the
former.[11] Three particularly prosperous and populous areas
existed in the Lower Yangtze, the Canton Delta, and the Middle
Yangtze. Since such areas became centers of both social change
and economic expansion, any political analysis requires an
awareness of core-peripheral distinctions. The disorderly populace of the peripheral areas had always presented military problems that were well understood by the imperial government,
but by the end of the eighteenth century one can discern the
potential for a different kind of challenge from the core areas,
with their increasing population, expanding social organization, and growing wealth.

There were certain built-in limitations to such changes. The
relatively balanced expansion toward integrated marketing systems that occurred within late imperial China[12] did not cause
major class realignments or destroy communal structures. The
new social tendencies associated with commercialization were
most developed in the areas that made the largest contributions to state finances and produced disproportionate shares of
upper-degree holders—who enjoyed high levels of influence

and patronage in the existing political system. Although officials had difficulty controlling this elite, its members still had good reason to identify with the state because they enjoyed access to its representatives. An explanation of the conflict between the merchant-gentry elite of such areas and the state must offer reasons why the gentry component forsook its long allegiance to the political structure.

Foreign trade and imperialism also affected the equilibrium of the nineteenth-century economy and society. China did not become a colony, and foreigners did not displace the existing Chinese rulers and elites. Nor could the large, commercialized, but only partially integrated, agrarian economy of Qing China be completely redirected by imperialist capitalist powers for the benefit of their own economies.[13] External forces were felt most strongly in the coastal areas and major river valleys that were already among the most urbanized parts of the country. Therefore the foreign intrusion first reinforced, and then redirected, the social changes that were already slowly occurring. Within the Lower Yangtze, for instance, the silk trade provided a definite economic stimulus from the mid-nineteenth through the early twentieth century.[14] New opportunities encouraged entrepreneurial activity, created new wealth, and further increased career options. The economic surge further fused the merchant and the gentry elites. Merchants made wealthy by foreign trade were accepted into the gentry. Trade—and later, industrialization—provided the gentry with lucrative and socially acceptable alternatives to scholarship and officeholding. Additional wealth strengthened the elites, and thus their organizations, vis-à-vis the officials.

The factors that reinforced the consolidation of a powerful elite stratum also initiated a fragmentation into new components that, by the end of the Qing, included capitalists, professionals, an urban intelligentsia, and military officers.[15] By the end of the nineteenth century, industrialization had also started to have an impact on the class structure. Newly defined social groups, which were particularly visible in the large cities, began to breach the existing integrative social mechanisms and to erode the links between the elites and the government. This process was just getting under way when the dynasty was overthrown, and it was not by itself enough to explain the 1911 Revolution. The logical conclusion is that the old-regime elite also mobilized against the imperial government. Understanding how this situation came about requires a consideration of the Qing state and its relationships to the elites.

State and Society in Late Imperial China

The term "centralized bureaucratic monarchy" (*junxian*) conveniently sums up the major features of Qing imperial rule through an administrative hierarchy. The general system dated back to the Qin (221–209 B.C.) and Han (206 B.C.–220 A.D.) dynasties, became entrenched during the Song (980–1279), and survived with modifications to 1911. Although contrasted in Chinese thought with an earlier system of decentralized "feudalism" (*fengjian*), it had long been accepted as the only viable political structure.[16]

In theory this was a unified, integrated structure. Authority was centralized in an emperor, whose claims to rule were buttressed by his spiritual role as the intermediary between human society and heaven and legitimized by Confucian ideology. His autocratic power was exercised through a highly educated, relatively small bureaucracy of about twenty thousand regular civil officials during the Qing.[17] Members of the upper classes were tied to the state structure by official examinations, which simultaneously offered a route to participation in government and reinforced the ideological justifications for the existing system. The personal loyalty that officials felt to the emperor was supplemented by complex systems of bureaucratic surveillance and regulation. Local independence was discouraged by a rotation of officials and a "rule of avoidance" that prevented them from serving in their home provinces. There were no effective institutional checks on absolutist power, and the ability of the government to act independently of outside groups was constantly reinforced. One prominent interpretation of Chinese history[18] maintains that absolutism increased throughout the late imperial period as successive dynasties built upon the legacies of their predecessors and nomadic conquerors imposed their rule upon the Chinese. Individual dynasties were subject to cyclical decay as ruling families degenerated, their finances and armies weakened, and corruption invaded the bureaucracy, but the general system survived and solidified.

Although this view requires considerable modification, some of its elements are important to the state-societal relationships stressed in this study. In contrast to the absolutist monarchies that established themselves in Europe from the fifteenth to the seventeenth century, the Qing inherited a well-developed system of centralized government. The Manchu invaders did not have to engage in the extensive process of state formation required of the early modern European rulers,[19] even though it took them several decades to establish military control over all of China. They were able to take over an existing bureaucracy, system of taxation, and legitimizing ideology; they had already developed their armies before the conquest. The concept of a unified, vertical political system was deeply ingrained in China, leaving little room for outside political activity. These kinds of strengths unquestionably retarded political organization and opposition until close to the end of the dynasty.

How then could this power be breached? The rise of European absolutism has sometimes been connected with the early stages of capitalism—in which case it can be argued that monarchs made concessions to the bourgeoisie emerging in the towns in order to enlist its support against the feudal nobility. Alternatively, absolutism has been interpreted as emerging from the crisis of feudalism in Europe. In this view, absolutism reallocated the resources of the existing feudal society to protect the nobility from war and peasant rebellion. It nonetheless allowed room for rising market economies and new classes by linking increases in monarchical power to the protection of private property and the mercantilist promotion of trade and industry.[20] Neither of these cases fits the Chinese situation, and it has generally been assumed that the Qing fell because of a combination of dynastic decline,[21] imperialist pressure, and a belated surge of capitalism.

Detailed research on the Qing government has suggested,

however, that this state structure was not as autonomous as has often been assumed and that the changes during the course of the dynasty were neither in the direction of increased autocracy nor explicable mainly in terms of cyclical decline. The early Qing rulers had not only reestablished the effectiveness of a tax system that had become riddled with devices for evasion; they had also centralized authority in the metropolitan boards more strongly than the Ming rulers before them.[22] They had, moreover, created the Grand Council to institutionalize their personal authority in government. Nevertheless, by the mid-eighteenth century most policy decisions were made collegially by leading members of the bureaucracy, and the imperial ability to make decisions was severely circumscribed.[23] Although emperors sporadically tried to assert their personal power in the early nineteenth century, authority shifted from the throne to major metropolitan officials and subsequently toward governors-general in key provinces. These officials remained supportive of the throne. Therefore, although the rise of the bureaucracy limited personal autocracy, it mitigated the effect of the decline of the ruling house by allowing the government to continue to function during the reigns of young or weak emperors.

Thus the bureaucracy was as important an element in the Qing state as the monarchy. Although early Western travelers had been greatly impressed with the long-established system of selecting officials by merit through the examinations, twentieth-century historians often took a less favorable view, considering the imperial Chinese bureaucracy inferior in differentiation, specialization, and rationalization to those of modern Western states.[24] Bureaucratic corruption and conservatism have also received a share of the blame for China's inability to resist Western imperialism. Nonetheless, detailed studies of the bureaucracy show that it was a sophisticated, highly structured system, governed by its own complex regulations, allowing room for specialization, and capable of adjusting to new situations.[25] It governed the empire for centuries, and the examinations qualifying men for bureaucratic posts connected the interests of the elite to the state by providing status, possibilities for administrative power, opportunities for financial gain, and ideological justifications for the system.[26]

Actually, the state was much less dominant in late imperial society than these views from the top would suggest. The Qing government was chronically underfinanced and therefore superficial.[27] It sought to dominate the critical aspects of political, fiscal, and military power, but it did not penetrate much below the level of the district administrative centers, and it intervened only when it considered its interests clearly at stake. Despite the use of Confucian ideology to instill loyalty to the emperor and obedience to authority, the claims of the Chinese state over the populace do not seem as extensive as those deriving from the organic concept of a strong, interventionist, integrated state that developed in parts of Europe and Latin America.[28] Nor did the Qing rulers seek to impose servile conditions on the peasantry to support a hierarchical system of unlimited service obligation as the Russian tsars did during the sixteenth and seventeenth centuries.[29] Instead the state often relied on the social elite to carry out important functions with relatively little supervision.

The Qing system thus depended to a considerable extent upon shifting adjustments between governmental and societal elements, in which the state was as much an arbitrator as a dictator. Without denying the importance of military force in the early years, it has been suggested that the landholding gentry accepted Manchu rule in the seventeenth century in return for the confirmation of their local positions, the restoration of order, and a continuing share in the government.[30] After the large estates of the Ming dynasty were broken up, the gentry did not appear threatening to the Qing rulers. Various local balances could therefore be established between the interests of elite society, officials, and peasants who had won some customary guarantees of security.[31] Such adjustments were precarious and might well favor landlords over peasants. However, they functioned well enough to maintain stability in prosperous periods, and both the officials and the elite recognized the advantages of a system in which each checked the destabilizing abuses of the other.

This minimalist form of government was an effective and inexpensive way to govern a large agrarian country during periods of economic stability or slow expansion. It was poorly suited for a governmental effort to develop the country's resources and was ill equipped either to deal with major crises or to maintain state control in periods of sustained or rapid socioeconomic change. It also allowed considerable latitude for elite activity outside the state structure.

The local elite role vis-à-vis the state and society has often been conceptualized as brokerage. Gentry, with connections to both the state and local communities, interpreted the needs and mediated the demands of one to the other—but maintained considerable freedom to pursue their own interests. Members of the elite supported, or were kept in check by, the state during periods of dynastic vigor but asserted private kinship, local, or class interests as the dynasty weakened. Officials in China were thus involved in an endless, fluctuating game of balancing local conflicts and cooperating with, or controlling, local elites.[32] For all its permutations, this was ultimately a static game in which the total amount of political power remained about the same. Conflict was integral to the political system, and although it might be an overstatement to say that it served to integrate state and society, it did not in the long run tear them apart.

This interpretation overemphasizes the unchanging natures of both the state and the social elites in late imperial China, but it does again point to some significant differences between Chinese and European history. The European states were established at the beginning of a period of rapid economic expansion that altered the class structure and the relations between government and society not long after absolutism was firmly established, whereas the basic elements of the Chinese late imperial state persisted through centuries of slow economic growth. By the nineteenth century, however, population growth and commercialization had begun to exert pressure for fundamental changes in China as well, thereby upsetting the existing balances between state and society.

noting management by the people (*min*) or gentry. The word public, itself, was perhaps first applied in water control—a basic sphere of collective activity where there were obvious differences between projects that benefited individual land-owners, projects that involved the whole locality, and large state-sponsored projects that affected wide areas. It was easily extended to other activities such as famine relief, education, and care of the aged, poor, and sick, when they were undertaken by local men who were not officials. By the time of the New Policies after 1900, the categories of official, public, and private routinely appeared in governmental documents.[34]

These spheres were not altogether functionally distinct. Private interests might be pursued under the guise of community action. Trade, kinship, and religious organizations might perform services beneficial to the whole community.[35] Officials retained the right to intervene, even when they did not supervise public activities directly. Under the unitary structure of the late imperial polity, public could not be defined by interest groups making demands upon the state or competing with each other. Neither was it synonymous with the interests and activity of the state. The significance of the public category lay in providing an intermediate arena where the state and society met. In the nineteenth and twentieth centuries it was a dynamic and expanding sphere, which neither governmental nor societal leaders could fully claim as their own. Late Qing officials might look upon public activity as community implementation of government policy. Elites, however, might take initiatives in pursuit of community goals that led them into making policy outside of bureaucratic channels. The public sphere became a place where new power might be sought, new conflicts could arise, and new relationships could develop.

The public sphere grew during the Qing as population size and mobility, growing trade, increasing numbers of market centers, and expanding social organization made the administrative capacity of the bureaucracy obsolete.[36] By the end of the eighteenth century, the Qing government could no longer intervene vigorously in such matters as grain distribution and population movement.[37] After its failure in the eighteenth century

State-Societal Relationships During the Late Qing

Nineteenth-century Chinese history is filled with manifestations traditionally associated with dynastic collapse: ineffectual rulers, bureaucratic corruption, decay of water control systems, foreign invasions, and popular unrest. Such indications help explain governmental weakness in the face of social change but not why the imperial system, as opposed to a specific dynasty, ended in 1911. More corrosive changes came from the movement of elites away from their established relations with state power. These changes can be seen in two phenomena of the latter half of the nineteenth century: the growth of public spheres of activity outside the bureaucracy, and the emergence of oppositional public opinion.

The public sphere. The concept of public activity was well established in China by the mid-nineteenth century. In Confucian theory, public (*gong*) concern was a general good define by the state, as opposed to the private, selfish (*si*) interests one or a few. Officials, as the representatives of imperial ber olence, were the ideal public guardians.[33] In any locality t' was also a generally recognized area of community inter which consensual decisions were articulated by comm leaders and services were managed by local men. Al most visible in the villages, such spheres existed at hi ban levels as well. Because the state did not routine vene, the informal means of local decision-making w' developed.

As I use the term here, "public" retains a consid' munal element but refers more specifically to the alized, extrabureaucratic management of matte' important by both the community and the state agement by elites thus contrasted with official (*guan*), and with private (*si*) activities of indiv' religions, businesses, and organizations that fied with the whole community. Public wa' used without need of explanation, that impl' tionship to the government from those of gories. This use of "public" may have evol' noting management by the people (*min*) or gentry. The word public, itself, was perhaps first applied in water control—a basic sphere of collective activity where there were obvious differences between projects that benefited individual land-owners, projects that involved the whole locality, and large state-sponsored projects that affected wide areas. It was easily extended to other activities such as famine relief, education, and care of the aged, poor, and sick, when they were undertaken by local men who were not officials. By the time of the New Policies after 1900, the categories of official, public, and private routinely appeared in governmental documents.[34]

These spheres were not altogether functionally distinct. Private interests might be pursued under the guise of community action. Trade, kinship, and religious organizations might perform services beneficial to the whole community.[35] Officials retained the right to intervene, even when they did not supervise public activities directly. Under the unitary structure of the late imperial polity, public could not be defined by interest groups making demands upon the state or competing with each other. Neither was it synonymous with the interests and activity of the state. The significance of the public category lay in providing an intermediate arena where the state and society met. In the nineteenth and twentieth centuries it was a dynamic and expanding sphere, which neither governmental nor societal leaders could fully claim as their own. Late Qing officials might look upon public activity as community implementation of government policy. Elites, however, might take initiatives in pursuit of community goals that led them into making policy outside of bureaucratic channels. The public sphere became a place where new power might be sought, new conflicts could arise, and new relationships could develop.

The public sphere grew during the Qing as population size and mobility, growing trade, increasing numbers of market centers, and expanding social organization made the administrative capacity of the bureaucracy obsolete.[36] By the end of the eighteenth century, the Qing government could no longer intervene vigorously in such matters as grain distribution and population movement.[37] After its failure in the eighteenth century

State-Societal Relationships During the Late Qing

Nineteenth-century Chinese history is filled with manifestations traditionally associated with dynastic collapse: ineffectual rulers, bureaucratic corruption, decay of water control systems, foreign invasions, and popular unrest. Such indications help explain governmental weakness in the face of social change but not why the imperial system, as opposed to a specific dynasty, ended in 1911. More corrosive changes came from the movement of elites away from their established relations with state power. These changes can be seen in two phenomena of the latter half of the nineteenth century: the growth of public spheres of activity outside the bureaucracy, and the emergence of oppositional public opinion.

The public sphere. The concept of public activity was well established in China by the mid-nineteenth century. In Confucian theory, public (*gong*) concern was a general good defined by the state, as opposed to the private, selfish (*si*) interests of one or a few. Officials, as the representatives of imperial benevolence, were the ideal public guardians.[33] In any locality there was also a generally recognized area of community interest in which consensual decisions were articulated by community leaders and services were managed by local men. Although most visible in the villages, such spheres existed at higher urban levels as well. Because the state did not routinely intervene, the informal means of local decision-making were highly developed.

As I use the term here, "public" retains a considerable communal element but refers more specifically to the institutionalized, extrabureaucratic management of matters considered important by both the community and the state. Public management by elites thus contrasted with official administration (*guan*), and with private (*si*) activities of individuals, families, religions, businesses, and organizations that were not identified with the whole community. Public was a working term, used without need of explanation, that implied a different relationship to the government from those of the other two categories. This use of "public" may have evolved from phrases de-to finance and expand local government, it was forced to rely upon an unpaid, or very low-paid, sub-bureaucracy of clerks and runners. Since the regular bureaucracy remained about the same size, this level of government must have expanded in order to collect taxes and to control the growing population. The endemic corruption fostered by the sub-bureaucracy undermined bureaucratic effectiveness and created tensions with the local residents. Their aversion to this stratum of government contributed to the development of elite management outside the bureaucracy. Although operating within narrower bounds, it became an institutionalized, extrabureaucratic counterpart of the administration, and by the latter part of the nineteenth century the leading managers displayed many characteristics of the generalist magistrates.

This managerial expansion can be traced back to the late Ming, when private contributions began to supplement taxes and gentry sometimes joined officials in managing water control projects—using hired workers instead of corvée labor. Private contributions increased more rapidly than gentry management, but the changes produced by population growth and commercialization gradually increased the amount of nonofficial management in the eighteenth century. This management may have focused initially upon water control because more land had to be cultivated to feed the growing population and because water routes had to be maintained for traders. As the trend continued into the first half of the nineteenth century, educational, welfare, and relief activities also increased. Management then assumed new dimensions, propelled by the need to respond to recurrent crises during and after the Taiping Rebellion.[38]

As public activity increased during the nineteenth century, it displayed many attributes of both collective action and community orientation, but it did not normally involve balancing organized group interests or mobilizing the populace.[39] Instead, it was carried out by relatively small elite groups that could organize themselves easily. These men were to some extent self-selected by their desire for such employment, but usually their roles were also sanctioned by the backing of an influential

segment of the elite community and the approval of the officials. Just as the late imperial state was not completely autonomous in its relation to society, public management was not as
independent of the central bureaucracy as is local civic activity
in pluralistic Western societies. In practice the Chinese system
allowed for a wide range of relationships. In the latter half of
the nineteenth century, the elite managers often appeared to
enjoy a considerable latitude in establishing, funding, and running public institutions, and in some cases they were clearly
aware of the autonomous aspects of their activities.

These were the men who appear in the records as gentry
managers (shendong); I will generally call them elite managers,
because they did not necessarily have formal gentry qualifications or engage in such gentry occupations as scholarship,
teaching, or estate management. There will be many examples
of such men in subsequent chapters. Here I simply stress that
they did not come from any one substratum or occupational
segment of the elite. The members of the managerial elite reflected the characteristics of the local societies in which they
operated, and they frequently moved into other occupations or
combined management with scholarship or trade. They were
connected by horizontal personal networks that cut across the
conventional social divisions between upper and lower gentry,
merchants and gentry, or sojourners and local inhabitants. We
may best envision the managers as members of small, and often
self-perpetuating, elite networks, who claimed (accurately or
otherwise) community sanction for their activities.

Management can be distinguished from several other elite
roles in public affairs during the late imperial period. It differed
from the lijia system of service obligation, through which the
founder of the Ming dynasty had sought to curb arbitrary official power by strengthening local participation while maintaining a strong state presence in rural areas. The breakdown of this
system resulted in the decline of formal elite involvement in
local government in many places and the expansion of the bureaucratic substratum to carry out necessary functions.[40] Eventually, the ad hoc emergence of local management reestablished
local participation on a different basis of salaries and local financing, which tended to reduce the state presence.

This supplementary organization by local elite leaders had different implications from those of gentry acting as brokers to mediate between officials and the local populace.[41] The brokerage function was informal, it was based on personal ties, and ideally it reinforced the existing system by reducing conflict within it. The managers, on the other hand, occupied formally defined positions that became a necessary part of local organization. Even though they initially maintained high levels of public services and order, in the long run they posed a challenge to state authority from the top levels of society.

The managers also constituted a group that was separate from the disreputable lower gentry, who connived with yamen clerks and runners.[42] This non-elite, but native, sub-bureaucracy has been characterized as a channel for local and private interests in contrast to the magistrate and his personal secretaries who represented the public interests of the state.[43] I prefer to place the sub-bureaucracy with the bureaucracy inside the state structure, drawing a line between it and the managerial elite that competed with the yamen-centered configurations in running local affairs. Even though the distinction was not complete, by the late nineteenth century elite public-management was a serious alternative to administration through the sub-bureaucracy. The managers tended to be drawn from respectable and often influential layers of local society, and they preferred to keep their distance from the clerks and runners.

Both configurations produced their own ranges of corruption, although that of the sub-bureaucracy was more pervasive. The structural relations between the two groups and the government were different. The sub-bureaucracy may have been an administratively dysfunctional and socially oppressive element, but it does not appear to have been a channel for systemic change in the late Qing. Rather, the clerks and runners favored a status quo in which they profited by their attachment to the bottom of the bureaucracy. The managers often had closer and more equal ties with the regular officials, but their crucial characteristic was their expansiveness outside the state structure. Therefore I do not follow the distinction commonly made between the bureaucratic gentry, meaning upper-degree holders qualified for office, whether actually in the bureaucracy or not, and the *shengyuan* or other lower-degree holders who were not so qualified. As management became connected to national politics at the end of the dynasty, the crucial distinction was between people operating inside and outside the state structure.

There is ample evidence in gazetteers and newspapers that extrabureaucratic activity expanded during the latter half of the nineteenth century. This expansion reflected a more general growth in social organizational capacity, which tipped the old balances toward social organization and away from the state as the scope of public functions increased. Activist momentum also expanded geographically across administrative and regional boundaries, and by the late nineteenth century management was becoming less and less constricted by local contexts. Expansion was fostered in many ways: by economic growth and foreign trade, population mobility, overlapping elite networks, combined local and external interests, and successive internal and foreign crises. The general growth of social organization and widening of interests affected the interaction of the bureaucracy and the elites in the public sphere. At the end of the dynasty, when major changes were introduced in the public structure by the Qing New Policies, the Lower Yangtze elites were already a more dynamic element than the state within this sphere.

Another effect of social expansion was to undercut the effectiveness of the examinations in tying gentry interests to the state. Although men still studied for the examinations, strict quotas kept many qualified candidates from passing. Even so, there were far more degree holders than could be absorbed into the static regular bureaucracy. The pressure was somewhat alleviated by the growth of clerical, private secretarial, and specialized posts outside the old framework. The growing numbers of social organizations, particularly in the expanding cores, provided other kinds of employment. Although the purchase of degrees, titles, and offices showed that the political structure was still powerful,[44] its hold inevitably weakened as other activities expanded.

The end of the late imperial system was to a large extent brought about by this outwardly expanding and coalescing

elite activism, which rapidly extended the public sphere—
nationally, locally, and across the old boundaries differentiating
it from the official and private sectors. My perspective differs
from interpretations that look upon managerial growth as a
symptom of the devolution of power from the state center to
the local and rural elites. These interpretations see the significance of the shift in balance between the elites and the bureaucracy in the rise of self-interested or locally defensive activities
and in the struggles between the officials and the gentry for
control of local affairs. The terms of the struggles changed in
the twentieth century. Governments established new institutions, attempting to extend administrative control down to the
villages and to end their dependence upon the local elites,
which were seeking to evade state control and run local affairs
independently. However, the origins of the struggles lay in an
essentially cyclical shift from state to gentry dominance in
local government.[45] Although these local struggles certainly occurred at the end of the Qing, I believe that they did not have
the same revolutionary significance as did the societal expansion that brought both old-style and new elites into conflict
with the imperial state.

The rise of oppositional public opinion. Whereas the expansion of public organization was clearly related to demographic
and commercial growth, the history of public opinion (*gonglun,
yulun*) was more intimately connected to relations between the
scholar-gentry elite and the state. Opinion formation was never
entirely independent of social organization, but in the 1880's
the two processes began to interact in ways that soon led to political mobilization. The concept of public opinion also had a
long history in China, although it had not acquired institutional underpinnings or legal protection. Partly for this reason,
it contained a large element of informal consensus that could
influence behavior strongly even when not backed by formal
power. The idea of a local community consensus defined by elite
leaders had old roots in Chinese thought.[46] Also well established
was the notion of the public opinion of the literati, inside or
outside the bureaucracy, about national affairs. Their opinion,
often formed through private social gatherings of friends or liter-

ary groups, became increasingly audible as crises multiplied in
the late eighteenth and nineteenth centuries. Although Qing
intellectual history is still imperfectly understood, it can be
suggested that the late Qing opposition was heir to several
stages of first apolitical and then political concern over current
affairs. As public opinion developed, so did more activist conceptions of the scholar's role, which also served to redefine
elite connections with the state.

Many scholars had withdrawn from politics in the seventeenth century because of their distress over the bloody factional disputes in the late Ming court and bureaucracy as well
as their opposition to the Manchu invaders. The Qing rulers severely suppressed any unfavorable references to the Manchus
but generally did not try to control philosophy, scholarship, and
private expression.[47] The first phase in the reformulation of
political criticism can therefore be found in the muted, in-
operative, anti-autocratic sentiments that were expressed privately or were inherent in philosophical writings. Some scholars primarily engaged in classical textual exegesis during the
eighteenth century arrived at interpretations that slowly undermined the ideological foundations of autocracy. These ideas
circulated among the prestigious Lower Yangtze academic communities, which had a life and institutional structure of their
own—apart from the government's program of educating men
for bureaucratic service.[48]

The second phase emerged from the first, as scholars became
concerned over social disorder and other political difficulties
during the late eighteenth and early nineteenth centuries. They
had never completely abandoned the study of practical affairs
for textual research, but now they put greater emphasis on
statecraft, studying current problems and the use of classical or
historical research to seek contemporary solutions.[49] They may
also have expressed their views more overtly; at least there are
references to public opinion within the bureaucracy in the
early nineteenth century.[50] A third phase began when these
contemporary concerns began to develop clearly political dimensions and to focus on foreign encroachment, during the de-

bates over opium suppression and the conduct of the Opium War (1840–42).[51]

This progression was interrupted by the Taiping Rebellion and the post-rebellion reconstruction, when most people were preoccupied with staying alive, defeating internal enemies, rebuilding devastated areas, and revitalizing a shaken government. Renewed foreign pressures, coinciding with the end of the most urgent reconstruction, inaugurated a fourth phase in the 1880's by refocusing attention on external problems. By then circumstances had changed. Levels of social organization were greater, imperialist pressure on China had increased, and power at the highest level of government was more fragmented.[52] It was at this point that the disenchantment with the government began to interact with the growing organizational capacity of society. Public opinion was used increasingly by political outsiders as a weapon against the power holders to express the frustrations of those who felt excluded.

During the nineteenth century a discrepancy had developed between the growing amount of social organization and activity and the continued political monopoly maintained by the throne and the higher levels of the bureaucracy. The centralized bureaucratic monarchy still did not tolerate independent political activity, and opportunities to criticize administrative policy were narrowly circumscribed even within the bureaucracy. The frustrations arising from such a situation may have been blunted by the large numbers of attractive careers opening up to the elite. Managers did not constitute a distinct, economically and socially constricted stratum like the service samurai of Tokugawa Japan. Nonetheless, the idea that a frustrated social group associated with the existing power structure can have a revolutionary potential, is relevant to the late Qing as well as to Japan.[53] The lower levels of the metropolitan bureaucracy, managerial and scholarly circles, and the treaty ports all provide examples of environments that fostered discontent within the existing sociopolitical system. Interconnecting personal networks originally facilitated the transmission of analogous demands from one area to another, and by the end of the nineteenth century people from all three were combining to form associations that led to political mobilization.[54]

Frustration arose within the low and the middle grades of the metropolitan bureaucracy because highly educated *jinshi*-degree holders occupied prestigious-sounding positions but had little role in policy-making and little chance of receiving substantive appointments quickly. Their frustration was expressed in moralistic, self-righteous "pure discussion" (*qingyi*), through which officials lacking in authority criticized leading policy-makers and the throne.[55] Pure discussion stayed within controllable limits in the early and mid-nineteenth century, but by the end of the century it was beginning to offer proposals for sweeping reforms and for new institutions to give political outsiders a role in governmental decision-making.

The elite managers, for their part, developed autonomous ambitions that were not fully reconcilable with official supervision. They also saw their work in terms of statecraft, and as the amount and scope of their activities increased so did their expectations of greater influence. Their attitudes did not directly challenge official control, but they suggested a larger extrabureaucratic role than could easily fit into the existing system of local government. Because of the degree of interchange between Lower Yangtze scholarly and managerial circles, we can hypothesize, but not prove, that there was interaction between anti-autocratic and autonomous sentiments. More incontrovertibly, scholars disillusioned with governmental policy or deeply concerned over current affairs turned to local arenas in their search for solutions to national problems. What I will call activist eremitism had a decided impact on management in Zhejiang.

Within the treaty ports, urbanization and foreign contact interacted to produce another set of expansive social elements whose ambitions were obviously being frustrated. Foreign trade increased the rewards for entrepreneurs and created new brokerage opportunities that were exploited by the compradors. Merchants chafed under governmental taxation and regulation and soon became suspicious of the official supervision of modernizing industrial enterprises.[56] By the late nineteenth century they were raising demands for better legal protection and greater freedom of economic activity. The foreign affairs experts among both the scholars and the merchants had skills that initially could not be used easily in Chinese society. They also had a knowledge of foreign political, military, and economic organization that made them aware of alternative systems and the need for reforms to protect their country. At the beginning of the twentieth century, the scholars, students, and intellectuals who congregated in urban centers were intensely frustrated by their powerlessness in the face of what they considered to be disastrous political and foreign crises.

Culturally somewhat peripheral, but economically central, the treaty ports provided effective channels for new influences and interests that spread by continuous interchange with surrounding areas. As new urban social groups began to mature at the beginning of the twentieth century, the treaty ports became dynamic political centers where people organized, expanded their demands, and advanced alternatives to the imperial system. New social elements continued to have close contacts with managerial elites and sometimes joined in new forms of management themselves as, for instance, school administrators or members of the chambers of commerce. Frustrated officials also joined provincial or local movements for change when bureaucratic avenues closed. The interaction intensified in the late nineteenth and early twentieth centuries, and the urban centers became more important in generating discontent.

Two specific factors, one institutional and one ideological, facilitated the convergence of opinion and the rise of opposition. One was the press. Daily newspapers appeared in the largest treaty ports during the 1870's, changing the way opinion was formed and transmitted and increasing open criticism of governmental actions. The second factor, patriotism, was most directly responsible for the growth of criticism, which was spread by the press as well as through elite networks and oppositional memorials.

A major interpretation of Chinese history has contrasted the traditional loyalty of the scholar class to Chinese culture—and to the emperor as its central symbol—with nationalism, which subsumes racial, linguistic, and other identities in its loyalty to the nation-state. According to this interpretation, a critical shift came during the 1890's, when nationalistic loyalty to China superseded the older commitment to the emperor and Chinese culture.[57] However, the patriotism that developed in response to foreign incursions during the nineteenth century seems to have bypassed this dichotomy. Resting upon people's impulses to defend their territory, possessions, social power, or political structure against foreign attack, it did not require any fundamental change in values. People both within and without the government sought to defend their country. Outside the policy-making levels of government, however, patriotism combined with the growth of social organization and initiative to foster what I call participatory self-strengthening, as distinguished from the self-strengthening programs sponsored by major officials. This brand of patriotism placed a premium on social mobilization, fostered demands that public opinion influence governmental policy, and eroded faith in leaders who could not protect the country.

The merging of patriotism with public opinion mobilized the old-regime elite and the still-very-few representatives of new social groups, encouraging them to assume more activist roles. Equally important, patriotism played a large part in undermining their loyalty to the existing governmental structure. Without rejecting Confucian harmonious and unitary ideals, scholars revived critiques of autocracy from earlier centuries and searched out precedents for the idea that social initiative might propel men and opinions upward to formulate national policy. This growing opposition among segments of the old elite was similar to what had occurred in France under the ancien régime, when members of the nobility lost their faith in the monarchy.[58] It opened the way for political cooperation between old and new elites and for the selection from Western history of representational institutions that the centralized bureaucratic monarchy had not allowed to develop in China. With this background of oppositionist patriotic opinion and public social activism, political activity was able to develop very quickly during and after the Sino-Japanese War in the mid-1890's. The challenge to the government was therefore not only to initiate reforms to strengthen China against foreign attack but also to absorb and satisfy this social initiative. Its failure to do so resulted in a new phase of escalating conflict.

Social Mobilization Versus Late Qing State-Building

The politics of the last Qing decade can be viewed in terms of the clash between the continuing mobilization of core-area elites and a new attempt at aggressive state-building by the Qing government. This state-societal conflict, which had little precedent in China, took place within the rapidly expanding and changing public sphere. It was definitely stimulated by foreign pressures and was more important than the rise of new classes per se in ending the imperial system. Both sides desired similar reforms to create a strong, wealthy, unified China. One wished to rely on social mobilization outside the bureaucratic structure, however, and the other wished to extend state control over society while enlisting its support. The balance between the centralized bureaucratic monarchy and the elites had already tipped toward the societal side during the nineteenth century. The incompatible claims advanced by each side in the early 1900's upset it completely.

Under stable economic and social conditions, the effect of the nineteenth-century increase in the number of social organizations might have remained simply quantitative, with more and more institutions performing similar functions under the general umbrella of the imperial state. Given the strengths of the bureaucratic monarchy and the still considerable identification of the elites with the political system, such an elaboration was a real possibility, and the growth of jobs outside the bureaucracy might simply have relieved discontent and frustration by employing educated men. However, the crisis-ridden nineteenth century stimulated qualitative changes in the organization of society, making it more expansive, activist, interconnected, and potentially oppositional.

Following the Taiping Rebellion, state power, too, had begun a transformation. After initial disagreements and vacillations, officials were provoked by rebellion and foreign intrusion to try to control and mobilize China's resources more effectively. Their policies were reminiscent of state-making in early modern Europe,[59] but the Qing officials were faced with a task of restructuring the existing imperial state that was not the same as creating new states out of feudal domains in Europe. Commercial *lijin* taxes were their most visible attempt to broaden and increase revenues. The official self-strengthening and foreign affairs movements began to modernize the armed forces, promote industry, and add new specialized bureaus at the national and provincial levels. Certain aspects of the old state structure, such as the prior existence of a bureaucracy that brought able men into government, facilitated change. The government was seriously hampered, however, by a lack of funds that was the heritage of the Qing's previous policy of low taxation. The sub-bureaucracy, which had been growing in size and complexity during the Qing, was another major barrier to structural change, because of its corruption and its hold over revenue collection.[60]

Despite a predictable resistance to taxes, social elites did not perceive state power as generally threatening until near the end of the dynasty. State power had not hopelessly decayed in an absolute sense, but it was shrinking rather than expanding in relation to the strength of social organization. When state and local (or social) interests clashed, the disputes remained specific and isolated. The elites still derived privileges from their association with the state, and conflicts with officials were likely to create a desire for improved contacts within the government rather than foster collective demands for separate political power.

This situation had already changed substantially during the late 1890's, and the Qing New Policies, which mandated sweeping administrative reforms after 1902, completed the disequilibration. The ways in which the New Policies affected the elites in Zhejiang will be examined in Chapters 6 and 7; a few points generally relevant to the state-societal framework should be mentioned here. The New Policies can best be assessed in terms of their impact upon an already existing sphere of public activity. They changed the structure of the sphere, but they did not create it. While the state was extending its presence, elite activists in central and south China were expanding their roles and claiming a public character for new organizations of their own. Political and public power expanded rapidly during this period as the result of both state and elite activity, but the ambitions of the central officials and the social elites expanded even more rapidly. Conflict, not adjustment, resulted. The basic issue was political power rather than the desirability or the content of reform.

A characteristic of the last Qing decade was the simultaneous outward extension of local and provincial elite activism to the national level. This nationalistically inspired and soon highly politicized process overshadowed the local defense of elite interests against the state, and ultimately it pulled the most dynamic organizations of the public sphere into revolutionary politics. A conflict between social mobilization and the centralized extension of state power was inherent in the situation and would have occurred whether the dynasty was Manchu or Chinese. Neither the state's effort to extend its control by the New Policies nor the elites' mobilization that made use of the new institutions initiated a decisive trend. The Qing and the republican governments that followed did not succeed in controlling the elites bureaucratically, nor did the elites translate their public positions into a permanent control of state power. The most lasting legacy of the New Policies period was the expansion—both institutionally and conceptually—of the public arena, which continued to be redefined during the Republic by the fluctuating competitions to control it.[61]

The evolution of the conflict in the late Qing resembles (if we allow for differences in motivation and timing) a model suggested by Charles Tilly to explain social mobilization and collective violence in western Europe during the nineteenth and twentieth centuries.[62] In Europe capitalism produced changes in social structure, which led to the organization of groups, the mobilization of the groups to acquire control over resources, and then the use of the resources in collective action to acquire more power. This collective action was likely to be violent, and the repressive responses of the state or other social groups caused more violence and further mobilization.

Capitalism had not progressed far enough in China to produce major changes in the social structure, but commercial growth and the consequent consolidation of a merchant-gentry elite similarly fostered social organization. Such a process was possible under the centralized bureaucratic monarchy precisely because at first it did not challenge the state politically. China's progression to mobilization and collective action was, unlike Europe's, triggered from the outside; foreign intrusion also stimulated the emergence of new classes, which provided some of the constitutionalists and revolutionaries, and patriotism or nationalism, which had a broader politicizing effect. Within elite society, collective action was not often violent before the republican period, but the conflict with the state was nonetheless serious.

In the Chinese case, the period of organizational growth within the slowly evolving society and polity had been very protracted, but the crisis-induced transition to mobilization and collective action was very rapid. This variation on the European pattern reflected other differences. Tilly has argued that in Europe there was a progression from communal violence, before the development of capitalism, to largely reactive violence against state-building and industrialization and then to "proactive" violence as new groups organized and reached out for power under the new socio-political system.[63] In China these developments were more accretionary than progressive. Because capitalism did not develop fully in Chinese peasant society, communal violence did not recede as it did in Europe—but neither was it important in the 1911 Revolution. Both reactive and proactive conflict played a role, but the two were telescoped as elites reached out for more power at the same time that the state sought to remake itself. Chinese and European nationalism had different consequences. In Europe foreign wars helped rally the populace behind the rulers of the emerging states. In China widely shared nationalism split the government and society apart. Although the elites prevailed in 1911, neither they nor the bureaucratic state was fully prepared for the contest. Neither side could win completely, and the unresolved issues of bureaucratic centralization and social mobilization reappeared in the disputes during the Republic.

The question then arises, what was the place of the radicals and the revolutionary parties in the 1911 Revolution? My emphasis on the broad elite social basis of the core areas and on the long preparatory period of developing social organization diverts attention from the people who have generally been considered revolutionary leaders. Radicals did indeed come to the fore in precipitating the revolution. Their contribution was twofold. They unambiguously advanced republican alternatives to the existing political system, and they were willing to use violence to realize their political goals. Violence was a logical outgrowth of the organization, mobilization, and political disputes at the end of the Qing. The members of the elite who were disillusioned with government policy had warned repeatedly since the 1880's of the possibility of violence. Nonetheless, they shrank from pursuing the implications of their own rhetoric because of their residual loyalties to the old system and their fears of social disorder. The radicals, who were less bound by old ties, were better able to take this step, although their willingness to take action did not free them from the need for a supportive audience. There were only a small number of committed revolutionaries, and they lacked the organization and military power to establish a new national government. Their weaknesses suggest that the 1911 Revolution could not have succeeded to the extent that it did without broad support from both the old and the new elites in central and south China.

In the following chapters I will trace these processes in Zhejiang. It will be useful to keep in mind a number of factors that may account for the special characteristics of the province. First, Zhejiang contained some of the most highly commercialized districts in China, and the core economic areas were among those places that produced the largest numbers of upper-degree holders. The opportunities for social interchange and overlapping economic interests between prestigious high-level scholars and merchants were therefore unusually well developed.

Second, rebellion, foreign trade, and imperialist encroachment interacted to foster social organization and mobilization. Only Jiangsu suffered comparable destruction during the Taiping Rebellion. Reconstruction needs in Zhejiang were therefore greater than in most provinces. The rise of foreign trade in Shanghai, abetted by the foreign demand for silk, changed trade patterns and injected new money into the commercialized areas of Zhejiang. The managerial activities of the surviving elites were therefore strengthened at the same time that reconstruction was providing additional incentives for public involvement. Not only did foreign trade have a relatively large impact on the parts of Zhejiang within the Shanghai hinterland, but the Zhejiangese were also sensitized to foreign military dangers because of repeated threats to the coast.

Third, the military and administrative situations in Zhejiang had special features. Because most of the province was not militarized, influence arising from trade did not have to compete seriously with military power, and military force was not as important in maintaining administrative control as it was in some provinces. The provincial capital of Hangzhou was not one of the major administrative centers in the country, and the governors-general residing in Fuzhou, Fujian, were rarely involved in Zhejiangese affairs. Although most late nineteenth-century governors were able, few were comparable to the powerful restoration and reformist officials who dominated the administrations in other key provinces. The vigorous elites of Zhejiang had a freer hand than their counterparts elsewhere, and elite activities were less concentrated in the provincial capital. Given the balance between bureaucratic and societal elites, multicentric patterns were further encouraged because there were several economic centers in the province and economic activities were also pulled outward toward the Shanghai metropolitan center.

Despite all these special circumstances, a study of Zhejiangese elite activities need not be approached as an isolated exercise in local history. As the centers of political change, the core areas were important during this phase of Chinese history. Managerial efforts in the peripheral parts of the province were less historically significant. They demonstrate the extent of elite entrenchment in local affairs, however, and they suggest that forms of organizational growth should also be investigated in the less prosperous and commercialized parts of the country.

TWO

Socioeconomic Contexts of Public Management

Scholarship, Rebellion, and Trade

Public management was inherently situational, responding to events and being shaped by socioeconomic and ecological factors. Some of these factors were fundamental in defining the elite in different localities, structuring the ways in which external events affected local societies, and shaping the problems addressed by, and the opportunities open to, the elite managers. The next chapter will examine the ways in which the managerial elite fitted into local societies. Here I will sketch out a number of disparate-sounding, but actually interacting, elements that constantly affected public activity in Zhejiang: the regional zonation within the province, the academic and intellectual establishments, the destruction caused by the Taiping Rebellion, and the economic expansion and restructuring encouraged by foreign trade.

Zhejiangese Regions During the Late Qing

Zhejiang has usually been characterized by the prosperous silk-producing regions of its northern prefectures, but actually the province varied greatly in terrain, productivity, wealth, and culture. It is almost impossible to compile rigorous core-peripheral data for the mid- to late nineteenth century. Aside from the unreliability and spottiness of the population statistics, the depopulation of most of the core districts during the Taiping Rebellion meant that population density bore little relationship to economic levels for much of this period. Supplementary data on such institutions as guilds and banks are also too fragmentary to be used systematically.

Keith Schoppa has used the more complete statistics available in the 1930's to divide Zhejiang's districts into inner and outer core and periphery areas.[1] This distinction can be applied with some commonsense modifications to the late Qing. The general outlines of the Zhejiang economy predated the Taiping Rebellion. After the rebellion, commerce developed without serious interruption from the late 1860's through the 1920's, spreading slowly outward from the most prosperous regions. One would expect therefore that core-peripheral relationships would remain roughly the same. In the nineteenth century, however, there were fewer inner-core districts and more peripheral ones, and economic centrality was more concentrated in the northern half of the province.

The inner core districts formed a great semicircle around Hangzhou Bay, bulging inland south of Tai Lake and ending with Yin district in Ningbo. They included Jiaxing, Xiushui, Jiashan, Pinghu, and Tongxiang districts of Jiaxing prefecture; Wucheng, Guian, and Deqing districts of Huzhou; Qiantang, Renhe, and Haining of Hangzhou; Shanyin, Guiji, Xiaoshan, and Yuyao in Shaoxing; and Yin, Zhenhai, and Ciqi in Ningbo.[2] An important aspect of urban development in these districts was the emergence of large market towns or small cities with populations of five to twenty thousand. These were major commercial centers in their own right, even when they were near larger cities. In Huzhou, for instance, the two districts of Guian and Wucheng, which shared the large prefectural capital of Huzhou, had four other dynamic commercial centers at Nanxun, Shuanglin, Wu, and Linghu.[3]

In general, peripherality increased as one moved south and southwest or went inland toward the hilly border areas. There were two other, more minor areas of development. One on the southeast coast included parts of Linhai and Huangyan districts (Taizhou) along the Ling River and its major tributary the Yongning, parts of Yongjia (Wenzhou) on the Ou River, and the environs of the ports of Ruian and Pingyang districts. These places had traded with ports in Fujian and Guangdong to the south for centuries. After Wenzhou became a treaty port in 1877, commerce slowly expanded and was partly reoriented north toward Ningbo and Shanghai. Trade eventually encouraged economic development in all the coastal districts of Wenzhou and Taizhou. In the late Qing, however, these areas had not achieved the levels of urbanization and commercialization found in the five northern prefectures.

The second minor area of commercial development existed along the middle and upper reaches of the Qiantang River. This was a very old, outdated trade route that ran across border passes, connecting Zhejiang to Jiangxi and Fujian provinces. Lanqi in Jinhua was the major commercial city, and the districts of Longyou and Qu immediately upriver in Quzhou prefecture were secondary trading and handicraft centers. This area had never fully recovered from the wars of the seventeenth century, and it declined again in the nineteenth century because of the Taiping Rebellion. Some cities were involved in inter-regional trade, but agriculture was far less commercialized and local marketing structures were more rudimentary than the core areas of the north.[4]

Probably the contrast between the inner-core districts and the rest of the province was greater in the late nineteenth century than during the republican period, when the outward spread of commerce had broadened intermediate developing zones. Foreign demand for silk, for instance, spread sericulture to new parts of Hangzhou, Shaoxing, and Huzhou. Improved river transport and finally, in the 1930's, a railway line helped break down the insularity of the peripheral districts in the center and southwest.[5]

These core-peripheral zones were superimposed upon four larger subregions, which had their own ecological variations and characteristic agricultural and commercial organization: the northern (Jiangnan) prefectures of Jiaxing, Huzhou, and

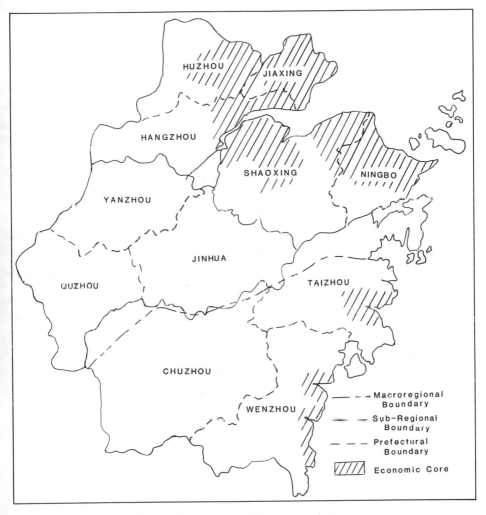

HUZHOU   JIAXING

HANGZHOU

SHAOXING   NINGBO

YANZHOU

JINHUA

QUZHOU   TAIZHOU

CHUZHOU

WENZHOU

— — — Macroregional
        Boundary

———— Sub-Regional
        Boundary

— — — Prefectural
        Boundary

///// Economic Core

Map 2. Prefectures and Regions in Zhejiang

Map 3. Districts of Zhejiang

Key to Map 3

JIAXING		HUZHOU		HANGZHOU	
Haiyan	4	Anji	11	Changhua	18
Jiashan	1	Changxing	8	Fuyang	20
Jiaxing/		Deqing	9	Haining	13
Xiushui	3	Wucheng/		Lin'an	16
Pinghu	2	Guian	7	Renhe/	
Shimen	6	Wukang	10	Qiantang	14
Tongxiang	5	Xiaofeng	12	Xindeng	19
				Yuhang	15
				Yuqian	17

SHAOXING		NINGBO		YANZHOU	
Cheng	26	Ciqi	28	Fenshui	34
Shanyin/		Dinghai	30	Jiande	37
Guiji	22	Fenghua	32	Qun'an	36
Shangyu	23	Xiangshan	33	Shouchang	39
Xiaoshan	21	Yin	31	Suian	38
Xinchang	27	Zhenhai	29	Tonglu	35
Yuyao	24				
Zhuji	25				

JINHUA		QUZHOU		CHUZHOU	
Dongyang	42	Changshan	49	Jingning	74
Jinhua	44	Jiangshan	52	Jinyun	68
Lanqi	43	Kaihua	48	Lishui	67
Pujiang	40	Longyou	51	Longquan	71
Tangqi	46	Qu	50	Qingtian	70
Wuyi	47			Qingyuan	73
Yiwu	41			Songyang	69
Yongkang	45			Suichang	65
				Xuanping	66
				Yunhe	72

TAIZHOU		WENZHOU	
Huangyan	57	Luoqing	60
Linhai	56	Pingyang	64
Ninghai	54	Ruian	62
Taiping	58	Taishun	63
Tiantai	53	Yongjia	59
Xianju	55	Yuhuan	61

NOTE: Double names separated by a slash are those of districts that divided the provincial capital of Hangzhou, and the prefectural capitals of Jiaxing, Huzhou, and Shaoxing during the Qing dynasty. These districts are best analyzed as single social and economic units and were combined after 1911.

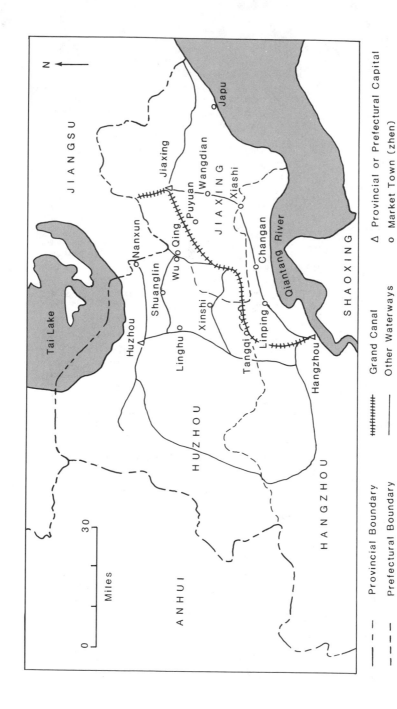

Map 4. Major Market Towns of the Three Northern Prefectures

Hangzhou; Ningbo and Shaoxing; Jinhua, Yanzhou and Quzhou in the center and southwest; and most of Taizhou, Wenzhou and Chuzhou in the southeast and south.[6]

The Jiangnan prefectures divided into a coastal area, a central section of well-watered alluvial plain, and hilly border districts adjoining Anhui or southwest of Hangzhou city. Cotton was grown along the coast, and the agricultural plain was the major silk-producing region in China during the second half of the nineteenth century. Agriculture was relatively specialized; in the 1920's, for instance, 18 to 35 percent of all agricultural land in the ten major silk-producing districts was planted with mulberry trees.[7]

Such product specialization went hand in hand with commercialization and urbanization. Good systems of rivers and canals connected and integrated the marketing systems. The silk- and cotton producing areas supplied spinning and weaving centers in northern Zhejiang and Jiangsu for centuries. Besides the provincial capital of Hangzhou, the prefectural capitals of Jiaxing and Huzhou were major cities, although the latter did not fully recover its pre-Taiping position. The large urban population and the specialization of agriculture meant that this region—like other core areas in Shaoxing and Ningbo—was not self-sufficient in rice. The three northern prefectures, like the adjacent part of Jiangsu province, paid both a land tax and a heavy grain tribute to feed the national capital in Beijing. Even if the tribute had been eliminated, Jiangnan would have had to import rice to feed its large numbers of town dwellers,[8] but profits from silk, cotton, and trade enabled the area to remain prosperous.

Although the hill districts increased their practice of sericulture during the nineteenth and twentieth centuries, they continued to lag behind the wealthier plain and littoral. The character of Jiangnan was defined by the sericulture, cotton culture, and water transport that supported trade, handicrafts, and large urban configurations. It shared these characteristics with the Jiangnan region of Jiangsu across the provincial border, and the two economies had been closely entwined for centuries.

Shaoxing and Ningbo prefectures grew steadily more prosperous and more commercially integrated during the Qing. Waterways were well developed in the flat-lying areas, where agriculture became more commercialized in the late nineteenth century as cotton production expanded south of Hangzhou Bay and sericulture was introduced in Shaoxing, Zhuji, Xiaoshan, and Cheng.[9] Tea had long been grown in the hilly inland areas, and the wines produced near the prefectural city had a national reputation.

Specialized agriculture and trade supported a large urban population in the cities of Shaoxing and Ningbo and other, lesser centers. An extensive regional trade in handicrafts and agricultural produce was augmented by inter-regional coastal trade during the nineteenth century.[10] The resulting prosperity did not extend to the inland hills or isolated coastal settlements, but the core areas of these prefectures were catching up to the older commercial centers of Jiangnan. Although set apart by different dialects, the two subregions shared major economic characteristics.

The southern half of Zhejiang presented a different picture. Except for the part of the two northernmost Taizhou districts that lay in the Lower Yangtze region, the prefectures of Taizhou, Wenzhou, and Chuzhou were within the Lingnan macroregion of Fujian.[11] Coastal trade helped turn Yongjia (the prefectural city of Wenzhou) into a major city in the twentieth century. Much of Wenzhou and Taizhou was densely populated. Most of the region was also hilly and poor, however, and there were few large land holdings. Tea grown in Wenzhou and Chuzhou had the largest sales of Zhejiang teas, but it did not equal those of Fujian as a regional specialty.[12] Small-scale mining and fishing were important in the economies of some districts, and oranges were shipped to northern Chinese cities after steam navigation speeded transport. Wenzhou umbrellas were the most famous of the local handicrafts, but, in short, commerce was only moderately developed.

Wenzhou was set apart further because the local dialect could not be understood by anyone else in Zhejiang. Inland Chuzhou was even more isolated. English Maritime Customs officials ruefully observed the area's lack of commercial integration with the coast after Wenzhou city became a treaty port. Throughout the 1880's, goods arriving by steamer for delivery to the Chuzhou prefectural capital of Lishui were often not sent directly up the shallow Ou River. Instead they followed the other three sides of a rectangle, going north by junk to Ningbo, west along the canals of Ningbo and Shaoxing, south on the Qiantang River to Lanqi, and then across the macroregional divide to Lishui.[13] It is not surprising that Chuzhou was little involved in events affecting the rest of Zhejiang.

The rural poverty and peripherality of this region was reflected in the unruliness of its populace. The southern border with Fujian was often restless, but Taizhou had a worse reputation among officials.[14] Its combination of a mountainous interior with a rugged, island-strewn coastline made an ideal terrain for combined banditry and piracy. Rebels and bandits could move on and off the water, prey on shipping, and combine piracy with legitimate fishing. Further inland were inviting *lijin* tax stations and opportunities to make forays into the adjoining districts of Shaoxing and Jinhua prefectures.[15] This disorder, which extended into Wenzhou, probably reflected not only the poverty of the area but also the disruptions and opportunities caused by expanding commercialization and by the contrasts between the relatively well-off trading centers and the hill country.

The southwest was defined by the Qiantang River drainage that extended into the central prefecture of Jinhua. The districts along the extensive border had more in common with the adjacent districts in Jiangxi, Anhui or Fujian than with the core areas to the north. Except for the commercial towns along the river, the products were typical of poor, mountainous land. Some tea was grown, but cotton and silk production was miniscule. Small-scale mining was practiced in Quzhou and Jiande. Tong oil was produced in Yanzhou prefecture, and lumber or other forest products were an important part of the economies of many districts.

Although Longyou profited by paper-making, its handicrafts were poorly developed. Jinhua had more agricultural potential, and hams and miscellaneous produce from several of its districts were sold in cities to the north. However, most of this prefecture, which also had its own dialect, had been isolated for centuries. The trade of some districts was declining in the late Qing, and there is little evidence of fresh impetus until the last ten or fifteen years of the dynasty.[16]

As in the southeast, the border populace was unruly, but the area's isolation also gave it stability. Jinhua had academies that traced back to the Song dynasty. Land turnover was slow in at least some districts.[17] Neither economic changes nor even the serious destruction caused by the Taiping Rebellion had seriously undermined existing social arrangements.

Because of these differences in economy, ecology, and local culture, it is difficult to discuss Zhejiang as a single unit. Different parts of the province participated in events in different ways, depending upon their geographical location and economic levels. The variations meant that, although gentry and merchants shared some general characteristics throughout the province, the composition and the interests of elites were not the same all over. Academic and cultural resources were, for instance, not spread evenly, and foreign trade had varying impacts. In the nineteenth century, only the Taiping Rebellion cut across these economic distinctions, but they reasserted themselves as soon as the fighting was over—channeling ways in which public management would develop. In many respects the distinction between core and periphery was more fundamental than that between urban and rural, unless the latter also takes careful account of the differences in the economic zones.

The Zhejiangese Scholar-Elite

Zhejiang had been part of the cultural center of China since at least the Southern Song dynasty (1127–1279), when Hangzhou was the imperial capital. At that time, high culture spread throughout the province in academies and scholarly communities. The Song and early Yuan (1280–1368) dynasties marked a high point in the academic histories of many of the districts in the southern half of the province, but the wealthy districts of the north continued to be famous throughout the Ming (1368–1644) and Qing for their scholarship and their success in the metropolitan examinations leading to the *jinshi* degree. Jiangsu was the only province with more metropolitan graduates. Hangzhou produced more *jinshi* than any other prefecture in China, and Jiaxing, Huzhou, and Shaoxing were also among the top nine Chinese prefectures during the Qing.[18]

This scholarly eminence had several important effects on the composition of local elite societies in Zhejiang. Because there were more upper-degree holders—people who were qualified for government office—than in most other provinces, there was a close interaction between the state bureaucracy and the top level of elite society. Government-conferred status bound the elite to the state, but, under certain circumstances, the social prestige derived from this status also strengthened the position of members of the elite when making demands upon or opposing the state. Local leaders drawn from the elite, upper-class pool were likely to have received educations and acquired connections that made them relatively cosmopolitan rather than parochial in their views. There was a strong scholarly cast to district-level local leadership even in districts where there was little examination success. The high educational levels meant that there were more qualified examination candidates in Zhejiang than in most other provinces. Because the number of upper-degree holders was severely limited, educated men were encouraged perforce to find an alternative to governmental employment. The gentry, narrowly defined, were relatively likely to seek alternative careers and to turn to trade in places where it was profitable.

Such factors were operative throughout much of the Qing. They are of interest in this study because they affected the way state-societal relationships changed during the last fifty years of the dynasty. Aspects of this academic-cultural background as well as economic changes were reflected in the processes of organization, mobilization, and politicization that will be traced in subsequent chapters. The differences between districts, which were ultimately reflected in varying levels of political involvement, are indicated by the numbers of upper-degree holders—which, in turn, suggest variations in state-societal relationships. A district-by-district breakdown of Zhejiangese who obtained the *jinshi* degree during successive fifty-year periods of the Qing (Appendix A) shows how marked these differences were and how they correlated with economic zonation. A total of 91 percent (2,404) of 2,545 *jinshi* came from the five northern prefectures, and 82 percent (2,289) came from their fifteen inner-core districts. Most *jinshi* from these prefectures were also from districts where the chief administrative city was located. Hangzhou was not only the provincial capital but also an old cultural and commercial center. All these factors combined to produce an extraordinary concentration of 720 *jinshi* in Renhe and Qiantang districts: 26 percent of the provincial and 80 percent of the prefectural total. Such concentration was most extreme where there were large core-peripheral differences within a single prefecture. In Huzhou an analogous 75 percent of *jinshi* came from the two districts sharing the prefectural capital, but in Jiaxing, where most districts were highly commercialized, only 33 percent were from the two capital districts. Shaoxing, with 54 percent of prefectural *jinshi* in the administrative center, and Ningbo (55 percent) fell somewhere in between, both in terms of the evenness of economic development and of the distribution of degree holders.

Where core districts contained large prosperous market towns, a significant number of *jinshi* came from these secondary centers (see Table 1). Although some of these men undoubtedly moved to the administrative city, others were active in their native towns. Both the concentration of upper-degree holders in the economic cores and their relatively wide distribution across the urban hierarchy of the economically advanced areas facilitated elite communication.[19] Such factors also contributed to the formation of horizontal managerial networks, when elite public organization increased after the Taiping Rebellion.

Success in the examinations correlated with other kinds of success. Shaoxing, and to a lesser extent Hangzhou, produced large numbers of clerks and secretaries, providing a lower-level route into government service.[20] Good educational facilities provided more jobs for scholars and teachers, in addition to in-

TABLE I
Upper-Degree Holders in Jiangnan Market Towns
During the Qing

Place	Jinshi	Juren
Linghu, Guian (to 1893)	34	157
Nanxun, Wucheng	19	74
Shuanglin, Guian	16	66
Wu-Qing, Wucheng/Tongxiang	37	122
Puyuan, Tongxiang	9	60

SOURCES: Town gazetteers as listed in the Bibliography. Note that these figures are inflated compared with the district totals in Appendix A (see note to Appendix A).

creasing the chances of students' passing the examinations, and districts that sent out large numbers of men to be officials created better opportunities for patronage. Because academically successful districts were also economically prosperous, some members of the elite forsook study for trade. In the long run, however, profitable commerce and scholarship reinforced each other. As a result, leading members of the elite in core districts were likely to be distinguished by high prestige and wealth that was tied to both outside and local interests. They had contacts in Beijing, they knew scholars and officials in other provinces, and they were likely to be aware of, if not directly involved in, national affairs. All these factors affected the evolution of public management.

In the rest of the province, there were not only far fewer jinshi, but the composition, status, and prospects of all upper-degree holders were also different from those in the northern cores. Only 259 jinshi came from the southern half of Zhejiang, and the more peripheral districts of the north did scarcely better. The southern jinshi were less likely to come from the district that contained the prefectural city, but the locations of their homes still correlated well with levels of commercial activity. Only Qu, which was also the economic center of Quzhou, had more than 50 percent of the prefectural total, and the commercial center of Lanqi (Jinhua) had only one fewer jinshi than the administratively central district.

The other side of the picture is that, even though the aca-

TABLE 2
Upper-Degree Holders in Selected Districts During the Qing

District	Jinshi	Juren	Gong-sheng	Total	Juren/Jinshi	Gong-sheng/Jinshi
Shanyin/Guiji (S)	614	2,318	826	3,758	3.8	1.3
Wucheng/Guian to 1884 (Hu)	315	954	611	1,880	3.0	1.9
Haining (H)	143	606	433	1,182	4.2	3.0
Yin to 1877 (N)	129	569	488	1,186	4.4	3.8
Jiaxing (Jx)	100	355	270	725	3.6	2.7
Ciqi to 1899 (N)	93	446	323	826	4.8	3.5
Zhuji (S)	57	173	270	500	3.0	4.7
Changxing to 1890 (Hu)	41	140	234	415	3.4	5.7
Shimen to 1878 (Jx)	33	146	187	366	4.4	5.7
Qu (Q)	22	101	293	416	4.6	13.3
Jiande (Y)	19	93	197	309	4.9	10.4
Linhai (T)	11	71	181	263	6.5	16.5
Xinchang (S)	10	68	216	294	6.8	21.6
Kaihua (Q)	8	29	357	394	3.6	44.6
Xiaofeng (Hu)	3	22	205	230	7.3	68.3
Suichang (C)	2	9	70	81	4.5	35.0

SOURCES: District gazetteers (chapters on degree holders).

demic elite was small in peripheral areas, upper-degree holders did exist and had local influence. A look at the distribution of *gongsheng* degree holders (senior licentiates), who ranked below *juren* but qualified as upper gentry, suggests how the composition of this upper strata differed in the core and the periphery (see Table 2). Well-off men from districts least likely to be successful in the provincial and metropolitan examinations were relatively more likely to become *gongsheng*, because the degree of senior licentiate by seniority (*sui gongsheng*) was awarded to scholars who had repeatedly taken the provincial examinations without obtaining a *juren* degree.

The more poorly prepared scholars from peripheral districts were more likely to fail examinations, but they also kept on trying—in part because they had fewer career alternatives than the men in the cores. Although left behind, they were not totally outside the process of elite formation and interaction stemming from the examinations. Senior licentiates by seniority were eligible for certain offices and traveled repeatedly to the provincial capital. They did not normally have the same variety of options as *juren,* however, and they were more likely to end up as managers or teachers near home, where their status was high in the local context. The distribution of degree holders suggests that the managerial pool in many poor districts had an academic slant reminiscent of the cores, but that members of the elite there would be relatively parochial in their interests and experiences.

Data on academy locations and a brief consideration of local scholarly traditions provide additional dimensions to the observations derived from statistics on degree holders. About 290 public academies operated in the province during part or all of the nineteenth century (Appendix B). Although this number was considerably smaller than the 415 of Guangdong,[21] they nonetheless provided members of the elite with considerable opportunities for advanced education, which were supplemented in some areas by family and lineage facilities. Not surprisingly, some districts that produced many *jinshi* also had a large number of academies, but, for a number of reasons, the locations of the academies do not correlate very closely with the distribution of *jinshi* or economic zonation.

The Qing regulation that every district should have an academy encouraged dispersion—and all but two districts did have at least one. Since the academies in the major centers were likely to be larger with more distinguished teachers, even if they were few in number they were more effective. A famous institution like the Gujing Jingshe in Hangzhou not only attracted eminent scholars but also was successful in educating students to pass the provincial examinations. The major academies of the northern core, particularly in Jiangnan, were moreover part of academic complexes where important libraries supported by wealthy patrons encouraged scholarly research.[22] Old academic centers also existed in districts like Fenghua (Ningbo) where picturesque settings attracted men from the surrounding areas.

Even allowing for all these factors, we still must explain why students were not channeled upward into a few dominant institutions in the provincial capital, as was the case in Guang-dong, and why 55 percent of the academies were in the south-ern prefectures. A long-standing diffusion of wealth and educa-tion in the core areas worked against centralization. Districts that had been academically distinguished for centuries had de-veloped their own prestigious institutions; scholars were pulled toward important centers in Jiangsu as well as to Hangzhou. The large numbers of academies in the peripheral areas represented the lower end of the same kind of academic diffusion. Members of the elite in such districts might seek to improve education in the hope of examination success. Meanwhile the academies educated future local leaders and provided facilities for local scholars. In the growth of local managerial establishments, the academies were among the key public institutions, and there was interaction between the managerial and the academic elite.

Members of the elite drew upon local intellectual traditions, which had been kept alive in the academies or revived by local scholars, to conceptualize current problems, criticize govern-mental structure or social conditions, and justify proto-political demands. Even many peripheral districts had their own local scholarly heroes. Aside from minor variations, three major in-tellectual traditions affected the way members of the elite ap-proached problems in the post-Taiping period. One tradition arose from the various schools of learning that flourished in Jiangnan during the Qing.[23] Scholars in the three northern pre-fectures were part of the brilliant Lower Yangtze center of clas-sical scholarship. They often looked to the writings of the seventeenth-century Jiangsu scholar-reformer Gu Yanwu for guidance in statecraft, and they could also turn to the works of numerous lesser local figures like the eremitic Confucian so-cial moralist Zhang Lüxiang of Tongxiang.

Scholars from Shaoxing and Ningbo were often found in the provincial capital. However, these prefectures were also the home of the Eastern Zhejiang Historical School,[24] and Shaoxing was the native place of both the philosopher and official Wang Yangming and the seventeenth-century social and political critic Huang Zongxi. Farther south, Jinhua had been the center of the pragmatic, institutionalist, and statecraft-oriented Yongkang (district) school of the Southern Song, whose chief representative was Chen Liang. Wenzhou had produced the closely allied Yongjia school, which included Ye Shi and Chen Fuliang in the twelfth century. Original Confucian thinkers with a utilitarian bent had come from Jinhua prefecture during the Yuan dynasty, and, although eclipsed by Zhu Xi's Neo-Confucianism, their schools attracted the attention of statecraft reformers from Zhejiang in the seventeenth and nineteenth centuries.[25] None of the "schools" was exclusivist, and the Eastern Zhejiang Historical School was particularly ill defined. Nonetheless, such traditions gave a different tenor to scholarship in different places and at times provided reasons for study unrelated to success in examinations.

All three local traditions included oppositionist writers who had formulated critiques of autocracy in earlier centuries. Gu Yanwu, who was well known for advocating that members of the local elite assume responsibility for running local affairs, was perhaps the most widely read of such writers in the Lower Yangtze. Some scholars from the southeast coast turned deliberately to the Southern Song writers as they debated the shortcomings of government, and other vaguely eremitic scholars made similar use of other representatives of recurrent substrains within the Confucian thought of the area. This recycling of ideas raises the possibility that there were persistent tensions between the centralized government and the scholar-gentry elite and that recurring weaknesses or perversions of the centralized bureaucratic monarchy had produced similar complaints over many centuries. Because the twelfth, thirteenth, seventeenth, and nineteenth centuries were all periods of dynastic weakness, foreign threat, and social turmoil, it is also possible that there was an oppositionist critique that surfaced when the state was weak.

This idea has definite limitations in interpreting the political changes at the end of the Qing. Confucian scholars had spoken out periodically against the political structure, nineteenth-century scholars were aware of the earlier criticisms of the government, and this awareness probably encouraged them to express their own complaints. However, extremely detailed comparisons would be required to determine just what was being extracted from the earlier writers and how earlier ideas were being reinterpreted. The economic, social, and political contexts were too different at the end of the Song, Ming, and Qing to assume that there was a static oppositionist tradition. On the most obvious level, by the late Qing commercialization in the core areas had reached the point where the kind of anti-mercantile Confucian reaction that had contributed to late Ming oppositionism had no political force. The threat from international capitalist imperialism was quite different from the pressures from the nomadic societies of the northern and northwestern steppes. The late nineteenth-century scholars slid easily from the selections they made of past critiques into Western theories that would express their political demands. Thus the revival of old writings reflected social and political changes at least as much as continuities.

Social changes within the scholarly elite are suggested by changes in both the numbers and the distribution of *jinshi*-degree holders and academies during the Qing. The average number of Zhejiangese *jinshi* per year declined from 12.9 during the period 1696–1745 to 10.2 during the period 1795–1850. The Taiping destruction caused a sharper drop to 9.0 from 1851 to 1904. Although the Jiangnan prefectures continued to lead the province, the numbers of *jinshi* from that area declined steadily from a high of 464 in the period 1696–1745. Its percentage of the provincial total slipped from 74 percent in the period 1745–96 to only 46 percent in the period 1850–1904. On the other hand, Shaoxing men became markedly more successful in the nineteenth century; the number of *jinshi* from Ningbo, which had declined sharply after the seventeenth century, also rose again after 1850. By then, the economic development in Shao-Ning was producing an academic surge that made these prefectures almost equal to Jiangnan, where academic structures had been badly battered by the rebellion.[26] This increase was duplicated on a much smaller scale along the southeast coast, where beginning economic development, better transportation, and elite political involvement all contributed to an academic revival. However, the dominance of the five northern prefectures was in no way challenged. Possible stirrings in Jinhua were cut off by the Taiping Rebellion, and the other southern prefectures remained academic backwaters.

While the number of Zhejiang *jinshi* was declining in the second half of the nineteenth century, the number of academies was increasing; small institutions were becoming more broadly dispersed in towns throughout the core and developing parts of the province. 85 academies (30 percent) were founded between 1850 and 1900 (mostly after the Taiping Rebellion) in contrast to 51 (18.5 percent) inherited from earlier dynasties and 53 (19 percent) established during the sixty-year Qianlong reign (1736–95).[27] Much of this increase occurred in Taizhou. However, more academies were founded in the five northern prefectures as a whole from the Xianfeng (1851–61) through the middle of the Guangxu reign (1875–1908) than in any comparable earlier period, whereas foundings declined in the other prefectures of the south and southwest.

The new academies were more likely to be located in growing commercial towns than in administrative cities or rural retreats. Members of the elite in wealthy market towns wanted a close, convenient educational institution of their own,[28] and they had the money to pay for it. Two of the three new academies established during the Tongzhi (1862–74) in the districts containing Huzhou city, for instance, were located in such towns.[29] In Linhai (Taizhou) academies were concentrated on the lower reaches of the Ling River, nearer the rising port of Haimen than the prefectural city.[30] Of about 65 academies established during the Tongzhi and Guangxu reigns, 49 were outside the environs of the administrative centers.

This increase and the form it took had implications for the relationship between the state and the scholarly elite. Paradoxically, the increase in the number of academies after the Taiping Rebellion signified a weakening rather than a strengthening of ties with the state. The new academies provided still more employment alternatives for upper-degree holders. Although they still aimed to prepare students for the official examinations, they were likely to be oriented toward local scholarly communities and not just the bureaucracy—especially at the lower urban levels. They also partly reoriented the geographical academic foci and encouraged circulation of members of the elite, which in turn facilitated the networking that fostered more extrabureaucratic activity.

Before the Taiping Rebellion, scholars in the three northern prefectures had been very oriented toward the academic centers of southern Jiangsu. These structures were shaken by the rebellion, and, in the late nineteenth century, there is evidence of considerable contact with other parts of Zhejiang and academic interchange between higher and lower urban levels in the same area. Graduates from the Gujing Jingshe in Hangzhou taught in Taizhou. A succession of retired *jinshi* headed a minor academy on the small island of Daishan in the group of islands forming Dinghai district (Ningbo). Upper-degree holders from district cities also sometimes headed academies in market towns.[31] This burgeoning academic activity came at a time when success in the examinations was declining in the old academic core of Jiangnan, when career opportunities outside the bureaucracy were rapidly expanding, and when scholars were beginning to look to a new intellectual center in Shanghai. All these coincidences suggest possibilities for growing elite institutional organization in a context of loosening bureaucratic ties, which will be explored more fully in following chapters.

The Taiping Rebellion in Zhejiang

Although some of these changes were underway by the mid-nineteenth century, the Taiping Rebellion profoundly affected social and economic arrangements for the rest of the century. Shi Dakai's Taiping armies had passed through southwestern Zhejiang in 1858, but the main fighting came relatively late. Most of the province fell to the Taipings in 1861, and Zuo Zongtang led protracted campaigns to recover the province from 1862 to 1864. Fighting was moderate in the southeastern prefectures, Ningbo, and part of eastern Shaoxing. The three northern prefectures and the southwest suffered tremendously. Hangzhou city endured a terrible two-month seige before falling to the Taiping leader Li Xiucheng at the end of 1861. It changed hands twice more before Zuo Zongtang's government troops besieged, bombarded, and then sacked what was left of the city a little over two years later. Similar misfortunes were visited upon the innocuous district city of Fuyang, south of Hangzhou, on Bao village (a center of resistance to the Taipings in Zhuji, Shaoxing), and on numerous other towns. Parts of Huzhou prefecture changed hands several times, and the countryside was only slightly safer than the cities.[32]

The Taiping invasion also triggered local secret society rebellions in, for instance, Zhuji (Shaoxing) and Ruian (Wenzhou), and defense forces were organized by local gentry or commoners.[33] Although the Zhejiangese people were not passive observers, many of the battles were nonetheless between outside troops. The Taipings were invaders, almost always called "Guangxi rebels" in the writings of Zhejiangese gentry, and Zuo Zongtang commanded an army of Hunanese. The Taiping armies numbered 750,000 to 1,000,000. Zuo's forces were somewhat smaller, but they were still larger than any force that could be mustered within the province. Local militias were frequently overrun, and Zhejiangese died in vast numbers—more often from starvation, exposure, and disease than in battle.[34]

Depopulation was the most dramatic result. There were about thirty million people in Zhejiang in 1850 but no more than eighteen million in 1873, nine years after the rebellion. In 1957 the population was still only 25.3 million.[35] Incomplete though the figures may be, available gazetteers repeatedly record declines of 50 to 85 percent in the most affected prefectures. Because most of these figures come from years well before or well after the rebellion, the actual losses are understated in Table 3. Despite the disarray of records and the probability that some displaced people went uncounted, the figures are too consistent to be ignored.

Deaths were matched by property damage. Public buildings, shops, and often most urban residences were destroyed. In the countryside mulberry trees were cut down, rice terraces overgrown, dikes and irrigation ditches destroyed, and roads neglected. A few years after the rebellion, some cities still had only a few inhabited homes, and villages were still abandoned.

TABLE 3
Population Loss During the Taiping Rebellion

District	Pre-Taiping population	Post-Taiping population
Jiaxing/Xiushui (Jx)	1,272,437 (1838)	292,687 (1873)
Tongxiang (Jx)	132,596 (1828)	40,579 (1874)
Haining (H)	93,343 (1759)[a]	33,579 (1873)[a]
Xindeng (H)	80,196 (1858)	10,643 (1864)
Zhuji (S)	956,556 (Qianlong)[b]	30,424 (1899)
Jinhua (Jh)	279,376 (1822)	119,427 (1874)
Yiwu (Jh)	513,878 (1785)	265,409 (1910)
Jiangshan (Q)	354,895 (1858)[a]	179,973 (1864)[a]

SOURCES: District gazetteers, population sections; Ho, *Population*, p. 241.
[a] Adult males.   [b] 1736–95.

About 5,786 acres of fields still remained unclaimed in the southwest at the end of the 1870's, and over 605,200 were unregistered in the three northern prefectures.[36] Even in the 1880's, extensive uninhabited areas were found right outside the Hangzhou city walls, and burned-out shells dotted the city. Squatters, drawn to the capital by jobs, congregated in encampments of highly inflammable grass shacks.[37]

Such destruction presented tremendous tasks of relief and reconstruction, but the rebellion also brought new opportunities. Population density dropped from an estimated three hundred persons per square kilometer on the eve of the rebellion to only about 117, some forty years later in 1898.[38] The decrease in population pressure created more favorable conditions for economic growth and even improved the living standards of the survivors. The other effects were of two kinds. Some threw existing socioeconomic relations into turmoil, without fundamentally changing them in the long run. Others merged with the changes produced by foreign trade, producing more lasting realignments.

Large (but often temporary) changes in land relations, immigration with its attendant social tensions, and general low-level disorder fell into the first category. The rebellion not only left much land uncultivated, but it also destroyed village registers.[39] The loss of the records was particularly serious, given the fragmentation of land holdings and the frequency of absentee ownership in Zhejiang. Landlords died leaving ownerless property. Those who survived had difficulty locating their land or proving title when they could find it. There was also an extreme labor shortage. Even if a person could prove his ownership, there were often no tenants to cultivate his plots.

Land prices therefore fell drastically. In Jiangnan some land that had been worth about forty thousand cash could be obtained for one thousand. To the southwest in Longyou, good agricultural land had sold for thirty yuan a *mou* and poor land for twenty. Right after the rebellion, prices had dropped to four and two yuan. Prices crept back up as recovery progressed, however. In the (early?) Guangxu reign good land cost eight yuan. By 1910 prices had inflated to 44 yuan, and they reached 70 yuan in the 1920's.[40]

Rents and tenancy followed a similar course. In Tangqi (Jinhua) wealthy families fell into straitened circumstances, and 70 to 80 percent of the fields were farmed by their owners after the rebellion. Rents also fell. Landlords who were trying to get land back under cultivation offered several years free of rent. Tenants were virtually able to set rates, and landlords could not evict defaulters. Particularly the immigrants, who were unbound by local ties, felt little obligation to the landlords. In Yanzhou, for instance, the three to four pecks (*dou*) of rice collected per *mou* in the late 1870's equalled less than half the old rent. Moreover, tenants refused to maintain irrigation systems and follow planting schedules.

Permanent tenure spread in Zhejiang after the rebellion, but rural social relationships were not completely altered. By the end of the century, tenancy had crept back to its old level of about 50 percent, and in the 1910's 60 to 70 percent of the fields in Zhejiang as a whole were cultivated by tenants. There were, however, subtler changes relating to the new wave of commercial expansion. In the core areas, the peasantry probably became more differentiated, household handicrafts were a growing source of family income, dependency on the market increased, and very possibly more peasants found urban employment. Social relationships in general became more market oriented.[41]

Migration also affected rural society. Uncultivated land in the north and west almost immediately began to attract immigrants (*kemin*) from Wenzhou, Taizhou, and Chuzhou; from parts of Shaoxing and Ningbo; and from such other provinces as Henan, Hunan, and Jiangxi. Some disbanded Hunanese soldiers settled in Zhejiang rather than returning home. Members of work gangs, recruited from the undamaged areas for major water control projects, also stayed on.[42] These immigrants formed their own cohesive communities, which then attracted more settlers from the same original area. Thus in western Huzhou immigrants in Anji district were mainly from Hubei, those in Xiaofeng from Shaoxing, and those in Wukang from Wenzhou. In some districts like Lin'an (Hangzhou), they far outnumbered the native population (*tumin*).[43]

The new settlers were almost always poor, but they varied considerably in respectability. In one township near Hangzhou people from Wenzhou and Taizhou came in family groups that banded together for mutual support. They were experienced farmers who were well regarded and able to intermarry with the local populace. Unlike them, the settlers from Hunan and Hubei, were mainly unmarried, disbanded soldiers. They were unskilled and remained poor; some were suspected of robbery.[44] Officials tried to control the settlers by organizing them into *baojia* or communal groups with headmen, but social strains and disorder were inevitable.[45]

Immigration merged therefore with several other general manifestations of late nineteenth-century social disruption. There was a constant movement of impoverished, vagrant, or migrating people. Emigrants setting out deliberately for new areas overlapped bands of distressed people (*nanmin*) fleeing natural disasters, disbanded soldiers, and permanent vagrants.[46] Increased female infanticide during and after the rebellion soon created a surplus of potentially rootless, poor, unmarriageable males.[47] Bandits and smugglers were particularly active in the hilly peripheral districts, along the coast, or around Lake Tai in the north. Conscientious officials organized *baojia*, and bureaus in large cities like Hangzhou were essentially police forces managed by members of the elite under official supervision.[48] However, the vagrancy, the raids, and the robberies, which were symptomatic of rural imbalances, could not be stopped.

Another factor that contributed to the larger picture of rural violence was frequent clashes between immigrants and the local populace. Both the officials and the remaining landlords had initially encouraged settlement to bring the land back into cultivation. It was, however, hard to collect rent, the local people often resented the outsiders, and immigrants occupying vacant lands became embroiled in disputes with the real or fraudulent former owners. The lack of records opened boundless opportunities for litigation and corrupt clerical manipulation of tax registers.

Clashes were particularly frequent in the border districts of western Huzhou, but no part of the north was immune. The immigrants were accused of robbery and smuggling by the local people. Sometimes they formed illegal cults, and there were incidents of rape. Different groups of immigrants also fought each other. In some places the clashing interests of the poor hill-people and the better-off townsmen further augmented tensions. By the early 1880's simmering feuds escalated into substantial battles —as in Jiaxing and Huzhou prefectures during the spring and summer of 1882—that required the repeated intervention of government troops. Subsequently the violence receded, but the tensions remained.[49]

Anti-tax riots were another prominent aspect of rural unrest during the post-Taiping years. The newspaper *Shen bao* recorded ten or eleven major incidents from 1872 through 1883, in which community sentiments were mobilized against abuses in land tax or grain tribute collections, manipulation of silver-copper ratios, new taxes for special projects, or *lijin*.[50] Banditry had also increased, and the rural societies of some peripheral areas had become militarized during the rebellion. This phenomenon was most evident in Taizhou prefecture, where militias originally organized against the rebels became allied with the bandits. Bandits organized as local defense forces, attacking other localities and easily eluding pursuit in the rugged terrain. A series of frustrated officials unwisely resorted to harsh methods that provoked hostility to government authority even among the respectable people—who resented the soldiers' indiscriminate killing and looting. The tensions culminated in a rising from 1881 to 1884 loosely led by the boxer Huang (Wang) Jinman, who was popular in the villages because of his Robin Hood policies of robbing the rich and helping the poor. Although the rising was finally suppressed, lesser disorders continued.[51]

As a whole, Zhejiang was not militarized by the Taiping Rebellion. In the hardest hit areas, the time was too short and the destruction too great. Thus the Shouchang (Yanzhou) gazetteer records that the militiamen initially organized against the Taiping armies were badly outnumbered. After most fled along with the troops and the officials, the small remaining bands played no decisive role in the subsequent fighting. By the end of the rebellion, 80 to 90 percent of the population had died, and the rest were destitute.[52] There simply was no one to militarize.

Although militias had larger roles in areas that were not so drastically overwhelmed, they were likely to be disbanded after the rebellion. Thereafter, local forces were mobilized periodically, but they were not continuing local features. Outside of Taizhou, evidence for militarization comes mainly from the decidedly peripheral districts, which were isolated from the main events of the late nineteenth century. Even there, neither bandits nor militias appear to have undermined seriously the position of the officials.[53]

Aside from the initial numbing effects of the destruction, the lack of militarization can best be explained by the economic resurgence of the core areas. Trade and money-making, not military competition, was the order of the day. A good deal of the unrest in such areas arose from opportunity; conflicts arose over who would benefit from expansion. Disorders and robberies occurred frequently, but they did not shape social organization, and they did not define the trends in the parts of the province that became political arenas at the end of the Qing.

How did the conditions created by the Taiping Rebellion in the core areas interact with those arising from the Shanghai foreign trade? It has been suggested that diminished population pressure raised living standards, allowed more latitude for agricultural specialization, and left more surplus for investment. Destruction of old-style silk-weaving establishments in Nanjing, Suzhou, and Hangzhou facilitated the reorientation of Jiangnan sericulture toward foreign trade.[54] The large population losses in the big cities of the north also encouraged new urbanization patterns. One general estimate suggests the Hangzhou population dropped from 600,000 to 80,000 between 1860 and 1864.[55] This city recovered its population in the twentieth century. Huzhou and Jiaxing, on the other hand, still had only about 100,000 inhabitants in the 1920's and were overtaken by Ningbo, Shaoxing, and Yongjia.[56]

Not only did the location of the major urban centers shift eastward, the balance between the cities and the market towns in Jiangnan also changed. Some sizable market towns recovered more quickly than the cities of Jiaxing and Huzhou. Those that did so were aided by profits from foreign trade. Their economies were oriented toward Shanghai, and they drew commerce away from the larger north Zhejiang cities. In the early twentieth century Zhejiang was distinguished by large towns with ten to twenty thousand people.[57] Its increasing urbanization fitted poorly into the Qing administrative structure, which gave little direct supervision to towns below the district level.

The Taiping Rebellion also contributed to the fusion of merchants and gentry. The elimination of many members of the old elite did not destroy the old social structure, but it did open up room at the top—most notably for merchants enriched by foreign trade. For a time, land was an uncertain investment, and gentry who depended heavily on rents fared badly. People with trading interests did better, and the availability of cheap land right after the rebellion created opportunities for mercantile wealth. Rich merchants also raised their status and acquired leverage with officials through contributions and services performed during the rebellion. Moreover, many members of the Jiangnan elite who survived the Taipings did so because they made their way to Shanghai. Refugees intermingled, developed new contacts in the city, and became familiar with circles that were involved in foreign trade. Some post-rebellion businesses and managerial ventures originated in this refugee experience.[58]

Finally, the Taiping Rebellion set the stage for sharper core-peripheral distinctions during the rest of the nineteenth century. Destruction did not respect zonal boundaries; the big difference lay in recovery potentials. The economic stimulus of foreign trade in the Jiangnan and Shao-Ning cores created a major new impetus on top of the economic edge that these areas had long had over the border districts and the southwest. The places that were drawn into the Shanghai trading sphere recovered and forged ahead. Other badly destroyed areas stagnated until at least the beginning of the twentieth century.[59]

Economic Expansion After the Taiping Rebellion

There were three dynamic sectors of the Zhejiang economy between the end of the Taiping Rebellion and the 1911 Revolution: silk, cotton, and coastal shipping. All three directed the economies of parts of the province in the direction of Shanghai and foreign trade. At the same time they stimulated economic organization, production, and trade within the parts of Zhejiang where they flourished.

This economic activity concentrated in the existing economic cores and, to a small extent, along the southeast coast. There are no reliable figures for the amount and location of trade in this period, but *lijin* statistics provide a rough indication.[60] The distribution shown in Table 4 underlines the existence of large core-peripheral differences and the lack of economic vitality in Chuzhou and the southwest.

Commercial agricultural crops. Silk was the most expansive sector of the Zhejiang economy in the post-Taiping years. As shown by Table 4, it produced a high percentage of *lijin* revenues. Jiangnan had been the center of Chinese sericulture since the Northern Song dynasty (960–1126), when it produced one-fourth of the country's silk. Production became commercialized during the Yuan dynasty, as peasant households sold home-reeled raw silk to urban weaving households. Peasant market-oriented production and urban weaving continued to

TABLE 4
Lijin *Stations and Collections in Zhejiang, 1897*

	Stations		Collections		
Prefecture	Main	Branch	Taels (tea)	Yuan (silk, cotton)	Strings of Cash
Hangzhou[a]	12	39	6,992	292,471	377,474
Jiaxing[a,b]	14	81	0	393,817	404,698
Huzhou[a]	7	44	1,332	1,532,727	748,387
Ningbo	8	14	116,854	155,100	584,628
Shaoxing[a]	11	53	97,424	581,945	660,616
Taizhou	6	20	1,781	2,840	112,344
Wenzhou	10	10	29,312	19,900	145,743
Chuzhou	4	0	1,487	0	66,741
Jinhua	1	4	5,031	10,430	69,688
Quzhou	5	9	39,740	4,000	428,563
Yanzhou	3	2	28,588	3,000	62,510
TOTAL	81	276	328,541	2,996,230	3,661,392

SOURCES: Luo, pp. 257, 260–61, amended for Wenzhou and Chuzhou from *Zhejiang tongzhi lijin mengao,* 2:65a.
[a]Including separate silk and cocoon stations.
[b]Before late 1897 reduction in the number of stations.

expand during the Ming and Qing, giving rise to collection centers like Shuanglin, Puyuan, and Shimen and causing the development of weaving to the technological limits of traditional science in the factories of Nanjing, Suzhou, and Hangzhou.[61] The domestic markets for silk did not expand in the nineteenth century,[62] but a sharply rising demand in Europe and the United States during the 1850's opened new markets abroad. Production was depressed in the 1860's because of the destruction of mulberry trees and traditional weaving establishments during the Taiping Rebellion,[63] but by about 1870 the silk regions had revived and had begun to direct production to the more profitable foreign trade.

Chinese silk exports as a whole continued to increase in both amount and value until the 1930's, even though China's share in the world market shrank after 1895 because of Japanese competition and China's own failure to improve technology and agricultural methods. From the 1870's through the 1890's, about 70 percent of the exported silk was shipped from Shanghai. The Shanghai percentage declined when more treaty

TABLE 5
Raw Silk Production in Zhejiang, 1878 and 1879
(Piculs)

Prefecture	1878	1879
Huzhou	29,252	33,042
Jiaxing	7,775	8,537
Hangzhou	8,211	9,352
Shaoxing	1,317	1,954
Ningbo	33	52
Total Zhejiang (white)	46,588	52,937
Shanghai exports (white, yellow)	51,278	60,358
Total China	67,000	81,000

SOURCES: IMC, Silk, pp. 76–82; IMC, Trade Reports, 1879, p. 109; Hsiao Liang-lin, pp. 102–6.

ports opened in the late 1890's, but the Lower Yangtze provinces as a whole retained their preeminent position.[64]

Zhejiang's share in the Shanghai silk trade lay in exports of raw, re-reeled, or steam filature white silk. Its dominant position in Yangtze Valley sericulture during the 1870's can be seen from a survey conducted by the British consul in Shanghai (Table 5). His estimates, based on lijin statistics, are far above the figures for Jiangsu silk production in those years. Thus a high percentage of exports must have come from Zhejiang, particularly from Huzhou, which aimed much of its production at the foreign market.[65]

Zhejiang continued to specialize in white silk into the twentieth century, but its share of the total Yangtze Valley production declined as yellow silk was introduced to new areas of Jiangsu, Anhui, and the Middle and Upper Yangtze. Sericulture also spread in Zhejiang, but the high production levels in the original areas left little room for growth without marked technological change. More ominously, by the early 1900's silkworm disease had begun to limit quantity and quality.

Even so, assuming that most Shanghai white silk exports continued to come from Zhejiang, silk remained a highly profitable aspect of the provincial economy (Table 6). After slump-

TABLE 6
Five-Year Averages of Shanghai Exports and
Re-exports, White Silk, 1876–1910:
Raw, Re-reeled, Steam Filature

(Nearest 100 piculs)

Years	Piculs	Years	Piculs
1876–1880	53	1896–1900	50
1881–1885	38	1901–1905	42
1886–1890	37	1906–1910	46
1891–1895	51		

SOURCES: Shanghai Annual Tables of Export and Re-export of Native Products, IMC, *Trade Reports*, 1879–1910; IMC, *Silk*, p. 85. Figures for 1880–81 and 1885 in IMC, *Trade Reports*, combining white and yellow silk adjusted downward 6,500–7,000 piculs.

ing in the 1880's, these exports recovered in the 1890's. The more moderate decline in the 1900's may not have represented any actual loss of Zhejiang silk production. An average of 1,850 piculs a year was exported through the new Maritime Customs station at Hangzhou from 1900 to 1910. Cocoons were also sent directly from Hangzhou to Japan, and the whole structure of silk production became more complex and specialized.[66]

The continuing profitability of sericulture during the last decades of the Qing had important effects both on Jiangnan society as a whole and on elite society and elite relations with the government. New areas were planted with mulberry trees. The distinctions between merchants and gentry were reduced still further as scholars and degree holders were lured into business by the profits to be had from the silk trade.[67] In subsequent chapters there will be repeated examples of the significance of this elite prosperity for the development of public activities.

How much peasants benefited depends upon the still unknown factors of taxes, rents, and the ratios between their expenses and silk or cocoon prices. New opportunities arose, including more work for women. Dependence upon foreign trade added new uncertainties to those already created by weather conditions and fluctuating domestic demand. Peasants owning land or enjoying secure tenure in sericultural regions appeared to gain, although those not so favorably situated lagged behind economically.

Cotton production expanded somewhat later than sericulture, and it benefited different parts of the province. Rising demands from mills in Japan and Shanghai caused more cotton to be grown in the coastal districts of Xiaoshan, Yuyao, and Ciqi (Shaoxing and Ningbo) during the 1890's. In 1887 the cotton crop of those districts was estimated at 96,000 piculs, and virtually all that was not used in Zhejiang was sent by junk to Fujian.[68] By 1893, 99,000 piculs of cotton was exported through Ningbo Maritime Customs to Shanghai (83,000 of which was sent on to Japan). In addition, 50,000 piculs was shipped to Fujian, and the growing handicraft weaving industry used unknown amounts within the province. Exports through Maritime Customs continued to rise rapidly, reaching an average of 155,000 piculs in the period 1906–10 (see Table 10). Cotton overtook tea as Ningbo's major export about 1900. During the next decade Ningbo was the second- or third-ranking treaty port in cotton exports, although its volume remained far below that of Shanghai.[69]

Zhejiang's cotton crop never rivaled that of Jiangsu, and the province did not become a textile center in the twentieth century.[70] The initial expansion at the end of the Qing, however, stimulated the economies of Shaoxing and Ningbo at that time. The demand for cotton yarn encouraged a few modern spinning mills and a larger number of small workshops using simple machinery.[71] By 1900 Zhejiang was producing about 300,000 piculs of cotton yarn; in that year two mills in Ningbo each manufactured 35,000 piculs of yarn. Although yarn exports rose after 1905, most was used by domestic weaving households. Foreign imports of cloth slowed this handicraft growth but did not prevent it.[72] The increase in cotton culture in the late nineteenth century was important because it increased elite financial resources in areas not well suited to sericulture.

The third major cash crop in Zhejiang was tea. Most was consumed in China, although a portion of Wenzhou tea shipped to Shanghai was then sent to the United States and England.[73] Tea remained economically important in Wenzhou, Quzhou,

TABLE 7
Tea Passing Through Maritime Customs,
1875–1910
(Thousands of piculs)

Year	Ningbo	Wenzhou	Hangzhou
1875	126		
1880	148	2	
1885	167	3	
1890	152	5	
1895	189	21	
1900	69	15	81
1905	87	18	109
1910	111	26	146

SOURCES: IMC, *Trade Reports*, reports from these three ports for the above years.

NOTE: Increased exports from Hangzhou in 1900 and 1905 probably reflected new record-keeping after the Maritime Customs was established. Some teas previously exported from Ningbo were diverted to Hangzhou (IMC, *Trade Reports*, 1901, p 537), and others presumably had previously been exported via Shanghai. Some of the exported tea was grown in Anhui, not Zhejiang.

and Yanzhou at the end of the Qing, but it was not an expansive commodity. As shown by Table 4, tea in Shaoxing was producing fewer *lijin* receipts than cotton and silk by the late 1890's, and exports from Ningbo had stagnated (Table 7).

Quantitative considerations aside, tea production was less likely to bring local prosperity than silk or cotton. Tea was grown in poor hill areas, and the trade was organized by outside merchants (often from Anhui or, sometimes, from Shaoxing), who could dictate terms to the local producers. The profits were exported, and the tea-growing areas did not develop strong merchant classes of their own. Moreover, tea was not a major entrée for Zhejiangese into the Shanghai business world. Even in Hangzhou, Zhejiangese-owned tea firms were outnumbered by those owned by Anhui men. New tea-processing companies appeared in Wenzhou, and some new techniques were introduced into tea finishing before 1911.[74] Nonetheless, tea merchants did not furnish the same financial and local leadership as the silk merchants, bankers, and shippers of the five northern prefectures.

The coastal trade. Ningbo was opened to foreign trade after the Opium War because it was already an important shipping center. The integration of marketing systems within the prefecture during the eighteenth century had provided a firm basis for the city to become a major transshipment point for goods going to or from Ningbo, Shaoxing, southwestern Zhejiang, and the adjoining districts of Anhui and Jiangxi. It was important in the north-south inter-regional coastal trade because of its location between the Yangtze Valley and the southern ports of Fujian. Because Fujianese already dominated both Ningbo's trade to the south and its silk trade with Japan, Ningbo merchants were pushed north to Shanghai. They became entrenched there well before Shanghai's opening as a treaty port, and during the nineteenth century they expanded up the Yangtze Valley to Hanzhou and north along the coast to Manchuria. With this background it was almost inevitable that they would acquire an important share in foreign trade.[75]

The linkage between Ningbo and Shanghai was a major factor in Zhejiang's development. Since the economies of the three northernmost prefectures had long been entwined with that of adjacent Jiangsu, silk naturally followed the existing trade routes to nearby Shanghai. Ningbo merchants brought different parts of the province and different economic activities into the Shanghai trading sphere.

Ningbo's role in foreign trade is somewhat obscure because it conducted little direct trade with other countries. In 1910, for instance, goods that were headed abroad through Ningbo Maritime Customs were worth only H.K. taels 5,688 compared to H.K. taels 10,313,848 worth of merchandise bound for Chinese ports. The value of direct imports in 1910 increased to H.K. taels 2,133,642, compared to 947,673 in 1900 and 372,951 in 1890.[76] Most of these goods were probably from Taiwan or Japan, however, and part of the increase may have been the result of the cession of Taiwan after the Sino-Japanese War, which turned an old domestic trading partner into part of a foreign country.

Nonetheless, two-thirds to three-fourths of Ningbo's imports through Maritime Customs were foreign goods. Most were transshipped at Shanghai, and some of the goods sent from Ningbo to Shanghai were exported. Ningbo men, either in Shanghai or at home, were the intermediaries. After Wenzhou opened as a treaty port, its foreign trade (and that of Taizhou), was also pulled northward, while the older southern trade with Fujian continued in junks.[77] The establishment of a Taizhou guild in Shanghai in 1902 reflected the growing business connections of Haimen and other Taizhou cities.

Ningbo thus became a secondary center through which such foreign goods as opium, cotton yarn and piece goods, kerosene, nails and iron bars, sugar, soap, and matches came from Shanghai. Tea, cotton, and handicraft items like hats, mats, fans, and umbrellas were shipped abroad and to other parts of China by way of Shanghai; lumber, agricultural specialties like oranges, medicines, and alum passed through Shanghai on their way to the Yangtze Valley or northern cities. In the process, Ningbo and Shaoxing men extended their influence within Zhejiang, both along the southeast coast and in the southwest. Although statistics are not available, in the late nineteenth century the trade route across Ning-Shao to the Qiantang River valley seems to have rivaled the more direct route between the southwestern prefectures and Hangzhou. Trade patterns began to shift around 1900, however, with the opening of a treaty port at Hangzhou in 1897, the use of steam launches on the Qiantang River, and the completion of the Shanghai-Hangzhou railway line in 1909.

A perspective on Ningbo's trade is provided by the comparisons with other treaty ports in Table 8 that show Ningbo in an intermediate position: similar to Fuzhou or Amoy, far below Shanghai, but substantially above Zhejiang's other two treaty ports. These figures only show trade passing through Maritime Customs, but they can reasonably be interpreted to mean, first, that the coastal trade had a considerable economic impact in Zhejiang, and, second, that the broad range of items on which the trade was based had not overtaken Jiangnan silk.[78]

Selected aspects of the Ningbo trade appear in Tables 9 and 10.[79] They show fairly stable trade levels through the 1870's and 1880's, with imports increasing after 1890 and exports after

TABLE 8

Relative Value of Trade at Treaty Ports, 1900

(Thousands of H.K. taels)

Place	Gross value[a]	Net value	Rank among 26 ports
Hanzhou	78,490	57,051	2
Canton	53,405	53,037	3
Swatow	44,031	43,245	4
Tianjin	32,635	31,921	5
Fuzhou	15,857	15,342	12
Ningbo	15,414	15,227	13
Amoy	18,122	13,943	14
Hangzhou	9,464	9,434	15
Wenzhou	1,625	1,460	24
Shanghai white raw silk exports	17,174		

SOURCE: IMC, Trade Reports, 1900.

NOTE: Trade was generally depressed in 1900 because of the Boxer Rebellion, but only the relative standing of Tianjin (usually 2) was changed.

[a]Gross value is the value of all imports and exports passing through Maritime Customs. Net value is gross value less imports re-exported to other treaty ports or abroad.

TABLE 9

Average Annual Trade, Ningbo Maritime Customs, 1876–1910

(Thousands)

Period	Imports (H.K. taels)		Exports (H.K. taels)		Tonnage	
	Net	By junk	Net	By junk	Out	Inland steam
1876–1880	7,782		5,784		282	
1881–1885	7,604		4,348		332	
1886–1890	7,630		4,993		412	
1891–1895	9,156		5,631		507	
1896–1900	11,084		4,871		494	75[a]
1901–1905	13,211	5,415[b]	6,832	5,277[b]	521	86
1906–1910	14,579	6,140[b]	9,031	4,605[b]	883	153

SOURCES: IMC, Trade Reports, 1882, pp. 219–20; 1890, pp. 273–74; 1900, pp. 272–73; 1910, pp. 516–17, 521.

[a]1897–1900 only.

[b]Nov. 1903–Nov. 1905, and Nov. 1906–Nov. 1910.

TABLE 10

Average Annual Imports and Exports in Selected Items, Ningbo Maritime Customs, 1876–1910

(Thousands)

Category	1876–80	1881–85	1886–90	1891–95	1896–1900[a]	1901–5[a]	1906–10[a]
Imports							
Kerosene (gallons)	422	972	1,595	2,219	2,701	3,148	2,562
Matches (gross)	426	154	219	318	342	313	264
Cotton goods (pieces)	680	539	750	343	753	782	727
Cotton yarn (piculs)				15	10	14	8
Iron (piculs)	27	36	35	29	19	14	8
Sugar: white, brown, refined (piculs)	30	35	90	103	224	12	5
Exports							
Green tea (piculs)	127	150	150	173	90	91	100
Raw cotton (piculs)	24	6	13	54	89	106	155
Cotton cloth (pieces)						12	13[b]
Cotton yarn (piculs)					2	1	19
Hats (pieces)	7,826	7,665	8,908	2,324	4,121	3,840	4,623
Fans (pieces)	758	933	2,112	2,507	2,358	2,028	2,513
Alum (piculs)	32	54	58	80	82	71	67

SOURCES: Same as for Table 9.

[a] After Hangzhou became a treaty port in 1897, some of the Ningbo trade, especially imports, was diverted to that city. Declines may not reflect total Zhejiang shrinkage because Ningbo trade with eastern and southwestern districts still grew (IMC, Trade Reports, 1898, p. 331).

[b] In 1902–10 an additional average 200,341 pieces of nankeen were exported by junk through Chinese customs.

1900.[80] The composition of the trade reflected the needs and capacities of commercialized peasant society in Zhejiang as well as demands of the inter-regional Chinese urban market and foreign countries. Household consumption of certain foreign items like kerosene, matches, and sugar increased as it did elsewhere in China. Exports of local handicraft specialties (hats, fans) and minerals fluctuated considerably.[81] The Zhejiang market for foreign cotton goods expanded slightly, but it was limited by peasant income levels and the rising local spinning and domestic weaving industries. The slow economic recovery of the southwestern prefectures presumably limited the market for household imports, and there was no rapidly rising export besides cotton. The picture was thus one with no dramatic changes, but there was long-term expansion, particularly after 1900.

Industrial modernization. How important was economic modernization in precipitating the social and political changes in Zhejiang at the end of the Qing? Factories using Western techniques of machine-powered production began to be established in the late nineteenth century.[82] Innovation was, in part, a response to the needs of commerce and, in part, a conscious effort to build up Chinese enterprises to resist foreign economic encroachment. According to one very inclusive definition, slightly over 2,000 factories had been founded in Zhejiang by 1911—more than in any other province. These were mainly small establishments that did not use power-driven machinery. In 1918, 2,490 factories in Zhejiang employed only 75,900 workers compared to 198,350 employed by 1,420 factories in Jiangsu.[83] Capital investment was also less than in the other leading provinces. Thirteen major industrial enterprises established in Hangzhou between 1895 and 1913 had a combined capital of 1,552,000 yuan, compared to eighty-three in Shanghai with capital of 23,890,000 yuan, seventeen in Tianjin with capital of 24,000,000, and sixteen in Canton with capital of 5,791,000.[84] Figures from this period can not be taken too literally, but they indicate that Zhejiang's modern industry was dwarfed by its commerce and that changes in production techniques often occurred by modifying existing handicraft technology.

Industrial development was limited because Shanghai had become a regional center for silk and cotton textiles and it was difficult for Zhejiangese factories to compete with the better-financed and staffed Shanghai establishments. The province also lacked large coal or iron deposits, which were necessary to support the kind of heavy industry that grew up in the Wuhan area. Gentry and merchants set up companies to explore and mine deposits in Taizhou, Chuzhou, the southwestern prefectures, and western Hangzhou border districts. The deposits were small, however, and even when mining actually began it is doubtful that the methods were very modern.[85]

Partly because of its limited potential for heavy or military industry, there was relatively little governmental investment in Zhejiang.[86] The Japanese were the main foreign investors, but, on the whole, foreign capital was discouraged by nationalistic opposition.[87] Most funding came from Zhejiangese in Shanghai or from gentry and merchants within the province.[88] Investment fell into three categories. The largest was a variety of usually small, often consumer-oriented enterprises like the electric companies and flour mills in Hangzhou and Ningbo; match, soap, candle, camphor, paper, and a few machine factories; or brick kilns, food-processing plants, and printing presses.[89]

Silk filatures and cotton mills occupied a second, special category of light industry, intimately related to the province's two main commercial crops. They first appeared in the mid-to-late 1890's in Hangzhou, Ningbo, and the cotton-growing district of Xiaoshan. At least eight silk filatures and eighteen mechanized spinning or weaving establishments had been established by 1911. Some of the biggest had start-up difficulties and capital shortages. The first major mill in Ningbo failed in 1911, for instance, and its counterpart in Hangzhou required both governmental and foreign loans to keep going. Nonetheless, a small modern textile industry aimed at both foreign and local markets was permanently established (Appendix C).

The third and probably the most significant area of modernization in Zhejiang was transportation, which attracted investment as an adjunct to commerce. During the 1880's the government had discouraged the establishment of private companies that would undermine the monopoly of the China Merchant's

Steam Navigation Company in coastal shipping, but private initiative outran official controls by the close of the century. Fifteen to twenty Zhejiangese-owned steamship companies operated out of provincial ports at the end of the Qing. The largest was the Ningbo-Shaoxing Steamship Company (*Ning-Shao lunchuan gongsi*) established by Yu Xiaqing in 1909 with a capital of one million yuan. Its ships operated between Ningbo and Shanghai. Smaller companies ran lines between Ningbo and other coastal cities. Still others owned steam launches that towed barges on the rivers and canals between Ningbo and Shaoxing districts, between Hangzhou and Suzhou, to ports along the Qiantang River, and along the canals and the Ou River in Wenzhou (Appendix C). Steam navigation on inland water routes increased rapidly, rising from 16 to 817 launch passages at Wenzhou between 1905 and 1910 and from 108 to 1,531 at Hangzhou. Since the faster and more efficient steamships and launches took business away from old-style junks without completely replacing them, these companies were good investments.[90]

The Zhejiang Railway Company was by far the largest modern enterprise in the province. By 1912 it had a paid-in capital of 10,600,000 yuan,[91] all raised from sale of stock. A line from Shanghai to Hangzhou was completed in 1909 in cooperation with the Jiangsu Railway Company, and work had begun on an extension to Ningbo. However, the company was already beginning to run into the construction problems and capital shortages that led to its sale to the government in 1914.

The political impact of the railway far outweighed its economic effect in the late Qing (see Chapter 7), but some changes were evident even in the first few years. By 1911, daily trains linked with steam launch service to Suzhou were speeding passengers, mail, and light freight. British observers, angry over resistance to the English loan in 1907, criticized the quality of the construction, but German and Japanese comments were more favorable.[92] Some of the work had to be redone in the 1910's, but the provincial companies had built a functioning line quickly.

Faster transport led to new urban markets for perishable farm produce, causing local wage and price rises and some shortages and disruptions. Trains were also more reliable than the launches on the deteriorating canal systems, and businesses in towns along the line began to relocate near the train station. Freight traffic grew more slowly than passenger receipts because of competition from the launches and barges, complications at the border *lijin* station, and the inconvenient location of the Shanghai terminal. In early 1911 the Jiangsu railway receipts were still only 25,000 to 40,000 yuan per month, and those of Zhejiang must not have been very much higher.[93] The railway did not really become economically important until the republican period, but the success of the Zhejiang company compared to the other provincial railways of the late Qing was another indication of the financial strengths and organizational capacities of the Zhejiangese elite.

In sum, economic modernization began in Zhejiang with a burst of investment after the Sino-Japanese War, lagged in the early 1900's, and began to pick up some momentum from 1905 on. Quite predictably, most modern factories were located in the two biggest cities, Ningbo and Hangzhou. Most of the rest were in the five northern prefectures, although not necessarily in their administrative centers because locations were usually determined by private investors rather than officials. The proximity of Shanghai may have retarded industrialization within Jiaxing and Huzhou. In the southern half of the province a few widely scattered enterprises were established by progressive members of the elite, but modern industry scarcely penetrated the area.[94] Modern enterprise mainly followed existing patterns of commercial development. It was undertaken privately and, with a few exceptions, on a small scale. Trade remained the key to economic changes in Zhejiang by stimulating agricultural production, creating wealth, and channeling the surplus available for investment and consumption.

Some Social Ramifications of Commercialization

Commercial growth indirectly shaped autonomous activities in the core areas by creating geographical and social linkages, enhancing elite independence, and strengthening leadership capacities. Several factors contributed to the process, including temporary occupational migration, the stimulation of mercantile organization, and the rise of Zhejiangese merchants in Shanghai.

Occupational migration. Men from all social levels traveled in pursuit of business or trade. Iron workers in the town of Qing (Jiaxing), for instance, came from Wuxi in Jiangsu province every fall and returned home in the summer.[95] The same was true of tinbeaters in Hangzhou city, who came from parts of Ningbo.[96] Both merchants and scholars traveled frequently, and cities normally had sizable sojourning communities of men from other areas with or without their families. This kind of geographical mobility differed from both permanent migration to empty lands and the wandering of people driven to the road by natural disasters and poverty. It indicated commercial growth rather than destruction or social disintegration. It was less alarming therefore, but nonetheless it was beyond the control of the officials, who generally preferred to have people remain in one place.

There is no way to chart the size and directions of these crosscutting movements that led practitioners of specific trades to certain cities, failed to conform to marketing-system hierarchies, and directed people to prosperous market towns and metropolitan centers. Figures on steamship passengers arriving at and leaving Ningbo give some indication of the magnitude of just one of the patterns of travel through that particular city. In the 1880's and 1890's there were two or three daily steamers between Shanghai and Ningbo, and there were more after 1905. Initially there were only three monthly steamer trips to Wenzhou, which were later extended to Amoy and finally to Canton in 1909. By the 1900's, however, smaller launches made multiple daily trips between Wenzhou and Haimen or Ningbo and between Haimen and Dinghai. Fares between Ningbo and Shanghai were cheap: a price war in 1891 reduced, at least temporarily, the late 1880's price of fifty cents to twenty-five. Travel from Wenzhou was far more costly: three yuan to Ningbo and four to Shanghai when steam passage was initiated.[97] Even so, the steamship was a cheaper and easier mode of transportation to the north than were junks or overland travel.

TABLE 11

Chinese Steamship Passengers, Ningbo, Selected Years, 1882–1910

(Thousands)

Passengers:	1882	1890	1895	1900	1905	1910
Arrive Ningbo	74	123				
Depart Ningbo	71	121				
To Shanghai			114	125	151	467
From Shanghai			102	160[a]	148	470
To Taizhou/Wenzhou[b]			0.4	28	48	32
From Taizhou/Wenzhou[b]			0.6	29	48	30
To inland/other						300
From inland/other						296

sources: IMC, *Trade Reports*, 1882, p. 270; 1890, p. 274; 1895, p. 313; 1900, p. 374; 1905, p. 330; 1910, p. 525.
[a]The Boxer Rebellion caused an exodus from Shanghai in 1900.
[b]Wenzhou passengers numbered 3,000+ in 1910, about 1,000 in 1900 and 1905.

We do not know how much of the total coastal passenger traffic is recorded by the figures in Table 11, or how much of the increase was achieved by the diversion of passengers from junks as steam fares declined. There was almost certainly some real increase as travel became easier and trade and industry created more jobs. Moreover, the travel was not all in one direction. Even if we assume that cheaper, but unrecorded, junks carried more passengers to Shanghai than away from it, people were still coming back to Ningbo in substantial numbers. Thus the influx of Ningbo natives (and, by analogy, of other Zhejiangese) into Shanghai was not a permanent loss to their home areas. Men and money moved in both directions with little official supervision. Along with them went ideas, contacts, and organization, blurring the differences between higher- and lower-order urban areas.

Mercantile institutions: banks and guilds. Old-style banks, occupational guilds, and native place associations are the best recorded of the many institutions that expedited and regulated the expanding trade or provided support for traders. Zhejiangese established such organizations both within the province and in the cities outside it where many provincials did business or served as officials. By the late nineteenth century there was considerable interplay between Zhejiangese institutions in Shanghai, their counterparts within the province, and associations of natives of other provinces doing business in Zhejiang. Old-style banks (qianzhuang) were small, private institutions that were licensed but not closely controlled by the government. Capital ranged between ten and fifty thousand taels. Although some banks lasted over fifty years, business fluctuations often caused failures.[98] These banks had risen to finance trade in the Lower Yangtze during the eighteenth century. Their number increased as trade grew during the last decade of the dynasty, reaching 245 in Zhejiang in 1912, with a combined capital of 3,376,700 yuan.[99]

Hangzhou and Ningbo were the financial centers within Zhejiang. Haining (Hangzhou) became a secondary center in the twentieth century; relatively few banks were founded in Jiaxing or Huzhou, where credit was presumably handled from Shanghai. The banks in the provincial capital handled transactions growing out of the silk and tea trades, commerce with the southwestern prefectures, and trade with Anhui and Jiangsu. Ningbo banking was, of course, closely connected with the coastal trade. Qianzhuang were found in five of the six districts in that prefecture. They also concentrated in Shaoxing city and in Yuyao district, where merchants had strong connections with Ningbo financiers. Not surprisingly, there were far fewer banks in the southern half of the province. Even in the 1930's these were still largely limited to a few cities like Huangyan and Taiping in Taizhou, Yongjia and Ruian in Wenzhou, and Lanqi, Jinhua, and Qu in the southwest.

Zhejiangese (particularly Ningbo men) had become leaders in Shanghai banking in order to finance their businesses in that city. From about 1870 to 1910 the Fang, Li, and Ye families of Zhenhai, the Dong and Qin families of Ciqi, and the Xu of Huzhou developed especially wide banking interests. Shaoxing families like the Xie of Yuyao gained entrée as managers of banks established by Ningbo natives. These Shanghai bankers also established banks in Zhejiang cities, which thus became links in the macroregional financial networks.[100]

Such connections meant that poor business conditions or financial panics in Shanghai were likely to trigger bank failures in Zhejiang. The 1910 crisis caused by rubber speculation threatened temporarily to wipe out banks owned by the major Zhejiang banking families and caused secondary crises in Hangzhou, Ningbo, and other provincial centers.[101] Credit facilities of the *qianzhuang* were never long impaired, however, and these banks can be considered the archetypical—and most crucial—institutions of the late Qing commercial expansion in Zhejiang.

When modern banks (*yinhang*) began to appear in the 1900's, Zhejiangese financiers also moved quickly into both governmental and private institutions. In 1908 they established a branch of the Shanghai-based Ningbo Bank (*siming yinhang*) in Ningbo and founded the Industrial Bank of Zhejiang (*Zhejiang xingye yinhang*) to handle the Zhejiang Railway's finances. Although the capital of just these two institutions was one-third that of all 245 old-style banks, even during the republican period the older institutions flourished along with modern banking.[102]

While the *qianzhuang* mobilized credit, the guilds and native place associations organized trades and served as support groups. Native place associations (*huiguan*) were organizations of sojourners rather than strictly mercantile organizations. In Beijing or the provincial capitals many members were likely to be officials or scholars, and the Association of Shaoxing Natives in Shanghai also included scholars. However, many of the native place associations within Zhejiang and Shanghai grew out of trade, and in such cases a high percentage of their members were merchants. Their functions overlapped those of guilds when a particular line of business in a given city was the preserve of men from a specific locality. Both types of institutions performed protective, educational, welfare, and religious functions. The guilds also regulated business practices, set prices, determined standards, settled disputes, and disciplined members. They promoted business solidarity, reinforced personal linkages, and provided avenues for entering trades.[103]

While theoretically subject to official supervision, they actually exercised day-to-day jurisdiction over important aspects of commerce. Their development in the Lower Yangtze was encouraged by trade expansion during the Qianlong reign (1736–95). The number of guilds and associations rose gradually during the first half of the nineteenth century. They were founded frequently after the Taiping Rebellion and increased still more rapidly after 1900. Aside from the quasi-public functions they sometimes performed directly, these organizations were a source of funds for elite-run public institutions, and they took part in the politicized mobilization of the last Qing decade.

Because of the increasing orientation of the economic cores of Zhejiang to Shanghai, some of the most significant organization of Zhejiang merchants occurred in that city. The Zhe(jiang)-Shao(xing) Association had been founded during the Qianlong and the Siming Guild of Ningbo natives in 1797. Huzhou men established an association after the Taiping Rebellion. During the Guangxu period (1875–1908) native place associations were founded by men from Jinhua, Jiaxing, Taizhou, and Haining (Hai-Chang gongsuo). Dinghai men organized a group about 1910, and there were additional, more inclusive associations of Ningbo, Shaoxing, and Huzhou natives residing in Shanghai.

Besides these associations based on locality, Zhejiang merchants also moved into the Shanghai guild structure. Ningbo shippers had founded their own guild in 1819. Ningbo wine merchants and Jinhua ham-sellers opened theirs in 1880. More important, Zhejiangese dominated some of the major Shanghai trade organizations. Ningbo men, for instance, controlled the banking and shipping guilds, while the silk guild established in 1888 was the territory of men from Huzhou.[104]

Within Zhejiang itself, there were two similarly overlapping patterns. Native place associations established in the trade centers throughout the province, either by men from other provinces or by Zhejiangese from other prefectures, revealed patterns of externally controlled commerce. Guilds that were established either by local men or by outsiders indicated important areas of commerce without reference to internal or external control. Large commercial cities like Hangzhou, Ningbo, and Shaoxing had both kinds of institutions,[105] but the sparse records from the smaller cities and towns do not give a precise idea of the distribution elsewhere.

We do know that merchants from Fujian, Jiangxi, and Anhui (the Xin'an guilds of men from Huizhou district) established associations dating back to the Kangxi period (1662–1722). Jiangxi traders operated mostly in the south and southwestern prefectures. Tea dealers from Anhui ranged over much of the province, establishing institutions in market towns from Huzhou in the north to Lishui (Chuzhou) in the south. Fujian traders founded organizations in the coastal cities but also had associations in the southwest and even in Jiangnan. Ningbo and Shaoxing men were the other major founders of native place associations. Their trading seems to have begun slightly later than that of the merchants from the adjoining provinces, although some of their associations dated back to the late eighteenth or early nineteenth centuries. The Ning Shao men went to the southwest and to the southeast coast as dealers in wine, tea, medicines, and other merchandise and as specialists in banking, shipping, and the distribution of foreign goods. They also traded in some Jiangnan towns and were strongly represented in Hangzhou. After the Taiping Rebellion business activities and trade organizations of Ningbo and Shaoxing men also interacted with the permanent migration of settlers from parts of these prefectures to Jiangnan.[106]

Outside traders in major commodities like tea established themselves in the largest Zhejiang cities, and men from peripheral areas with a particularly profitable specialty like Jinhua hams also organized to bring their goods to the urban markets. However, the distribution of native place associations in much of Zhejiang traced the movements of merchants from economically dynamic areas into the peripheries. Once begun, such trends tended to perpetuate themselves because outside merchants were best prepared to organize further trade. Sojourning merchants might then become active in the public affairs of their places of business, or they might clash with local men trying to assert their prerogatives.

The core areas of Jiangnan were a major exception to this

pattern. Natives moved into Shanghai and other flourishing Jiangnan cities, but they did not go in force into the less developed parts of their own province to the south and east. The wealthy Jiangnan districts attracted outsiders, but the numerous, prosperous, and organized local merchants continued to control trades in which they had a special interest. The silk trade, for instance, was organized by native traders who were often inextricably connected to gentry landowners. Occupational guilds are more widely recorded in this area than in other parts of Zhejiang. Although it is possible that guilds elsewhere are simply neglected in the available sources, it is striking that they are listed in the market towns as well as the cities in Jiangnan. Thus there were rice and silk guilds at Xinshi (Deqing). Shuanglin town had rice, silk, and medicine guilds, Nanxun had a silk guild, and Puyuan had guilds for silk goods, raw silk, rice, and millet.[107]

The occupational guilds and native place associations were only one facet of the complex organization of trade. Large associations in the big cities were often divided into several subgroups.[108] Guilds were supplemented by smaller agglomerations of neighboring stores and shops dealing in the same items (*hang, zuo*).[109] Brokerage firms (*yahang*) organized silk production and distribution in Jiangnan or Shaoxing and controlled tea and other trades in Wenzhou and the southwest.[110]

These institutions competed with one another, but collectively they strengthened both the mercantile stratum and the elite as a whole. Merchants in the late Qing were more able than ever before to finance and regulate large volumes of trade, articulate and protect their interests, and bring new recruits into the existing structures. In these respects the mercantile associations may be compared to institutions like the academies or libraries that provided underpinnings for the scholar-gentry. Both these segments of elite society were expanding their distinctive organizational capacities while they were being drawn together in different ways by family and lineage connections, occupational interchange, or joint interests in public affairs. The resources of such expanding economic organization then strengthened the positions of members of the elite in public management.

The Zhejiangese merchants in Shanghai. Many of these late Qing trends are illustrated by the merchants who flocked to Shanghai during the nineteenth century. Biographical materials on the most successful of these men are more readily available than information is on their counterparts in the cities of Zhejiang. However, these big Shanghai merchants did not live in a world apart. There were particularly promising business opportunities in Shanghai, but there were many other opportunities in the expanding commercial cores during the late nineteenth century. Because the trade of these cores was becoming increasingly linked to Shanghai, intermediaries connected merchants in district seats and market towns to those in the urban center, and local businessmen had investments in Shanghai just as Shanghai merchants had economic interests at home. The histories of these Shanghai merchants tell us what was happening to society in the cores of Zhejiang; they also show some of the social effects of the growth of foreign trade and the development of a macroregional urban center within the Shanghai trading region. Who then were these men, and what were their connections with other members of the elite, with foreigners, with the rest of the Shanghai business world, with their home areas, and with officials? The history of the Li family of Zhenhai (Ningbo) is one good place to start looking for answers.[111]

The founder of the Li fortune, Li Mi, arrived in Shanghai in 1822 as a poor, fourteen-year-old apprentice to a flour shop. The shop also sold wine, which Li carried to the ocean-going junks anchored at the South City wharves. When a captain invited him to join his crew, Li took advantage of his right to bring extra goods to trade on his own account. In this way, he saved enough money to buy his own ship and to establish a firm with his older brother, Li Chengfu. At the height of their operations they owned one of the Shanghai wharves and a fleet of junks worth several tens of thousands of taels each. These ships carried raw cotton, paper, and other goods from Ningbo and Shanghai to the northern ports and brought back oil, beans, and wood products to the southeast. Soon the brothers expanded into finance by contributing money to a new *qianzhuang* bank, which was headed by a man who had arranged loans for their shipping. Later they established three banks of their own.

The Lis won favor with provincial officials when they built a warship that defeated the pirates off the coast of Fujian and Guangdong during the Daoguang period (1821–50). Li Mi's reputation for pirate suppression won him a commission to carry grain tribute by sea to Beijing. Subsequently he was awarded the sixth rank for his grain transportation and was given a salt transport franchise. Li Chengfu was commended for his contributions during the Taiping Rebellion.

By the time the two brothers died in the late 1860's, the family fortune was securely established. Business was carried on by Li Mi's son Li Jia, who increased his capital to several million taels, and by Li Cheng-fu's eldest son, Li Yuan. A younger brother studied and became a *jinshi* in 1876. Li Jia spent some of his fortune on a beautiful house and garden. He was also noted for his philanthropies in Shanghai, Ningbo city, and Zhenhai, and all three cousins cooperated to establish the lineage charitable estate that their parents had desired.

The dominant figure in the third generation was Li Houyou who, with his brothers, expanded the family banking business until it was wiped out by the panic of 1910. The Li fortunes were not seriously damaged, however, because Houyou had also continued the shipping business, established new trading companies, invested in Manchurian land development, and moved into modern banking by providing part of the capital for the Siming Bank. He did business in his native Zhenhai as well as Shanghai and was one of the first promoters of railway construction in Zhejiang.

During the last Qing decade Li Houyou was an officer of the Shanghai Chamber of Commerce and served on the Shanghai City Council. He had an important part in the mobilization of the 1900's as an organizer and a director of the Zhejiang Railway Company and a friend and business associate of Tang Shouqian, Zhang Jian, and other constitutionalists. He himself was a member of at least one constitutionalist organization and took part in nationalistic demonstrations; one of his cousins was a revolutionary. Lis of the fourth generation continued as businessmen, bankers, and compradors in Shanghai, and at least one was still living there in 1959.

This success story illustrates a number of the characteristics of Shanghai merchants in general and those from Zhejiang in particular. First of all, Zhejiangese had a very important place in Shanghai business by the second half of the nineteenth century. Ningbo natives surpassed Cantonese as the largest outside community in the city. Shaoxing natives were the next largest Zhejiangese contingent, and there were sizable communities from the three northern prefectures. Although Ningbo men dominated banking and shipping, those from Huzhou predominated in the silk business. The first Chinese-owned modern silk filature in Shanghai was founded in 1881 by Huang Zuoqing of Huzhou, for instance, and in 1897 almost all the 23 Chinese filature owners were from Huzhou, Hangzhou, Shaoxing, or Ningbo.[112] Below the very rich merchants were many other Zhejiangese businessmen and bankers, small traders, artisans, and workers making money at different levels.

Despite their numerical importance, Zhejiangese merchants did not "colonize" Shanghai like the outside merchants who dominated the trade of cities in some less developed parts of China. They had too many competitors among the merchants from Guangdong, Jiangsu, and other provinces. The Lower Yangtze economy and the commerce funneled through Shanghai was too large and too varied to be dominated by natives of one province. Conversely, Zhejiang did not simply become an economic dependency of Shanghai. There was some tendency in that direction, but the Zhejiangese cores were already highly commercialized. Certain aspects of their economies—most obviously sericulture and banking—were affected by Shanghai business conditions, but there was no one-way drain of human, material, or financial resources in the late Qing.

Trade fostered social mobility and the rise of new families, often from specific towns or districts that were well situated to profit from the new opportunities. Success came through hard work, frugality, and entrepreneurial talents.[113] When business empires persisted for several generations, it was clear that profits were neither being dissipated in conspicuous consumption nor diverted excessively into "gentry" investments in land, usury, or education. The initial entrepreneurial impetus was, however, normally replaced by a safer dispersion of assets among numerous lines of business and in land or lineage facilities. This method of limiting risks was fostered by the lack of legal protection. It did not always discourage long-term investments, but it did spread capital more thinly. It also contributed to the integration of vigorous new capitalists into the existing social and economic structures.

There was constant interaction between domestic and international business, with the role of foreign trade increasing sharply in the mid-nineteenth century. The Lis and the even older Fang family of Zhenhai[114] began their rise before Western trade became important in the Lower Yangtze. Fortunes of some slightly later merchants like Ye Chengzhong and Dai Siyuan of Zhenhai or Liu Yong of Nanxun were more closely connected to foreign trade.[115] It was, in any case, typical for men who had made large fortunes in one sphere to move into the other as well and also to become involved in modern industry and finance.

Shanghai merchants therefore had a complex and seldom totally dependent relationship to foreign trade and foreigners. Some merchants like Yu Xiaqing, another poor boy from Zhenhai, rose as compradors and were lifelong employees of foreign firms.[116] Nonetheless, being a comprador was only one of many overlapping routes to business success in Shanghai. As compradors became rich, they, too, founded independent firms, managed government enterprises, and engaged in philanthropic activities.[117] Merchants who had already become rich also became compradors as part of their multiple activities. Still others traded with foreigners without being employed by them, and the Fang family set up a separate company to handle foreign bank accounts—thus creating an institutional rather than a personal comprador. In contrast with the colony of Hong Kong, there were very few opportunities for Chinese with foreign expertise to rise in the Western political and social institutions of the Shanghai International Settlement or the French Concession. Their social positions were defined in Chinese contexts, pulling them back from becoming a distinct, peripheral, foreign-oriented stratum. Even a man like Yu Xiaqing, who had very close relations with foreign firms, could take the lead in opposing French land claims.[118]

The successful Shanghai merchants tended to broaden their connections with other elements in elite society, both in Shanghai and at home. At the same time, the profitability of foreign and inter-regional trade pulled local gentry into business. Thus scholar-gentry landlords in Jiangnan dealt in silk, while banking and shipping attracted gentry in Ningbo and Shaoxing.[119] While rich merchants were obtaining degrees and directing their sons to study for the examinations, gentry were sending their sons into trade. The core districts of Zhejiang were dotted with landlords who had business interests in Shanghai,[120] and rich merchant families who adopted gentry life-styles did not thereby give up the businesses through which they made money. The cooperation of gentry and merchants in modern industry and politics in the 1890's and 1900's was one outgrowth of this fusion of economic and social characteristics.

Philanthropy and public management were other arenas of elite interaction. Zhejiangese merchants helped run welfare institutions in Shanghai. They served on the Shanghai City Council after it was established in 1905, and, starting with Yan Xinhou, most presidents and many directors of the Shanghai Chamber of Commerce came from Zhejiang.[121] Some merchants active in Shanghai also did business and made contributions within their native province. Yan was a major investor in the first cotton mills in Ningbo, and Yu Xiaqing financed a bank and shipping company. Other Shanghai merchants backed the early silk filatures and cotton mills in Hangzhou and Xiaoshan.[122]

Shanghai merchants founded or contributed money to local public institutions in their home areas and helped to manage them after retirement. The Lis were also not the only family newly enriched by Shanghai trade to establish a lineage charitable estate. Four such families in the prosperous town of Nanxun did so in the 1890's and 1900's.[123] In many respects the relationship of Shanghai merchants to their home areas was similar to that of successful scholars who pursued other careers as officials. They invested money at home, provided leadership in initiating projects, and dispensed their own kind of patronage by providing jobs for men from their lineage or locality.

Rebellion and war broadened the roles, the public reputations, and the opportunities of merchants. Li Mi made his mark in pirate suppression, but the Taiping Rebellion created greater demands for merchant skills and money. Governors and army commanders asked Shanghai merchants to make contributions, manage revenue-producing monopolies, and procure supplies for troops.[124] Contributions drained the merchants' capital, but their fortunes were increased by administering monopolies and procurement. Such services also brought prestige, awards of rank, and future business. Thus the silk merchant and financier Hu Guangyong developed a long-lasting relationship with Governor-General Zuo Zongtang, and Yan Xinhou had a similar connection with the prominent self-strengthening Governor-General Li Hongzhang.[125] Officials were indebted to Shanghai merchants for help in suppressing rebellion, and both officials and gentry needed their aid in reconstruction. Just as the Taiping Rebellion stimulated elite management as a whole, it gave impetus to mercantile involvement in both official and public projects.

A very large part of Shanghai business activity was only loosely under official control. The Qing government had no program to foster private industry and commerce until the last few years of the dynasty, and the well-known system of "official supervision and merchant management" (*guandu shangban*) was characteristic of only a few early capital-intensive modern enterprises. Quite possibly, the disillusionment of merchants with this system and their fear of official encroachment upon highly visible private modern industry had the untoward effect of encouraging investment in better-protected foreign enterprises and thus retarding the growth of Chinese-owned modern firms.[126] Such problems did not stifle commerce. On the contrary, growing financial strength and organization fostered mercantile autonomy. Shanghai merchants were in a particularly good position to accumulate wealth and develop independent businesses, contributing to the surge of elite activity outside bureaucratic control—and many of these merchants were from Zhejiang.

Whatever happened in the future, Zhejiangese merchants in Shanghai still retained the attributes of sojourners during the last decades of the Qing. They were away from, but still geographically close to, their original homes during a period of improving transportation and diminishing travel times. One part of their social significance lay in the new characteristics they acquired in the city. The other lay in their continuing ties back home. Sometimes local ties actually broadened as successful merchants founded lineage organizations, made philanthropic contributions, and established equal relationships with other members of the elite in their native areas. They were leaders in the complex process through which commerce—and particularly foreign commerce—introduced changes into the core areas of the Lower Yangtze.

This multi-dimensional view of the Shanghai merchants leads on to the issue of the Chinese bourgeoisie.[127] The prosperous Zhejiangese merchants in Shanghai were part of the small capitalist class that emerged in the late nineteenth century. Their history amply illustrates the importance of foreign trade and capitalist intrusion in stimulating capitalism in China, although it does not prove thereby that this was the only way that Chinese capitalism might develop. On the other hand, inter-regional commerce was already vigorously expanding when foreign trade and investment entered Shanghai. Some older businesses were hurt by foreign competition and new technology. New traders and businesses arose in conjunction with foreign capital, but some established merchants also made the transition to more profitable lines of business.

The biographies of Shanghai merchants indicate that it is difficult, if not impossible, to separate these men into distinct nationalist, comprador, and bureaucratic capitalist categories, since they might fall easily into two or all three of these categories. What does seem politically important is that by the end of the nineteenth century the nationalistic bourgeoisie was dominant among the major Shanghai merchants, regardless of the origin of their capital.

Little attention has been paid to the possible overlap between what has been called the bureaucratic landlord class and the treaty port merchants—other than through the medium of government-dominated bureaucratic capitalism. In the Lower Yangtze there is reason to believe that this distinction is often artificial. The treaty port merchants continued to invest in land, purchase rank or degrees, and support kinship and educational institutions. Gentry with business interests were one source of capital for modern enterprises. Such investment patterns were consistent with the fusion of gentry and merchants that I have suggested occurred during the Qing. They also were reflected in the political cooperation found in the railway movement at the end of the dynasty. The incomplete differentiation of the bourgeoisie from the older social elite thus may have been a source of political strength rather than weakness vis-à-vis the late imperial state, and the bourgeoisie's continued involvement in kinship and local networks may have reinforced the economic effects of foreign trade in bringing about social change during this period.

In sum, the Zhejiangese economy and society were characterized by large core-peripheral differences, but a long history of economic prosperity and academic excellence had created a strong elite stratum. In the mid-to-late nineteenth century, first rebellion and then foreign trade disrupted the old patterns and interjected new elements. The old social outlines withstood this twin onslaught, but there were changes within the existing structures. On the elite level, for instance, the balance between office holding and trade as a source of status and income shifted. New families rose to prominence, new occupations developed, and the levels of social organization increased. New transportation, trade patterns, and technologies pulled parts of the province together, tying them more closely to Shanghai and connecting local economies to larger domestic and international markets. Men writing in this period spoke of social disruption. They lamented the decline of the old ways while moving to take advantage of the new, and they sought ways to deal with the problems they perceived. Elite reconstruction efforts, reactions to imperialist attacks, and political commitments were all molded by such broad trends even when they occurred in local settings.

THREE

The Post-Taiping Reconstruction
The Rise of the Public Sphere

It has often been assumed that an autonomous public sector did not develop in China until the very end of the nineteenth century and that this development involved the importation of Western institutions. In reality, the already growing number of public functions outside the bureaucracy were decisively increased in Zhejiang by the need to repair damage after the Taiping Rebellion. Physical reconstruction was a large part of the Tongzhi Restoration on the local level. Surviving elites expanded managerial roles and increased extrabureaucratic organization in the course of rebuilding community institutions.

Although officials and members of the elite undertook these tasks together, men outside the bureaucracy acquired more responsibility. Ironically, the very success of local reconstruction contributed to the proliferation of social organization beyond government control—ultimately undermining the political system that the elite still sought to preserve. The effect of post-Taiping reconstruction on state-societal balances can be seen in the growth of independently financed institutional complexes, the rise of managerial activism, and the development of rationales justifying autonomous initiative to benefit one's home area and recreate community solidarity in a perilous age.

Reconstruction Institutions

Welfare and education are the keys to understanding the expansion of local public institutions during reconstruction. These long-established spheres of elite activity assumed new urgency after the rebellion. Moreover, because charitable organizations and academies did not directly threaten government control, officials were likely to encourage such elite initiatives to promote social stability. Organization might expand therefore without confronting state power.

Although welfare and education emerge in the gazetteers as the most dynamic spheres of institutional development, they merely illustrate a still larger process of local organizational growth. Members of the elite also assumed responsibility for maintaining dikes, canals, roads, bridges, and public buildings. In some places, these functions tended to fuse with welfare immediately after the rebellion, because all were aspects of reconstruction. In the long run, however, they remained separate categories of local activity.

Water control in particular had long been managed by members of the elite in Zhejiang. There were local elite-run bureaus,[1] and water control attracted an increasing portion of community resources at successively lower levels of the urban hierarchy. Despite its quantitative importance, the water control sphere was not a propelling force in the post-Taiping managerial expansion for a number of reasons. The largest projects, like the repair of the seawall around Hangzhou Bay, were so enormous that they were paid for by the provincial government. Gentry managers were hired and contributions were solicited, but officials kept close track of progress.[2] On the other end of the spectrum, water control often involved divisive local issues.[3] Even when communities cooperated to dredge channels or maintain dikes,[4] the scope was geographically limited. In addition, water control was a specialized field that did not necessarily lead to wider involvement in local affairs.[5] In contrast, welfare and education were often at the core of expanding managerial establishments, and in many cities the men who supervised important water control projects were drawn from such complexes.[6]

Local welfare complexes. Gazetteers list a great variety of organizations that were established to store grain; distribute gruel to the hungry; care for the ill, aged, widows, and foundlings; correct wayward youths; dispense money to the poor; save the shipwrecked; ferry people across rivers; help scholars travel to examinations; and bury the dead. Firefighting and the collection of wastepaper with characters written on it were also among these services. Government-sponsored public relief homes (*yangji yuan*) had existed for centuries. They had not always operated continuously, however, and, in any case, many were destroyed during the rebellion. From the reconstruction period on, local welfare was often coordinated by officially sanctioned united welfare agencies (*tongshan tang*) that were organized and managed by elites to combine a variety of welfare functions.[7]

Agencies with this name pre-dated the 1860's,[8] but they multiplied along with relief and reconstruction bureaus (*shanhou ju*) after the rebellion. Zhejiang merchants and gentry in Shanghai had already organized relief for refugee communities during the fighting.[9] Fragmentary gazetteer accounts indicate that, as soon as their home areas were recaptured from the Taiping armies, members of the elite moved quickly with or without official leadership to import rice, set up gruel stations, and distribute clothing to the destitute populace. One particularly well-connected *jinshi*-degree holder from Tongxiang (Jiaxing) immediately secured a tax remission for his district from Governor-General Zuo Zongtang and set up a relief bureau. The next year he went to Hangzhou to ask the governor for more formal permission to found a relief and reconstruction bureau.[10]

In some places, these bureaus suppressed bandits and rebuilt dikes or bridges as well as dispensing relief.[11] After the initial crisis had passed, managers went on to establish academies,[12] foundling homes,[13] and a variety of other charities.[14] Most bureaus were eventually phased out or converted to permanent united welfare agencies, and united agencies continued to be established throughout the rest of the century—particularly in Shaoxing and Ningbo[15]—because they were a convenient way to organize and supervise local welfare. Sometimes an agency in a district city established branches in market towns.[16] More often, it coordinated district-level activities through subsidiary offices or quasi-independent institutions. Thus the agency in Linhai (Taizhou) oversaw grain equalization operations, the foundling home, one or more academies, and the organization that gave financial aid to men travelling to Hangzhou to take the provincial examinations (*binxing*).[17]

The scope of welfare functions was never formally defined, and agencies sometimes expanded their activities beyond what would normally be called welfare. The Hangzhou united welfare agency was a major presence in the provincial capital, housing several charities, financing a number of projects, and supervising fund raising. Officials enlisted its aid in such matters as fire-prevention, and in 1878 the agency even provided money for patrols to protect silk firms against a wave of robberies.[18]

United welfare agencies were not confined to any one part of the province or to administrative centers, but they are most often recorded in core or economically developing districts. Almost everywhere, welfare was not casual philanthropy, but rather a considerable effort to bolster social stability under elite dominance. It was not always well or honestly managed, and welfare agencies with too many managers became more of a burden than a benefit to the community.[19] Nonetheless, organizers in some places established regular accounting procedures, sought to limit the number of managers, and tried to ensure that they did not become entangled with yamen underlings. Like some chambers of commerce during the last Qing decade, welfare agencies played a central role in public affairs that might go beyond their formally defined functions, and officials treated the men running them with respect.[20]

Foundling homes enjoyed a special vogue through the end of the nineteenth century. Such homes had appeared and disappeared for centuries. Rampant female infanticide during and after the Taiping Rebellion stimulated their creation in the 1860's and 1870's. The many waterways of Zhejiang made drowning a convenient way for poor families to dispose of babies they could not afford to raise, and the floating corpses appalled both officials and members of the Zhejiangese elite.[21] An imperial edict of 1866, which singled out Zhejiang as one of the worst provinces, ordered the establishment of homes for foundlings. By then action had already begun in some districts, and by the 1890's homes existed in most districts of every prefecture. Occasionally they grew out of a small operation in which a local philanthropist hired a boatman to fish bodies out of the water and give them a decent burial. More often, founders and managers included some of the most prominent and high-ranking local elite activists, who were also involved in other institutions.[22]

The homes were mainly of two types. "Homes to nourish foundlings" (yuying tang or ju) actually housed and cared for children. "Bureaus to protect foundlings" (baoying ju) made cash payments directly to parents for the first six months to two years of the child's life. This second method became more popular during the late nineteenth century because it was simpler, less costly, more effective, and encouraged family solidarity.[23] Some places without full-fledged homes had "offices to receive foundlings" (jieying suo), which forwarded babies to other centers.

Homes accepted boys as well as girls, but they were primarily institutions for females. Many infants were weakened by exposure and malnutrition; dependent on a fluctuating supply of wet nurses, they died in even the best-run homes. Administrative abuses, including the sale of older girls as prostitutes, were also common.[24] Nevertheless, these homes were a serious organizational effort. In some districts they were subsidiaries of the welfare agency, but elsewhere large, independent homes developed their own institutional hierarchies. In Fenghua (Ningbo), for example, the district society to protect foundlings had 102 branches in 8 rural districts. During the second month of every year for about ten years the society in one rural district dispatched representatives to the villages it served to register families and distribute cash.[25] Such complex structures significantly added to the public institutional matrix and increased the links between different levels in the urban hierarchy.

Academies were also a focus of managerial activity, as members of the elite rebuilt existing institutions destroyed during the rebellion and founded new ones. The benefits from education and welfare supplemented each other: education increased the chance of success in the outside world, and welfare fostered local harmony and stability. It is not surprising therefore to find that these two spheres of public activity expanded together. In some instances, welfare institutions and academies or schools were organizationally linked.

The internal organization of the academies is seldom well recorded, although the general pattern is familiar. Most had one head who might lecture, although he usually did not. The number and names of teachers are rarely given, and the size of the student body varied considerably. The chief academy of a moderately well-off district might have sixty students, who were divided into two levels. Prestigious institutions in important cities had considerably more, while those in very peripheral district cities and some market towns had only forty or less.[26]

Qing academies are generally considered official institutions because of their close ties to the examination system. In Zhejiang, however, members of the elite founded between two-thirds and three-fourths of the academies established during the entire Qing period, and they also participated at times in planning academies with formal official backing. The amount of involvement is strikingly higher than it was in the other educationally strong southern provinces of Jiangsu and Jiangxi, but it is similar to elite involvement in Guangdong after 1850.[27] Whether officially founded or not, academies were managed by gentry and integrated into local situations. Officials appointed heads and teachers, but apparently they did so in consultation with local elites. In contrast to Grimm's description of education in Guangdong,[28] there is little evidence of a province-wide hierarchy of academies leading up to a few major institutions in the capital, and official control seems to have rested more on shared definitions of education than on strict supervision. There is evidence of linkages with other local public institutions. The academies in Pinghu district city and in two market towns of Jiaxing prefecture, for instance, grew out of, and used the buildings of, the united welfare association or the relief and reconstruction bureau.[29] In still another Jiaxing market town the foundling home was responsible for the establishment of the academy.[30] Thus reconstruction encouraged local matrices of linked public institutions. One organization provided the impetus for others, and expansion produced a cohesive and not a fragmented public sphere.

Financing local public institutions. Normally these institutions were financed locally, and costs varied depending on their size, type, and locality. The initial outlay could be reduced by taking over an existing building such as a temple, but the actual construction costs of a modest-sized district or town academy could reach four to five thousand yuan.[31] Seven thousand strings of cash (eight to nine thousand yuan) was said to have been spent rebuilding Hangzhou's chief academy, the Gujing Jingshe, after the rebellion, and the complex of buildings housing the welfare institutions cost ten thousand silver ounces.[32] A badly destroyed city might well spend over a hundred thousand yuan reconstructing just the public educational and welfare institutions and the basic roads, dikes, and bridges of greatest interest to the local elite—let alone the official yamens, all the water control facilities of the surrounding countryside, and the private buildings.

Accurate figures on annual income and expenses are difficult to obtain. Managers may have hidden part of their institution's income. In other cases, it is hard to tell how much theoretical income from rents and interest was actually collected. In Huzhou city the two major gentry-run institutions, the relief and reconstruction bureau and the chief academy, had respective annual incomes of 6,000–7,000 yuan and 6,700 yuan during the Tongzhi (1862–74).[33] At the same time, the elite-run silk office in wealthy Nanxun town collected at least ten thousand yuan a year in taxes for welfare and reconstruction, using them for both capital and operating expenses.[34]

The expenses of successful welfare institutions increased as their operations expanded. In Haining (Hangzhou) the foundling home started out spending a modest 100,000 copper cash (about 87 yuan at a cash-yuan ratio of 1,150:1) to care for 50 children; by 1900 it needed as much as 8,800,000 (9,430 yuan at a ratio of 933:1) to look after 440.[35] By the first decade of the twentieth century, elite-run welfare could be big business. In 1901 the revolutionary-connected Shanghai newspaper *Minhu ribao* maintained that relief expenditures for rice gruel in Hangzhou city were over one hundred thousand (yuan?) a year and that the foundling home was spending forty to fifty thousand. In Shaoxing city the home's expenses were twenty thousand silver ounces.[36] Even allowing for the possible inflation of the figures in journalistic attacks on allegedly corrupt gentry management, these were considerable sums, and, although these particular institutions were all in major core area cities, even the Lishui united welfare association had five thousand silver ounces to use for gruel stations in the peripheral prefecture of Chuzhou.[37]

The money to establish and operate these institutions came from a few basic sources: official treasuries, individual or community contributions, endowments, and business assessments or taxes. Major institutions usually received funds from several sources, and the mix varied from place to place. The most consistent regional difference was the larger amounts of money available from trade and business in commercialized areas. Very soon after the end of the rebellion, it became clear that communities with connections to the Shanghai trade had a special advantage in building up their public institutions.

Prefects, magistrates, directors of education, and other officials sometimes made yamen funds available to important institutions.[38] Alternatively, they could transfer income from another local organization or a defunct bureau[39]—or they might authorize the use of buildings or endowments of Buddhist temples and monasteries.[40] Local officials did not have enough revenue to finance most activity. Since they normally only helped support major institutions in administrative centers, most funding had to come from outside the bureaucracy.

Donations from wealthy individuals, families, or lineages were a major source of support. Such contributions were an accepted part of elite social responsibility that increased the donor's prestige while benefiting the community and promoting social stability. Most were voluntary, although some were made under official pressure.[41] Large donors, like the wealthy landowner in Zhenhai who contributed ten thousand yuan to enlarge an academy in 1889,[42] were sure to be commemorated, but gazetteers often also recorded the names of people who made very modest donations. Sometimes people managed or continued to encourage institutions to which they had contributed, and some families supported an important local institution for generations. In Yongkang (Jinhua), four lineages cooperated to maintain an academy that dated back to the Song, and the Yings had contributed money to repair the Confucian temple since at least the late Ming. Another family made a series of donations to a newer academy from the Daoguang period (1821–50) to the 1880's.[43]

A few of these donors were women. There are scattered listings of female contributors in the Qianlong period (1736–95), and at least one from the Ming.[44] Late Qing and republican gazetteers record far more female investment from the mid-nineteenth century on. Much was for religious institutions or very local necessities like bridges, but women also contributed to academies and foundling homes. An unusually active matron in Xiangshan (Ningbo) established a charitable school and granary in the 1850's; she also helped found a charitable estate for her husband's lineage.[45] Such contributions did not mean that elite women were leaving the household to participate in community activity. They might, however, keep abreast with local affairs and have the authority to donate family money. This behind-the-scenes participation from within the family was a minor part of local investment, but it was recorded in gazetteers throughout the provinces.

Natives pursuing successful bureaucratic or mercantile careers away from home were a much more important source of local investment. In the late nineteenth century, for instance, the first man from Xiangshan district (Ningbo) to become a *jinshi* in 174 years contributed to grain equalization and helped establish a militia to fight against pirates.[46] By the second half of the nineteenth century, contributions from merchants, particularly those in Shanghai, were a major source of money in districts fortunate enough to be a part of external commercial networks. Liu Yong, like other merchants who made fortunes in the mid-nineteenth century, contributed heavily to institutions in his home town of Nanxun.[47] Another merchant used some of the profits from his Shanghai factories to establish a school in his native village in Shaoxing. He also built a bridge and a temple, restored the granary, and supported medical charity.[48] Mercantile contributions could be solicited systematically. Pinghu (Jiaxing) silk merchants in Shanghai annually contributed 1.8 coppers from the sale of each *bao* of silk to welfare in their home district.[49] Shanghai was also a good place to solicit funds for specific projects. Even an unimportant market town in a poor, mountainous rural township in northwest Fenghua (Ningbo) raised 508 yuan in Shanghai for a foundling home, as compared to contributions of 100 yuan in Ningbo and 510 strings of cash at home.[50]

Continuing annual operations required more automatic sources of income. The time-honored method was to acquire an endowment of agricultural land. A very few wealthy people might contribute the entire endowment, but often there were many, small donations, sometimes made over a long period of time. In poor areas like the southwest, managers resorted to systematic assessments on households throughout the district to rebuild city institutions destroyed in the Taiping Rebellion.[51] However they were acquired, the lands normally lay within the district or township where the institution was located.[52] The plots were very fragmented, so that dozens of pages might be needed simply to list a property.[53]

The size of endowments varied widely. A compilation of endowments of 127 charitable and educational institutions from gazetteers throughout the province shows 2 of over two thousand *mou*, 6 between one and two thousand *mou*, 18 between five hundred and one thousand, 47 between one and five hundred, 29 between thirty and one hundred, and 25 under one hundred.[54] Some institutions, like a charitable graveyard in Yuyao with one thousand *mou*,[55] were so over-endowed that one suspects they were tax dodges or that the income was also used for other purposes. Other institutions, which had very small endowments, were often little schools and burial societies that did not have high expenses.

The rent actually produced by these holdings was not the same throughout the province—more than three times as much rice was received per *mou* in Linhai (Taizhou) as in Longyou (Quzhou), for instance.[56] Endowment income did not necessarily cover expenses,[57] and the ravages of the Taiping Rebellion severely aggravated this problem. Institutional landlords, like individual landowners, suffered from lost records, clerical corruption, labor shortages, and difficulties in collecting rent. Managers of the Longyou academy complained in the mid-1890's that they were only collecting about one-third of the rent due. Their problem was temporarily solved by official help in rent collection, but the increased income soon disappeared into the hands of clerks when the rent was simply collected along with taxes.[58] In Ningbo and Shaoxing, where profitable, commercialized agriculture had not been so greatly disrupted, public institutions continued to rely heavily on income from land. In the districts that had suffered most during the rebellion, however, land was not always a dependable source of income, particularly during the expensive initial phases of reconstruction. Commercially based income therefore became crucial to local public programs.

In many districts, even in only moderately developed areas, endowments included urban property.[59] Investment in pawnshops was another profitable supplement mentioned in gazetteers of northern and southwestern districts.[60] Nevertheless, business contributions and trade taxes were the most effective solutions in the commercialized districts.

Even a quick look at the gazetteers that give details about financing shows the importance of commercial taxes. In Haining (Hangzhou) the major foundling home was supported by a 2 percent surcharge on *lijin;* contributions from rice, tea, and cotton firms, pawnshops, and other businesses; and rents from 148 *mou* and urban property. The chief academy received annual contributions from cotton, rice, and silk firms as well as rents from 133 *mou* and urban property. In Cheng (Shaoxing) the foundling home's income came from levies on pawnshops, tea, silk, paper, cocoon, and rice as well as from donations by the founder and his friends.[61] The salt trade was the most likely source of business support in the less commercialized parts of Zhejiang, but more general levies also occurred, especially in the cities along the main riparian trade route.[62]

The major innovation after the rebellion was the use of a portion of *lijin* taxes to support local welfare. Salt *lijin* financed the rebuilding of a foundling home in Lishui (Chuzhou) and an academy in Ninghai (Taizhou).[63] Academies and foundling homes in Jinhua and Langqi as well as the home for chaste widows in Qu also derived part of their income from this source.[64] Heavy reliance on *lijin* might lead to greater control by officials, if they distributed the funds for elite-managed famine relief, welfare, and construction. Gentry did submit requests to officials for *lijin* funds,[65] but actual control depended on such factors as the relative strength of the officials and the elite, the method of collecting *lijin,* and the location of stations.

Silk *lijin* provides dramatic examples of how this tax might foster managerial autonomy rather than bureaucratic control. In Zhejiang *lijin* was not collected in the same way on silk as on other goods. Because so much of the raw silk from this province was destined for export, officials had sought to forestall foreign claims for tax exemption by collecting *lijin* at the first point of sale rather than at stations along the transportation routes. Separate silk *lijin* bureaus were therefore set up at market centers where raw silk was brought from the surrounding countryside. Not only was the silk clearly a local product, *lijin* collectors might also have connections with welfare managers.

A generous amount of silk *lijin* was earmarked for the reconstruction of badly damaged sericulture areas. Actual calculations varied locally, but the basic silk *lijin* of sixteen yuan per *bao* officially included two yuan for reconstruction during the Tongzhi. Eventually, one yuan was permanently reserved for welfare. There were further additions for water control and, in Huzhou, for welfare in the town where the silk was first sold.[66] This major source of income supplied the income for the relief and reconstruction bureau in Huzhou city. Again in Huzhou prefecture, it contributed to the same type of bureau in the town of Shuanglin, it supported virtually all elite-run enterprises in Nanxun town for at least ten years, and it provided most of the funds for the Deqing district foundling home. In adjoining Jiaxing prefecture it was the main source of money for the Tongxiang district academy, supplemented the foundling home's income, and supported academies in the towns of Qing and Puyuan in that district.[67] It seems to have virtually replaced land endowments in Huzhou prefecture, where land registers had often been destroyed. However, silk or other *lijin* was also an important source of income in the cores of Hangzhou and Jiaxing.[68]

The way in which silk *lijin* supported expansive, autonomous elite-management is illustrated in the town of Nanxun, where a silk-tax bureau had been set up in the late 1850's with the stipulation that some of the revenue would support local charities. This unusually early bureau was staffed by local men, including one landowner who was active in welfare during the next twenty years. It disappeared during the Taiping occupation, but as soon as the town was permanently recaptured in 1864, local leaders established a relief and reconstruction bureau. The next year silk merchants petitioned for a new silk office (*siye gongsuo*) "to collect taxes and protect merchants." The bureau had a subsidiary charitable office, in which one of the managers was a *jinshi*-degree holder who was probably related to wealthy silk merchants and another was a merchant who was probably related to the men who had run the old bureau. The reconstruction of the badly damaged town was supported by *lijin* for the next ten years, and managers of the charitable office were among the founders of the academy, the charitable schools, the foundling home, the granary, and the welfare association.[69] This system, in which members of the managerial elite financed their activities through the silk taxes that they themselves collected, eventually aroused the suspicions of the Huzhou prefect. The silk office was dissolved in 1874, but the system may have remained intact, since no alternative funding is indicated for ongoing institutions.

Wealthy and prestigious members of the Nanxun elite, in a town removed from the administrative city, achieved an unusual degree of financial autonomy. In view of the wide use of *lijin* to support local welfare, however, they could not have been unique. Powerful gentry in nearby Suzhou (Jiangsu province) used rent bureaus to gather "donations" from tenants for welfare, reconstruction, and military expenses,[70] and powerful gentry and merchants of Zhejiang silk-producing areas fastened upon *lijin* collections to finance their projects.

I will consider the implications of this autonomy later. Here I wish to look at some of the changes in the structure and scope of public activities. Although the local public institutions of the reconstruction period were not new, increases in numbers and structural complexity distinguish them from those of earlier periods. Looking mainly at the earlier years of the Qing, Ch'ü T'ung-tsu has suggested that public institutions were concentrated in the prefectural capitals, although gentry and magistrates also established them in district cities.[71] In the later period, this was no longer the case, and better access to sub-district records would probably show even more institutions at low urban-levels.[72] In addition, lineages provided another, private matrix of dispersed educational and charitable institutions, which substantially added to public facilities and fused with them in single-lineage villages.[73]

On the district level, welfare was managed through complex, multi-level organizations. These were not simply agglomerations of discrete institutions under bureaucratic auspices; nor were they random products of individual philanthropy. Institutional complexes that existed within cities or between different levels of the urban hierarchy provided effective bases for growing public activity outside the bureaucratic system. As organization became more sophisticated, it augmented the public sphere; particularly in the core areas, this effect was reinforced by small welfare institutions outside the umbrella of the united agencies.[74]

An ability to tax business and commerce was crucial to the expansion of public institutions. Prompt reconstruction in the cores of the northern prefectures was thus one manifestation of regional prosperity connected to foreign trade. Such commercially based funding also lessened the direct financial burden of public institutions on the communities. Whether or not the incidence of *lijin* and other taxes was ultimately passed on to the peasants, a good part of local business profits was being generated from Shanghai. Contributions from sojourning merchants tapped the wealth of the macroregional economic center (and of foreign trade) even more directly. Until the last Qing decade, the level of public activities in the core districts of Zhejiang does not seem to have seriously strained local resources.[75] Even more important from the viewpoint of developing management, the Shanghai foreign trade changed the balance between official and extra-bureaucratic initiative simply by making available to local institutions more money that was free of yamen control.

Such was not the case in the peripheral districts. It was possible to sustain and somewhat expand earlier levels of public activity with local, agriculturally based income, but this source was not adequate for post-rebellion reconstruction. The complex financing in the southwestern districts indicates that there was no ample source of money; and where institutions in the district city were supported by district-wide household levies, the financial burden was more visible than in the cores with their commercially based funding. Despite the similarities of institutions established in core and peripheral areas, the significant quantitative distinctions suggest a qualitative difference in the expansiveness of public management.

The Taiping Rebellion had a decisive impact on public activities. The magnitude of the crisis elicited a strong elite response, and it defined the major area of post-rebellion expansion. Members of the elite focused on welfare because they considered it to be integral to reconstruction. The welfare agency often became the chief public institution of a locality, in the sense of being prestigious, well financed, and central to public decision-making. The expansion of welfare was thus the leading edge of a more general growth of the public sphere. Managing this expansion were members of local elites, who were both propelled and enticed into public activity by the needs and opportunities of the period.

Local Managerial Establishments

The second important departure in the post-Taiping period was the rise of activist managers, who expanded local institutions while acting as local opinion leaders and spokesmen. This activism contributed to the growth of the public sphere in the latter half of the nineteenth century. It raised new problems, which were different from the static or cyclical kind of local-private vs. state-public tension that had long been a factor in the relationship between the government and local elites. Two consequences—which might appear independently or together—were, first, the emplacement of long-lasting managerial establishments of socially linked, prestigious men who ran complexes of local institutions, and, second, the association of their local activity with issues of concern to all the country. The existence of this activism was important to the political evolution in the last decades of the Qing, and its general significance is independent of questions about the disinterestedness or efficiency of individual managers.

The reconstruction activists. The most famous manager of reconstruction in Zhejiang worked in Hangzhou. Ding Bing was the son of a wealthy scholar who had maintained shrines and temples. Bing began his public career as early as 1838 by establishing gruel stations and repairing temples and other buildings near Hangzhou, sometimes supervising projects underwritten by his father. During the Taiping Rebellion he managed relief, both in Hangzhou between occupations and in other Lower Yangtze cities. After Hangzhou was finally retaken, he threw himself into the task of reconstruction, establishing and managing the welfare agency; rebuilding the academies and other public buildings; repairing bridges, temples, and shrines; dredging waterways and repairing dikes; heading the Zhejiang Printing Office; establishing a foundling home; supervising the charitable ferry and lifesaving association; setting up gruel stations and homes for the destitute; and collecting money for relief as needed. In 1878, after fifteen years of heading the welfare agency, he stepped down but remained publicly active on a gradually diminishing schedule until he died in 1899. Ding Bing was a famous bibliophile, noted both for his own library and for his efforts to reassemble the scattered texts housed in the famous Hangzhou Wenlange. These accomplishments contributed to his prestige in the high scholarly circles of Hangzhou, but he was a power in the city and was consulted by provincial officials because of his public activities.[76]

Although Ding Bing operated in the provincial capital, the kind of energetic, expansive management he represents was by no means confined to the large cities. It was a response to crisis that appeared in much of the province. In some places it originated during the rebellion. One of the most powerful and respected managers of welfare and education in Pingyang (Wenzhou) during the Tongzhi (1862–74) had earlier helped his uncle and cousins organize a militia.[77] In other cases, leading postrebellion activists began their local involvement with reconstruction. Some left official careers to return to what seemed to be more urgent tasks at home.[78] Some, especially those who had fled and survived while relatives and friends died, seemed to feel a special responsibility for their family and community.[79]

This reaction did not appear in all districts. We are told that in the poor district of Fuyang (on the Qiantang River south of Hangzhou), scholars were content with their private pursuits and did not become involved in public affairs (gongshi). The populace there avoided officials, feared litigation, and looked upon yamen runners as tigers. Even the great suffering the district endured during the rebellion did not shake this apathy. With few economic resources, Fuyang remained stagnant during the rest of the century. There was only one academy and charitable school and very few welfare institutions. The foundling home, revived after the rebellion, closed for lack of funds.[80]

More typically, management gained and maintained momentum as local leaders emerged to undertake necessary tasks. Men who became managers reflected the distinctive social characteristics of the elite in the locality where they were active, but they were generally alike in coming from the broadly defined upper levels of local elite society. Management in this period was a respectable—even a prestigious—occupation; it overlapped the associated roles of founder and contributor, which had long been honored in the local records.[81]

More precise social categorization is difficult because gazetteers are not very reliable guides. Nor are they complete; the names of most managers were never recorded, and many of the men who are mentioned are not further identified. Everyone— gazetteer compilers, officials, memoir writers, newspaper reporters—used "gentry manager" as a functional, not a social, term to describe people running local institutions. Activities specifically organized by businesses, such as night patrols in urban commercial sections, might be called "merchant-managed" (*shangban*),[82] but merchants (who might have purchased rank or degrees) were usually simply included among "gentry managers." Similarly, some gazetteer compilers carefully specified the degrees held by upper gentry. Very often, however, loose classifications like "gentry," "gentry and wealthy men" (probably merchants), "district gentry," "district men," and "local men" or "villagers" (*liren*) were used interchangeably with, or in the same context as, "gentry managers." It was all too possible to call a *jinshi*-degree holder a "district man" or a "villager," like any low-status local notable.[83] Because of the scholarly orientation of the elite in much of Zhejiang, local managerial complexes were likely to include upper-degree holders. One possible social range in a core district is indicated by a list of "gentry managers" who reestablished the granary in Nanxun town (Huzhou) about 1880: two *jinshi*, one *juren*, three *shengyuan*, two major Shanghai merchants from Nanxun, one local(?) merchant, one purchased *jiansheng*-degree holder, and one wealthy landowner with purchased rank.[84]

Upper-degree holders were also likely to be among the leading managers in administrative centers of peripheral districts, although they were of course drawn from a smaller and lower status-pool. One of certainly no more than a dozen living *juren*-degree holders from the depressed prefectural capital of Yanzhou went into local affairs after the Taiping Rebellion.[85] *Juren* and, more commonly, *gongsheng* appear among local activists in other prefectural and district cities of the southwest or south. In Longyou (Quzhou) the high percentage of *gongsheng* active in local affairs meant that a substantial number of the district's examination elite was going into management.[86]

The lack of an upper degree did not necessarily indicate low gentry status, for such men might belong to prominent families. The founder and manager of the welfare association in the town of Wangdian (Jiaxing), for instance, was a poet and scholar whose older brother was a member of the Hanlin Academy. Membership in a strong lineage might also ensure prominence, as could even a reputation for honest public management.[87]

Merchant participation in local public affairs followed similar patterns. Wealthy merchants not only contributed to local institutions while residing away from home but also managed them if living in their native place. Prominent managers in the town of Qing (Jiaxing) and the district city of Longyou in the southwest were, for instance, merchants. It is impossible, however, to estimate how many managers were merchants, because they are not systematically identified in gazetteers. Given the coalescence of mercantile and scholarly classes, probably many unidentified managers in core localities were either merchants or combined scholarship with trade.[88]

The role of sojourning merchants is still more difficult to determine. Some sojourning communities established their own institutions, such as schools and burial societies, and non-local merchants also contributed to repairing bridges and dikes.[89] Salt merchants from Anhui supported the foundling home in Qu (Quzhou), but the available evidence is not sufficient to say whether such sojourners were routinely active in the chief welfare institutions of Zhejiangese cities as they were in Shanghai or Hanzhou.[90]

Biographical information fades as one moves into the peripheral districts or down the urban hierarchy below administrative market towns (*zhen*). The managers in the villages were probably recognized community leaders.[91] In the peripheral districts, managers might include military *shengyuan*,[92] who were rarely in charge of important institutions in the academic cores, and we may assume that in really violent areas they included local strongmen. These men were likely to be at the top of the social structure in their home areas, and the leading figures in the commercial or administrative centers of the peripheries were likely to be identified with the interlocking gentry-merchant elite. The Taiping-era militia leaders on the southeast coast who continued their military careers did so away from home, and they were not among the major post-Taiping district managers.[93]

Such locally prominent men were likely to be socially conservative, but their status facilitated the expansion of the public sphere. Although from the upper class, managers did not necessarily come from, or act as representatives of, the most socially prominent families. Rather, they were members of the elite stratum who had, for various reasons, gone into local public affairs. High status increased their effectiveness as local leaders, because they were likely to be accepted by the elite community and respected by officials. Although they used their positions to help their own families, they also used their personal social networks to bolster public institutions by enlisting the aid of wealthy or high-status friends and attracting a following of relatives, associates, and protégés. Less prominent managers were likely therefore to be socially connected to highly placed members of the elite. Their connections contributed to an assertive direction of local public affairs during reconstruction. This activity was not a simple expansion of old elite advisory roles and informal leadership. New aspects were introduced as activist managers seeking to surmount the problems of rebellion and reconstruction fused old roles with new, elaborate institutional structures.

The managerial establishments. The resulting establishments were generally headed by one or a few prominent men in charge of major local institutions. Gradations among managers appear in several contexts. First, the most important men sometimes chose and supervised the managers of subsidiary institutions within a city or in smaller towns.[94] Second, managers at various levels in the sub-district administrative hierarchy acted on behalf of managers in the district city.[95] Officials used these low-level men to carry out government-ordered relief and other tasks. In at least some districts, however, they were separate from the local constabulary (*dibao*), and, as men of community standing, they acted as local spokesmen with their own connections to members of the elite at higher urban levels. Finally, there were distinctions within institutions between the most prominent managers and their associates who were delegated specific responsibilities.

The extent to which one group dominated local institutions is often difficult to determine because of incomplete information in the gazetteers. An unusual collection of six complete lists of managers in Longyou (Quzhou) from the late 1880's through the mid-1900's shows how interconnected separate institutions were.[96] Three of the lists are almost identical, and the five men who appear on all four of the lists from the 1890's may be considered the top managers of the decade. A *gongsheng*-degree holder and a paper merchant linked this leadership to the relief and reconstruction immediately after the rebellion. As the old guard changed in the 1900's, a few active managers of the 1890's remained and provided continuity, even though the original restoration management had faded away.[97]

This picture of a distinct group running the most important local institutions is repeated in a more fragmentary way in a significant number of gazetteers. Some of the best examples come from Huzhou prefectural city and the town of Nanxun, Tongxiang district city (Jiaxing) and the town of Qing, and Ruian (Wenzhou) on the southeast coast. A closer look at these cases gives an idea of the managerial establishments that became embedded in the economically expansive areas of Zhejiang for the rest of the nineteenth century and well into the twentieth.[98]

The Tongzhi reconstruction in Huzhou city was supervised by an exceptionally prestigious group of three *jinshi* and the *juren* scholar and bibliophile Lu Xinyuan.[99] They had all held middle-grade official posts in Beijing or the provinces. At least one had contributed to local relief before the rebellion. Lu and relatives of two of the others had organized an anti-Taiping militia.[100] After the rebellion they worked closely with the Huzhou prefect, Zong Yuanhan, to provide relief; rebuild the prefectural academy and another academy; dredge silted channels in Lake Tai; compile a new prefectural gazetteer; and construct, repair, or head various other welfare and educational institutions.[101]

Unfortunately, there is little information about Huzhou city after the Tongzhi, but accounts of an almost equally imposing collection of managers in Nanxun town cover nearly fifty years. Nanxun has already been mentioned repeatedly as a flourishing commercial center. Wealthy merchants and prestigious gentry from the town far overshadowed the low-ranking subordinate officials present there, and officials are scarcely mentioned in the local history. Public affairs were dominated by the Jiang family, who were landlords and lower scholar-gentry, and the wealthy merchant-gentry Lius, Zhous, Zhangs, and Pangs, who were connected by both marriage and business ties. Managers thus had access to some of the wealthiest Shanghai merchants as well as *jinshi*-degree holders and high officials.[102] Jiang Tang, who had raised contributions for government troops during the rebellion and had helped organize relief in Huzhou city, was a main link between town leaders and the prefectural establishment. However, the members of the Nanxun elite operated independently. They competed somewhat with the prefectural group, and they achieved considerable financial autonomy.

During the 1860's and 1870's the dominant public figures were Jiang Tang, by virtue of his wealth, his entrenched position in local society, and his participation in the silk bureau that collected *lijin* surcharges for reconstruction, and Pang Gongzhao, who was a *jinshi* teacher at the new academy, a relative of wealthy silk merchants, and a founder of the charitable bureau that administered the funds raised through *lijin* surcharges. Both men were among the founders of the academy, the two charitable schools, and foundling home. Pang's high degree was useful in petitioning officials in the prefectural city, while Jiang appears to have been a vigorous manager and local politician. In the late 1870's, he was still active enough to lead in reinstating and managing the public granary at the time of the first major post-Taiping famine.

Major merchants like Liu Yong and Zhou Changfu contributed to, helped found, or briefly managed local institutions, while mainly living in Shanghai. Two *jinshi*-degree holders besides Pang helped found the granary. Still other Shanghai merchants simply invested in local institutions or aided relatives left destitute by the rebellion. Less prestigious local men (like the *shengyuan* with merchant relatives who was a manager of the silk bureau, academy, foundling home, granary, and relief) probably did much of the day-to-day work.[103]

In the next generation, members of the same four merchant families organized the militia during the Sino-Japanese War. Thereafter, various Lius, Pangs, and Zhangs established a home for poor widows in 1896, an association to aid victims of fires in 1897, a society to support scholars' widows in 1899, and a restructured academy curriculum in 1898. Very prominent members of these families continued to found both new and old-style institutions through the New Policies period after 1900—although they were much involved in business and politics elsewhere, and the actual managing may have been done by their less prominent relatives.[104] Nanxun is a striking example of how the local managerial establishments of towns in core areas displayed characteristics normally associated with elites in much larger administrative cities.

Prestigious members of the elite also dominated local public affairs in adjacent Tongxiang district, but here there was a much closer meshing of the district city and the market town establishments. The leading figure from the end of the Taiping Rebellion through at least the early 1880's was Yan Chen, a *jinshi* and Hanlin scholar from a well-off scholar-gentry family, who had spent much of the 1840's and 1850's in Beijing. In 1862 he retired from office to spend the rest of his life teaching, studying, writing poetry, and managing local affairs. His large family had marriage ties with prominent officials and gentry outside the district. He also maintained the friendships he had made in Beijing, and such high connections were useful in obtaining prompt approval of his local institutions.[105]

Yan was the man who set up and managed the Tongxiang relief and reconstruction bureau and the foundling home. He also reestablished the academy and headed it for ten years; he

founded the charitable school and a home for old people, supervised the repair of the Confucian temple, and managed the granary. He headed the academy in the market town of Qing for 27
years and was the first head of the academy in Puyuan town.[106]
In addition, he was a spokesman for the district gentry in a protracted struggle to reform grain tribute collection. He recorded
all these activities in the gazetteer he compiled in 1881.

Yan also had a full social and literary life. He was indeed a
busy man, who necessarily delegated some of his managerial
duties.[107] Besides his subordinates, he was joined by a few close
associates. One was a *juren* from the district city, but his chief
collaborator was the merchant Shen Baoyue, from the town of
Qing, who owned and operated the long-established family iron
foundries in the small market center of Lutou between Qing
and the district city. Shen was from a mercantile line within
one of four branches of a lineage dispersed about the district.
The other major line in this branch was oriented toward scholarship and produced several upper-degree holders in the nineteenth century.[108]

Like Yan, Shen contributed to relief and organized it in Qing
town during 1864. On the district level, he helped Yan establish
the relief and reconstruction bureau, found the orphanage, and
rebuild the academy. In Qing, Yan joined Shen in establishing
the town academy and setting up a foundling home. Yan is also
credited with founding the charitable school, and Shen independently established still other foundling homes and a burial
society. He had his own set of associates in Qing and could solicit donations from merchants in Shanghai. Continuing the
interaction between managers in the town and the district city,
the man who succeeded Yan Chen as head of the district academy was a scholarly cousin of Shen Baoyue.[109]

There is little information about managers in the district
city after Yan Chen published his gazetteer in 1881. In Qing,
Shen Baoyue's descendants were among those who dominated
town affairs into the Republic.[110] The managers in Qing were
not as prominent as those of Nanxun, but they were still prestigious. Shen Baoyue was known in the provincial capital for
his local activities—he received commissions and rank from

two governors and rejected office to remain at home.[111] Leaders in Qing and Nanxun may have been particularly prominent. On the whole, however, they exemplify situations in the rich core districts of northern Zhejiang where people of great wealth and degree-holding status were not only numerous but also somewhat spread out through the urban hierarchy. Men who were prominent enough to have a place in larger sociopolitical arenas were found managing affairs at relatively low urban levels.

In Ruian (Wenzhou) the leading managers were also high-status members of the scholarly elite, but they were operating in the less economically developed, socially turbulent, culturally distinctive southeast coast. The managerial establishment there was not typical of most of the southern periphery. It was important, however, because it produced a number of scholar-reformers of provincial or national significance. It also illustrates the combined impact of a number of factors that were significant in other places: social disorder, gradual economic growth, the revival and reinterpretation of old intellectual traditions, and the foreign threat to the coast. This story, which began in the middle of the century, will be picked up again during the 1890's and in the first decade of the twentieth century.

The Sun family was central. This old kin group of modest scholar-landowners became prominent when first Sun Qiangming and then his brother Sun Yiyan became *jinshi* in 1841 and 1850. This extraordinary feat, in a district that had produced only three *jinshi* during the previous two hundred years, was duplicated about twenty years later by their younger friends, Huang Tili and Huang Tifang. In each case, one brother pursued an official career while the other spent a good deal of time at home managing family and local affairs.[112]

During the Taiping period, Sun Qiangming led other gentry in organizing a militia against the local rebellion of the Gold Coin Society. Although some gentry disapproved of their tactics, the Suns claimed credit for defeating the rising. Afterwards, Sun Qiangming established the foundling home, and the family was responsible for bridge repairs.[113] When Sun Yiyan retired from office in 1879, he taught at the academy and established a school. In contrast to men in Longyou and most southern districts, the leading Ruian activists were distinguished by broad external connections, intellectual sophistication, and reformist aspirations.

Their external connections were both national and regional. Sun Yiyan had made friends among officials and nationally known scholars as a metropolitan official, a protégé of major governors and governors-general, a member of the sophisticated intellectual circles of Hangzhou, and a well-known scholar in his own right. While lieutenant governor in Jiangsu, moreover, he was able to offer employment to scholars from Wenzhou districts. Sun Qiangming had an independent reputation acquired first in Beijing and then as a teacher in Lower Yangtze academies and as educational commissioner in Guangxi.[114] First Huang Tifang, and then his son and his nephew, Huang Shaoji and Huang Shaodi, provided continuous connections within the metropolitan bureaucracy from the 1860's to the mid-1900's. These two families had much to do with what must have been a general rise in the expectations of all scholars in Ruian. Not only could officials from the district provide aid and patronage, but the number of upper-degree holders also increased markedly—culminating in, for Ruian, an epidemic of eight new *jinshi* from 1885 through 1894.[115]

The Suns, at least, did not cultivate external connections at the expense of their local roots. The family was part of a complex of long-established, interconnected kin groups. Yiyan and his brother contracted marriage alliances with scholars and local managers in other southeastern districts, and joint efforts against the Gold Coin Society led to lasting ties with still other local leaders.[116]

Because of his successful official career and scholarly reputation, Sun Yiyan was a natural magnet in the district. He led the movement among local scholars to revive the utilitarian Southern Song statecraft school of thought named for Yongjia (Wenzhou). Theories of Southern Song scholars such as Ye Shi and Chen Fuliang reinforced both Yiyan's own institutionally oriented pragmatism and his advocacy of a greater role for gentry in local affairs. Upon retirement he attracted a bright collection of young scholars from Wenzhou districts. Among them were

Yiyan's own son, the classical scholar, reformer, and local activist Sun Yirang; the historian Chen Fuchen, who would be president of the Zhejiang provincial assembly; the institutional reformer Chen Qiu; and his more morally radical counterpart Song Heng.[117] Unfortunately, there is little information about the operation of local institutions in Ruian during the Tongzhi. From the late 1880's on, however, we shall see that men from the circles around Sun would be among the leaders in redefining reformism and in establishing new institutions in their home district.

Thus managerial establishments composed of locally prominent men controlling key public institutions initiated a pattern that continued into the twentieth century. One effect of such establishments was the introduction of an element of stability, if not conservatism, into local affairs. The same group of people and their heirs—either descendants or protégés—dominated local public institutions for many decades despite major national political changes. The influence of these men went beyond the institutions they managed, in part because of the combined weight of the interlocking managements and in part because the managers were sufficiently important to take over the old informal roles of advisers to officials and leaders of elite opinion.[118]

Another aspect of these establishments was less conservative; they subtly shifted the control of local government into the hands of local members of the elite. Managers were nominally appointed by officials and were subject to official authority. They could not overstep certain bounds, but the leading figures were local powers with, in effect, their own organizations. They enlisted the services of (and provided jobs for) friends and relatives, commanded funds, provided valuable services, and built up their own establishments.

In considering the implications, it is important also to remember a third characteristic: these establishments began amid crisis. Their beginnings were sudden and potentially disequilibrating, even though preceded by slower accretions to the existing system. The fear and sense of urgency created by the rebellion contributed to the expansionist activism of the reconstruction period and encouraged an influx of managers who could have had careers in larger sociopolitical arenas. These men were found mainly in core areas, further distinguishing ostensibly similar organizations in the core and the periphery. They approached management in light of their scholarly studies and external experiences as well as in terms of local interests, and their ideas give insight into the directions which local activism was taking.

The Challenge to Government: Alarm, Assertion, and Malaise

Managers were often also scholars who wrote in an unsystematic way about what they were doing. Their views are buried in incidental writings, tombstone inscriptions, poetry, and classical exegesis. The practical demands of their jobs combined with their understanding of contemporary problems to shape the ideas set forth in their brief essays. Looking for more general guidance, they turned to writers who had lived in earlier periods of change and turmoil—notably the Southern Song and the seventeenth century. The diverse literature of the post-Taiping period awaits examination. Here we can only look at a few aspects: its renewed commitment to statecraft, its concern for social stability, its tendency toward autonomy, and its doubts about the drift of government.

From the time of the late eighteenth-century social disorders, statecraft studies had often occupied scholars. The Taiping Rebellion reinforced this practical interest. Yan Chen wrote sadly of Tongxiang district when he returned home. He saw fields that were a jumble of "raspberry briars and goosefool," while the pine and the chrysanthemum—those symbols of permanence—were wasted. Distress and suffering were everywhere, and the scholar's vocation was "to save the times" (*jiushi*).[119] Faced with such destruction, men turned to statecraft. They saw management as an application of practical studies. The public activities of the manager of the major city institutions in Jiashan for twenty years are described in the gazetteer as "seeking the truth from actual facts."[120]

In the three northern prefectures, this approach to reconstruction management was reinforced by the shattering of
the once-glamorous Lower Yangtze academic communities as
academies and libraries were destroyed and scholars and patrons
were killed or dispersed.[121] Much of the damage would be repaired, but the great scholarly establishments would not be the
same in the changing late nineteenth century. Some members
of this academic elite moved into management after the rebellion. Ding Bing and Lu Xinyuan were prime examples of scholars who became public activists, seeking to rebuild what they
could and to plan for a more secure future.

The conceptualization of management as statecraft occurred
amid a general academic shift toward practical studies. The
combination of philological, classical, and exegetical scholarship with practical concerns was not new. From the time of its
founding by Governor Ruan Yuan in 1801, scholars at the foremost Hangzhou academy, the Gujing Jingshe, had combined
statecraft study with the Han-learning tradition of detailed
exegesis.[122] Yu Yue carried on this combination during the last
three decades of the nineteenth century. Although famous as a
classical scholar, Yu also wrote on subjects ranging from water
control and charitable estates to the organization of government, national strengthening, and foreign technology—and he
often praised statecraft abilities in his biographies of officials
and non-officials.[123]

The Gujing Jingshe served as a model for similar institutions
in Jiangsu,[124] and its graduates taught in other Zhejiang academies. Lu Xinyuan and the other scholars who rebuilt the prefectural academy in Huzhou stressed the need for practical
scholarship,[125] and Lu himself wrote on such statecraft topics
as militia, foundling homes, and water control. Academy libraries included practical and technical books, and gazetteers con-
tain approving references to directors of education or teachers
who stressed practical studies and discussed statecraft.[126]

Zhejiang academies were not free from useless pedantry and
flagrant corruption,[127] but at least part of the academic establishment was slowly changing its emphasis. This trend continued; eventually it merged with the larger changes intro-

duced in the late 1890's. In 1879 Zong Yuanhan, who had been appointed prefect at Ningbo, sponsored the Literary Association to Foster a Discriminating Spirit (*bianzhi wenhui*); it offered provincial graduates six courses of study to teach them to extract useful knowledge for governing from the classics and literature.[178] It was not therefore a large step when a decade later an academy-like institution in a market town of Haining began to teach current affairs and foreign studies along with the principles found in the classical commentaries and the twenty-four histories.[129]

The academic revival was accompanied by a burst of printing after the rebellion to replace the enormous number of destroyed books. The Zhejiang Printing Office, established by Governor Ma Xinyi in 1867, led the way. With Ding Bing as its first head, the office attracted both major scholars and bright young men studying for the examinations.[130] There was also much private printing, and men revived both the works of neglected scholars and the writings of major intellectual figures from the past in addition to replacing recently destroyed books.

A good deal of the publishing in the nineteenth century was done by scholars who were also managers or had connections with managers. Among the books they reprinted were statecraft works that included dissident writings of the twelfth, thirteenth, and seventeenth centuries. Since a considerable number of these earlier critics were natives of, or sojourners in, the Lower Yangtze, honoring local traditions merged with searches for practical knowledge and alternative models.

Gu Yanwu, whose writings had never really gone out of print, was the seventeenth-century scholar most respected in Zhejiang. Sun Yiyan, Lu Xinyuan, and Yu Yue were among the prominent admirers who celebrated Gu's birthday in Hangzhou shortly after the end of the rebellion.[131] Sun Yiyan's publication of *A Collection of Writings from Yongjia* (*Yongjia congshu*) and *A Study of the Yongjia School* (*Yongjia xuean*) in the 1870's spearheaded the revival of a more specifically Zhejiangese intellectual tradition.[132] The works of Chen Liang and other scholars of the closely allied Yongkang school were reprinted twice by men from locally active families in Yongkang district (Jinhua),[133] while other scholars from Wenzhou and Jinhua studied their favorite authors from these schools.

Yan Chen similarly revived the works of the seventeenth-century eremitic Neo-Confucian social moralist Zhang Lüxiang, and Ding Bing printed the volumes in Hangzhou.[134] A study of Yan Yuan was completed in 1869 by Dai Wang, a New Text scholar from Deqing who had many friends among the Zhejiang literati. Tang Zhen's seventeenth-century attack on the evils of the late Ming bureaucracy and autocracy, *Writings in Retirement (Qianshu)*, was published in 1883.[135]

These works gave Zhejiangese access to many criticisms of the government in earlier centuries. There is no easy way to determine what the different members of the scholarly managerial elite took from these various works. A clue may, however, be found in the introduction to *A Collection of Writings from Yongjia*, which suggested that "past and present had similar misfortunes."[136] This cliché calls attention to the widely shared conviction that the post-rebellion period, too, was a time of crisis. Late nineteenth-century scholars did not necessarily draw the same conclusions as earlier writers had.[137] In searching for solutions to current problems, however, they turned to men who, in other critical periods, had written about the defects of government, the decline in social morality, rebellion, military weakness, and ecological breakdown. Members of the elite had only about twenty years to concentrate on reconstruction problems before changing circumstances again altered their intellectual frameworks. Their ideas were not coherently worked out, and we may question the efficacy of their solutions. Nevertheless, the underlying sense of urgency was real enough; to doubt it would be to underestimate the impetus to social activism in the post-rebellion period.

The Taiping experience led members of the elite to search for ways to bind up social wounds, while the continued turbulence of the postwar years kept their attention focused on the need to foster social morality and strengthen community bonds.[138] It is unlikely that such concerns led many gentry to favor rent reduction or similar measures in their private dealings, although labor shortages after the Taiping Rebellion forced them to accept contracts more favorable to tenants. Public management, however, aimed to foster social harmony and equity.

Welfare was often justified by the standard Confucian moral precepts of benevolence, compassion, love, righteousness, and propriety.[139] Gazetteer descriptions of foundling homes show, however, that gentry interpreted these unimpeachable virtues in light of the current social crisis. Stability, first of all, required the correction of customs that would weaken morality. Respectable members of the elite saw the poor as prone to a host of bad practices that included gambling, "lewd plays," boisterous festivals, opium smoking, and fortune-telling. Drowning girl babies was another obvious example. Moreover, female infanticide undermined the stabilizing principles of propriety and filial piety because so many girls were being drowned that men would not find wives to carry on their family lines. It was hoped that foundling homes would combat this social erosion.

The efforts to safeguard Confucian norms not only led back to moralistic homilies but also led on to broad ideals of morally infused sociopolitical action. Principles inspiring men to save the lives of infants were basic to a "government sympathetic to the needs of the people." The "love of the young and small" exemplified in foundling homes thus became a manifestation of statecraft—a "primary duty of the times," designed to strengthen the social fabric upon which order and prosperity rested.[140] This seems a large burden for a foundling home to bear. We should remember, however, that these homes did address, albeit weakly, a difficult demographic problem: a surplus of poor, unmarriageable males who produced an unruly element, difficult to integrate into communal society.

Education, too, was pressed into the service of improving popular customs[141] and fostering community solidarity. There was little consideration of how education might serve the needs of an agricultural populace.[142] The purpose was rather to bolster elite-defined social solidarity by combating heterodoxy. The sociopolitical goal lay in an ideal of social energy emerging from community cohesion. This ideal was sometimes expressed through an interpretation of the ancient institutions of the Zhou dynasty that stressed social integration and government for the benefit of the people. These socially stabilizing principles were believed to have been nourished by the Zhou schools, which played a central role in local communities. Schools in every village served as bridges between the villagers and the local officials chosen through the schools. People sought learning (and absorbed morality) because the upright and energetic could hold office on their own merits regardless of birth.[143]

Such arguments were often related to the issue of autonomy, but it was an autonomy that ideally rested upon community cohesion. In its outward thrust, the conception of local solidarity held by members of the post-Taiping elite resembled the ideas put forth by Gu Yanwu in the seventeenth century. The same account of the Deqing (Hangzhou) district academy that depicted education as a way to improve popular customs linked local traditions of scholarship to the country's need to collect talent and praised the academies as repositories of "our country's" civilization and virtue. The second half of the Zhou dynasty model embodied two ideas: locally based social stability as the foundation of national order and unity, and the need for talented men moving upward from local societies to govern the country.[144] In the reconstruction period the problem of local social cohesion attracted the most attention. In subsequent decades the latter half of this conception would provide one approach to Western representational concepts.

One picture of elite communal leadership emerges in Sun Yiyan's idealization of community self-defense in the rough-and-tumble society of Ruian during the Taiping period. Sun described his native village as the home of hard-working, law-abiding, educable people, living together under the protection of the fort built by his brother in 1850. He, too, refers back to the Zhou for a model of local leaders who taught the people the virtues of filial piety and loyalty. Even though advanced education had become "complex and sophisticated" over the centuries, Sun argued that scholars could still emulate the first rulers and unite the people. Thus they could achieve community solidarity similar to the mutual, though hierarchical, love between fathers and sons. Sun believed that solidarity had been as important as military organization in protecting his home area from rebels, and he thought that popular education to foster such solidarity should have high priority throughout the empire.[145] From what we know of Ruian history, there is also little doubt that he thought his own family well suited to the parental role.

Another view of community solidarity emerges in the petitions and propaganda written by Yan Chen during a protracted campaign to reform grain tribute collection in his native Tongxiang, within the Jiangnan core.[146] Yan proposed a number of changes to prevent clerks from adding excess charges or fraudulently collecting more grain than taxpayers legally owed by such practices as increasing the size of measuring pans. When none of the changes were successful, he changed his tactics and called for a system in which taxpayers would deposit their taxes directly into sealed collection boxes without the intervention of clerks—a reform often advocated by Lower Yangtze gentry during the reconstruction period. Clerks and runners found ways to circumvent these efforts to control them, so it is doubtful whether much was accomplished in the long run.

Yan underlined the communal aspects of the struggle with a plea to the city gods for help in removing tax abuses and a thanks-offering after a partial success. He dramatized in song the miseries of the people and the crimes of tax collectors, those extortionate and licentious "wild cats" who stole rice "grown and harvested with the people's sweat and blood." As "sons of the district," Yan and other gentry appear in standard roles as spokesmen for the people weighed down by corrupt government.[147] At the same time, Yan identified the interests of the upper gentry sub-community with that of the district as a whole in protecting weaker members. Violent tax resistance seemed a real possibility, and Yan did not want to be blamed for his early support of what turned out to be unpopular and easily manipulated regulations commuting payments in kind to cash. He did not wish a local reputation for "aiding officials to be tyrannical," nor did he wish officials to accuse him of crimes if there was a riot.[148]

Whatever Yan's fears of being caught in the middle of a tax protest, he was also following general principles of equity. Far from trying to obscure class differences, he did not even intend to modify the distinctions between privileged great households (*dahu*) and lesser households (*xiaohu*). He did think it unfair, however, that even after several stages of reform, the poorer tax-payers still had to bear the full brunt of corruption.[149] The kind of community consensus within hierarchical frameworks that Yan was seeking precluded such flagrant inequity.

Yan's tax reform efforts would probably have benefited small tax-paying landowners rather than tenants or poor landless peasants.[150] However, the idea of minimal standards of equity did underlie his proposals. It was also embedded in welfare, which helped the poor to maintain a minimal level of subsistence upon which conventional morality depended. Agencies to support infants at home tried to alleviate the poverty that caused people to abandon babies against their parental and moral instincts.[151] Members of the elite also founded low-interest pawnshops or bureaus to make loans to the poor. In the early Guangxu (1875–1908) the newspaper *Shen bao* urged that such bureaus be subsidiaries of welfare associations. At least one operated in Hangzhou in the early 1880's, and others are recorded in gazetteers of Yuyao (Shaoxing) and the town of Xincheng (Jiaxing). They could not, of course, have made much dent in lower class economic problems, and they were probably few and shortlived.[152] Like the settlement houses in the United States at the turn of the twentieth century, they are more significant for their indication of elite uneasiness over social problems than for their practical effect.

This old question of social equity was complicated further by an influx of wealth from the Shanghai trade, particularly in the silk-producing districts of northern Zhejiang. Even if the silk trade benefited the region generally—and made more money available for welfare—the gap was widening between exceedingly rich silk merchants and peasants raising worms and reeling silk. An awareness of this problem comes through in an 1883 *Shen bao* article praising the gentry and merchants in Nanxun town for distributing vouchers to the poor to use at gruel stations. The editorialist noted that during the past twenty years "learning the secrets of mercantile wealth and opening mines" had made the rich richer but had not helped the poor. Welfare, he suggested, could be a contemporary substitute for the Zhou dynasty well-field system (of a central common tract of land surrounded by private holdings) that had fostered economic equity in antiquity. This long-defunct system could not be revived, but there was still a need to distribute wealth somewhat fairly.[153] Again the lessons of the Zhou were pressed into contemporary service, this time by opinion leaders who occupied a position somewhere between an urban bourgeoisie and the old elite rooted in rural society.

Not all wealthy people shared these social concerns, but the members of the upper elite who went into high-level local public management after the rebellion were sensitive to the possibility that gross inequities or huge gaps in the standard of living might be socially disruptive. Social reintegration was pursued through welfare in tandem with physical reconstruction. Such goals gave public leadership a sense of purpose lacking in more ordered times, reinforced managers' sense of their own worth, and contributed to the prestige of managerial activity.

What then did all this public activity portend for relations between the managerial elite and the officials? It is again worth stressing that this elite was not challenging the political structure. Yan Chen referred to the state and to the officials as fathers and mothers, and he believed that in helping the people he was also benefiting the state.[154] Nonetheless, we see an indirect functional challenge as members of the elite increasingly took over local responsibilities from officials. We also observe that managerial activities fostered ad hoc autonomous conceptions, and we find inchoate suspicions of governmental power.

The overlap between the public and the official sphere is indicated by the biographies of magistrates whom gentry gazetteer compilers defined as good. Except for tax remissions and occasional troop mobilizations, these magistrates are praised for doing just what members of the managerial elite were doing.[155] Men who were officials and managers at different stages of their careers were often commemorated twice for similar acts. Thus a manager who had supervised the most important educational and welfare institutions in Jiashan (Jiaxing) became an official near the end of his life; as director of education in Zhenhai district, he repaired the Confucian temple, revived an academy, and organized relief.[156]

Functional overlap often resulted in cooperation between leading managers and officials, and official help could be crucial for the success of elite-run projects. Managers in Longyou made the most progress in establishing institutions during the tenures of two magistrates who were recognized by biographies in the gazetteer. Managers, however, enjoyed the same advantages of continuity and local knowledge as clerks did, in contrast to the constant stream of magistrates. In Longyou, where one member of the gentry was a public leader for about thirty years, there were thirteen magistrates during the Tongzhi and nineteen during the Guangxu.[157] Even though four of these magistrates served for considerable periods, managers must have had a far firmer grasp on the local situation. Elite assumption of local responsibility and the eclipse of officials in the field of welfare was by no means limited to Zhejiang.[158]

Moreover, members of the managerial elite used their institutional positions and duties to further unrelated *public* aims. When Yan Chen was pressing the magistrate and higher officials for tax reform in Tongxiang, he talked to the people and gathered information as he traveled all over the district managing his program to support the babies of poor families. That these tax reforms were no private venture is underlined by his description of them as "a renewal of government" (*xinzheng*).[159] When local managerial initiatives were so wide-ranging and when managers pushed ahead of officials in calling for reform, their actions took on dimensions that were different from a defense of private interest against officials but no less autonomous in implication.

This was the period in which Feng Guifen's essays urging a formal role for local elites in running the affairs of their home districts were gradually being published. We do not know whether the members of the managerial elite in Zhejiang were familiar with Feng's ideas. However, some literati managers must have been acquainted with Gu Yanwu's proposals for hereditary officials drawn from local elites or with works of other authors from earlier centuries who advocated a measure of local control. Ideas drawn from the persistent "feudal" model of government, which included local autonomy, a wider recruitment of literati talent into central decision-making, and a greater diffusion of authority, were circulating in the Lower Yangtze during the latter half of the nineteenth century.[160]

Accounts of public institutions indicate that managerial activities themselves also generated autonomous attitudes, without any need to prove connections to political theorists. The old conceptions of the "public selection" (*gongju*) of respected community leaders and the informal "public discussion" (*gongyi*) of important local issues were applied to the organization and operation of public institutions. Thus "public discussion" resulted in the organization of gentry-run night patrols in Hangzhou during the 1880's and the decision of Pinghu merchants in Shanghai to contribute to charities at home. The supervisors of the Hangzhou night patrols were "publicly selected," as were the directors of the Jiashan welfare association.[161]

Once established, major public institutions could serve as forums to discuss issues unrelated to their functions. In the spring of 1875, for instance, gentry gathered at the welfare association to "publicly discuss problems of examination administration in Hangzhou."[162] Such methods of making decisions and choosing leaders were routinely reported in the press without elaboration, and conceptions of community "public opinion" (*gonglun*) existed in places far from major urban centers.[163]

A crucial element was added by attaching the concept of "self" (*zi*) to public activity. The Pinghu merchants in Shanghai contributed money to extend "self-help" (*zizhu*) to welfare, and an 1891 account of a foundling home in Cheng (Shaoxing) called it "self-established" (*zili*, i.e., by members of the local elite).[164] Such terms had connotations of autonomy that foreshadowed the issues of self-government (*zizhi*) that arose in the 1900's. Indeed, an editorial in *Shen bao* on corruption in the Hangzhou house-tax collection during 1878 took an additional step by arguing that, in this instance, "self-government" was necessary to obtain the people's confidence—which was needed for successful governing on a larger scale.[165]

Elite managers did not ordinarily use these phrases, but their writings nonetheless suggest an underlying commitment to local responsibility for local affairs. One of the leading managers in Shuanglin town (Huzhou) maintained that "the power of officials to foster benefits and avoid harm to a locality is limited to sending out instructions and displaying documents. If no one from the place itself puts forth great effort, then absolutely nothing will be started, or, if begun, it will fail before completion."[166] He urged people not to think that public affairs were none of their concern and not to pursue only their personal ambitions.

Against whom, then, did the members of the elite see themselves competing for local control? Clerks and runners were the primary rivals. The corruption and oppressive practices of the sub-bureaucracy were cited to justify elite management of local institutions, and at least the top-level managers tried to distance themselves and their institutions from that aspect of local government.[167] There is reason therefore to look upon managerial development in terms of competition between the sub-bureaucracy and the respectable gentry for control of local activities.[168]

At the same time, there is evidence of competition with regular officials and distrust of them. At the very least, managers and officials had different perspectives on managerial functions. Officials might approve of elite management, agree that it was a remedy for clerical corruption, and endorse the "public selection" of managers.[169] They spoke of "contribution by the people and management by the people" (or gentry: *minjuan min(shen)ban*).[170] There was no determined opponent of gentry activism among high Zhejiang officials comparable to Governor Ding Richang in Jiangsu. In the last analysis, however, even accommodating officials remained suspicious of possible elite corruption, inefficiency, and empire-building, and they sought to keep local activism within a framework of "official supervision and popular (or gentry) management" (*guandu min-(shen)ban*).[171] Normally such a conception coexisted with the rudimentary autonomous ambitions of local leaders, but differences occasionally surfaced during disputes.

Muted conflict developed between the reconstruction leaders in Nanxun town and Prefect Zong Yuanhan in Huzhou city. Zong criticized the Nanxun managers for spending money on bridges instead of pursuing their alleged goal of academy construction. He also insisted that they reduce the reconstruction surcharge on silk *lijin* and contribute some of their collections to revising the prefectural gazetteer. The real problem seems to have been that they were behaving too independently for Zong's taste, even though he was often a strong supporter of managerial activity. The Nanxun leaders had to back down, but they did point out that their taxes had been levied on locally produced silk—and by implication should be spent as community leaders wished.[172]

More explicit statements were made in Longyou (Quzhou), where gentry spokesmen unequivocally blamed yamen clerks for shortages in educational funds, while the magistrate accused "worthless gentry managers" of taking a rake-off and dividing up the spoils. The eventual solution was the establishment of a rent bureau, which the magistrate called "official supervision and gentry management" but the academy head termed the "opening shot of gentry management" that would strengthen the "rights" of the district gentry.[173] Although this dispute came during the conversion of the academy to a new school almost three decades after the Tongzhi, the issues were very much the same—as was the failure to achieve a genuine meeting of minds between the magistrate and the managers.

Limited clashes sometimes rested on a deeper suspicion of the official establishment, which was the obverse of the distrust of the gentry shown by Ding Richang. Magistrates were accused of corruption, negligence, and incompetence. Sun Yiyan, although an official himself, was a proponent of local autonomy—at least for his native Wenzhou. Sun's most bitter criticism was aimed at magistrates in Ruian during the Gold Coin Rebellion. These men, he charged, had appeased the real rebels and persecuted innocent people so that they could report progress in restoring order. Their actions only fanned popular anger. With withering sarcasm, Sun pointed out that in the ensuing rebellion a few officials were killed, ten or so men received rewards, but several thousand people died. Building a commemorative shrine to the righteous dead was a hollow substitute for correcting the misgovernment that had caused the rebellion in the first place.[174] In contrast, Sun praised the defense efforts of the Wenzhou elite, comparing the exploits of a militia leader in Pingyang to those of famous Song dynasty generals from Wenzhou. Although this leader operated in only a small area, his accomplishments were great because, Sun maintained, he sought nothing from officials and officials could do nothing to hinder his power.[175]

In a different (but similarly ambiguous) way, Yan Chen, too, held himself apart from the bureaucratic establishment. He had a dispute with the district magistrate, whom he accused of manipulating the rates for commuting tribute-in-kind into silver. Being a good deal closer to the provincial capital and operating in the more settled reconstruction period rather than in the midst of a rebellion, he handled the immediate problem by the time-honored, respectable method of using his rank and connections to go over the magistrate's head. His more fundamental worries about social stability were not so easily solved. Yan argued that if corruption were controlled, the populace would be content and the government secure. The unstated corollary was that elite security also depended upon social stability. The members of the elite did not necessarily define this stability in the same way as officials. On the contrary, they sometimes linked it to the protection of community interests from harm by the government, and Yan once even implied that corruption that "cheated the ruler" (by depriving the state of revenue) but did not harm the people might be preferable to the reverse.[176] He also suggested that, if the magistrate made a practice of manipulating commutation rates, "not only would the people's hearts resist, it would also provoke a crisis in the structure of government."[177]

Such rhetorical flourishes were not political statements but expressions of vague unease. In "normal" times they would have had no practical implications whatsoever, but the reconstruction period was not normal. The effects of rebellion were still being felt, while the Shanghai trade was impinging upon the economy and society of the commercialized core. The poorly articulated doubts of elite public leaders were being set forth stridently in Shanghai by the newspaper *Shen bao*, which was quick to criticize the mistakes of the bureaucratic establishment. Within the first few years of publication, the paper protested against such infringements upon elite interests as what it considered the unjust punishment of a member of the gentry from Yuhang district (Hangzhou) in a murder case, the harassment of merchant boats by port underlings in Jiaxing city, and the proliferation of *lijin* stations in Jiaxing prefecture.[178] Even so popular and admired an official as Zong Yuanhan, who was usually praised by the newspaper, came in for criticism when he used too much pressure to elicit contributions from the Ningbo elite.[179] Frustrations erupted in a November 1879 editorial entitled "On Officials," which averred that officials were worse than bandits because their deprivations were constant and affected everyone. Not just the sub bureaucracy but all officials were indicted in a lengthy list of malpractices.[180] Whether *Shen bao* was leading or reflecting Lower Yangtze elite opinion, such an airing of grievances indicated that questions were being raised about the way government impinged upon people.

Prominent members of the elite, who had numerous options open to them but chose to return home to manage reconstruction, had placed the needs of family and native place above conventional careers. This choice suggested a belief that more could be accomplished outside the bureaucracy. Yan Chen wrote approvingly of how Zhang Lüxiang, fed up with late Ming politics, decided to "resist ambition and not go forth" in pursuit of wealth and honor but to cultivate frugality and right conduct, manage his farm, and study the agricultural economics of the "southeast."[181] Like Zhang's decision, Yan's retirement involved a little more than an affinity for rural simplicity. He had been reprimanded and marked down in 1862 for what the throne considered excessive praise of the two empress dowagers in a Hanlin Academy final examination. This humiliating incident evidently contributed to his decision to return to the Lower Yangtze.[182]

Although it is impossible to say how many high-ranking

members of the elite pursued careers at home because of the vicissitudes of bureaucratic politics or disagreements with government policies, one finds scattered examples of a phenomenon that became more evident as disillusionment increased during the last two decades of the century. Lu Xinyuan retired to scholarship and management in Huzhou, first during an extended mourning period and then in anger over Japanese claims to the Ryukyu Islands. In the end, he was permanently barred from office because of financial irregularities, which do not appear to have reflected upon his personal character or dimmed his reputation among Lower Yangtze literati.[183] Yu Yue, who was intimate with literati-managers as the foremost scholar and teacher in Hangzhou, had also been permanently dismissed in the 1850's for posing an unfortunate provincial examination question that allegedly showed disrespect for the empress.[184]

Such examples suggest that managerial activism absorbed an eremitic strain in this period. The two most influential models of behavior open to literati who believed that degenerate governments would not properly use their talents were the preservation of their integrity by retiring to private pursuits until the times were propitious for a return to office and the mixture of stubborn loyalty, dissent, and sacrifice exemplified by the fourth-century B.C. minister of Chu, Qu Yuan.[185] In the reconstruction period we see a third pattern, reminiscent of the seventeenth century, in which eremitic officials retired to local activity in the hope of making improvements at home that would eventually benefit the country.[186]

This muted disapproval and the determination to pursue solutions outside the bureaucracy are captured in Sun Yiyan's biography of his old teacher Zhang Zhenkui, a *juren* who died in 1867. Zhang had angrily resigned as director of studies at Zhenhai (Ningbo) during the Opium War, after higher officials had rejected his plan for local naval mobilization against the British. Zhang never again tried for office, but as a teacher in Wenzhou he influenced a generation of rising scholars and was consulted by officials on a wide range of local affairs. To his students he stressed "broad learning," in which scholars perused all the classics, history, ancient philosophy, poetry, and essays to extract currently useful lessons. With the qualities of the sages thus internalized, a person might devote himself to the dynasty and the court if he was eminent, but on a lower level he could also help a township or a district.[187]

Zhang was a quiet man whose local reputation derived from his knowledge and moral example. The managerial expansion in the Tongzhi provided a scope for a more active eremitism, practiced by men who did not fully approve of government policies. Like the officials and the court, they wished to restore the sociopolitical order—but not necessarily in quite the same way.[188] During the post-Taiping period, we see in the Lower Yangtze the faint beginnings of competition between bureaucratic and social activism that became better articulated under different circumstances in decades to come.[189] Arising as they did amid efforts to reintegrate the social order, the independent initiatives carried their own justification.

The post-Taiping period was thus characterized by the rise of local public spheres between the bureaucratic and private sectors. Both the requirements of reconstruction and the economic changes wrought by foreign trade contributed to this development. Continuing institutions and long lived managerial establishments ensured its permanence, and, once established, this sphere had a life of its own that went beyond its original components. Existing institutions continued to increase, but expansion also came through new activities as members of the elite responded to different crises. The problems of the Tongzhi, which were conceptualized in the capital as the restoration of dynastic power, were seen in the localities more in terms of reconstruction. Both approaches were reformist in the context of the day;[190] the one being of particular concern to the officials and the court, the other to the managerial elite. A legacy of reconstruction was public activism, which was backed by leadership and organizational capacity outside the bureaucracy. It was too restless and too concerned with the problems of the day to remain within bounds.

FOUR

Beyond Local Boundaries

The Extension of Public Activism

The reconstruction after the Taiping Rebellion was not completed in any one year, but the major damage had been repaired in the core districts by the end of the 1870's. The functions of the post-rebellion welfare bureaus and other agencies became more routine, and publicly active members of the elite began to respond to new crises. Reconstruction had directed elite attention inward to repairing damage done to their home areas. It would have been possible therefore for autonomous impulses and social concerns to continue to evolve in localistic contexts. Just when reconstruction was losing its urgency, however, new crises, which seemed to threaten the entire country, stimulated public opinion and organization across spatial divisions.

These new elite initiatives were grounded in the reconstruction; they were abetted by the cosmopolitanism of the members of the elite who became local leaders after the Taiping Rebellion. The change came in two stages. First, existing forms of local activism were pulled into wider arenas as public welfare expanded into a macroregional, nationally oriented organization for north China famine relief. Second, the way was paved for subsequent politicized mobilizations when renewed foreign attacks began to introduce qualitative changes in the nature of public activism. During both these stages Shanghai was an increasingly important organizational center, but the new impetus was generated even more widely by the elite activism that was coalescing in the local public spheres of the core districts.

The Emergence of a
Macroregional Managerial Establishment

By the end of the Tongzhi (1862–74), there was already a personally connected, open-ended establishment composed of activist scholars and managers in the Lower Yangtze. Horizontal networks of personal relationships linking managerial elites of separate localities were fostered as successful people made external connections while pursuing careers away from home.[1] We have seen that, as Zhejiangese merchants gravitated to Shanghai, they helped direct profits from foreign trade back into public management at home. The overlap between managerial and scholarly circles connected local management to the outside in different ways, which became increasingly crucial in pulling public organization outward into contact with national events. Men and institutions in Shanghai played pivotal roles in this process, and that city emerged as a new intellectual and organizational center from which public opinion was spread by the press.

These interlocking personal networks that led in all directions defy description except in restricted contexts. I am concerned here with the effect of ties between managerial and scholarly circles on the prestige and effectiveness of managers, the scope of management, and interchange within the public sphere. Such ties existed between Ding Bing, the most prominent manager in Hangzhou, and Yu Yue, the most eminent nineteenth-century Zhejiangese scholar. Although these were unusually well known men in the provincial capital, similar interchange appeared in other cities and towns.

Ding lacked Yu's academic status but derived literary prestige from his book-collecting. Both had fled to Shanghai during the Taiping Rebellion. Both set out on the post-Taiping phase of their careers with the support of the governor, Ma Xinyi. Ding rebuilt the academies at which Yu taught, and he headed the printing office that supplied them with books. Yu contributed to some repairs managed by Ding, and he wrote an introduction to one of the books Ding reprinted. Each had his own circle of protégés; they overlapped when students from the Gujing Jing-she, headed by Yu, found work at the printing office. The two men also knew many of the same scholars, officials, and managers. Both knew Lu Xinyuan of Huzhou, Yan Chen of Tongxiang, and the Suns of Ruian. They were also friends of merchants like Hu Guangyong of Hangzhou, Liu Yong of Nanxun town, and Shen Baoyue of the town of Qing.[2]

These few names can be considered the tip of a provincial establishment (or, more likely, interlocking establishments) of literati-manager-merchant activists centered in the wealthy, cultivated Jiangnan core.[3] Men from outlying districts, like the Suns of Ruian, were also included. They were, however, fewer in number and had to operate across longer distances between their homes and the provincial capital. The long-term expansion of career opportunities outside the bureaucratic track made such an establishment possible. When reconstruction added management to the prestigious alternatives previously provided by the Lower Yangtze academic complexes, scholars and bibliophiles like Lu Xinyuan and Ding Bing became public activists. At the same time, academic jobs were dispersed when rebellion disrupted the old centers of learning and high-ranking literati found employment in newly founded town academies. The town of Puyuan in Tongxiang, for instance, attracted a series of distinguished heads, starting with Yan Chen and continuing through a *juren* manager from the prefectural city, a *juren* from Shaoxing who had served as an educational official in Jiaxing prefecture, and two former members of the Hanlin Academy.[4]

The literati managers who served as district or prefectural educational officials provide another example of manager-scholar interaction. Gazetteers frequently record instances of men moving between management and the post of director or sub-director of education.[5] This combination of roles demonstrated the rising prestige of management and broadened the duties of local educational officials. Local educational positions in the regular bureaucracy were exempt in part from the "law of avoidance" that prevented officials from serving within their native province. During the Qing, educational officials normally were men from another prefecture within the same province.[6] *Juren* and *gongsheng* were eligible for these posts, which were not rotated as systematically as the position of magistrate. Governors sometimes used these officials to collect information outside regular channels, but the educational officials were also likely to have rapport with the gentry communities.[7] Educational directors did not often go on to hold official posts outside their own provinces, but some expanded their functions within the province to include welfare, construction, or defense.[8] It thus appears that this bureaucratic post was being pulled closer to the emergent public sphere and that the jobs of local educational officials were becoming closer to those of leading managers.

As a result of all these connections and interchanges, managers were able to make use of successful practices in other districts. The new charitable school and the burial society in Nanxun were considered excellent models, and gentry of distant Yuhuan (Wenzhou) copied the regulations of Nanxun's foundling home.[9] Yan Chen patterned the Tongxiang foundling home on homes in Shaoxing and Chenzhou (Hunan province), while Pinghu (Jiaxing) district managers combined Yan's model with that of nearby Shimen district.[10] Even when this kind of information was spread by officials, it still fostered managerial collegiality. Men looked to their contemporaries as well as to past ideals for models of public institutions.

These interchanges had fostered the growth of reconstruction institutions. The ties critical to the next stage of public activism fostered interchange between Zhejiang localities and Shanghai. Shanghai had begun to play a significant role in the expansion of elite managerial networks during the Taiping Rebellion, when men who later took part in rebuilding their home communities were thrown together as refugees in that city. Throughout the reconstruction period Shanghai became an intellectual magnet, displacing older disrupted centers, providing opportunities for the currently popular statecraft-oriented education, and offering new instruction in foreign subjects. The Longmen Academy and the Shanghai Gujing Jingshe (which merged with the still more practical Jiuzhi Academy in 1876) were the most important new academies founded there to impart knowledge useful for government.[11] Early schools of Western studies were the Institute of Foreign Languages (*guangfang yanguan*), established by Li Hongzhang in 1863, and the Chinese Polytechnic Institute (*gezhi shuyuan*), founded by John Fryer and Xu Shou of Wuxi (Jiangsu) in 1884.[12]

Because Zhejiangese were involved in these Shanghai institutions, they served as vehicles for expanding scholarly and managerial contacts across provincial boundaries. The founders of the two academies, Shanghai intendants (daotais) Ying Baoshi and Shen Bingcheng, were Zhejiangese officials with ties to local managerial establishments in their home districts. Both knew eminent Zhejiangese scholars or activists such as Yu Yue, Sun Yiyan, and Yan Chen.[13] Shen appointed Yu Yue the first head of his academy,[14] and other Zhejiangese held positions at these two academies during the last decades of the nineteenth century.[15] There were similar connections with the new Western-style institutions; a mathematics teacher at the Institute of Foreign Languages, for instance, was the nephew of Shen Baoyue of Qing town, whom we have met as a merchant, local manager, and associate of Yan Chen.[16]

Not only academies but also welfare institutions in Shanghai contributed to building up macroregional networks. Ying Baoshi founded a large composite welfare agency, soliciting contributions from silk merchants of Jiaxing and Huzhou as well as from Jiangsu natives. One of the most active managers was Jing Yuanshan, a merchant-philanthropist-reformer from Shangyu (Zhejiang) who directed the Shanghai Telegraph and other enterprises for many years. Jing used this agency and another to mobilize funds for north China famine relief, and he also enlisted support among Shanghai colleagues for projects in three different districts of his native Shaoxing.[17] Thus the symbiosis between the scholarly, gentry, and official worlds of Shanghai and Zhejiang resembled the commercial relationship of the two areas. Its effects appear repeatedly in accounts of the expansion, redirection, and politicization of public activity during the Guangxu reign period (1875–1908).

Important though they were, all these institutions fitted into the existing reconstruction mode. The press was a dynamic new factor. The Western-style newspaper *Shen bao*, established in the late Tongzhi, first contributed to the development of reconstruction public spheres and then facilitated their expansion in new directions. The growth of the press also boosted Shanghai's position as a center of public organization and opinion formation. After this period news could be disseminated without depending upon social networks; in central China this news was almost exclusively printed in Shanghai until the 1890's.

Shen bao had been preceded by several short-lived Chinese language papers, including the *Shanghai News* (*Shanghai xinwen*), established in 1862 by the *North China Daily News*. It was, however, the first major Shanghai daily aimed at a general audience. It was founded in 1872 by two English tea merchants, the brothers Frederick and Ernest Major, at the suggestion of their comprador. The editor, Qian Zheng, drew upon Wang Tao's journalistic experience in Hong Kong and made his paper an important source of national, foreign, and regional news.[18] *Shen bao* soon drove the *Shanghai News* out of business. Within ten years it was being sold in Beijing and Tianjin, a number of provincial capitals, and several other cities in Jiangsu and Zhejiang. In Zhejiang it had outlets in Ningbo and Hangzhou by 1880 and added another in Wenzhou in 1882. The paper must have been available—at least occasionally—to elite leaders in the five northern prefectures and along the coast.[19]

A number of *Shen bao* staff members in its early years were from Zhejiang and so may be presumed to have had ties with elites in that province,[20] but the paper's main impact came from its news coverage and editorials. During the 1870's it focused on the Lower Yangtze,[21] providing a mine of information about prices and business conditions, foreign threats and coastal defense, local administration and elite public management, natural disasters, riots, risings, robberies, murders, and even the lives of women.[22] Zhejiangese readers in Shanghai or at home could learn about the latest round of fires in Ningbo, local bullies in Hangzhou, a new book firm in Jiaxing, bridge repair on the Ningbo-Ciqi road, and economic conditions in the southwest.[23] This deliberately trivial list is meant to emphasize that *Shen bao* was not a narrow treaty-port newspaper. It was also the spokesman for the Yangtze Valley gentry-merchant managerial elite, and in the early 1880's it became a national paper. It not only published news of managerial activities but also commented on such subjects of elite concern as female infanticide.[24] Its propensity to criticize officials and its ability to place events in wider frameworks drawn from both Chinese and Western experience fostered conceptual changes and nurtured public opinion. Members of the elite acquired an alternative to informal connections or petitions in presenting their cases to authorities. Readers found their views rationalized in ways that suggested new ideas and demands.

In the late 1890's *Shen bao* held itself aloof from reformers in Shanghai and was therefore regarded as the spokesman for conservative official-gentry.[25] In the 1870's and 1880's, however, it was a progressive and even slightly disruptive publication that fostered elite activism. Six years after it was established, its articles encouraged a new stage of expansive, regionally based public activism through which managerial elites in the Lower Yangtze united to organize relief for distant northwest China.

Macroregional Mobilization:
The North China Famine Relief

Coming when the worst problems of post-Taiping reconstruction were over, the famine created by severe drought in Henan, Shenxi, and Shanxi riveted the attention of elite activists of the Lower Yangtze. The disaster caused economic dislocation south of the Yangtze,[26] but members of the elite were more worried about its threat to the national social fabric. Once their concern was aroused, the profitable silk trade of the late 1870's provided much of the money for new charitable ventures.

The relief effort in 1878 marked a series of departures in public activity. Welfare leaders in major cities raised funds, which they distributed in a different part of China. Newly formed committees in major cities enlisted existing local agencies and individuals to collect money at lower urban levels. Shanghai emerged as a center for elite activists from both Jiangsu and Zhejiang, and the press was used to promote public organization and fund-raising.

Western philanthropists, the Chinese government, and extra-bureaucratic institutions all aided famine victims. An Anglo-American Chinese Famine Relief Fund Committee went into action in Shanghai in January 1878. By the end of the year it had distributed some 190,000 taels for relief,[27] and it continued to raise money abroad and in China throughout the crisis. This committee consulted with Chinese officials and prominent Chinese individuals in Shanghai. Its organizational methods were an example for Chinese managers, and one of the stories of Chinese-Western interaction of the late Qing and Republic is found in gradually closer and more equal cooperation in relief.

The Chinese government was a little slow to recognize the magnitude of the famine, but by the spring of 1878 Li Hong-zhang had established a coordinating bureau in Tianjin. Wealthy Shanghai was a prime target for official fund-raising. Li relied upon directors of the Chinese Merchants Steam Navigation Company, the local daotais, and a few prominent, officially connected merchants including Hu Guangyong of Hangzhou. Ranks were conferred upon large contributors, and it was reported that a hundred thousand taels were raised in less than a month.[28] By mid-July the Zhejiang governor memorialized that 20,000 taels had been raised in Hangzhou, 25,000 in Ningbo and Shaoxing, and 11,000 in Huzhou. A very wealthy Hangzhou banker contributed another 30,000. Such officially solicited contributions were sent to the Chinese Merchants Steam Navigation Company in Shanghai for transmission to the bureau in Tianjin.[29]

My main interest is in the separate relief effort that emerged from the existing elite-run welfare organizations. There was already the precedent of Shanghai agencies raising money for non-local disasters in northern Jiangsu in 1876 and in Shandong and Shanxi in 1877.[30] Welfare managers were thus ready to act when they heard of the greater 1878 disaster. By summer special relief offices (*xiezhen gongsuo,* or simply *zhenju*) had been founded at two major Shanghai welfare agencies and the Taigu Steamship Company in the French Concession. There was a similar office at the Hangzhou welfare agency. Zhejiangese residing in Suzhou took the lead in forming a bureau there, and a fourth major bureau was set up in Yangzhou.[31]

Jing Yuanshan has left an account of how the major Shanghai relief bureau evolved. Jing raised one thousand ounces of silver from friends whom he called to a meeting at one of the welfare agencies. These men collected funds during the first months of 1878, and another friend published a pamphlet on the famine. By early spring about ten thousand ounces had been collected, and emissaries were sent with funds to Henan province. A larger meeting on May 15 raised another 13,500 ounces and established the Shanghai relief office with Jing as its head.[32]

Despite such haphazard beginnings, the four major relief centers cooperated to raise over a million taels during the next three years.[33] They accepted contributions from individuals, businesses, and public institutions. In prefectural and district cities and large market towns, local philanthropists or such public institutions as welfare agencies, foundling homes, granaries, and even *lijin* bureaus organized collections and forwarded money to one of the centers. Sometimes collection boxes were set up on the streets, or contributions were imposed upon local businesses.[34] It is not surprising that most of the Zhejiang donations came from the core districts in the northern prefectures. Collections in Jiaxing and Huzhou were sent to Shanghai, or perhaps Suzhou, as well as to Hangzhou.

The severity of the famine was well known to the literate public in at least the core districts of Zhejiang, and appeals elicited a broad response. Lists of donors printed in *Shen bao* typically started with a few gifts of two hundred taels or more and ended up with contributions of about a yuan—with a considerable number falling between ten and fifty taels. As in the case of local welfare, a few contributors were women.[35] There is no way to tell how effectively and honestly this money was managed, but the organizers took the effort very seriously and published frequent, though unsystematic, financial reports in *Shen bao*.

This deliberate support from the press was the most striking innovation in social mobilization. *Shen bao* began to carry reports and editorials about the famine early in 1878. It constantly covered activities of the elite-run offices, published their financial reports, and encouraged contributions with lists of donors. It printed extracts about official relief from *The Peking Gazette*, but most news articles focused on gentry and merchants. One editorial even suggested that elite-run famine collections be regularized through monthly assessments like those used to support welfare institutions in southern Jiangsu.[36]

The mobilization of prominent managers and philanthropists at different urban levels and across provincial boundaries was a second major development. Some of these men had been, or would be, employed in the bureaucracy, but they were operating privately so far as famine relief was concerned. The four main offices not only managed their own collections (albeit sometimes supported by an official decree urging contributions) but also distributed funds in the famine areas. Representatives set up Jiangsu and Zhejiang relief bureaus in Henan under a *juren* and a lower-degree holder from Jiangsu and an expectant daotai from Xiushui. These men formed a "united bureau" to distribute relief. They received funds directly from the four offices in Jiangsu and Zhejiang and addressed letters about conditions and operations to the "welfare heads" (*shanzhang*) of those offices.[37] Such extended extra-bureaucratic management was a definite step beyond the localized activism of the Tongzhi period.

Existing rationales for local public management were adapted to this new wave of macroregional initiative. Looking over recent history, a *Shen bao* editorialist suggested that famine and rebellion were alike in producing misfortune and loss of life. Southern provinces had suffered during the Taiping Rebellion, whereas the north had escaped destruction. Subsequently the south recovered, but now the north was suffering from famine.

It therefore behooved the once again wealthy southerners to give aid in what was perceived as a new phase of a continuing social crisis.[38] Members of the Lower Yangtze elite who visited the famine areas were genuinely appalled by conditions there; they mixed their humanitarian concerns with a hope of forestalling rebellion by limiting misery. A sociomoral commitment to philanthropy led to the idea of people from all regions working together to preserve the social stability of the country.[39] Invoking the image of the superior man (*junzi*), another *Shen bao* editorial exhorted people to put forth their best efforts without asking whether there was an official program, suggesting it was unlikely that the government's method of rewarding contributors with ranks would work indefinitely.[40]

Very clearly, the famine relief managers considered autonomy to be one of the virtues of their relief effort. *Shen bao* used the phrase "contribution by the people and management by the people" to describe the program[41] and questioned whether officially administered relief could deal with so widespread a disaster. Voluntary, independent relief (*yizhen*) was therefore an essential addition.[42] Jing Yuanshan was emphatic in advocating voluntary relief as far more honest and effective than official programs. Jing did not want a complete abdication of official responsibility, but he thought voluntary relief offices should manage both official and publicly raised funds, and he wanted to increase the resources available for non-official relief.[43] This confidence in extra-bureaucratic initiative was similar to the earlier preference for local elite management to circumvent clerical corruption. Members of the Lower Yangtze elite had more faith in their own agencies than in official ones. They were willing to contribute to famine committees although they resisted official demands for donations.[44]

The expanded, macroregional welfare organization did not die out after the worst crisis in north China had passed. In the winter of 1879–80 the managers shifted the operations of the Zhejiang-Jiangsu bureau to Tianjin, where they worked with the head of the Tianjin welfare association to combat new disasters in Zhili.[45] Two years later one of the original managers was running operations in north Jiangsu, and in 1882 a new famine relief office in Ningbo joined the existing ones in Suzhou and Hangzhou in collecting for Anhui flood victims.[46] By the summer of 1883 the focus had shifted to floods in Shandong.[47] In 1887–88 these offices aided victims of more serious flooding in Shandong and Zhili, and three years later, they turned their attention to the Yangtze Valley as well.[48]

During the 1880's and early 1890's, top managers evolved into professional high-level relief experts who operated wherever trouble arose.[49] The same kinds of bureaus continued in large cities of Zhejiang and Jiangsu. In Shanghai the center of relief operations shifted to the telegraph office (because Jing Yuanshan was employed there) and to the silk guild (which could tap the wealth of sericulture districts), but methods did not change.[50] Offices in urban centers raised funds in smaller cities and towns through local managerial structures, and *Shen bao* continued to publish reports of donations. Probably the Jiangsu-Zhejiang relief field office became less independent after it shifted its headquarters to Tianjin, but voluntary national relief retained its identity. Activity spread in Zhejiang, and similar initiatives appeared outside the Lower Yangtze.[51]

The north China famine relief was part of a post-reconstruction phenomenon—the extension of public organization in welfare. The man in Huzhou whose Confucian conscience and concern for order led him to aid starving peasants in Henan moved beyond localism. The manager from the Hangzhou office dispensing donations in the northwest extended the subtle mixture of support and preemption that characterized the relations of local managers to officials. The techniques of organization, fund-raising, and newspaper coverage were carried over into politicized movements of the 1900's, but the line of transmission was not straight. Famine relief made its main contribution to extending the public sphere in the late 1870's and early 1880's. Thereafter it, too, became routine, and foreign events furnished another impetus, which pushed elite activism in political directions.

Patriotic Activism

Foreign military threats made a different contribution to the evolution of the public sphere. Although domestic social crises produced an organizational response, there were only temporary and limited opportunities for autonomous military organization to repel invasion. Foreign incursions did, however, arouse the populace and involve elites in defense. In the 1880's foreign problems began to overshadow domestic concerns, and the Sino-French and Sino-Japanese wars altered the evolution of public opinion and the public sphere. The need to defend against external dangers enlarged people's conceptions of elite participation in their country's affairs and fostered a public opinion critical of governmental leaders. As before, ideas in the Shanghai press interacted with those of scholarly and managerial circles in Zhejiang. During this period, however, the uneasiness in the Lower Yangtze could be related to political controversies within the bureaucracy in Beijing. The result was only a proto-mobilization. Nevertheless, the themes that emerged—resistance to foreign domination, utilization of social energy, and suspicion of bureaucratic leadership—constantly appeared in the politicized movements to come.

The background of foreign intrusion. By the 1880's, Zhejiangese had been aware of foreign dangers for forty years. Military action in Zhejiang during the Opium War centered on the Ningbo coast, although British ships made brief forays along the south shore of Hangzhou Bay. Gentry and merchants contributed money for coastal defenses and organized militias in several Ningbo districts. A few local forces fought bands of English, while other local men were recruited into governmental armies to supplement troops from other parts of China. Some army commanders were Zhejiangese, and stories of heroic resistance were kept alive—as in the temple for the fallen general, Zhu Gui, in Ciqi district.[52]

From the little we know, the invasion had three effects on the local population. Frightened people immediately fled from threatened coastal points. The news also stirred up social disorder similar to that in the Canton Delta; banditry and rent resistance broke out in the poor littoral of Yuyao (Shaoxing) when foreign ships approached.[53] Finally, gentry organized militias, drew up defense plans, and put pressure on officials to fight the intruders. Mo Bingyuan, a fifty-year-old *gongsheng* from Shanyin, wrote the governor about the danger and then drafted warning memorials to Beijing when invited to join the governor's staff. Subsequently, as director of studies in Dinghai, he helped organize defense and reprovision the city after the war.[54]

Indignation and a sense of humiliation lingered in some academies and scholarly circles, inspiring reconsiderations of Chinese history. We have already seen that the defeat caused Sun Yiyan's teacher to give up governmental office for an academic life of statecraft scholarship. Mo Bingyuan, who had always stressed literary refinement while he was teaching in Ningbo academies, also shifted his focus. In his old age, he began reading about the Ming, which, he maintained, held better lessons for "later affairs" than more ancient history did.

The Taiping Rebellion cut off any political implications that might have developed from such vaguely disaffected historicism. The Arrow War, fought further north in the midst of civil war, did not make much impression on Zhejiang, and reconstruction occupied most elite activists for the first ten years after the rebellion. The reappearance of foreign troubles in the mid-to-late 1870's, however, began to refocus their attention on the vulnerable coastline.

The Japanese expedition against Taiwan in 1874, on the pretext of retaliating for the deaths of sailors from the Ryukyu Islands, produced a flurry of troop movements and defense preparations in Zhejiang. Rumors of an impending Japanese attack and "unfathomable misfortunes" circulated about Ningbo prefecture. People again fled from the coast into the mountains. Wealthy families transferred silver inland, and some small Ningbo banks failed because they had to pay up to .145 percent interest a day (53 percent a year) to keep accounts.[55] Uneasiness and rumors spread to Hangzhou, where banks were also shaken and the important tinfoil business was brought to a halt when tinbeaters refused to return from their usual summer vacations at home in the Ningbo districts.[56] Scholars noted the government's failure to take a strong stand against Japanese claims to the Ryukyu Islands, and it was at this point that Lu Xinyuan again left government service to return home to Huzhou.

The next year the diplomatic crisis over the murder of the

British interpreter A. R. Margary in Yunnan produced rumors of impending war with England.[57] Forts were readied at Zhenhai (Ningbo), and mines were laid in the river. A dispute with Russia over control of the remote Ili region in Turkestan brought new alarms in 1880 when Russian ships anchored off Dinghai (Ningbo). Chinese ships were sent to Zhenhai, and troops were transferred from Hangzhou. Men were conscripted in peripheral Chuzhou as well as in Ningbo city. Members of the Ningbo gentry did their share by raising twenty thousand yuan to purchase breech-loading rifles.[58] This concern over coastal defenses continued through the early 1880's. Officials in Wenzhou levied a special contribution of twenty cents a *mou* to improve fortifications,[59] governors made inspection tours, and ominous foreign warships appeared from time to time.

Shen bao carried news of foreign demands, negotiations, and troop or naval movements during these incidents. The articles stressed international dangers and offered two-pronged advice about how to meet military threats. On the one hand, they called upon the government to modernize its armed forces. On the other, they sought to mobilize members of the Lower Yangtze elite and argued that military preparations must be accompanied by the removal of abuses that were weakening society internally. During the Ili crisis, *Shen bao* singled out the contributors in Ningbo as models for members of the elite elsewhere in China. Coastal preparedness was a proper concern of all, it maintained, because the people as well as the state would benefit from a strong defense of China. Linking together themes of resource mobilization, elite activism, and modernization, the paper praised the Ningbo men not only for loyally and righteously raising money for defense but also for knowing that modern guns were needed.[60]

Such praiseworthy contributions from rich men led to questions about the way the government spent the money. An editorial a few days before the one on coastal preparations began by discussing the economic burdens caused by official corruption, and then it turned to military costs. Large amounts of *lijin* went into private pockets; the grain tribute was also a source of corruption. Such abuses harmed both the country and the people. Rich households in Jiangnan had already spent vast sums for military supplies, and now far greater expenditures for modern steamships and weapons were required.[61] Such statements indicate that at least some members of the Lower Yangtze elite entered the 1880's alarmed over foreign threats, ready to participate in defending the country, aware of the need for better armaments, and skeptical of the ability of the bureaucracy to modernize honestly and efficiently.

Patriotism during the Sino-French War. The war with France presented a much more tangible danger to the coast than the incidents of the 1870's had. French colonial expansion in Indochina led to hostilities along the ill-defined Annam-China border in the early 1880's. By late 1883 the fighting had escalated into battles between French and Chinese troops. An agreement negotiated by Li Hongzhang was rejected by the Qing court because of bureaucratic opposition to such concessions as the recognition of French sovereignty over Annam. Thereupon, the French fleet moved north, attacking Taiwan and destroying the Fuzhou naval yards in the summer of 1884. Although the French and the Chinese armies were more evenly matched, French naval superiority was enough to persuade the Chinese government to sign a peace treaty in the spring of 1885.

While members of elites in coastal provinces were supporting the war effort, literati-officials in the metropolitan bureaucracy were furiously attacking Li Hongzhang and others whom they blamed for the Chinese defeats and concessions to France in the peace negotiations. The leaders of this militant *qingyi* (pure discussion) criticism were members of the Pure Current (*qingliu*) group, who had arisen in the early 1880's from the Hanlin Academy and other education-oriented offices. The criticism reflected a wider uneasiness over governmental leadership, however, and revealed a general, deep anger at foreign invasion. Lower and middle-grade officials with no other way to influence policy called for broader consultations to somewhat diffuse decision-making within the central bureaucracy.[62]

Some of these metropolitan officials were from Zhejiang—most notably Huang Tifang, who was intimate with leading scholar-managers of Ruian (Wenzhou). The disputes in the capital had an effect on the younger scholars of that district, but there is no good indication of how closely they were followed in the province as a whole. Nonetheless, from the mid-1880's there was increasing interaction between political opposition on the national level and public opinion and activity within Zhejiang (and the Lower Yangtze in general). At no time, however, did the impetus come only from the center. During the 1880's, members of the elite responded to situations created within the province, and these situations produced reactions similar to those expressed by the much more politicized opposition in the capital.

Zhejiangese were first directly affected by the disruption of commercial coastal shipping when the French intercepted vessels suspected of bringing arms or supplies to Chinese forces on Taiwan. Then in February 1885 there was an engagement between Chinese and French ships off the coast of Ningbo. Soon after, the French blockaded Zhenhai to bottle up the Chinese ships that had withdrawn into the Yong River. Defenses were supervised by two exceptionally able officials, the reformist daotai Xue Fucheng and Ningbo prefect Zong Yuanhan. They began preparations before France attacked Fuzhou. Throughout the war they encouraged members of the elite to lead militias and contribute money. They sought to avert panic and, on the whole, prevented social unrest.[63]

Zhejiangese reactions were similar to those produced by earlier foreign incursions, but the scale was broader. Rich families once more fled their homes, and the people were filled with "fear and doubt." Rumors of French atrocities against Chinese boatmen circulated after the Ningbo blockade began.[64] Nevertheless, one foreign observer in Ningbo contrasted the "exasperation and anger" felt toward the French with the "abject fear" displayed as the Taiping armies advanced in 1861.[65]

This anger sometimes manifested itself in racial hostility to foreigners, and particularly to French missionaries. There were rumors of cannon hidden in Ningbo churches,[66] and attacks on both Protestant and Catholic missions in Wenzhou took place during the fall of 1884.[67] However, the main reaction can be better described as a determination to defeat the invaders than as indiscriminate xenophobia. English missionaries traveling about the northern prefectures after the war reported that people there knew the fight had been against France and did not necessarily blame natives of other countries.[68] Men in the Ningbo area were quick to present themselves for army service, even after the end of hostilities.[69]

Members of the elite aided the war effort in four ways: by organizing militias, tendering military advice, contributing money, and running the French blockade. Gentry used *baojia* registers to form militias in Zhenhai, and defense forces were planned or actually organized in some other coastal districts.[70] Gentry also joined officials in drawing up defense plans for Zhenhai and in figuring out how to block the river to prevent French ships from sailing upstream toward Ningbo.[71]

The most effective form of elite support was probably the monetary contributions by merchants and gentry from Ningbo, Shaoxing, Hangzhou, and other places. These men included Xu Shulan (who became an educational reformer in Shaoxing city during the 1890's), the former Shanghai daotai Ying Baoshi of Yongkang (Jinhua), and the banker, silk merchant, and perennial philanthropist Hu Guangyong of Hangzhou. The total contributions are not known, but those of the Ningbo-Shaoxing gentry exceeded 300,000 taels—which covered 20 or 30 percent of the provisions for Zhejiang troops during the crisis.[72]

Some merchants also transported supplies from Shanghai to Taiwan or Zhenhai. This was a risky undertaking because of the French blockade, although success presumably meant high profits and official honors. Among the people who volunteered to run the blockade was the merchant Dai Siyuan, who had made his fortune trading with foreigners in Shanghai and subsequently would establish a flourishing inland steam launch company.[73] Other Zhejiangese in Shanghai sent rice to Zhenhai to keep prices from rising too rapidly during the blockade.[74]

Such help from merchants and gentry shows an awareness of the danger to China and the willingness of at least some members of the elite to support a war. The officials were definitely in charge, however, and these elite activities did not lead to permanent organization. The important ingredient was simply their involvement in the defense of the country or, at least, their anger over the attack. This involvement brought members of the elite in Zhejiang face-to-face with a new range of problems concerning national defense and strengthening. The solutions toward which they began groping in the 1880's and early 1890's suggested wider participation in national affairs than ever before and pointed to new relationships between bureaucratic government and society.

Participatory self-strengthening defined. The events of the 1880's led some Zhejiangese to set forth a series of solutions that may collectively be called "participatory self-strengthening" to distinguish them from the well-known self-strengthening and foreign affairs (*yangwu*) movements within the government, through which officials like Li Hongzhang sought to improve China's military capacity and establish modern industry. Proponents of both approaches to China's foreign crises were found within and without the bureaucracy, and they might favor similar reforms. However, the implications for state-societal relationships were different. The official self-strengthening movement can be considered a forerunner of the state-building of the last Qing decade, and its leaders were cool to the idea of much social initiative in national and military affairs. Participatory self-strengthening, on the contrary, pointed in the direction of social mobilization.

By the 1880's participatory self-strengthening incorporated older suggestions for correcting misgovernment, militant criticisms of official failure to repel invasion, gentry concern for social solidarity, and pressures for a larger elite role in government that were generated by both reconstruction activism and the defeat by France. The internal and external disasters were considered mutually reinforcing, and good government to achieve social stability was seen as the solution to both. Elite activism and outside reinvigoration of the bureaucracy were integral to reformist concepts that involved greater scope for local elite initiatives and wider participation in national decision-making. Economic and military modernization could easily be included, but as complements to the other measures and not substitutes for them.

As always, there were many overlapping variations. Within the bureaucracy participatory self-strengthening was associated with *qingyi* movements, which criticized the willingness of dominant officials to accept unfavorable peace terms from foreigners and demanded wider consultations within the government. Ideas circulating in Zhejiang were similar to those developing within the capital and in other provinces. Rather than try to cover all the approaches to reform, even in Zhejiang, I will only extract some of the ideas expressed by Zhejiangese or circulated through the press that seem particularly important to subsequent elite mobilization and politicization. Examples of ideas relevant to participatory self-strengthening are found in the newspaper *Shen bao*, in short essays, and in major tracts by three Zhejiangese scholars: *Words of Warning (Weiyan, 1890)*, *Humble Proposals from Liuzhai (Liuzhai beiyi, 1891)*, and *Important Proposals to Save the Times* and *Extensive Discussions of Statecraft (Jiushi yaoyi* and *Jingshi boyi, 1892).*[15] The author of *Words of Warning*, Tang Zhen (Tang Shouqian), had ties to militant officials in Beijing; fifteen years later, he would lead the provincial railway movement. Song Heng and Chen Qiu, who wrote the other tracts, were part of the group of Wenzhou scholars who gathered around Sun Yiyan in Ruian. They, too, had indirect links to metropolitan *qingyi* groups through the Suns and other officials from that district.

The immediate catalyst for rethinking political relationships came from militant reactions to foreign invasions. Since the Opium War, this militancy had arisen both within the bureaucracy and among scholars in the provinces whenever foreigners threatened. Although some prominent *qingyi* militants of the mid-nineteenth century had opposed most foreign practices, military modernization was no longer a major issue dividing them from bureaucratic self-strengtheners. The distinctions revolved about the fundamental militant premises that Chinese had to mobilize popular armies to fight invasion and that determined resistance would provide a more effective defense of China than new technology or diplomatic negotiations.

Policy-making in the central government still tended to be controlled by a small number of high officials, often members of the Grand Council, and a few powerful figures in the court.

The anger at imperialists, the suspicion of officials who gave in to foreign demands, and the frustrations of men who could not influence the policies that they condemned gave militant patriotism an oppositionist caste. Opposition was not yet aimed at the political system, but focused on high officials like Li Hongzhang who were blamed for humiliating defeats. However, the political conflicts in the capital and the dissatisfaction among elites in the provinces did affect the political structure. It further weakened already incomplete governmental control over a mobilizing elite society, and undercut the strategy, associated with Li Hongzhang in the late nineteenth century, of negotiating limited concessions to buy time for officials to improve the military and establish industries.[76] The approach that would have increased government control over internal resources as part of policies to strengthen China internationally was thereby weakened. On the other hand, new social initiatives were fostered, and those people who disapproved of official foreign policy were encouraged to look for new ways to make their opinions heard.

Shen bao was the chief conduit of militant views in the Lower Yangtze during the 1880's. Over a year before hostilities were declared against France, it maintained that war was inevitable and even favored by most officials in the capital. China had to fight—if not on sea, then on land where its armies would have an advantage. If the government yielded once, it would have to give way repeatedly, and foreigners would gradually dominate the country.[77] *Shen bao* published racial abuse of the French,[78] but it mainly emphasized mobilizing the populace against invasion. The paper praised the irregular Black Flag forces that were fighting the French along the Tongking-Chinese border under the secret society leader Liu Yongfu. It called generally for militias—stressing that the strong resolve of the people and the scholars would keep the French at bay.[79] Throughout the war it criticized high officials and opposed the peace negotiations. Such articles inevitably brought the paper into conflict with the peace faction backed by the court. At least two imperial edicts directed Jiangsu officials to discipline *Shen bao*, but without effect.[80] By the end of the war a standoff had been achieved. While the press could criticize governmental policy but not dictate it, the government could not control its critics.

The militant emphasis upon popular mobilization led to other aspects of participatory self-strengthening. Governmental abuses had to be corrected and social order had to be maintained, if the people were to defend the country. One example of the connections drawn between foreign invasion and internal unrest appears in a *Shen bao* editorial on a sectarian rising in 1883. It suggested that social unrest might be curbed by putting vagrants to work building railways, mines, and facilities for water control and by obtaining officials competent to control and indoctrinate the populace. "If we wish to withstand foreign misfortunes, we must first control internal rebellion. If we wish to control internal rebellion, we must first pacify men's hearts, and if we wish to pacify men's hearts, we must seek officials to [i.e., who can] govern. Great officials who direct [government] on high and lesser officials who carry it out below must recognize true methods and strictly and precisely reward or punish. They must thus reform internal government, and foreign misfortunes will then also be settled."[81]

The basic view of the government's role stemmed from the old Confucian argument that the foundations for a strong state lay in government beneficial to the people (the philosophy of *minben*). Yu Yue set out this idea in his essay on self-strengthening,[82] beginning with Mencius's advice to the King of Qi in the ancient Warring States period (403–221 B.C.): if he truly benefited the populace, lightened punishments, and reduced taxes, the people would be content and neighboring peoples would be attracted. Yu interpreted this formula to mean that Chinese should strengthen the foundations of the state by improving government, rather than being too impressed by the machines devised by Western technology. The key was to reform the local bureaucracy by obtaining good men, giving them longer terms in office, and allowing them fuller authority so that they might foster orthodox culture and promote agriculture. Then the people and the officials would be like one family, and the people would do their best to defend the government.

As Yu saw the problem, actual conditions in China were directly opposed to this "first principle of self-strengthening." Officials were like "hired strangers" who "planned for a year's profit" in office. Without rapport between the officials and the people, it did not matter how strong armies and fortifications were. Soldiers would abandon their posts and do nothing to save their leaders. Although Yu himself underrated the importance of technological modernization, his views can not be labeled simply a conservative reaction to progressive Westernizing reformism. Chen Qiu, who unquestionably favored adopting many Western methods and institutions, also maintained that the question of local magistrates was of primary importance for self-strengthening.[83] The general theme that governmental defects underlay national weakness kept appearing in various combinations. Yu's critique could have been answered by administrative reforms, but such concerns could also lead toward a more fundamental alteration of existing authority structures.

One manifestation of a malaise that would not be assuaged by minor modifications can be found in uncompromising attacks on existing evils. In his *Humble Proposals*, Song Heng dramatically described the miseries of the people—mired in poverty, ruined by flood and drought, beset by bandits and local bullies, oppressed by clerks and yamen-runners, and subjected to harsh punishments. He accused officials of losing sight of the basic principles of peace and order while they concentrated on the goals of wealth and power. Since the Song dynasty, officials had been "ostensibly Confucian but covertly Legalist," relying on cruel punishments and extracting taxes.[84] This critique could be expanded into a broad attack on the centralized bureaucratic monarchy that echoed criticisms made in the Southern Song and late Ming. After the Qin dynasty ended "feudalism," he argued, tyranny arose as authority was increasingly concentrated in the emperor. Rulers then followed false teachings that promised them more power and kept it from the people. Such oppression had killed the harmony, intellectual vitality, and societal initiative fostered by the schools during ancient Zhou. It also contributed to the foreign humiliations visited upon China since the late Tang dynasty (618–906), because truly able men did not become officials and the neglect of popular needs eroded support for government.[85]

Song Heng was extreme but not unique. The perception that all was not well with agrarian society was also behind the founding of societies of local scholars who were groping toward utopian or broadly Confucian, humanitarian solutions. There is no indication of how numerous such societies were, but there are records of two separate groups in Ruian (Wenzhou) and Shaoxing.

In Ruian, a scholar who had long been unable to realize his statecraft ambitions led "comrades . . . into the mountains" in 1882 to establish a peaceful, egalitarian community for commoners (*buyi*) that would approach the harmonious accord between heaven, the multiple things on earth, and man known in Confucian thought as the Great Unity. He enlisted some of Sun Yiyan's protégés, including Chen Qiu and Chen Fuchen. His inspiration came from *The Record of the Peach Blossom Spring* (*Taohua yuanji*), a utopian story by the eremitic scholar Tao Qian (365–427) about people who had lived happily isolated for centuries after fleeing into the wilderness to escape the rebellions at the end of the Qin dynasty (255–206 B.C.). The Ruian group combined this vision of arcadian simplicity with elaborate regulations governing clothing, architecture, ritual, ceremonies, and elections, which seemed to owe more to the *Rites of Zhou*. Neither the organizational details nor the unsolved question of whether—or how long—this community actually existed seem as important as this scholar's conversion of statecraft into slightly eremitic utopianism under the pressures of an uncertain decade. As the name "Village to Seek our Resolve" (*qiuzhi she*) indicates, these men were not just withdrawing but aspiring to build a better society.[86]

The similarly named Society of Determined Study (*zhixue hui*) in Shaoxing was established by a local teacher and younger scholars, including the future reformer Zhou Yunliang. Their sociomoral principles came from interpretations of the seventeenth-century scholar Zhang Lüxiang. Seeking a society with no evil, no sickness, and no poverty, they called the people (*min*) their brothers (*tongbao*) and argued that a lack of education kept commoners from reaching their potential. One member lauded the diligence and benevolence of the ancient sage kings and praised the local schools and the well-field system of land distribution during the Zhou dynasty for fostering social equity and community harmony.[87]

Such an explicit focus on popular social conditions suggests an uneasiness that was pushing beyond restoration thinking, but these ideas were not carried very far at this time. On the whole, elite perceptions of social problems were similar to those in the post-Taiping years and well within the bounds of Confucian social philosophy. Members of the elite wanted popular education to reinforce Confucian norms, and their concepts of equity reflected a rational altruism that would ensure order and strengthen social structures.[88] For the time being, the idea that the people were necessary to China's defense was particularly compelling. The repeated invocation of Zhou society in the 1880's and early 1890's suggests a vision of local social cohesion achieved under elite leadership, which would swell upwards to reinvigorate the central government. Such ideas had been broached during reconstruction, but the stakes now included the preservation of the country against foreigners.

Connections between social mobilization, elite local control, and defense emerge clearly in Chen Qiu's introduction to his account of the militia he organized in Wenzhou.[89] Chen maintained that militias were the key to military self-strengthening. In antiquity, soldiers had been a part of the communities defined by the schools and the well-field system. This link between the military and society dissolved when "feudalism" disappeared. Thereafter China gradually weakened because educated men would not be soldiers. Soldiers had been set apart and used only to suppress rebellions, but militias offered new hope of reintegration.

Although Chen established his militia against foreign invaders, he also saw internal dangers. Vegetarian sects were "spreading everywhere in the empire, the Elder Brother Society (*gelao hui*) lurked in all four corners, and wandering braves, disbanded soldiers, local bullies, and reckless fellows were feasting and drinking, slaughtering oxen, and hating and killing each other." How could "all anxiety be about foreign barbarians"? Militias might solve both problems by serving as instruments of coercion, vehicles for reestablishing harmony, and the means of mobilizing against foreigners. Gentry were the natural organizers—and Chen believed that corrupt local government, not local elites, stirred up unrest.

Other gentry writers also believed that, if community consensus and solidarity could be revived, if the people could be strengthened by prosperity and their spirits developed through proper education, the resultant locally based revitalization would, by extension, provide support for the central government.[90] They wrote in terms of reforging the unity between high and low,[91] ruler and ruled, but their arguments rested upon the premise that the government needed the support of the people—which for practical purposes began with its elite stratum. Zhou Yunliang of the Shaoxing Society of Determined Study openly argued that military strength without popular support was a weak reed for a ruler to rely upon. Both Napoleon in Europe and the fourth-century King of Qin, Fu Jian, were successful generals, but they could not survive defeat because their governments lacked a solid foundation.[92] The conception of a militia for both defense and social control developed by Chen Qiu contained a measure of ambiguity. Twentieth-century events would show that elites found it hard to control the people if they were really mobilized. Nevertheless, a more limited application of the idea of mobilization within the elite stratum of society acquired political importance in the railway and constitutional movements of the last Qing decade.

The final major aspect of participatory self-strengthening was its insistence on an enlarged role for members of the elite in government. Local self-government that would give administrative authority to local men was an obvious theoretical outgrowth of locally based activism, and precedents could also be found in the "feudal" theories of earlier centuries. The idea was raised only very cautiously: it was a more dangerous challenge to centralized power than the pleas for better officials were. Feng Guifen's tract that included this idea was written in the 1860's but not published until 1885. Even so wide-ranging a reformer as Chen Qiu limited himself to the suggestion that head jailors be chosen from among *shengyuan,* although he advocated the formalized consultation of gentry in local assemblies.

More attention was paid to finding ways to give greater weight to public opinion. Those who undertook this search still assumed that the political system was unified in vertical hierarchies converging on the emperor, and their aim was still to strengthen the existing order by eliminating the many impediments to sociopolitical harmony. Comprehensive tracts combined ideas for wider participation with proposals to strengthen administration by reforming the bureaucracy and eliminating corruption.[93] Among the Zhejiangese reformers, particularly Chen Qiu and Tang Zhen called for economic change and industrialization as well. Nonetheless, if there was little thought that the interests of private groups and the state might conflict, there was a feeling that unity was being impaired by excessive centralization and governmental insensitivity to societal concerns. Song Heng had put the case most strongly, but Chen Qiu, for instance, also argued that the bonds between "high" and "low" had been severed when the centralized bureaucratic monarchy replaced "feudalism."[94]

The search for new political relationships was expressed in two different ways. One called for officials who were more responsive to outside views. The other urged increased opportunities for outside opinion to influence policy. The former aim led to renewed pleas to enlist men of talent (*rencai*). In the Lower Yangtze, this perennial nineteenth-century aim now expressed the interests of a number of somewhat competing groups. One consisted of literati who had to endure long waits for appointments after painstakingly obtaining the *jinshi* degree. Another was made up of men with practical knowledge not tested by the examinations: legal specialists, merchants, and new specialists in foreign affairs and economics. A third consisted of disaffected literati who wanted to get what they considered right-thinking people into government. The dissatisfactions felt by members of these groups began to coalesce under the foreign pressures of the 1880's.[95]

As usual, *Shen bao* was instrumental in defining the new

combination. An editorial of December 1883 complained that foreign misfortunes and internal disasters were accumulating even though China had opened mines and purchased machines, steamships, and guns. The problem was that government had not achieved the internal order that was the best defense against outside enemies. Different able men had to be recruited, who would heroically pursue policies to improve domestic conditions and resist foreigners. Military and economic modernizations were necessary, but they should be undertaken by "able men" who would not postpone resistance to foreigners until after the current shaky and uncertain efforts were completed.[96]

If the literati critics had had full confidence in the national political leadership—or if the government had been willing to accommodate or able to control them—they might have rallied behind the court and the Grand Council. Because of political dissension in Beijing and the growing distrust of government, the recurring nineteenth-century demands for better communication between literati and the throne began to include ideas for structural change. Searches for national unity veered toward institutions that would augment local elite roles and give public opinion more weight in national policy-making. Early suggestions drew heavily upon the literature of Chinese "feudalism" and the *Rites of Zhou*.[97] After the Sino-French War writers began to pay more attention to Western institutions. A shift toward fundamental institutional reform among Zhejiangese scholars arose from their reaction to the contemporary political-military situation, their previous searches of Chinese history to find vehicles for elite activism and ways to curb autocratic centralism, and their discovery that Europeans and Americans had developed more effective institutional methods than existed in the Chinese context.[98]

The early 1890's reform tracts arising from militant patriotism were characterized by proposals for assemblies at different levels of government. A few Chinese had written about Western parliaments during the 1870's, and knowledge had spread further among Chinese scholars during the 1880's. Early in that decade, *Shen bao* had advocated parliaments to search out what was valid in public opinion, create unity between ruler and people, and dispel doubts—particularly over the conduct of foreign affairs.[99] Militant memorialists during the Sino-French War knew that parliament limited the authority of French officials.[100] Discussions in the press and by individual writers increased after the war. Among the Zhejiangese reformers, Chen Qiu and Tang Zhen advocated assemblies.[101]

Ramifications of the growing interest in parliaments had already been suggested by a *Shen bao* editorial in the spring of 1887.[102] The author began by contrasting Chinese government, in which all power lodged in the ruler and flowed downward from him, with Western systems that invested sovereignty in the people (*minzhu*) or divided it between rulers and populace. The Western systems had the advantage of dividing up responsibilities and eliciting popular support. The editorialist reiterated the claim that in antiquity ruler and people had governed together. The schools of the feudal state of Zheng had provided avenues for discussing national policy and evaluating governmental acts; Confucius, too, had favored popular debate. Thus there had been parliamentary sprouts in the Zhou period, but they had been cut off by the centralized bureaucratic monarchy.

Turning to the present, the editorial called for a hierarchy of assemblies whose members would be "publicly chosen" by elites living in units at the next lowest level in the administrative hierarchy. Such assemblies would foster understanding between high and low in two ways. Public selection and parliaments would bring talented men into government by circumventing rigid qualifications and using public opinion to judge officials. In addition, popular sentiment (*minqing*, i.e., elite public opinion) would be emphasized, to manifest the ruler's virtue and unite the hearts of the masses. By basing policy on public opinion, the ruler could unite with the masses and achieve the good government of antiquity. Tyranny, as exemplified by harsh laws and the misdeeds of clerks and runners, would disappear, and the people would not abandon the government. Military reforms could then be successfully undertaken, and officials could pursue economic policies that would create opportunities for merchants to make money in ways beneficial to the nation.

The proposals and emphases varied, but the ideas that new men should be brought into government, that policy should reflect at least elite public opinion, and that merchant-gentry initiatives could contribute to national strength were current by the early 1890's. Elite reformers wanted unity between ruler and ruled, but a unity that would require the central authorities to make a place for outside initiative and opinion. This was essential to achieve the less tyrannical and corrupt, more effective, responsive, and benevolent government that they deemed a prerequisite for self-strengthening. The divisive potential of participatory self-strengthening would emerge shortly, after elites refocused their public activities and began to compete with the government in pursuit of reform.

The Effect of the Sino-Japanese War

The Sino-Japanese War completed the merger of nationally conscious public opinion with the managerial activism that was the heritage of the reconstruction period. People in Zhejiang reacted to the war in much the same way that they reacted to the previous foreign crises, but on a larger scale. Rumors of imminent invasion caused families to flee or move their assets inland; they disrupted business in Ningbo and Hangzhou.[103] More volunteers than could be absorbed into the armies arrived in Ningbo from the interior districts.[104] Militias were again organized in Ningbo prefecture and also appeared in places like the town of Nanxun (Huzhou), where they had not been formed during the war with France.[105] Merchants and gentry made individual donations to support government troops, while guilds pledged funds or cooperated in collecting special taxes.[106] War also rekindled social unrest. Piracy increased on the Ningbo-Taizhou coast. Anti-missionary sentiment became more evident, particularly in places like Wenzhou that were already markedly hostile to Christianity.[107]

A significant development in 1894–95 was the further expansion of the press. By 1894 two major Shanghai dailies besides *Shen bao* were circulating in Zhejiang: *Hu bao* (*The Shanghai News*) and *Xinwen bao* (*The News*). The latter paper, which was founded in 1893, was especially militant and prone to exaggerate Chinese military successes.[108] All three papers spread news, with varying degrees of accuracy. They criticized Li Hongzhang and other high officials, opposed the peace treaty, and supported opposition to the cession of Taiwan to Japan. Privately printed collections of newspaper articles and editorials as well as compilations of pro-war memorials also appeared. Finally, there were fictionalized accounts of battles and of the resistance on Taiwan, with Taiwan governor Liu Mingquan idealized as a national hero.[109] This literature reached a significant segment of the literate audience in Zhejiang. In Wenzhou a stall was set up near the examination hall; it carried booklets and cartoons about the war and attracted large crowds of students who were in the city for the prefectural examinations.[110]

Reactions in 1894–95 were not only sharper because defeat by Japan was particularly humiliating. They also reflected the cumulative frustrations of previous defeats, the effect of wider press coverage, and the preoccupation with self-strengthening that had grown during the previous decade. Once again, patriotism was a politically divisive as well as a mobilizing force. Both militant officials and the press blamed the defeat on leaders in Beijing and protested their failure to endorse popular resistance. The hostility to Li Hongzhang and his associates that had arisen during the Sino-French War persisted through the late 1880's and early 1890's. During the war with Japan, it was linked to questions about the empress dowager's role in government, and to the idea that elite activists should have a voice in Beijing.[111]

The ideological rationales that emerged in newspaper editorials went beyond a strident criticism of leading officials to argue that the people (presented as an undifferentiated whole) were more reliable defenders of the country than the government was. A *Shen bao* editorial in July 1895 ran through a list of humiliations since 1840 and declared that China could not give up Taiwan to Japan. "The ruler can be cheated, but the people can not be cheated. Officials can be trifled with, but the people can not be trifled with."[112] Another editorial described the short-lived Taiwanese republic as a product of "the public deliberations of the masses of people" and praised Liu Ming-quan for announcing that he would withdraw into the hills and continue to resist. The issues of loyalty to the dynasty and to the country were raised, but not yet broken apart. Loyalty was simply equated with fighting to defend China. In disobeying orders to turn Taiwan over to Japan, Liu was more faithful to the emperor than those generals and officials who would not fight.[113]

The question of loyalty and patriotism was dramatized by the case of Jian Dashi, a Taiwanese resistance leader who was arrested and handed over to the Japanese after fleeing to Amoy. Jian publicly avowed his allegiance to the Qing, but officials were both susceptible to Japanese pressure and suspicious of leaders of popular armies. Newspapers, however, backed Jian. One editorial contrasted the righteousness of the people, who would not accept humiliation, with the chicanery of the officials, who abandoned the people to protect their own riches and honors.[114] Frustration and distrust pervaded the editorial. People who fought "the enemies of the ruler-father" died; those who did not resist lived. The assertion that the country's existence or demise (*cunwang*) depended upon whether or not the people supported the government in their hearts was not simply a restatement of the old role of the people as passive indicators of heaven's will. It was a call for political leadership that would give expression to the popular will to resist. The line between patriotism and nationalism had been becoming increasingly blurred throughout the 1880's. By the 1890's there was little meaningful distinction, and the militant variety of patriotism and nationalism had become attached to demands for participation.

Jing Yuanshan explicitly related patriotic mobilization to elite activism and representational participation in government.[115] Drawing on his background in welfare and relief, Jing compared the current military crisis and foreign humiliations to floods and famines. People had contributed to relief from natural disasters, and the current situation presented a still greater threat. Chinese land was being cut up, and the people's wealth was being used for indemnities—causing "one hundred generations to cry out and burdening tens of thousands of people." If the Chinese yielded they would not be able to fight again; cultural heritage, country, and livelihood would all be lost. To prevent this national and cultural demise, Jing called upon the "loyal and righteous heroes and scholars of the empire and excellent and benevolent men all to contribute voluntary donations to aid in obtaining voluntary supplies and to call together voluntary troops to raise a voluntary army." "Looking above," these activists would "requite the country" and, "looking below," they would "save the people."

Jing proposed establishing bureaus in provincial capitals with branches in major commercial ports. These bureaus would unify the plans of upper gentry (*shidafu*) who "understood the country." By uniting the hearts and strength of the four hundred million Chinese people, they would pacify the interior and drive out the foreigners. Once again Jing stressed that all the people belonged to China and that their urgent task was to save the country.

These bureaus and the troops they commanded were to be outside of, but not antithetical to, the bureaucracy. The heads of local bureaus were to be gentry chosen by public opinion (*yulun*). On top of the provincial structures, Jing proposed a "publicly selected" general bureau in Beijing, which could receive petitions from the provincial bureaus and memorialize the throne. Military commanders would be chosen for their ability and would not have to be officials. Troops would be taught foreign drill, and weapons would be furnished by Chinese who could manufacture machinery and armaments or were skilled in chemistry.

This proposal to link militias into an elite-organized and controlled army was decidedly subversive of central bureaucratic control. Jing stated clearly his criticism of the existing political leadership, with its dislike of extra-bureaucratic initiatives. The misfortunes and disorders of the empire had arisen because few "heroes knowledgeable about affairs" had been brought into the government. The usual qualifications must be waived to bring forth able men, particularly those who understood Western studies. It was crucial to have leaders and institutions that would unite the spirit of the "masses" by bringing forth their wisdom and strength. The old idea of seeking out talent had been expanded beyond a desire to improve bureaucratic performance; it encompassed innovations that would change the nature of government.

During the spring of 1895 a growing number of metropolitan bureaucrats who were opposed to the peace negotiations tried to contact patriots outside the government. Throughout the spring officials in the capital maneuvered for political advantage, held meetings, and submitted joint memorials opposing the peace negotiations. It was in this atmosphere that Liang Qichao led metropolitan examination candidates to submit reform proposals to the throne. Once more the militants were overruled by the court, but the opposition was stronger and did not lose as much power as it had in 1885.

By the mid-1890's there had been several important developments in the public sphere. It was now possible to speak of a nationally conscious public opinion, nourished by the press. Although its boundaries were not clear, this opinion was oppositionist in origin and distrustful of authoritarian leadership. Immediately after the war, a new national consciousness redirected the expansive edge of public management in Zhejiang into projects for self-strengthening. This was a mobilization of elite energies for nationalistic rather than overtly political purposes. On the national level, however, the pressure for broader participation in government that had begun during the wars did not abate. From this time on, the growing portion of local public spheres that was involved in self-strengthening could not avoid being affected by national politics, even if local elites were not politicized themselves.

FIVE

The Reorientation of Elite Management

1895-1901

The years from 1895 to 1901 encompassed the 1898 Reform Movement, the political reaction against it, the Boxer Rebellion, a new wave of imperialist penetration, and another reaction to the court policies held responsible for internal and external disorders. Normally these years are divided into the 1898 Reform Movement, which climaxed in the "One Hundred Days" during the summer of 1898 when reformers in Beijing enacted sweeping changes in the name of the Guangxu emperor, and the conservative reaction to the reform movement, which led to the Boxer Rebellion. In the longer framework of late Qing political history, the years form a coherent whole, which is less neatly divisible into reformist and conservative phases and which is characterized by rising social activism, new levels of imperialist penetration, and the politicization of national affairs. Institutional change and open political activity distinguish this period from the 1880's and early 1890's. The incipient and tentative nature of its changes, as manifested in widely fluctuating governmental policies and extreme political uncertainty, distinguishes it from the sustained competition between centralizing bureaucratic reformism and societal movements of the last Qing decade.

The events of these years had a complex impact on the public sphere within Zhejiang. Foreign intrusion stimulated organizational change, and the most expansive areas of public activity began to shift from welfare and old-style education to industrial and commercial institutions, Western-style schools, and organizations to promote social improvements. Organization for these purposes was built upon previous managerial experience, but it also began to change the public sphere. It provided a more immediate basis for political activity in the 1900's than the reconstruction and post-reconstruction institutions did. At the same time, local activists began to be more directly affected by national politics, and it became increasingly difficult to separate locally based initiatives from national issues and policies.

During this period, some Zhejiangese consciously promoted what studies of Hunan have called progressive-elite reform or self-strengthening reform.[1] Both designations define aspects of developments in Zhejiang as well. Members of the elite sought new sources of profits in industry and modern transportation. Reformers tried to introduce Western-inspired institutions, technology, methods, and information to increase productivity, raise educational levels, improve social conditions, and thereby strengthen China. The changes were not simply viewed as Westernizing, however; they arose from elite managerial experience and statecraft scholarship as well as the experience of newer urban social groups and foreign examples. Reformism during the 1898 period in Zhejiang contrasted with the more radical variety introduced by Liang Qichao and his friends in Hunan, because it did not challenge Confucian morality and social structures. It also differed from the program of leading official self-strengtheners because, like the participatory self-strengthening movement of the 1880's and 1890's, it placed less emphasis on military technology and had overtones of social initiative and mobilization. By the beginning of the twentieth century, such differences in emphasis were politically important.

Institutional Innovations

Change in Zhejiang during the second half of the 1890's has been ignored, largely because associates of Liang Qichao and Kang Youwei were not active there. Nor was there a well-known reformist governor. Change was mainly generated by members of the Zhejiangese elite. With established scholars and managers often in control, there was little dramatic radicalism. Nonetheless, the record of reform in Zhejiang compares favorably with any other province, even though the innovation there was overshadowed by the more intense and concentrated activity in Shanghai.

Foreigners noted Zhejiangese eagerness for change following the Sino-Japanese War. One observer even suggested that there was a Chinese middle class, "smothered by the great weight of the mandarinate," whose members were chafing to supply the capital and intelligence to carry out "grand works of improvement."[2] If this picture of an incipient liberal, capitalist industrial revolution is a bit overdrawn, the impression that Zhejiang merchant-gentry were ready to take new initiatives was quite correct. Like merchant-gentry in other provinces, they concentrated on modern industry and schools, and they founded a few newspapers and voluntary associations.

Most of the major modern cotton mills and silk filatures established in the province before the end of the Qing appeared between 1895 and 1900, along with flour mills, electric companies, steam launches, and other modern enterprises. The first plans for a railway were also drawn up in this period. Much of the financing came from rich Shanghai merchants who were Zhejiang natives.[3] Shares were also offered in financial markets of Hangzhou, Shanghai, and probably Ningbo. The shares were expensive (one hundred yuan for the mills in Hangzhou and Ningbo). Nonetheless, although we do not know how widely they were held, there were reports of enthusiastic responses resulting in initial oversubscriptions.[4]

Information on the press and voluntary associations is extremely fragmentary. There had already been a short-lived foreign-backed paper in the Ningbo treaty port but no journalistic development like that of Shanghai or Hong Kong. The availability of Shanghai papers undercut the need for a provincial daily, and Zhejiangese journalism began with small, less-frequently published papers that specifically advocated reform. The *Hangzhou Journal* (*Hang bao*) appeared during the Sino-Japanese War. Reformers in Ruian (Wenzhou) founded a paper during 1897.[5] Its Hangzhou office soon expanded into the separate *Journal of Statecraft* (*Jingshi bao*). The *Pinghu Vernacular Journal* (*Pinghu baihua bao*) began publication about the same time, and the *Ningbo Journal* (*Yong bao*) appeared in the winter of 1898–99. After the Boxer Rebellion, the future revolutionary Sun Yizhong established the *Hangzhou Vernacular Journal* (*Hangzhou baihua bao*) in 1901, and at the end of the year plans were laid by a group of Shanghai merchants and gentry for a paper in their native districts of Shangyu and Yuyao (Shaoxing).[6] In addition to being more numerous, newspapers also became easier to obtain. A privately established library in Shaoxing city, for instance, carried new books and newspapers in 1897, and in 1898 reading rooms were opened in Shangyu and Yuyao. Schools, bookstores, and other institutions, including salt and telegraph bureaus, were outlets for Shanghai reformist papers.[7]

There are also scattered records of new associations, although they were still few in number, they indicated a further enlargement of the public sphere. Scholars had always discussed current affairs among themselves, but now autonomous societies were also being formed to address issues of general interest to society and government. An interest in improving women's conditions was indicated by an anti-footbinding association founded in Huzhou in 1897, and a desire to improve agricultural methods led to sericulture institutes in Hangzhou and Ruian (Wenzhou).[8] After the end of the Boxer Rebellion, a debating society (*yanshuo hui*) appeared in Hangzhou, and a Society to Broaden Knowledge (*guangzhi hui*) was formed in Jiaxing.[9] Since small, short-lived, privately founded groups were likely to go unrecorded, this list is by no means complete. It does, however, indicate that organizations modeled on study society groups were appearing in Zhejiang, pulling some inhabitants into the reform currents of the day. Although these associations were privately established, they often interacted with the new institutions, such as schools, that were being added to the old public sphere. The same people might found both, or separate founders might hold similar conceptions of social action and expression. From the beginning, the enlarged and redirected public sphere emerging in Zhejiang included social action that was rapidly outgrowing even the previous elastic bounds of public initiative.

An expansion of social initiative is also seen in new institutions that were established to serve public purposes more directly. Like other provinces, Zhejiang introduced schools that taught Chinese classics, literature, and history combined with Western science, mathematics, language, and history. Table 12 summarizes information compiled from gazetteers and newspapers about all kinds of schools, including specialized schools and reorganized academies. Some were supported by official funds. The provincial treasury paid the first modern school in Hangzhou, the Qiushi Academy, nine thousand taels annually for the first three years,[10] and its successors continued to be financed by the provincial government. The military school in Hangzhou was, of course, a government institution. Probably the second new academy and the sericulture institute in Hangzhou as well as the Chucai Academy in Ningbo and the new school in Qiande received official support. Most of the others, however, were privately funded by wealthy local gentry and merchants or by contributions from Shanghai.

Money was raised among Shanghai merchants from Yuyao and Shangyu to start agricultural and industrial schools in those districts, and the Yuyao school founded in 1900 was converted from a charitable school that probably had been supported by the locally prominent Xie lineage.[11] In Cheng a school received money from an institute established by a local *shengyuan* to raise funds for education after the Sino-Japanese War.[12] Other schools in Nanxun, Zhulin, Shaoxing, Qu, and Ruian were financed by local gentry or merchants.[13] Quite possibly, a greater number of new institutions were privately financed in Zhejiang than in other provinces.[14] In any case, private funds

TABLE 12
New Schools Recorded in Zhejiang Before 1902

Prefecture; district/town	Number	Year	Urban level
Hangzhou			
Qiantang/Renhe	8+	1896–99	Provincial capital
Haining	2	1892,?	Zhou city
Huzhou			
Guian/Wucheng	1	?	Prefectural city
Deqing	1	1901	District city
Nanxun	3	1899–1901	Zhen
Jiaxing			
Jiaxing/Xiushui	2	1898	Prefectural city
Zhulin	2	1900	Standard market?
Shaoxing			
Shanyin/Guiji	1	1897	Prefectural city
Cheng	1	c.1896	District city
Xinchang	1	1898	Qu
Yuyao	2	1898,1900	District city
Shangyu	1	1898	District city
Ningbo			
Yin	1	1897	Prefectural city
Zhenhai	1	1901	Qu
Xiangshan	2	1898–99	District city
Wenzhou			
Yongjia	1	?	Prefectural city
Ruian	4	1885,1895–96	District city
Yanzhou			
Jiande	1	1901	Prefectural city
Quzhou			
Qu	1	1898	Prefectural city
TOTAL	36+		

SOURCES: *North China Herald*, Dec. 11, 1896, p. 999; Apr. 23, 1897, p. 711; May 7, 1897, p. 815; Jan. 21, 1898, p. 84; Jan. 28, 1898, p. 135; June 20, 1898, p. 1069; Jan. 30, 1899, p. 169; *Hangzhou fuzhi*, 17: 1a–2a, 9a–b; *Haining zhouzhi gao*, 4: 14b; Shen Yuwu, p. 168; *Deqing xian xinzhi*, 3: 9a; *Nanxun zhi*, 3: 2a, 3b–4a; Chiang Monlin, *Tides from the West*, p. 41; *Cheng xianzhi*, 16: 44a; *Xinchang xianzhi*, 5: 62a; *Yuyao Liucang zhi*, 15: 9b; Jing Yuanshan, 2: 53a–56a; *Zhenhai xinzhi beigao, xia*: 15a; *Zhenhai xianzhi*, 11: 17a; *Xiangshan xianzhi*, 14: 31b, 36a; Chen Mi, "Dong-Ou," pp. 7, 10; Zhu Fangbu, p. 69; *Zhejiang chao*, 4: 182 (Apr. 1903); *Jiande xianzhi*, 6: 25b; *Qu xianzhi*, 3: 24a; *Zhulin bayu zhi*, 4: 3a, 6: 37b.

were definitely available to establish new schools, and the more difficult problem of financing continuing operations did not have to be faced until later.

The geographical distribution shown in Table 12 reinforces the evidence for significant merchant-gentry involvement in educational reform and suggests patterns that would continue through the next decade. Like the post-Taiping reconstruction institutions, most new schools were established in the core districts of the five northern prefectures or on the southeast coast. The similarity of geographical distribution did not, however, indicate that older trends simply continued. During the second half of the 1890's, the old differences in the amount of managerial activity in cores and peripheries began to include new qualitative differences. The new schools that concentrated in core areas are examples of a more general shift in the focus of activities of managerial elites of those places, whose many external contacts brought them into touch with national politics and reform. New influences were not totally absent from the rest of the province, but existing gaps tended to widen during the next decade and peripheral areas did not fully share in the commercial development, organizational proliferation, or political activity of the early 1900's.[15]

Within the cores, new institutions were quite broadly distributed in different districts and across levels of the urban hierarchy. This diffusion also recalls reconstruction patterns and suggests that innovations are best understood as products of an uncoordinated movement within elite society. The movement reflected the diverse elements already shaping Zhejiang public activism: the accumulation of managerial initiative and organization, the geographical mobility of members of the Zhejiang elite, their economic connections with Shanghai, the impact of foreign trade and the treaty ports, and patriotic anger at foreign invasion. It was not, however, simply a replay of the past. The new institutions as well as new political circumstances soon began to transform the nature of public activism and the goals of reformers.

The Reformist Activists

Who established the first new institutions? There were no students returned from study abroad and few new professionals. Full-time revolutionaries and reformers did not yet move about Zhejiang looking for political opportunities. On the whole, initiative came from the existing merchant-gentry-manager establishment.

Although there was no unusually dominant governor in Zhejiang, officials provided some leadership as well as the more passive support or tolerance that was still necessary for elite initiatives. From 1894 to 1898 Governor Liao Shoufeng encouraged reform. He rewarded merchants who founded industries, aided establishment of the Qiushi Academy in 1897, and sent five students to study in Japan in 1898.[16] The Hangzhou prefect also helped establish new schools, and in 1898 he encouraged academies to buy newspapers dealing with government or education.[17] Liao's successor was probably chosen because he was not associated with reform, but the two governors from late 1900 to the fall of 1902 had been part of the reform movement.[18]

Even in Hangzhou, however, initiatives also came from existing managers, Zhejiang merchants and scholars living in Shanghai, prominent gentry, and patriotic scholars within the provincial capital. The two men credited with founding the first Hangzhou cotton-spinning mills and silk filatures were Pang Yuanji, a wealthy Shanghai businessman from Nanxun town, and Ding Bing, the aging dean of gentry managers.[19] The Qiushi Academy was established at the urging of Hangzhou gentry, who first suggested a modern school in 1896 and then pressed the governor to continue when plans threatened to fall through for lack of money. Among the early planners was Wang Kangnian of Qiantang, who before he became a *jinshi* and an official had helped establish a medical dispensary in Hangzhou during a plague in the 1880's. By 1896 he had resigned from government to promote reform and edit the reformist *The Chinese Progress* (*Shiwu bao*) in Shanghai. Wang was also one of the organizers of the Hangzhou sericulture institute.[20] Another was Fan Gongxu, a retired member of the Hanlin Academy who had gained brief fame in 1885 when he challenged the empress dowager's moves to end overt opposition to peace negotiations with France by closing the lines of communication to the throne (*yanlu*). After leaving office, Fan had managed welfare activities; he would direct New Policies institutions in the 1900's.[21]

Local leadership structures established outside the provincial capital in the reconstruction period often persisted into the twentieth century. In such places, new schools and other institutions were added to existing public complexes by externally connected local activists who saw a need for change. The institutions these men sponsored did not usually disrupt local structures or violate the consensus among the influential members of the local elite.

Xu Shulan of Shaoxing is an outstanding example of a gentry manager who became a reformer. Xu's father was a merchant who had taken his family to Shanghai to escape the Taiping rebels. There he had contributed money to buy provisions for government troops. Shulan's brother Youlan purchased a *jiansheng* degree and briefly held a post in Beijing during the mid-1880's, but he soon returned home to study and carry on the family business in Shanghai. Shulan obtained a *juren* degree, also held office in Beijing, and was appointed a prefect. He never took up the post because his mother was unwell; instead, he devoted himself to local and lineage affairs. These included water control, an endowment in 1893 for the foundling home in his mother's native district of Cheng, a public home for chaste widows, and charitable fields to support lineage members. He was also one of the men commended for their financial contributions to armies in Zhejiang during the Sino-French War.

Youlan helped establish one of the first Chinese-run modern silk filatures in Shanghai in 1894. After the Sino-Japanese War, Shulan concluded that Chinese had to act rapidly to strengthen the country if they were not to lose out in an international social-Darwinistic struggle for existence.[22] Therefore, in 1897 he established the Chinese and Western School and a library of classical and western books, with a reading room and a newspaper room open to the public. Financial help came from his brother and from a wealthy salt merchant who was also deeply involved in Shaoxing public activities and his own lineage's affairs.

Shulan did not abandon his previous managerial activities when he began to promote modern education. He managed famine relief in 1898. At the same time he was in touch with Shanghai reformist circles, not only through his brother but also through his own friendships with Zhang Jian and other Lower Yangtze progressives. At one point he joined the agricultural study society established by Wang Kangnian. There is no evidence that Xu considered these activities incongruous or incompatible or that they challenged the local social networks of which he was part.[23]

An even stronger continuity between "old" scholar-manager circles and "new" reformers is illustrated by the widening scholarly networks that had originated around Sun Yiyan in Ruian (Wenzhou) during the 1870's and 1880's. During part of the 1880's and 1890's, Chen Fuchen taught at and headed the academy in Luoqing, where some of his students later went into public management.[24] He and Chen Qiu also founded a hospital in Ruian and later used part of the building for an elementary school.[25] Besides managing the militia during the Sino-Japanese War, Chen Qiu expanded his reform projects to include a Western-style school and newspaper. Far more important, the war prompted Sun Yiyan's son, Sun Yirang, to become active in district affairs. His first steps were to establish a school to teach chemistry and mathematics in addition to Chinese subjects and to found an agricultural society.[26]

The local anti-missionary risings in Wenzhou during the Boxer Rebellion stimulated the next burst of activity by renewing fears of social disorder and foreign intervention. Chen Qiu was a member of the Ruian *baojia* bureau, while a Society to Study Military Preparedness (*wubei xueshe*) was established by another scholar who would soon join Sun Yirang's associates in founding new schools. The militia in neighboring Pingyang district was also organized by an acquaintance of the Suns.[27] However, the focus soon shifted back to civil affairs. Chen Qiu and Chen Fuchen developed plans for lake-dredging, and in 1901 they founded a society to promote public works, reform the foundling home, and generally improve the conduct of local affairs.[28] The post-Boxer initiatives led directly into the concerted effort led by Sun Yirang during the New Policies period to introduce changes that would revitalize local society to strengthen the whole country.

Merchants and other men living in Shanghai also introduced

new institutions into their native areas. This action was not disruptive, because sojourning donors and sponsors followed customary patterns of investment at home and relied upon local contacts. Among these men was Jing Yuanshan. Although very much a part of Shanghai business-scholar-manager and (by 1898) reform circles, Jing maintained his local and kinship ties by reorganizing welfare in Shangyu and setting up a charitable granary in his native village in the early and mid-1890's. In the 1898 period he planned newspaper reading rooms in the district cities and eventually in even smaller centers of his native Shangyu and adjoining Yuyao. A subsequent proposal for agricultural and industrial societies and schools appears to have fallen through. However, Jing was back in the winter of 1901–2 with a scheme to establish a newspaper at the district academy that would be sold by lineage organizations in every ward (*du*) of the district.[29]

Jing Yuanshan's detailed accounts describe the informal consultation, mobilization, and fund-raising that took place between local elite activists and Shanghai sojourners. Jing began plans for his schools by consulting a reformist friend in Shanghai whose lineage was located in Shangyu.[30] When this man promised financial support, Jing drew up a list of managers from Yuyao and Shangyu, tactfully including the wealthy Shanghai banker Xie Lunhui. Jing's friend was the nominal head; because he only returned to his ancestral home once or twice a year, the real manager in Shangyu was to be a retired merchant. The supervisor in Yuyao was to be a man already involved in the reading rooms.

Jing acquired additional endorsement by soliciting a congratulatory letter from his influential superior in the telegraph administration Sheng Xuanhuai. Agricultural and commercial societies broadened the support in Shanghai among natives of the two districts. The societies met at several locations familiar to historians of the 1898 Reform Movement, including the popular meeting grounds at Zhang's garden, the telegraph bureau, and the offices of *The Chinese Progress* and the *Agricultural Studies Journal* (*Nongxue bao*). There were arguments over agricultural priorities and problems, but the members endorsed the schools and some pledged money. Funds were to be deposited in an old-style bank in Shanghai that was owned by a friend of Jing's from Yuyao and then transferred to a related bank in that district.[31]

The proposed locations of the newspaper reading rooms in Yuyao and Shangyu underline Jing's importance as the contact between his Shanghai friends and local society. Papers were sent to the telegraph bureau in Yuyao (where Jing would have had connections) and to the welfare association. In Shangyu they went to the welfare association (which Jing had helped reorganize) and the mathematics institute. Town reading rooms were to be housed in private homes, including one belonging to a member of the Jing lineage. Although the plans for the schools were aborted, they show how new institutions and activities could be filtered through existing managerial, kinship, business, and other networks. There is also evidence that existing local managerial establishments began to focus on new institutions. Jing asked at least three men already involved in his newspaper reading rooms to run agricultural and industrial schools. Several other planners in Shanghai and Yuyao were among the organizers of a town higher primary school in 1902.[32]

Men like these were not separate from local elite society. In fact, much of their strength derived from local networks. Nevertheless, although in general they were not deliberately disruptive, their involvement with new institutions and with explicitly reformist groups in Shanghai was beginning to alter the nature of local management. The shift was also reflected in their external connections. Like the reconstruction and postreconstruction managers, the founders of new local institutions were pulled together by their outside ties. After the Sino-Japanese War provincial and macroregional establishments began to appear that were based on reformist rather than welfare institutions.

The press again played a crucial role. By 1898 ideologically reformist newspapers were supplementing the general coverage of the major Shanghai dailies. In early 1898 *The Chinese Progress* went to eleven cities in Zhejiang.[33] The *Hangzhou Vernacular Journal*, which was sold in ten Zhejiang cities as well as several in Jiangsu,[34] performed a similar function. Besides introducing new ideas, these papers encouraged local initiative by telling people what was done elsewhere and by bringing together men interested in promoting new institutions. Managers in Ruian (Wenzhou) learned of the establishment of a new school in Nanxun (Huzhou) from the newspapers,[35] and the *Hangzhou Vernacular Journal* publicized the need of funds for projects in the provincial capital.[36]

Local reformers also began to congregate in major cities after the Sino-Japanese War. Reform in Zhejiang was not directed from Hangzhou, but the provincial capital did become a meeting place for reformers from different parts of the province. The *Journal of Statecraft* is a good example of such coalescence. It was started by Chen Qiu, Chen Fuchen, Song Heng (of Ruian scholar-manager-reformer circles), and two Shaoxing scholars. The future railway president Tang Shouqian of Shanyin and the future revolutionary Zhang Binglin of Hangzhou also contributed. These men were friendly with reformist intellectuals in the provincial capital like the bannerman Guilin, and they were recognized as a distinct (although ephemeral) group within its scholarly circles.[37]

The emergence of Shanghai as the Lower Yangtze center of new reformist activity and organization in the mid-1890's was still more important. Zhejiangese had long been involved in Shanghai academic life and business, and they were also heavily involved in the new organizations. Wang Kangnian was probably the best-known Zhejiangese reformer in Shanghai in the 1898 period. He founded a reformist Chinese Association (*Zhongguo gonghui*), helped establish and edit *The Chinese Progress*, and co-founded an agricultural and an anti-footbinding society.[38] His Zhejiangese associates included the scholar Ye Han, who founded the *Journal of Elementary Education* (*Mengxue bao*),[39] Xu Shulan, who helped found the agricultural society, and Jing Yuanshan, whose girls' school had the support of *The Chinese Progress*. Zhang Binglin, who wrote for *The Chinese Progress*, was another well-known Zhejiangese reformer. Song Heng spent much time in Shanghai, and Chen Fuchen visited the city from time to time. Rather than a direct, one-way line of transmission from Shanghai to localities in Zhejiang, there was a constant circulation of scholars who had become interested in reform either at home or in the large cities. It was, however, in the large cities, particularly in Shanghai, where these men encountered a significant number of like-minded people. The protection afforded by the foreign-run International Settlement also became important as oppositionist organizations began to appear. The number of new associations in Shanghai overshadowed associations in other Lower Yangtze centers,[40] and, as reform became politicized in the late 1890's, Shanghai became a focal point surrounded by the activist elites of the Lower Yangtze core.

The Meaning of Reformism in Zhejiang

Given what we know of the people who established new institutions in the 1898 period, there seems little doubt that these men were consciously committed to reform. Their ideas reflected the intellectual currents in the treaty ports and drew upon Western theories, institutional models, technology, and science. They did not, however, come to their views by rejecting or even thoroughly reworking Confucian values. Nor did they necessarily go as far as Liang Qichao did in articulating theories of participatory nationalism and a new view of the world order.[41] Nonetheless, a broad spectrum of elite activists was moving in the direction of Liang's thought by extending statecraft, reacting against imperialism, and seeking ways to deal with the rapidly changing circumstances of the late nineteenth century. Liang drew upon the same ideas about corporate groupings, citizenship, service, activism, and the social-Darwinistic struggle that appear in more fragmentary form in the writings of managers and scholars—who may or may not have read his work. Political change was in the air, and ideas justifying it were circulating among people concerned over current affairs.

The more historical and indigenous side of Zhejiangese reformism is illustrated by two very different examples: Jing Yuanshan's speeches in favor of agricultural and industrial schools and his regulations for them, and Sun Yirang's much more comprehensive reform tract. Operating in the very different milieus of Shanghai-Shaoxing and the southeastern coast, both men introduced new institutions into their home localities. Their views of reform emerged from their elite interests, their managerial experience, recent fears of foreign invasion, and nineteenth-century concerns over social stability and local government. They proceeded beyond the strong heritage of statecraft thought and altered older solutions by incorporating foreign examples and nationalistic goals.

Jing justified his schools as a way to strengthen China. He spoke of wiping out national humiliation, sought national enrichment and military strength, and stressed the importance of an educated, knowledgeable populace in self-strengthening. This was not an abstract nationalism. Like the militant patriotism of the 1880's and mid-1890's, it had a strong territorial element, which Jing's rhetoric brought down to the most local level. Foreign dangers threatened the villages. If national sovereignty was lost, families would not be able to protect their fields or hand them down to their sons and grandsons. Jing also related self-strengthening to current agrarian problems. In rural Shaoxing 1898 was better known as a year of poor harvests, high rice prices, and social unrest than as a national political watershed. Jiang argued that improvements in industry and agriculture would enhance the living standards of the poor while gradually strengthening the country.[42]

Jing presented his ideas for agricultural and industrial training as an extension of the elite-managed welfare in which he had been so active—with a similar aim of achieving social stability. He argued that all the welfare and relief of the past twenty years had neither eliminated poverty nor solved the chronic difficulties of the people. If policies merely alleviated disasters without fundamentally aiding the poor, the poor themselves would eventually rise up and create a crisis. Jing hoped to implement basic solutions—which he also called welfare (*shan*)—by promoting agriculture and industry, providing education, and cultivating barren land. This reform would also help the rich, because there would be fewer robberies and less unrest; it meant "benefiting oneself while benefiting others."[43] Responding as Jing did to a national emergency by trying to improve rural conditions was in the interest of the elite because it would buttress the existing social order. It did not even necessarily require modernizing change. Indeed, some of Jing's associates argued that, given the scarcity of money, it would be better to concentrate on water control and opium suppression. Jing himself wanted to introduce new techniques, however, and his view prevailed within the associations he organized.

Whereas Jing's arguments reflected his background as a business administrator and a welfare manager, Sun Yirang's views emerged from his classical studies and the Sun family's role as scholar-managers in Ruian. When reform again became a matter of governmental policy after 1900, he directed *The Political Essentials of the Rites of Zhou* (*Zhouli zhengyao*) toward the national scholar-official community, but his views were formed earlier.[44]

These views reflected Sun's long association with scholars who saw the solution of social and local governmental problems as a prerequisite for national strength and unity. By the mid-1890's, however, he was also looking for new ways to increase economic productivity and mobilize society. In discussing the national bureaucracy, Sun advocated such rationalizing statecraft reforms as a reduction in the number of existing posts to eliminate overlapping functions, a clarification of responsibilities, and a training program to enable metropolitan officials to replace clerks.[45] At the same time he proposed new governmental organs for commerce and banking. Nevertheless, Sun was not primarily interested in reforming the central administration. The heart of his ideas lay in proposals that would expand participation in government and mobilize the populace.

Within each district, Sun wished to replace clerks with "gentry managers." Quoting Gu Yanwu and referring to examples from the Zhou and the Han dynasties and English local government, he proposed eliminating virtually all existing governmental structures below the district magistrate and choosing officials responsible for education, law enforcement, and tax collection from the local gentry.[46] He downplayed the bureaucracy as a means of linking lower and higher levels of government. Instead, he emphasized institutions and methods in Western states that circumscribed governmental power by informing the people, conveying public opinion to officials, and controlling the ruler: newspapers, assemblies, outside evaluations of government, and law. He recommended that national, provincial, sub-prefectural, and district assemblies debate policy and convey opinions. Since Sun assumed officials would accommodate ouside views, he believed that the results would be harmonious.[47]

Political changes of this kind required the integration and mobilization of the populace for national purposes, and Sun sought these ends more in societal reform than in bureaucratic leadership. The education of citizens (*guomin*) was his key. Sun bitterly criticized existing education—the people learned nothing while scholars studied the wrong things—and strongly advocated Western mathematics and science and translations of Western books. His conception of the school system arose from an idealized notion of Zhou dynasty education in which a large number of local schools formed a basis for both communal and political life. Through the schools, men would have the chance to participate in public affairs according to their abilities, and the most talented could advance up the educational ladder to positions of governmental responsibility. For the most part, schools would turn out a literate, skilled, and socially indoctrinated people, who could use modern agricultural techniques and whose sense of both local and national community would cause them to rally behind the government in emergencies.

This view of education is clearly both elitist and socially conservative. Sun believed that education not based on the Confucian three bonds and five relationships would allow room for heterodox ideas, but any methods might be used if firmly grounded in these Confucian principles. Elementary education to nourish citizens' characters while enlarging their general knowledge seemed to him much safer than university education, which might foster rebelliousness.[48] In rural areas, this kind of education would also promote an increase in productivity. A well-educated peasantry was needed if agricultural output was to be raised by using foreign methods, machinery, and fertilizers. Sun did not elaborate upon how such a program would be implemented, but he saw its benefits in terms of alleviating rural distress—hence promoting order—as well as creating a surplus for use in national development.

His views on taxation were consistent with these goals. In contrast to the traditional gentry aversion to surveys and registration, Sun and his associates in Wenzhou attached great importance to cadastral surveys as a way to gather information for maintaining order, utilizing resources, controlling corruption, and collecting taxes.[49] Sun saw these surveys as a gentry project. Recognizing that revenue was needed to support locally run institutions as well as the central bureaucracy, he also suggested that gentry collect taxes. He may also have been looking for an equitable system that would foster his own version of rural regeneration. To circumvent the corruption associated with the land tax, he proposed a new system based on a slightly graduated head tax, a small stamp tax on all transactions, and miscellaneous commercial levies.[50] In the late Qing, there was no chance of testing such a plan to see whether it would raise more revenue more fairly or merely benefit landowners and shift malpractices into a new system.

Sun's conception of commercial and industrial development also emphasized social action. Sun proposed a ministry of commerce and a national bank to promote industry, set national standards, and protect Chinese businessmen from foreigners at home and abroad. The real key to his plan, however, lay in corporate social initiative. People, he argued, had acquired power over the "ten thousand things" because they could extend their material strength and knowledge by operating collectively (*qun*). Western scholars, farmers, and merchants all had corporate (*hequn*) associations; joint stock companies and chambers of commerce were the equivalent mercantile organizations. Sun envisaged a layered commercial structure analogous to his hierarchies of assemblies and schools, with corporations at the bottom, hierarchies of chambers of commerce in between, and the ministry of commerce at the top. The chambers of commerce, composed of local men, were to be very active in formulating regulations, debating issues, and bringing consensuses to bear. There would be an upward flow of opinion and initiative to the ministry of commerce, which would use the power of the nation to protect the merchants' accumulated power. This protection was needed for China to "establish itself" (zili) in a global trade war. Just as opinions expressed in assemblies were to shape political policies, national economic policies were to reflect what the chambers of commerce wanted. A similar identification of private commercial and industrial interests with those of the nation as a whole was found in the work of such other Zhejiangese reformers as Sun's friend Chen Qiu.[51]

From 1895 until his death in 1908, Sun tried to implement aspects of this program within Wenzhou. Since it was never a real possibility, we must see it as a statement of patriotic, progressive gentry interests, a sweeping plan to construct national unity out of the initiatives that had been developing in elite society, and an effort to weld old concerns for agrarian stability to new programs for increased output. From both Sun's and Jing's writings we can understand why "reform" found supporters among established members of the Zhejiangese managerial elite.

Neither Jing nor Sun defined elite interests as distinct from those of the state or other classes. Sun showed no tendency to divide or limit governmental powers or to carve out specific spheres of autonomous activity—even when he proposed institutions that had been used for such purposes in some Western countries. Instead, he turned the flow of authority upside down and used the Rites of Zhou to justify social mobilization. Previously, managerial activism had eroded governmental authority. Sun's tract went further by suggesting a different relationship between elite civic leaders and the state. Even though Sun continued to see political power as undivided and with a national center, his conceptions could easily lead to greater tensions with officials. Although members of the elite differed from the coming generation of students educated in Western subjects, these ideas opened possibilities of cooperation.

The Beginnings of Political Opposition

Although patriotism fostered oppositionist politics during the Sino-French and Sino-Japanese wars, the reform movement in Zhejiang was relatively apolitical during the mid-1890's. Although public opinion was angry and disillusioned over Li Hongzhang's policies, people were less disposed to think that a broad confrontation with the government was necessary. Pressures for reform were also building up within the bureaucracy, and there was a growing hope of altering the political balance of power in Beijing. Most members of the elite pursuing reform in Zhejiang were not associated with any one political faction. They were individuals, connected in part by horizontal social networks, who shared the patriotic belief that they could contribute to strengthening China by introducing changes where they lived.

Nonetheless, they came from the stratum of elite society that was conversant with national politics, and some had direct political ties. From the end of the Sino-Japanese War through the summer of 1898, trends within the bureaucracy were favorable to change in the province. When national politics then took a turn against elite activists, domestic conflict reinforced the doubts about governmental leaders that had first been aroused by foreign danger. From 1898 through 1901, the groundwork was laid for the oppositionist movements in the Lower Yangtze during the last Qing decade. During the same years, radicalism that went beyond moderate elite reform first appeared.

The impact of national political trends: the 1898 period. The major events of the 1898 Reform Movement are among the most studied in Chinese history. Very briefly, after the end of the war with Japan, there was protracted jockeying for political advantage among reformist officials—often men who had been associated with the "Emperor's Faction"—and supporters of Li Hongzhang or the empress dowager. At the same time, frustration over Chinese defeats led to the founding of numerous reformist study societies and newspapers ideologically committed to reform. The short-lived Society to Study Self-

Strengthening (*qiangxue hui*) in Beijing and the separate organization of the same name in Shanghai were seminal unions of oppositionist officials and scholars founded in the summer of 1896. Before long, however, differences could be seen between the many advocates of moderate reforms and a smaller number of radicals like Kang Youwei, Liang Qichao, and Tan Sitong, who attacked the Confucian hierarchical social structure and favored a more rapid extension of political participation.

The sympathetic Governor-General Zhang Zhidong invited Liang and other ardent reformers to teach in Changsha, giving them a foothold in Hunan. At the beginning of 1898 Grand Councillor Weng Tonghe introduced Kang Youwei to high officials and recommended him to the emperor. Kang never acquired power in the government, but the Guangxu emperor was receptive to the reformers in general. In June the emperor took control of the government he had nominally headed. During the following "One Hundred Days" of reform, imperial decrees reorganized administration, implemented aspects of the old statecraft agenda, and established new policies and institutions. In September, however, the empress dowager reasserted control over policy with the help of officials and courtiers who feared for their jobs and their lives. Six leading reformers were executed in the capital. The radicals in Hunan, who had already aroused moderate opposition by attacking Confucian norms, were ousted, and the emperor became a virtual prisoner in the palace.[52]

Few if any Zhejiangese were part of Kang Youwei and Liang Qichao's inner circle.[53] Some had been active in the reform movement in the capital, however, and even more were involved in Shanghai. Significant numbers had promoted changes in Zhejiang. Although reform in Zhejiang had been largely locally inspired, it still required bureaucratic endorsement. When opponents of the reform factions took control in the capital, innovation in the provinces became more risky—not necessarily because of local opposition to change, but because of political uncertainty.

Membership in societies is the most concrete, provable link between members of the Zhejiang elite and national reformist politics. At least ten members of the Societies to Study Self-strengthening in Beijing and Shanghai were from Zhejiang, including Wang Kangnian, Zhang Binglin, the aged Huang Tifang of Ruian, and Huang's son and nephew.[54] There were also fifteen Zhejiangese in the Society to Protect the Country (*baoguo hui*), founded in Beijing in the spring of 1898.[55] Soon thereafter, Wang Kangnian, Cai Yuanpei, Chen Qiu, and Chen Fuchen joined other Zhejiangese in Shanghai to form the Society to Protect Zhejiang (*bao Zhe hui*), because they did not fully agree with the policies of the national organization.[56]

We have already seen that some of these men and their friends in Shanghai had direct connections with reform scholars or activists in Zhejiang. The defeat by Japan had initiated a new wave of retirement by officials who felt compromised by their oppositionist policies or were pessimistic about initiating change from within the government. The most portentous retirement in the Lower Yangtze was that of Zhang Jian, who became the next decade's best-known gentry-reformer and constitutionalist, but Zhang was not alone. Among the Zhejiangese, Wang Kangnian, for example, left office for organizational and newspaper work in Shanghai. Sheng Bingwei, a leader of educational and other innovations in Ningbo and Zhenhai during the next two decades, left the government in 1895 on the excuse of caring for his aged mother.[57]

Such movement out of the bureaucracy introduced more men into Zhejiang who were disillusioned with governmental leadership. Shanghai also emerged as an oppositionist political center at this time.[58] Until September 1898, however, national events mainly affected Zhejiang indirectly by creating an atmosphere favorable to autonomous initiatives. The expansive upsurge of patriotic reformism received considerable support from elite public opinion in many provinces, and it appeared to have a chance of becoming the wave of the future.

The political impact of the Boxer Rebellion. The reassertion of the empress dowager's authority, therefore, dramatically changed the political context in which elite activists operated. The problem in Zhejiang was not a general "conservative" backlash. Zhejiang reformers, unlike those in Hunan, were not generally ideologically radical and were well integrated into local social structures. Despite reports of criticisms by local opponents of change, there is little evidence of broad cultural antipathy to Western innovation. Some new institutions closed and others never opened, but there was enough local support to keep some going,[59] and a few more were even added in 1899 and 1900. The unsettling question was how far the now-dominant officials would go in retaliating against their opponents and tightening their control over the provinces. In addition to the executions, arrests, and dismissals immediately after the palace coup, rumors persisted of Weng Tonghe's impending arrest. The southern tour by Manchu Grand Secretary Gangyi during 1899 could be interpreted not only as a way to extort money but as a prelude to further arrests and demotions. The court also began to replace Chinese officials in central and south China with its supporters, who were often Manchus. The provincial judge for Zhejiang who was appointed in the spring of 1900, for instance, was a young Manchu nobleman who had been only a prefect the year before,[60] and progressive provincial officials like Liu Kunyi were under a cloud.

The numerous members of the Lower Yangtze elite with reformist records could not help but feel uneasy. For the next two years, issues pertaining to the control of the court, the safety of the emperor (and those who had introduced changes in his name), and the dominance of the Manchu princes and Chinese officials close to Empress Dowager Cixi overshadowed the question of reform per se. The court, under the control of Cixi and her followers, pursued policies that would lead to open support of attacks on Westerners by the Boxer sect in 1900, to the capture of Beijing by the allied Western force sent to rescue foreigners there, and to the flight of the court to Shanxi province. Meanwhile, new imperialist threats and rising social disorders increased the political unease in Zhejiang. News of Italian demands for a concession at Sanmen Bay (south of Ningbo) in 1899 brought about strong anti-imperialist protests similar to the reactions of the past twenty years.[61] The renewed enthusiasm for expelling foreigners[62] did not, however, lead members of the Zhejiangese elite to support pro-Boxer elements at court.

They had few political ties with this dominantly Manchu group, they were alarmed by the adventurism that so blatantly risked foreign retaliation, they were financially hurt by the sharp drop in foreign trade caused by the war, and they were disturbed by growing social unrest in Zhejiang as rumors about the Boxers spread around the province.

During 1900 there were minor anti-foreign incidents as well as several serious attacks on foreigners. Most occurred in Wenzhou and Taizhou. During the summer an anti-missionary band also burned churches and missionary homes in Zhuji (Shaoxing). The most serious incident was instigated by Fujianese bandits, who captured the district cities of Jiangshan and Changshan on the Jiangxi border. When the prefectural city of Qu briefly fell to the rebels, several missionaries were killed.[63] Nevertheless, there were no large scale risings. Most officials tried hard to prevent disorder, while members of the elite organized militias and self-defense forces.[64] The uncertainty was indeed unsettling; it prompted, for instance, large numbers of Ningbo natives to return home from Shanghai to escape possible trouble.

The events of 1899–1900 led to an even broader disillusionment with the government. More officials left office after Cixi's coup. Some of these men, like Tang Shouqian or the future editor Zhang Yuanji, had been members of the "Emperor's Faction" and would be leaders of the Zhejiang railway and constitutionalist movements. The departure of more obscure men, like Yuan Zutang of Shaoxing, indicates that alienation was not confined to the most politically involved reformers.

Yuan had studied law and worked his way into the regular bureaucracy from secretarial posts specializing in legal, commercial, and industrial affairs. In 1898 he went to Beijing with a recommendation from Governor-General Liu Kunyi, but the coup occurred before he received a post. Yuan found the political situation discouraging. China's problems seemed to derive more from the court struggle between "the new and the old" than they did from foreign misfortunes. Because there seemed to be little that an average official like Yuan could do, he returned home in 1899. He was then greatly distressed by the

Boxer incident. Considering the state of the times and his own poor health, he decided he could not hold office again. During the last three years of his life, he devoted himself to public and lineage charity and education. Yuan did not reject the political structure; he simply saw nothing for him to join in the government.[65]

Once more the press led in expressing public opposition, and prominent members of the elite openly defied the court on the related issues of its support of the Boxers and the future of the Guangxu emperor. The Shanghai press criticized the court for supporting "rebels" (thus unleashing unrest in the empire) and for provoking foreign intervention (thus adding to national humiliation).[66] Reformers accused pro-Boxer officials of shutting out progressive Western knowledge and opposing people who turned to new ideas to combat foreign encroachment. Some journalist critics saw a logical progression from conservatism to the reassertion of the empress dowager's regency, to attempts to depose the emperor, to the use of the Boxers to drive out foreigners.[67] There were also calls to revive programs of self-strengthening reform. The demands for wider political consultation and participation in government that had surfaced during and after the Sino-Japanese War were also revived in suggestions, for example, for a meeting of provincial representatives and for the use of gentry managers to pacify the people and rally them behind a program of reform.[68]

One type of criticism was aimed directly at Manchus. It seems probable that the failure of the 1898 Reform Movement was a turning point in the rise of anti-Manchu feeling at the end of the Qing. Persistent racial awareness and latent hostility tended to acquire political overtones when Chinese officials or members of the social elite felt personally threatened. Cixi's reassertion of political authority eliminated the possibility of the Guangxu emperor as an alternative leader, which advocates of participatory reformism favored. The empress dowager's most conspicuous supporters were Manchu, and indications that Manchus were replacing Chinese provincial officials provided another reason for animosity.

Zhang Binglin had idiosyncratically proclaimed his anti-

Manchu position from the relative safety of Taibei in late 1898,[69] and racial hostility was woven into revolutionary ideology up to 1911. In times of political stress, however, such sentiments were not confined to radicals. In an editorial of July 1, 1900, *Shen bao* openly attacked the Manchus. It particularly blamed the associate grand secretary, Prince Gangyi, for court support of the Boxers, and called for his execution, but it also indicted the other pro-Boxer Manchu princes in Beijing. The court, the paper claimed, relied more on Manchus than on Chinese and made it easier for them to advance in the bureaucracy. Manchus, not Chinese, had incited rebellion in "our country." They only knew how to practice rites and ceremonies, exchanging toasts and indulging in waste, extravagance, and arrogance. If the most highly placed Manchus were bad, there was little hope for others of the race. Even if Gangyi and his associates were punished, the "disorder in the empire" could not be brought under control.

This indictment, which gave a racial underpinning to the vague warnings of disaster common during the Sino-French and Sino-Japanese wars, was somewhat modified by a second editorial in August that said some Chinese officials were as much to blame as the Manchus.[70] Nonetheless, an even slightly imaginative reader could have picked up the suggestion that there was little hope for China as long as Manchus controlled the government. Such antipathy did not operate all the time, nor did it necessarily lead to rebellion. However, it was one more element undermining faith in the government and intensifying opposition already aroused by other factors.

In 1900 leading members of the Zhejiang elite cooperated politically with other men from the Lower Yangtze, particularly from Jiangsu, on two important issues. In June 1900 Tang Shouqian and Shen Cengzhi acted with Zhang Jian and other prominent gentry from central and south China to help Chinese provincial officials work out the agreement with foreign consuls that kept Boxer hostilities out of the Yangtze Valley.[71] These three men had all been members of the "Emperor's Faction" and had left office because of policy disagreements or because it was too dangerous in Beijing. Tang and Zhang led the provincial movements in their respective provinces during the coming decade. However circumspect and respectable the role of members of the elite in these negotiations, their defiance of court policy in 1900 was another step in defining the nature of the Lower Yangtze reformist establishment and in drawing its leaders into national politics.

During the same year other Lower Yangtze activists openly organized and protested against the government. This movement started in January, when the Guangxu emperor publicly announced that he was ill and appointed an heir apparent. About the same time, Gangyi and Li Bingheng, the most prominent Boxer supporter among Chinese officials, impeached Weng Tonghe. These moves were widely interpreted as a step toward deposing and eventually murdering the emperor, thereby solidifying the control of Cixi's faction. Jing Yuanshan led a protest in Shanghai, placing his name at the head of a telegram with 1,231 signatures. Angry telegrams from all over China contributed to the decision to shelve plans to depose the emperor—indicated by the announcement of preparations to celebrate his birthday later in the year.[72]

This small victory for public opinion did little to change policies or power distribution in Beijing or to allay the suspicions and fears of progressive members of the elite. Indications that more arrests were in store[73] increased their anger over policies that were provoking a disastrous foreign invasion. Public opinion was further infuriated by the executions of two popular literati-officials from Zhejiang for opposing the court's pro-Boxer policies.[74] Zhejiangese were not involved in the rising led by the Hunanese Tang Caichang in August, but a number of Zhejiangese in Shanghai were members of the related National Association (*guohui*) that was organized on July 26.[75]

The National Association was a discussion group incorporating a broad range of opposition; it was not a rebellious organization. Some members would soon revolt and others would later join revolutionary parties, but many were respectable members of the Lower Yangtze elite with ties to prestigious scholars and rich merchants. The full name, Chinese Deliberative Association (*Zhongguo yihui*) suggests that members of the elite were once again affirming their right to discuss national issues and influence government by expressing public opinion. The demands in 1900 were different from the demands of the mid-1890's because people had become aroused as much over domestic as foreign issues, they were aiming their opposition more at the court than at Chinese officials, and they were meeting at a time when some Chinese intellectuals were beginning to take up arms against the government. Opposition was still not fully mobilized, but members of the elite had become more politically aroused. The National Association symbolized the indistinct boundary between outraged, non-violent expressions of opinion and revolutionary action. Revolution was about to become a major political factor, and the two streams would overlap increasingly in the coming decade.

Differentiation within the opposition. In the 1880's and early to mid-1890's, oppositionist politics encompassed public criticism of leading officials and policies, a desire for wider consultation in policy-making, and a spreading sense of the inadequacy of governmental structure, leaders, and programs to solve domestic problems or defend against foreigners. These still poorly defined sentiments encouraged malaise and eremitism, but they did not inspire elite action against the state. On the contrary, they fed into the participatory reformist drive of 1895–98. After the Sino-Japanese War, however, more radical tendencies appeared within or alongside this main political stream; they were encouraged by the rebuff to participatory reformism in the fall of 1898.

These tendencies were most marked in Hunan, Guangdong, and Shanghai. The first, small manifestations of radicalism within Zhejiang also appeared after 1898. During the next decade, political radicals were distinguished by their willingness to use violence to overthrow the governmental structure. Initially, however, they were less clearly defined, except that their criticisms and activities did not fit comfortably into the activities of the progressive scholars and managers who were introducing changes in the 1898 period. They appeared in a small way in schools and local societies, spinning off from reformers who were more closely integrated into local establishments.

One such person was the future revolutionary and educator Cai Yuanpei, who was one of the disillusioned officials who left the bureaucracy at the end of the One Hundred Days of reform. Cai turned to local reform, becoming a superintendent at the Chinese and Western School in his home city of Shaoxing. Unlike most reformist members of the elite, he found the dominant faculty members and local officials too conservative for his taste and soon left for the more congenial atmosphere of Shanghai.[76]

In Hangzhou in 1899 or 1900, a group of scholars who subsequently joined radical or revolutionary groups formed an association to discuss current events and nationalism known as the Zhejiang Society (*Zhe hui*).[77] In 1900 Song Heng and Chen Fuchen were popular teachers at the two modern academies in Hangzhou. A former student at the Qiushi Academy recalls that Song discussed tyrannical government and explained why the scholar-gentry were shameless, why society was debased and the people were miserable, and why the country was beset by barbarians. Although never criticizing the Manchus outright, he praised his friend Zhang Binglin's anti-Manchu tract *Book of Raillery* (*Qiushu*)—thereby making students want to read it even though he never described its contents. Books at the school that year included the seventeenth-century reformer Huang Zongxi's critique of Ming autocracy, *Mingyi daifang lu*, and two famous accounts of Manchu atrocities during their conquest of China, *Ten Days at Yangzhou* (*Yangzhou shiri ji*) and *The Massacre at Jiading* (*Jiading tu cheng lu*).[78]

Chen's students at the Yangzheng Academy believed him to be an outstanding historian. His lectures contained anti-barbarian references and drew upon ideas of Huang Zongxi and Mencius. In an essay written about this time, Chen maintained that poverty and hunger were as much a problem as the tyranny of cruel rulers. Therefore people who simply identified freedom with democracy and tyranny with monarchy missed the point that starving people had to be helped as well. Like Song, Chen also focused on the misery caused by cruel laws; he discussed the ideas of earlier scholars like Lu Xuan of the Tang dynasty, Sima Qian, Ye Shi, and Gu Yanwu, who had written about such problems. Chen concentrated his attacks on the Legalists, the officials he considered their present-day successors, and the militarists who preyed upon the people. He believed that government policy should focus on "saving the people," but he wanted old customs that were not corrupt and evil to continue.[79]

Although neither Song nor Chen ever advanced from an extreme dissatisfaction with existing systems to revolutionary activity, some of their students did. There was a manifestation of anti-Manchu sentiment during the summer of 1901 that made it necessary for Sun Yizhong, the editor of the *Hangzhou Vernacular Journal*, who was then teaching at the Qiushi Academy, to leave the provincial capital. The next step for some of the students was study in Japan, and at least eight who attended the Qiushi Academy at that time eventually joined the revolutionary movement.[80]

A final example of the beginnings of radicalism comes from the small market town of Zhulinmiao, about four miles southeast of the prefectural capital of Jiaxing. Three young men purchased a hundred *mou* there in 1899 and established an agricultural society to teach sericulture, animal husbandry, and other farming techniques. The next year they founded an elementary school. Finally, in 1903 one of them organized a militia to fight against salt smugglers and bandits. This force lasted until 1909, although it was not well drilled and had little local support.[81]

The wealthy, educated founders of the institutions in Zhulinmiao came from merchant and gentry families. They had become concerned over current affairs during the Sino-Japanese War. One was later active in the New Policies public sphere as a teacher and another as a member of the chamber of commerce in the prefectural city. There seemed little to distinguish them from other patriotically inspired manager-reformers in the late 1890's. Nonetheless, they were not well integrated into the local leadership of Zhulinmiao. One of the men who remained within New Policy managerial circles eventually sympathized with the revolutionary movement. The third man was already a member of the relatively radical Zhejiang Society; later he had contacts with radicals and revolutionaries in Shanghai and Zhejiang. Their goals in Zhulinmiao are unclear. In part these men were an extension of 1898 reformist managerial establishments. In part they were forerunners of the revolutionaries who five years later would contact illegal societies and use their connections with local elites to establish front organizations.

In sum, before the central government moved toward systematic reform in 1901, there were two important developments in Zhejiang that would later affect the official New Policies program. First, foreign intrusions produced both organizational changes and a proto-mobilization of the social elite. New kinds of organizations appeared in the public sphere, and the most expansive activity began to shift to new institutions. The public sphere was also enlarged by organizations that had formerly been genuinely private or non-existent. Voluntary organizations to address public issues and express public opinion were often accorded a public character rather than being considered private interest groups. Private industry and transportation also took on a public aspect when they were linked to national strengthening and when their founders received official rewards for acting in the national interest. Thus an organizational base for new kinds of public activity began to emerge. By the same token, members of the manager-scholar-business elite committed themselves to change and took initiatives to found schools, industries, newspapers, and associations. They continued the pattern of the reconstruction period, spreading networks of personal connections across the urban hierarchy of the core areas and into the reformist establishments in the big cities. Ideologically committed reformers were joined by people who were more attracted to industry, new education, and other innovations as avenues to profitable new careers. The social initiative that had been discouraged after September 1898 resumed as soon as it seemed safe.

Second, the societal mobilization under way in Zhejiang became politicized by domestic as well as foreign events. The assumption in the earlier reform literature that the government would listen to outside views had been sorely strained. From the fall of 1898 onward, a few of the Zhejiangese elite took openly oppositionist stands and began to join revolutionary movements. A larger number showed a willingness to defy governmental policies that they believed threatened both China's interests and their own. They did not yet seriously question the legitimacy of the imperial system, but they did believe that people in control of the court between the coup against the Guangxu emperor and the foreign occupation of Beijing had behaved illegitimately. The erosion of their faith was not yet irreversible, and another chance for accommodation may have existed in 1902 after national leadership and policies again changed. Nevertheless, "local" public activists had come into touch with national policy. To satisfy these critics, government leaders would have to allow effective outside participation in national policy-making, as well as undertake self-strengthening reforms. The legacy of rising political aspirations and growing distrust formed a background for the new and still more irreconcilable conflicts that arose between officials and members of the elite during the Qing New Policies period.

The Changing Structure of Public Management

*The Qing New Policies
in Zhejiang*

During the latter half of the nineteenth century, public activity had expanded more rapidly than state power. Its earlier momentum revived quickly after the Boxer Rebellion and contributed to the new heights of social mobilization reached during the last Qing decade. A new ingredient after 1902 came from the governmental decision to embark upon a sustained effort at bureaucratically directed state-building through the New Policies (*xinzheng*). These official initiatives were far broader than the uneven nineteenth-century efforts to bolster revenue through *lijin* taxes or to improve the armed forces and foster industry through the self-strengthening movement.

One category of reforms reorganized and rationalized the bureaucratic structure, replacing the Six Boards in the capital with Western-style ministries and eliminating outmoded or redundant official posts. The structure of local government was also formally changed when new elite-run functional organizations were added in such spheres as commerce, education, and agriculture and a comprehensive national school system was devised. Some of the organizations formalized functions al-

ready being performed by elites, and others had been anticipated by institutions established by reformers in the 1890's.
There had never before been a systematic legal basis for such
institutions, however. After some hesitation, the court also endorsed a program to gradually establish limited constitutional
government over a nine-year period. Elected local, provincial,
and national assemblies were to give elites a role in policy-
making. An appointed cabinet of high officials was to replace
the Grand Council, and local elites were also to participate
in local administration through "self-government" executive
councils under the district magistrate.

There was not enough time to carry out these reforms before
the Qing was overthrown in 1911. Nor did the government
have the manpower or control to implement all the new laws
throughout so large a country. Social elites and local officials
were the ones who carried out the provisions affecting local
government, and in these circumstances the speed of implementation and the actual form and performance of new institutions varied greatly. Nonetheless, the institutional structure in
which local elite activists operated was permanently altered.
The New Policies created new organizational resources and
new opportunities for either cooperation or conflict between
extra-bureaucratic elites and the Qing state. As the New Policies were put into effect during the first decade of the twentieth
century, the political significance of the conflicts overshadowed
that of the instances of cooperation.

Disagreements did not arise over the stated aims of central
officials responsible for the New Policies. By the beginning of
the twentieth century, nationally conscious members of the
elite favored policies for rationalizing administration, promoting economic and military modernization, revising education,
devising new legal codes, and extending the functions of government. Problems developed over the implications of the New
Policies for state-societal relationships, and over the often unstated intentions of national officials that the New Policies
serve to centralize power.

The New Policies extended the range of state activities; they meant that the state would become more interventionist and would have to extract more taxes from the populace to pay for new programs. The Ministry of Finance and other new ministries in the capital would also attempt to supervise provincial officials and finances more carefully to ensure that national programs were carried out. Although the officially mandated functional organizations opened new roles to elites, they were also a possible way to end the superficiality of the late imperial state by bringing formal government structure down to lower administrative levels and attaching local managers to the bottom of the bureaucracy. If the government had succeeded in extending the state structure in this way, the New Policies would, in effect, have increased state penetration into society, recentralized power on a denser institutional basis, and allowed officials to mobilize the populace for government-defined national purposes.

Not all the official architects of the New Policies had consciously arrived at such aims, and some might not even have agreed with them. However, in the course of the first decade of the twentieth century, governmental goals of centralizing and extending power became increasingly explicit. It may well be argued that such centralization was necessary to implement sweeping national reforms, but for it to be effective the government would have had to reduce the autonomous societal activities of members of the core-area elites. Because these activities were already so highly developed, and because members of these elites had already displayed a national political consciousness critical of governmental leadership, one may well ask whether the institutions established by the New Policies would serve as vehicles for centrally directed mobilization or for continued social mobilization beyond governmental control. This chapter will address questions concerning the type, number, and location of new institutions in Zhejiang, the kinds of elites running them, the extent of their autonomy, and their linkages to earlier forms of public organization as well as to the growing body of private organizations. The next will describe the political clash between state-building and social mobilization that ended the imperial system.

The New Institutional Context

One of the first signals of decisive change in governmental policy was an edict of October 10, 1901, calling for educational changes and a national school system to replace the old academies that trained scholars for the examination system.[1] Two more years were required for reformist officials to solidify their positions within the metropolitan bureaucracy, ensure court backing, and map out policies. By 1904, however, the government was ready to embark upon change. In January 1904 a detailed plan for a national school system, drafted by Zhang Zhidong and Zhang Boxi, replaced the vaguer proposals of 1901. The court accepted their suggestions for a hierarchy of elementary and primary schools below the district level, higher primary schools in district cities, prefectural middle schools, a provincial higher school (college) in each provincial capital, and a national university in Beijing. The old examination system was abolished during the following year, and a ministry of education was established. District offices to promote education (*quanxue suo*) were to assume responsibility for encouraging, overseeing, and, in part, financing the new schools.

Numerous other governmental laws and regulations directly affected elite activists. In the economic sphere, chambers of commerce (*shang hui*) were authorized in 1904 to improve trade, compile statistics, sponsor technical schools, protect merchants, and present opinions to officials on economic affairs. Laws governing commercial practices and the formation of limited liability joint-stock companies were promulgated for the first time in the same year. In 1905 a Ministry of Police (later Ministry of the Interior) was established. Agricultural associations (*nong hui*) were formally authorized in 1907. After several years of study, the court finally also endorsed limited constitutional government in China. Regulations for provincial assemblies were issued in 1908, and assemblies were elected in 1909. Preparations for local self-government were to be undertaken by elite-run self-government affairs offices (*zizhi shiwu suo*) and self-government study offices (*zizhi yanjiu suo*). District assemblies and councils or executive boards in lower administrative divisions were introduced in regulations of 1908 and 1910 and began functioning in 1910.

The significant New Policies institutions in Zhejiang and elsewhere dealt with old areas of elite concern: education, trade, agriculture, and the general supervision of local affairs. Therefore it was easy for existing members of the elite to move into management of these new institutions. Opportunities for more contact with the bureaucracy were also created because specialized bureaus and posts were being established about the same time, mainly at the provincial or prefectural levels. Because personnel in such positions were not necessarily subject to the "law of avoidance," elite managers of new institutions sometimes dealt with governmental specialists who were also from Zhejiang. There is very little evidence about the relationships between these officials and local activists, but we may assume that common geographical origins fostered cooperation. In one instance, a special circuit-level governmental bureau to promote education in Wenzhou and Chuzhou prefectures simply strengthened the hand of existing Wenzhou elite activists by giving their leader an official position.[2]

The new local public institutions. The New Policies quickly changed the institutions through which members of the elite exercised local leadership. Although they were established by governmental decree, these organizations may be considered additions to the already-existing local public spheres. They gave impetus to the new directions of public activity begun in the 1890's and did not necessarily mean a loss of elite initiative or increased official control. Members of the elite moved into New Policy positions to further community or private purposes, and both the major spheres of activity and the distribution of new institutions throughout the province reflected previous trends.

In the 1900's members of the elite exercised most of their influence through chambers of commerce, educational institutions, and the various offices to prepare for self-government. Police forces also appeared throughout the province. Officials and members of the elite shared an interest in order, but the officials' interest in keeping the police under bureaucratic control resembled their earlier attitude toward militias. After the center had been drastically weakened by the 1911 Revolution, police (or similar forces to keep local order) often were vehicles for militarized elite control over local societies, but they do not seem to have been a good vehicle for the autonomous expansion of elite power during the Qing—and, at least in some districts, local forces did not multiply until after 1911.[3]

Agricultural associations (including sericulture institutes) are only infrequently recorded before the end of the dynasty. Gazetteers give little information about them, and few clues are provided by their locations, which range from the provincial capital to low-level market towns, and from the Jiangnan core to peripheral Chuzhou.[4] There were probably not many of these associations. They were likely to concentrate on the stated reformist purposes of elites who established them, and were not yet significant vehicles for control over peasants—as they would be in some places during the Republic.

There was no single pattern of local dominance by chambers of commerce, educational institutions, or self-government organizations. At the end of the Qing, when these institutions were being established unevenly throughout the province, any one had the potential for becoming a center of decision-making by local elite establishments (like united welfare associations during the late nineteenth century). The exact local balances of power depended on such factors as commercial levels, numbers of degree holders, place in the urban hierarchy, and previous managerial patterns. Gazetteers seldom give enough information to sort out such variables, but, as we shall see, memberships in the new institutions sometimes overlapped. Elite leadership networks could operate through the new institutions in the same way they operated through the old-style organizations of the previous decades.

Chambers of commerce and educational associations appeared about the same time in the core areas.[5] The first chambers of commerce were founded in Hangzhou, the prefectural capitals of Wenzhou and Quzhou, and the twin towns of Qing and Wu (Jiaxing-Huzhou) immediately after they were authorized by Beijing in 1904. The provincial educational association was also founded in that year. These institutions spread rapidly in the core districts and more slowly into the peripheries. By the end of 1907, there were at least 41 chambers of commerce (three-fourths of which were in the five northern prefectures), and 55 educational associations or offices to promote education with 827 members and incomes totaling 27,657 yuan. Three years later, there were 85 chambers of commerce; only fifteen districts did not have one, and at least twenty-three market towns did. Educational organizations also approximately doubled in number, and their membership and income increased still more markedly. In 1911 there were one hundred organizations, with 3,538 members and a combined income of 93,557 yuan. Although these new institutions were well distributed by the end of the Qing, they were more widespread and better financed in the economic cores. In 1911 almost all the subdistrict chambers of commerce were in core districts; except for Haining, all fifteen district cities without chambers of commerce were peripheral, and mainly in the southern half of the province. Suian (Chuzhou), where trade was very undeveloped, did not have a chamber of commerce until 1921.

Both the educational and the commercial organizations introduced new factors into local affairs. Educational associations and offices were initially conceived as advisory, research, and promotional groups, but they, or their individual members, also took an active part in founding and running new schools. Scholars and gentry had long been involved in both the public and private educational affairs of their home areas, but the new organizations enabled them to exert their influence through institutions authorized to plan and implement educational programs and raise funds for these purposes. Educational associations and offices attracted locally prominent men and served as locales for decision-making about non-educational subjects. During the famine of 1910, for instance, a meeting was held at the Jiaxing educational office to discuss relief, after which local leaders set up an elite-managed price equalization society under the self-government affairs office.[6] Educational associations were also drawn into the national political issues of the 1900's.

Chambers of commerce were a greater innovation because, despite the importance of trade in parts of Zhejiang, commercial organizations had not normally been part of the old public sphere, even though guilds performed public functions like fire-prevention and welfare. The chambers of commerce now formally brought private guild leadership into the public sphere. A substantial portion of chamber members came from guilds,[7] but other prominent members of the elite participated as well. The chambers of commerce were powerful representatives of economic interests and also became involved in other aspects of local affairs. They, like earlier merchant associations, organized militias and other patrols. Since many of the nationalistic or anti-governmental movements at the end of the Qing involved economic issues, chambers of commerce, perhaps even more than educational associations, were drawn into the wider political movements that will be discussed in the next chapter.

Institutions to prepare for self-government were not formally authorized until 1909. However, some members of local elites began to establish preparatory organizations as early as 1906, when the Qing government first indicated that constitutionalism and local self-government were serious possibilities. These organizations were called public benefit bureaus (*gongyi ju* or *she*), as well as self-government offices. They were more likely to appear in cities than in rural areas.[8] They were also founded in prosperous market towns like Xinli in Jiaxing or Luqiao in Taizhou, however, and town leaders even made their own connections with village heads.[9] Like the reconstruction managers before them, members of early twentieth-century elites copied regulations of associations already existing in other towns and cities. Some of these groups were more like voluntary associations than government-mandated institutions following a uniform pattern.[10] These organizations were precursors of the executive councils that assumed broad responsibilities in local public affairs, but they were also heirs of the reconstruction and post-reconstruction institutions—whose activities had sometimes been broader than narrow definitions of their functions would indicate. Although institutions were changing, ideas of local public needs were not. Although these preparatory organizations and the councils and assemblies that succeeded them were new local organs, they were not simply injected from the outside. To a considerable extent they were the outgrowth of existing local elite activities, which had already been formally recognized in earlier public institutions.

This perspective is indicated by the rather sparse records of the activities of the new institutions. The self-government public benefit society in Xiaofeng (Hangzhou) planned local activities in four spheres during 1907: education, police, welfare, and industry.[11] The regulations of the Yin district self-government association in Ningbo city delineated its duties as the prohibition of gambling and lewdness, the elimination of opium, the improvement of social customs, the control of bandits, and the promotion of education.[12] Another association in a Ningbo market town displayed a similar preoccupation with order, the control of social customs, opium suppression, and education.[13] Such preparatory groups also established welfare institutions.[14] Elite societal leaders elected the members of these associations. In some localities members of the elite seemed to be pressing ahead of the government schedule for local self-government.[15]

The formal implementation of local self-government had just begun when the 1911 Revolution occurred. Assemblies or councils had been established in only seventeen districts, six market towns (zhen), and fifty-nine rural townships during 1910–11.[16] They were too few and too recently established to have much impact before the national political and governmental context changed. Given the very restricted electorate and the indirect methods of selecting candidates, these bodies were more likely to confirm than to challenge existing managerial structures, methods of running local affairs, and social hierarchies. Nevertheless, councils and assemblies began to consolidate the supervision of public functions. Thus in 1910 the Qing town council took over the administration of the foundling home, and in 1911 the Shaoxing self-government council assumed responsibility for the granaries that had been run by the Xu family (of Xu Shulan) using a local tax surcharge.[17] Like other New Policy institutions, the assemblies were sometimes assertive and difficult for magistrates to dominate.[18]

The Social Impact of New Policy Institutions: Distribution and Financing of Schools

The school was the new institution most frequently founded during the New Policies period. Although schools are not normally considered loci of power, they are by far the best indicators of the growth, distribution, and impact of the new forms of local organization. There were enough schools to give a clearer picture of core and peripheral distinctions than chamber of commerce records can provide; more important, statistics published by the national Ministry of Education for the period 1907–9 give detailed information that is not available about other institutions. These figures probably leave out many family, lineage, and other small, privately founded schools that were also changing their curricula. They may therefore greatly underestimate total local educational resources.[19] Nevertheless, the data appear to be reliable enough to permit comparisons between districts and provinces.

The figures in Table 13 show that the number of schools and students in Zhejiang were increasing rather rapidly; by 1909 the school budget was a substantial 1.65 million yuan, and the percentage of official funds was increasing. Taken by themselves, these figures could be interpreted as the promising beginnings of a state-controlled school system, but other figures in the table suggest alternative lines of development. Sixty to seventy percent of school income was raised locally from elite-controlled sources. Sizable sums had to be raised quickly. Schools were operating at a deficit or just breaking even, and the number of students and schools were increasing more rapidly than income. Such information suggests that instead of one school system there were many local elite-run educational efforts and that the additional expenses might strain local resources.

More detailed district-by-district figures and annual breakdowns on school foundings favor the latter interpretation. Table

TABLE 13
Income and Expenditures of Regular Schools in Zhejiang,
1907 and 1909

Category	1907	1909
Income (yuan)		
Official	154,034 (14%)	364,541 (22%)
Public	277,103 (25%)	312,676 (19%)
Voluntary contributions	162,276 (14%)	236,159 (14%)
Involuntary contributions	166,949 (15%)	232,191 (14%)
Endowments	130,450 (12%)	164,561 (10%)
Interest	47,139 (4%)	68,952 (4%)
Student tuition	174,598 (15%)	206,214 (12%)
Miscellaneous	14,871 (1%)	89,413 (5%)
TOTAL	1,127,420 (100%)	1,674,707 (100%)
Expenditures (yuan)	1,184,546	1,665,895
No. of schools	1,120	1,911
No. of students	39,285	73,564
No. of students per school	35	38
Income per student (yuan)	29	23

SOURCES: Xuebu (1907), pp. 554, 564, 572; Xuebu (1910), Zhejiang 11, 21, 29.

TABLE 14
Regular Schools Established Annually in Zhejiang,
1902–1909

Year	Official	Public	Private
1902	34	33	1
1903	15	22	6
1904	13	40	7
1905	32	69	15
1906	53	286	93
1907	49	322	68
1908	40	300	31
1909	−5	347	22
TOTAL	231	1,419	243

SOURCE: Xuebu (1907), pp. 555–56; Xuebu (1910), Zhejiang 13.

14 shows that most of the schools were established by public, elite-run educational offices. Even in 1902, when the official category swelled because of the first wave of district academies converting to higher primary schools, official and public foundings were virtually even. Over the eight-year period from 1902 to 1909, the number of official foundings did not quite equal the undoubtedly under-recorded number of private foundings that appear in the ministry statistics. It is not surprising therefore that nineteenth-century managerial patterns carried over into the New Policies period.

Table 15 suggests that core-peripheral distinctions and previous levels of managerial activity were major factors in the location of new schools. The districts with the largest numbers of students were in the economic cores of the north and the southeast coast.[20] The combination of administrative and economic centrality continued to be a powerful impetus to educational activity, but, although six of the ten most active districts in 1909 contained high-level administrative cities, this was not the only governing factor. For instance, Hangzhou was the unquestioned provincial educational center because colleges and law and technical schools were concentrated there, as shown in Table 16. However, the data on regular elementary through middle schools shown in Table 15 suggest that the districts of Qiantang and Renhe containing the provincial capital did not have as much educational development as might be expected, and we learn from other sources that gentry outside Hangzhou city were slow to establish schools.[21]

The local development of public management was thus a second factor in explaining the number of new schools established in a district. The strong educational programs of the Wenzhou districts of Pingyang, Ruian, and Luoqing was caused to a large extent by the continuation of the nineteenth-century managerial impetus into the New Policies period. This same local impetus may also explain why a surprisingly large number of schools were established in several districts of poor, isolated Chuzhou. Sun Yirang of Ruian not only encouraged education in his own district and prefecture, but from his quasi-official position as the head of the educational bureau for

TABLE 15

New School Students in Selected Districts, 1907 and 1909

		1909				1907	
Rank[a]	Place	No. of students	1907 rank compared		Place	No. of students	1909 rank compared
1	Yin (N)	4,025	—		Yin (N)	2,797	—
2	Zhuji (S)	3,957	+20		Qiantang/ Renhe (H)	2,354	+1
3	Qiantang/ Renhe (H)	3,800	−1		Pingyang (W)	2,032	+4
4	Shanyin/ Guiji (S)	3,715	—		Shanyin/ Guiji (S)	1,905	—
5	Jinhua (Jh)	3,305	+16		Cheng (S)	1,763	+8
6	Dongyang (Jh)	3,128	+12		Jiaxing/ Xiushui (Jx)	1,484	+2
7	Pingyang (W)	2,977	−4		Fenghua (N)	1,348	+4
8	Jiaxing/ Xiushui (Jx)	2,889	−2		Huangyan (T)	1,385	+10
9	Zhenhai (N)	2,721	+5		Ciqi (N)	1,115	+5
10	Yongjia (W)	2,000	+3		Xiaoshan (S)	1,025	+10
21	Ruian (W)	1,351	−4		Jinhua (Jh)	695	−16
22	Luoqing (W)	1,233	−10		Tongxiang (Jx)	658	+10
23	Ninghai (T)	1,194	+2		Qu (Q)	611	+4
24	Haining (H)	1,148	−9		Songyang (C)	579	+21
25	Shangyu (S)	1,148	+6		Ninghai (T)	568	−2
36	Xiangshan (N)	591	—		Xiangshan (N)	347	—
37	Jiangshan (Q)	585	+20		Jinyun (C)	343	+10
38	Qingtian (C)	556	−10		Deqing (Hu)	336	+12
39	Longyou (Q)	525	+4		Lishui (C)	311	+4
40	Dinghai (N)	509	+2		Xinchang (S)	300	−5
56	Wuyi (Jh)	257	−2		Xindeng (H)	113	+6
57	Jiande (Y)	235	−2		Jiangshan (Q)	105	−20
58	Yuhang (H)	232	−17		Taishun (W)	98	−6
59	Lin'an (H)	217	−13		Xuanping (C)	83	+1
60	Xuanping (C)	215	−1		Yuqian (H)	80	+3
70	Kaihua (Q)	83	−6		Jingning (C)	64	−6
71	Yunhe (C)	62	−44		Suian (Y)	67	−4
72	Fenshui (Y)	42	−30		Xiaofeng (Hu)	22	−7
73	Wukang (Hu)	36	−4		Fenshui (Y)	21	−1
74	Shouchang (Y)	25	—		Shouchang (Y)	20	—

SOURCES: Xuebu (1907), pp. 548–54; Xuebu (1910), Zhejiang 7–11. Based on regular schools, not including colleges and specialized schools.

[a]Rank refers to the district's performance in establishing a new educational system as measured by the number of students in new schools.

TABLE 16
College-Level and Specialized Schools, 1907 and 1909

Type of school	1907		1909	
	Schools	Students	Schools	Students
Hangzhou City				
Higher (college)	1	268	1	174
Law	1	231	2	460
Agriculture	2	125	1	71
Industry	1	101	2	278
Normal	3	278	4	661
TOTAL	8	1,003	10	1,644
All other districts[a]				
Law	1	47	0	0
Agriculture	2	68	4	117
Industry/Commerce	1	40	7	259
Normal	29	1,086	8	535
TOTAL	33	1,241	19	911

SOURCES: Xuebu (1907), pp. 544–47; Xuebu (1910), *Zhejiang* 2–5.
[a]Specialized schools outside Hangzhou were generally lower level, and they were located mainly in Shaoxing-Ningbo, the southeast coast, or Jinhua. Practically none were in Huzhou or Jiaxing.

Wenzhou and Chuzhou he did his best to promote education in neighboring Chuzhou with the help of a few scholarly friends from that prefecture.

A third factor was kinship organization, which affected schools more than other New Policies institutions. Gazetteers do not give a clear picture of the late nineteenth century levels of public activity in the Jinhua districts with a large number of schools, but available sources do indicate that kinship organizations were strong and that they had long supported educational institutions. This history, combined with the early effects of commercial growth, may have contributed to Jinhua educational development. There is more evidence to suggest that one reason for the vigorous educational programs in Shaoxing and Ningbo was the alacrity with which their lineages converted the schools to the new system.[22] Kinship organization could also have negative effects on the founding of new schools. It is possible that educational programs in the core districts of Huzhou and Jiaxing were not as successful as might have been expected because highly developed family and lineage schools added new subjects, retarding the need for new public schools.

Because schools reflected a general proliferation of local levels of public social organization throughout the urban hierarchy in the prosperous parts of the province, they were not simply concentrated in the administrative cities (although there were a large number in Hangzhou). By 1911, 43 of 55 wards (du) in Pingyang (Wenzhou) had at least one primary school, and only 7 of 124 schools were in the district city.[23] In Cheng (Shaoxing), most of the 9 higher-level primary schools were in the district city, but there were 16 two-level and 40 lower-level primary schools in market towns and villages.[24]

The information in Table 15 is roughly compatible with the data on degree holders and academies in Appendixes A and B. The three northern prefectures were still important centers but did not dominate provincial performance. Shaoxing and Ningbo continued their ascent. The relatively prosperous southeastern coastal districts were further expanding their educational institutions, and Jinhua was recovering the momentum that had been cut off by the Taiping Rebellion. Since the schools interacted closely with other institutions, their distribution reflected the distribution of other new institutions in the core districts. Once founded, the new institutions tended to pull members of the local elite into the new trends, just as members of the elite had been pulled into nineteenth-century public activity. Zhejiangese elite activists had begun to revise their educational system before the traditional examinations were ended in 1905. Although the end of the examination system was generally unsettling, in effect the new governmental educational program ratified or encouraged changes already underway in the Zhejiang cores.

The picture changes markedly in the districts with the fewest new schools and students. They were located in peripheral parts of Zhejiang, particularly in the south and along the Anhui-Jiangxi border on the west. Every district had at least one new school, and the autonomous and even democratic ideas associated with the schools and other new institutions found their way even to remote districts in Chuzhou prefecture.[25] In districts at the lowest end of the rankings in Table 15, however, educational facilities were likely to consist of the converted district academy and a few schools in the district city or a market town. The gap between the new education available in the more prosperous areas and the peripheral districts was growing: far more new schools and students were added in top-ranking and intermediate districts than districts at the bottom. By 1909 the Chuzhou districts that had started out well were dropping to lower rankings because they did not have the resources to continue the work begun by Sun Yirang. Even the Wenzhou districts of Pingyang, Ruian, and Luoqing could not maintain their initial impetus. Despite the strong educational commitment of a segment of the local elite, these districts did not have the incomes to match the considerably more developed cores to the north.

The district-by-district financial data in Table 17 reinforce the impression given by the figures on student and school distribution. There were obviously vast differences in the amounts of money available for education in core and peripheral districts. Educational expenses in the lowest-ranking districts were insignificant. In districts like Pingyang or Yiwu, which had many students but were not part of the most commercialized cores, educational managers had much less money to spend than managers in wealthier districts with comparable numbers of students. Financing in rich and poor districts did share one characteristic: income other than tuition was mainly raised locally by members of the local elite. Most official funds went to high-level and specialized schools in the provincial capital or to the prefectural-level middle schools whose incomes are recorded in Table 17. Farther down the administrative hierarchy and farther from the core areas, the chances of official funding were generally slight.

Other income was derived from mixtures of new taxation and old methods of financing local public institutions through endowments, interest, contributions, and taxes. Endowments for academies and other institutions were taken over by the chief new schools in the district cities or major market towns.

TABLE 17

Sources of School Income, Selected High and Low Districts, 1907

(Yuan)

District[a]		No. of students	Endow- ment	Interest	Official	Public	Students	Involuntary contri- butions	Voluntary contri- butions	Misc.	Total
Yin (N)	P	143	—	2,202	17,279	1,375	4,318	3,181	5,061	614	34,030
	D	2,654	5,551	2,096	—	10,532	17,105	610	24,527	98	60,519
Qiantang/ Renhe (H)	Pv	571	375	936	66,404	10,645	12,547	1,033	1,164	1,367	94,471
	P	1,185	138	5,896	19,019	18,403	7,370	2,954	3,369	374	57,523
	D	598	112	4,320	13,746	2,140	5,043	2,035	4,897	42	32,335
Pingyang (W)	D	2,032	2,098	180	—	2,252	5,306	4,564	2,894	230	17,524
Shanyin/ Guiji (S)	P	116	3,320	—	—	2,347	980	2,666	43	—	9,356
	D	1,789	7,549	1,032	3,550	9,402	1,917	7,111	12,291	976	43,828
Cheng (S)	D	1,763	5,524	194	240	8,554	9,377	3,163	4,490	1,597	33,139
Jiaxing/ Xiushui (Jx)	P	86	—	112	9,600	—	1,050	—	—	—	10,762
	D	1,398	1,592	326	32	8,542	7,329	10,612	6,747	455	35,635
Huangyan (T)	D	1,335	5,026	597	—	3,993	1,865	1,657	1,949	24	15,111
Ciqi (N)	D	1,115	798	1,502	2,689	5,841	6,489	1,435	8,646	881	28,281
Xiaoshan (S)	D	1,025	1,963	275	30	6,764	5,326	5,299	2,546	2,171	24,374
Yiwu (Jh)	D	1,021	1,178	114	—	953	3,148	435	1,851	215	7,894
TOTAL		16,831	35,224	19,782	132,589	91,743	89,170	46,755	80,475	9,044	504,782
Percent			7%	4%	26%	18%	18%	9%	16%	2%	

Yuqian (H) D	80	357	276	—	269	32	1,209	—	141	2,284
Anji (H) D	77	42	410	—	192	717	1,133	90	—	2,584
Xianju (T) D	73	1,000	620	—	220	180	—	480	—	2,500
Fuyang (H) D	71	807	—	999	390	200	754	—	—	3,150
Kaihua (Q) D	67	906	—	247	139	392	791	362	2	2,839
Xiaofeng (Hu) D	22	16	—	—	805	—	270	—	—	1,091
Fenshui (Y) D	21	61	149	—	276	—	111	—	—	597
Shouchang (Y) D	20	210	75	300	255	—	150	—	—	990
TOTAL	431	3,399	1,530	1,546	2,546	1,521	4,418	932	143	16,035
Percent	21%	21%	9%	10%	16%	9%	28%	6%	1%	

SOURCE: Xuebu (1907), pp. 558–64.
[a]P, prefectural-level schools; D, district or sub-district schools; Pv, provincial schools in Hangzhou.

TABLE 18
School Income and Expenditures,
Selected Districts, 1907

District	No. of students	Income (yuan)	Expenditure
Yin (N)	2,797	94,619	96,541
Pingyang (W)	2,032	17,524	29,317
Ciqi (N)	1,115	28,281	32,990
Yiwu (Jh)	1,021	7,894	11,182
Tongxiang (Jx)	658	11,309	12,566
Ninghai (T)	568	8,657	10,051
Deqing (Hu)	336	6,971	8,239
Lishui (C)	311	16,804	16,738
Yuqian (H)	80	2,284	2,416
Fenshui (Y)	21	597	985
Shouchang (Y)	20	990	662

SOURCE: Xuebu (1907), pp. 548–54, 558–64, 567–72.

Members of local elites also contributed money to establish new schools, which they then sometimes managed and supported;[26] Shanghai merchants invested in new schools at home as well as older local institutions.[27] Approximately 50 percent of all income came from involuntary and voluntary contributions (*paijuan* and *lejuan*), and taxes or tax-like levies accounted for most of it.

A systematic comparison between New Policies taxes and contributions and those of the reconstruction period is not possible. Initial reconstruction expenses had been heavy, and the high local levies for public purposes continued and in some places expanded in the post-reconstruction decades. Nevertheless, localities entered a new phase of substantially increased, continuing annual public expenditures during the New Policies period. Financing tended to shift from private sources to taxation. This transition was not easy. As Table 18 shows, in the early years reported school expenditures were likely to outrun reported incomes. This problem was most marked in systems undergoing rapid expansion, especially in districts like Pingyang and Huangyan where commerce was not as profitable as it was in the northern districts that benefited most from the Shanghai trade. Deficits appear in the finances of schools with both large and small incomes, although the amounts of the deficits in schools with the lowest incomes were probably too small to have a general impact in even the poorest peripheries.

Elite activists raised and administered school funds, except for the prefectural and provincial schools. In 1910 the provincial assembly recognized elite financial responsibilities in education and other local spheres of cities, market towns, and rural districts by establishing auditing offices of five to nine "gentry managers," who were "publicly selected by scholars and the people." These offices were to oversee the use of local public funds and properties, including expenditures for the publicly financed activities of private organizations such as guilds. Only institutions like ancestral temples, lineage charitable estates, and shrines were excluded.[28] The regulation gives a false impression of coordinated provincial policy-making, but it accurately indicates that New Policies management was in the hands of local elites.

How did the increase in the number of Zhejiangese local public institutions compare with increases in other provinces? School statistics again provide the best means of comparison. Table 19 shows that the number of schools and school incomes in Zhejiang fell in the middle range of all Chinese provinces, but official funds accounted for an unusually small percentage of school income. This information is consistent with a picture of strong elite initiative outside official control. Zhejiangese had reacted very quickly to the New Policies and had been among the leaders in establishing schools in 1902–3.[29] These schools remained gentry institutions,[30] but the relatively independent initiative did not produce as many new schools as promotion did by strong, modernizing governors-general like Yuan Shikai in Zhili, Zhang Zhidong in Hubei, and Xiliang in Sichuan. The Zhejiangese pattern of financing was closer to the patterns of Jiangsu and Guangdong, where official funding was low and 40–50 percent of income came from public sources or contributions and taxes. These similarities probably reflected common social attributes of central and southern coastal cores that were centers of foreign trade.[31] Independent-minded members of the elite may not have established as many institutions

TABLE 19
Provincial Educational Comparison, 1907

Province	School income[a] (1,000 taels)	No. of schools	Percent official funds	Percent public funds	Percent taxes/con-tributions
Hubei	2,050	1,467[b]	77%	5%	9%
Jiangning	907	643	51%	10%	14%
Jiangsu	832	921	25	22	20
Zhili	1,584	8,048	39%	6%	27%
Sichuan	1,421	7,750	—	—	—
Guangdong	1,067	1,487	18	41	9
Shandong	873	3,817	49	5	17
Zhejiang	789	1,120	14	25	29
Hunan	715	696	41	12	15
Henan	591	1,580	34	16	16
Yunnan	547	949	44	29	3
Jiangxi	247	432	46	12	11
Shanxi	495	651	40	11	13
Shenxi	468	2,007	36	7	11
Anhui	461	283	41	7	17
Guangxi	369	456	37	32	5
Fujian	365	361	40	16	21
Guizhou	233	402	23	13	38
Gansu	—	461	—	—	—

SOURCE: Xuebu (1907), pp. 35–36, 41–42.
[a]Zhejiang figures are calculated in yuan in the provincial tables, but converted to taels for comparison with other provinces. Hence, the amounts in this table are not consistent with those in Table 13.
[b]Hubei had relatively few schools, but large student bodies, because large expenditures on schools began only in 1906.

as officials who controlled state resources did, but the institutions established were usually part of local structures rather than official ones and they had to be financed without bureaucratic funds. Such areas were not typical of much of China, but it is possible that local initiative was beginning to challenge officials elsewhere as well. The number of publicly funded schools and the percentage of local financing was on the rise throughout the country by 1906–7, if not earlier.[32] Officials might therefore have trouble controlling the increasing volume of elite participation in public affairs, except where the state presence was so strong that members of the elite most easily expanded their power by attaching themselves to its lower reaches.

If the New Policies organizations were not closely attached to the bureaucratic structure, what was their relationship to other social organizations? Within the core areas of Zhejiang, New Policies institutions were established within a larger context of vigorous autonomous activity. The old range of welfare and other elite public activities continued. Additional welfare institutions, foundling homes, burial societies, and similar institutions were founded during the New Policies period.[33] Prosperous welfare agencies like the one in the provincial capital even used their funds to establish new kinds of institutions.[34] The old welfare institutions no longer dominated the changing, expanding public sectors of the core districts; the most prominent place was filled by a combination of offices to prepare for local self-government (before local executive councils were established), chambers of commerce, and educational organizations. By the same token, welfare was no longer so important in linking local activity to national concerns. Nonetheless, the old institutions still contributed significantly to the total mass of the public sphere, increasing its substance and contributing to its autonomy. Interchange between the management of major welfare institutions and the chambers of commerce[35] is one example of the way in which the new organizations built upon the old.

The New Policies institutions were established at a time when private organizations were also rapidly expanding. Although factory industry did not develop rapidly in Zhejiang, more and more foreign-style businesses appeared throughout the decade.[36] More Zhejiangese newspapers were established alongside the reformist and revolutionary journals and mass-circulation dailies that came from Tokyo and Shanghai. In addition to the slightly older *Hangzhou Vernacular Journal*, an *All-Zhejiang Daily* (*Quan-Zhe ribao*), and a *New Vernacular Journal* (*Baihua xinbao*) had been founded in the capital by 1910.[37] Shaoxing also had a newspaper, and occupational groups had begun to publish specialized journals. The Hang-

zhou Educational Association, for instance, discussed a periodical to promote Zhejiangese products, and students at the Hangzhou higher elementary school published a paper advocating
student self-government and a magazine of English-language
studies.[38] Although the record of publications is very fragmentary, it is probable that little local journals were also established outside major cities—there was even a *Journal to
Promote Education* (*Quanxue bao*) in out-of-the-way Taiping
(Taizhou).[39]

Local reformist and professional organizations also appeared
in increasing numbers. Some were hard to distinguish from officially mandated New Policies institutions, except that they
sometimes appeared before the governmental regulations were
formulated and they did not follow prescribed forms. They
often addressed older social concerns as much as new programs. Members of the elite formed associations to suppress
opium;[40] they organized societies to abolish superstitious practices or to end social evils like foot-binding and prostitution;[41]
they gave lectures on social morality.[42] The Improvement Association (*gailiang hui*) sought to promote industry and education, improve social morality, and provide a basis for local self-
government. The Commercial Education Association (*shangxue gonghui*) founded in 1909 and the Legal Studies Association (*faxue xiehui*) established in 1911 were among the professional associations appearing in Hangzhou. Similar bodies
appeared in at least some other large cities; by 1910 there was a
Political Research Society (*zhengzhi yanjiu she*) in Shaoxing,
and the superintendent of the normal school had founded an
Association to Discuss Educational Affairs (*jiaowu taolun
hui*), which met monthly and distributed a newsletter to over a
hundred schools throughout the district.[43] Such organizations
not only developed feelings of solidarity among men moving
into new professional fields but also provided opportunities for
increased linkages between prominent Zhejiangese and natives
of other provinces through meetings like that of the All-China
United Agricultural Association in 1910.[44]

Specifically political organizations will be considered in the
next chapter. Even the growth of non-political groups suggests

a process of elite redefinition and self-assertion—which was rooted in the nineteenth century but was accelerating and changing direction in the twentieth.[45] In Zhejiang the New Policies activists were closely linked to such changes through their public activities. For example, to use the example of the schools, the quality of education may not have been high,[46] and the subjects studied may not have been very different—particularly in the countryside where money was relatively scarce and new subjects were not relevant to daily life. Nevertheless, the schools did more than simply continue the old education under a new name. The mere idea of a theoretically (if not actually) standard curriculum that was based on new texts could introduce different subjects and styles of learning.[47] Students and educators developed a sense of identity that became increasingly marked as one ascended the educational ladder. The concentration of older students in the cities had definite political consequences at the end of the Qing and in the Republic. Teachers and gentry promoters of education in prefectural and district seats and market towns also developed a sense of their local or social identity, which could be linked to national issues but did not automatically imply an extension of bureaucratic state power. With the end of the old examination system and with the inundation of the old mainline bureaucratic posts by new positions, the challenge to the Qing was to ensure that the new systems were integrated into a renovated bureaucratic structure rather than either becoming localistic or fostering national political competition.

Aside from their significance in national politics, the New Policies institutions increased both local opportunities and local tensions. The New Policies added to the institutions through which local power could be exercised and rearranged them. In Zhejiang there was significant social support for these innovations, which were often treated as continuations of the reformist activism of the 1890's. Members of the elite competed to control the new institutions and their revenues. Managers of new functional associations were sometimes resented by people who were bypassed by the changes, and new financial demands or other disruptions led to popular protests.[48] Fifteen of twenty-three Zhejiangese riots recorded in *The Eastern Miscellany* from 1906 through 1910 involved attacks on schools, educational associations, chambers of commerce, and other New Policies organizations or personnel.[49] Some incidents, like the attack on a school, educational association, and statistical bureau in Shangyu district during the spring of 1910, were specifically triggered by new taxes.[50] Taxing a specific trade could lead to riots by merchants or producers being asked to bear the burden. The appropriation of temples for schools could also provoke popular protests, and cultural hostility was aroused more by threats to religion than by the foreign flavor of Western-style institutions. In other cases, new institutions aroused hostility because they were obviously run for the benefit of a special group. An expensive new school in a town of Jingning district (Chuzhou), for instance, served only the lineage of its head, although it was supported by surcharges on the salt and bamboo taxes.[51]

There were thus numerous reasons why new institutions might be attacked. In the Shangyu and Jingning cases, there are indications that members of the elite were divided over whether to support the New Policies. In most cases, however, either new taxes or the appropriation of religious buildings precipitated incidents. Particularly in 1909 and 1910 protests against New Policies institutions occurred amid food riots and demands for grain and land-tax remission. New local charges were particularly onerous because they came on top of natural disasters and poor harvests. To make matters worse, the 1910 Shanghai banking crisis shook financial and commercial institutions in the core areas of Zhejiang.

Nonetheless, the recorded number of violent protests is small compared to the number of new institutions founded. Although there must have been numerous small incidents that went unchronicled, either social control remained effective or opposition was not very deep. Dissatisfaction was typically specific and economic, breaking out when additional taxes were levied on special interests or on products important to peasant livelihood. Segments of the elite who felt threatened also incited protests.

This violence tended to follow earlier patterns of community competition or reaction to state or elite extractions. Local tensions sharpened as the New Policies increased the reasons for competitive or reactive violence; changes in local relationships foreshadowed even more social discord during the Republic. In some other provinces tensions had a more immediate effect, but they do not appear to have been a major political force in Zhejiang at the end of the Qing. Members of the elite did not divide themselves neatly into progressive and conservative segments, nor was there a marked class polarization. Members of the lower classes generally did not display a broad sense of class solidarity in their protests. Local incidents remained local and no more threatening than nineteenth-century unrest had been to the elite. Peasants had not yet started along the new progression of organization, mobilization, and politicization that elite society was following.[52]

In this period there was a sharpening of differences between core and peripheral areas in organizational levels and types of social activity. This was not an absolute gap. Just as there had been academies, upper-degree holders, and some welfare institutions in peripheral districts, there were now some new schools, chambers of commerce, and assemblies. The New Policies institutions were introduced more slowly, in peripheral districts, however, and, as the school data show, they were fewer in number. There were also fewer private societies and businesses, and this whole picture of elite social inertia rested on lower levels of economic development. As Keith Schoppa has pointed out in his study of Zhejiang during the Republic, the concentration of change in the wealthiest, most commercialized parts of the province meant that local activities and interests diverged in new ways, depending upon levels of economic development.[53] These factors contributed to the contexts in which members of the elite began consciously to redefine their relations with the state and to move into a new phase of politicized organization and mobilization.

The New Policy Activists

What was the effect of the New Policies on elite leadership? The sudden influx of new institutions could have radically changed the composition of the elite managerial stratum. Managerial networks had already been established in much of Zhejiang by the beginning of the twentieth century, however, and in core and developing areas these networks included men who were externally connected and cosmopolitan in their views. Reformers were already part of these networks in some districts. Since the New Policies institutions built upon existing public spheres, their appearance did not usually mean a sharp change in local leadership. The transition from the partly altered management of the 1890's to participation in the New Policies was not a major step.

Local activism under the New Policies. Existing managers often moved into the new positions. Heads of district academies might, as in Longyou, head the higher primary school into which the academy was converted.[54] In Hangzhou the first chairman of the chamber of commerce, Fan Gongxu, was the head of the welfare association, and for several years he held both positions.[55] Another prominent chamber of commerce member from a welfare-managerial background was Ding Bing's son, Ding Lizhong.[56] In other cities, too, welfare management was interchangeable with the presidency of the chamber of commerce or the educational association.[57]

One of the problems therefore is to sort out the balance between old and new elements among New Policies managers. The information on members of new policy organizations is too fragmentary to allow precise social classification,[58] but it does indicate that, as before, leaders were defined by their combined social and institutional networks rather than by their membership in a particular elite substratum. The social composition of activist groups varied according to institution. Members of educational associations had scholarly interests and credentials that allowed them to be called gentry. Presidents and vice presidents of these associations often had higher degrees,[59] and graduates of new schools also became members in the course of the decade.

Chambers of commerce, on the other hand, drew their membership more broadly. Some chambers of commerce were strictly mercantile associations, but even they expanded the public roles of the merchants dominating local trades. In places where trade was in the hands of outsiders the new institutions were sometimes controlled partly or wholly by non-natives—creating a situation that could lead to local friction.[60] Very often, however, the merchants in the chambers of commerce fitted into local leadership structures in the same way that merchants had been part of welfare management from the time of the reconstruction. So many gentry were involved in trade and the chambers of commerce were so influential that high-ranking gentry were also found heading chambers of commerce. *Jinshi* or *juren*-degree holders were presidents in the prefectural cities of Wenzhou and Qu, in the district seats of Ruian (Wenzhou) and Dinghai (Ningbo), and in the market towns of Shuanglin (Huzhou) and Qing (Jiaxing),[61] and the president in Hangzhou, Fan Gongxu, was a former member of the Hanlin Academy.

The varied social characteristics of members of district or town assemblies during the last year of the Qing and the first three years of the Republic suggest that they, too, came from a broad segment of the elite involved in public affairs. In studying fourteen assemblies recorded in gazetteers, Keith Schoppa found that all but two had one or more members who were upper gentry or school graduates. The overwhelming majority of members were not identified, however; presumably they were lower-degree holders, merchants, or other locally prominent men without degrees. Schoppa does not believe the assembly members were a new social group (although he considers them a new political and administrative elite), and he does not think the data adequate to support the hypothesis that lower-degree holders monopolized self-government posts.[62]

Very probably, all these institutions reflected the social compositions of existing local activist elites, but the increase in the number of positions also brought more men into the public sphere. Among the new entrants were men with a new education and new professional career aspirations. Even in 1904 some of these men were heading New Policies institutions, and their numbers increased as the new schools produced more graduates. They were sometimes abrasive additions, but in general the managerial establishments of the last Qing decade had many characteristics of their reconstruction predecessors. Networks radiated out from prominent activists who held several important positions and might remain active for many years.

In places like the towns of Qing and Nanxun, the New Policies structures had roots in the Tongzhi (1862–74). For instance, Shen Shanbao, who founded Qing's first modern school in 1902 and served as vice president of the self-government office and president of the agricultural association, was a descendant of the leading local reconstructionist, Shen Baoyue.[63] Men with no previous record of public activity also became well established during the New Policies. The person who founded and managed a school in his home market town in Zhenhai (Ningbo) in 1906 later served as president of both the district office to promote education and the self-government association. He became the second head of the post-revolutionary district civil government in 1911 and a magistrate in 1912; in 1916 he established and managed another school.[64]

Gazetteers of less commercialized districts, where smaller numbers of people were involved in public affairs, provide striking examples of kinship ties among people running old and new institutions from the 1890's well into the Republic. The Lus furnished several leaders in Xinchang (Shaoxing), including a *juren* who established the foundling home, contributed to the endowment for examination candidates, managed dike repairs in 1901, established and managed the district higher primary school in 1902, and was president of the office to promote education in 1907–8. Two *sui gongsheng* from the same kin group variously contributed to the endowment for examination candidates, revived a burial society in 1903, served as a member of the district assembly in 1912 and as president of the chamber of commerce from 1912 to at least 1917, and established a silk factory in 1917.[65] Although the New Policies leadership in the moderately prosperous southwestern prefectural capital of Qu was more varied, the Zheng family contributed several members. The *juren* Zheng Yongxi headed the agricultural bureau and the educational association. Subsequently, he headed the first prefectural government after the 1911 Revolution, served as a member of the district educational council in 1922, and compiled the 1929 district gazetteer. Zheng's brother helped establish the first girls' school in 1907, which was headed by his mother. His father supervised the middle school, and a cousin studied cartography and did surveying for the district.[66]

Not only are these examples similar to examples of managerial establishments during the reconstruction period, but all the factors that encouraged a cosmopolitan orientation in late nineteenth-century managers were also still operative. Men still mixed local and external careers, moving between the bureaucracy, public management, and trade or business.[67] Sojourning merchants continued to invest at home. Men still promoted public activities in their ancestral homes and at higher urban levels. Local reformist leaders viewed their efforts even more in terms of national frameworks than they had before. Although the biographies of some leading figures also suggest the beginnings of entrenched local oligarchies, the localistic legacy of the New Policies in parts of Zhejiang after the central government collapsed did not characterize situations in core areas at the end of the Qing.

In the absence of a thorough social revolution, continuities in the backgrounds of local leaders were inevitable. It is fairly rare to find evidence of a person filling a New Policies position whose biography does not fit the profile of the elite society where he was active. Such continuity did not mean, however, that the character of elite leadership remained fixed even though contexts and people changed. The New Policies institutions expanded local opportunities, interjected new relationships, and provided another set of hierarchies through which people could move upward on the basis of their locally assessed performance. Some students or graduates of new schools returned home to found new institutions. Thus one of four men who established a primary school in Haining city in 1907 was a graduate of the Hangzhou middle school, and two of a group that founded a school in a nearby market town were about to graduate from the Zhejiang higher school.[68] A law school graduate, a normal school graduate, and a student recently returned from Japan founded schools and headed the education association in Jiande (Yanzhou), and the president of the office to promote education in Songyang (Chuzhou) had studied education in Japan.[69] Such graduates were probably particularly significant in promoting change and filling new positions in less commercially developed districts that had fewer lines to the outside,[70] but opportunities offered by New Policies institutions attracted graduates home to core areas as well.

It was also possible for managers of new institutions to move from lower to higher urban levels. Xia Xinming from the market town of Puyuan (Jiaxing) illustrates this possibility on a modest scale. Xia had converted the town academy to a school in 1902 and helped establish another town school in 1905. Because of his educational reputation, he was invited to manage district educational affairs in 1905 (presumably as the head of the office to promote education). He then delegated responsibility for town-level schools to another man, but he continued to encourage the establishment of schools in his part of Puyuan—and they were founded well before schools in the adjacent areas of the adjoining district.[71]

Local activists also moved into the assemblies and executive councils that appeared at the very end of the last Qing decade. In Qu, for instance, the president of the assembly established in 1912 was a *shengyuan* who was active in welfare and had established and managed several schools. The vice president, also a *shengyuan*, was the son of one of the active local public figures during the Guangxu reign period (1875–1908).[72] One of the Tongxiang (Jiaxing) district assembly members was a *juren* who had been president of the self-government office in the district's main market town of Qing. Fourteen of thirty members of subprefectural, town, or rural township executive councils in Haining during 1915 had founded, managed, or headed schools between 1902 and 1911—or appear to be close relatives of men who did.[73]

The provincial assemblies elected in 1909 added an important new level to which local activists might aspire. In Zhejiang as well as other provinces, the assembly studied problems, passed laws, intervened in fiscal matters, and became aggressively involved in political issues. The Zhejiang assembly was a vigorous institution, in which members or private citizens introduced five times as many bills as the governor did during the first session. The assembly provided elites with a substantial forum to advance their interests on such matters as business or education and to complain about such problems as irregularities in the collection of grain tribute or trade surcharges and fees at *lijin* checkpoints.[74] The governor had no choice but to try to work with assembly members, who maintained their independence and had the power to delay the budgetary process. Although it did not create the political movements in which it became involved, the Zhejiang assembly had a substantial impact on the province. Most New Policies institutions enlarged local public spheres, but the provincial assemblies brought activists from further down the urban hierarchy into a more politically influential organ in the provincial capital.

Information available on 66 of the 112 assemblymen indicates that most were gentry of relatively early middle age. There were thirty-seven regular upper-degree holders, at least another eleven had purchased ranks and degrees, and at least fourteen had studied in Japan—usually after acquiring a degree in China. There were very few new-school graduates or professional men and only three or four merchants.[75] At least thirty-one of the sixty-six had been involved in New Policies institutions of their home districts: eight had been presidents of chambers of commerce, thirteen had headed educational associations, and sixteen had founded, managed, or taught at new schools. In contrast, only ten are known to have held official posts,[76] and only a few appear to have focused their careers on the provincial capital before their election to the assembly. Gazetteer information on local activists (in contrast to that on local men who became officials) is fragmentary; considerably more men may have come to the provincial assembly by way of unrecorded local public activities. In the selection of assembly members, local involvement seems to have been more important than prestige acquired by employment at higher urban levels.[77] The assembly also became a stepping-stone to national representational positions: in 1910 seven members moved on to posts in the National Consultative Assembly (*zizheng yuan*) in Beijing.

Cai Rulin (born in isolated Dongyang, Jinhua) illustrates

how prominent members of the elite worked for new institutions in their home and other districts, became involved in national issues, and moved upward to higher levels in the administrative urban hierarchy. Cai received a *juren* degree in the mid-1890's and studied in Japan in 1903. He then headed a school in Xinchang (Shaoxing) and supervised the prefectural middle school in Jinhua as well as a school in Hangzhou for natives of the four south and southwestern prefectures. Cai also served as director of two different educational organizations in Dongyang (Jinhua) and as director of the provincial educational association. He was a member of both the Qing provincial assembly and the different provincial assembly established immediately after the 1911 Revolution. He was politically active as an officer of the association to oppose the British railway loan in 1907, a member of constitutional organizations, and a participant in the Zhejiangese delegation to request immediate opening of a national assembly in 1910.[78]

The upward movement illustrated by Cai was not the only pattern, however. Other provincial assembly members remained closer to home and did not cut their local roots. For instance, Vice President Chu Fucheng remained an active member of the Jiaxing educational association, and at least twelve members of the assembly returned home and held local posts during the politically unsettled period immediately after the 1911 Revolution. If anything, improvements in water transport and the completion of the Shanghai-Hangzhou railway line increased the circulation of members of the elite from its already high late nineteenth-century level. In addition to movement related to business and careers, reformers and revolutionaries also began to travel about the countryside making speeches. Two members of such a group journeying through market towns of Huzhou and Jiaxing in 1903, for instance, inspired a father and son in Puyuan town to found a girls' school.[79]

National and local perspectives thus intermingled. Xia Xinmin, the founder of a school in Puyuan in 1902, wrote of the deteriorating international situation—using the anti-imperialist cliché of the 1900's "European wind and American rain." He explained that people familiar with public affairs were therefore fervently promoting education to provide new technical content and a new nationalistic public morality.[80] A Shanghai merchant from Haining (Hangzhou) used rationales reminiscent of late nineteenth-century participatory self-strengthening to justify new institutions. At home he established a girls' school and supported lineage facilities, in order to improve public morality and benefit the public interest. He argued that both Eastern and Western nations became rich and powerful when people's thoughts were nationally and socially oriented, so that they acted for the public good and opposed forces that would harm it.[81] Like members of the elite in the 1890's, a wide range of socially aware people supported local change. Even though many of these men were very similar to the people who had previously been involved in local public affairs, they were now caught up in larger changes.

New Policies management in Ruian and Wenzhou. The relatively well documented history of the New Policies in Wenzhou prefecture illustrates how all these aspects fit together in one place. Changes in Ruian district (and to a considerable extent in the prefectural city as well) were initiated by Sun Yirang, whose scholarly managerial background and reform activities during the 1890's have already been described. Local initiatives centered on education, but leaders of the dominant educational establishment also assumed other positions. The Wenzhou-Chuzhou daotai from 1901 to 1905 was a reformer who encouraged new schools, sent students to Japan, founded a sericulture school, and set up an industrial bureau to teach handicrafts to vagrants, criminals, and disbanded soldiers.[82] His friendship with Sun and other local leaders resulted in fruitful collaboration, through which gentry initiatives flourished with official backing.

Sun initiated changes in Ruian using friendships dating back to the activist circles of the 1880's as well as relationships with younger scholars. In 1902 he and Huang Shaoji converted the mathematical school established in 1896 into a middle school. Chen Fuchen converted an old-style school into a new one, and Sun was directly responsible for founding one of four other elementary schools established that year. Another old protégé of

Sun's father managed a second elementary school, and men directly connected with the Sun family were involved in the others. An anti-footbinding association, a reading room, and a debating society attached to the middle school helped mobilize and justify local reform from perspectives that had developed over the past twenty years. The Wenzhou reformers of the 1880's and 1890's Song Heng, Chen Fuchen, and Chen Qiu lectured there. Other members of the society soon became prominent educators in the prefecture.

The following year two girls' schools were established in addition to a higher primary school, an industrial school, and a commercial school. One of the regular lecturers at the debating society founded a society to study teaching (*shifan yanjiu hui*). This organization may have been inspired by interest in Wenzhou vernacular and folklore; it may also have been related to the idea of developing a writing system for the Wenzhou dialect that was being pioneered at that time by Chen Qiu.[83]

The prefectural middle school was established in 1902, and a Yongjia reading society was begun in early 1903. Several schools appeared in Pingyang during these two years, and in Luoqing two scholars who had once studied under Chen Fuchen began raising money to found a teachers' school. Sun Yirang helped plan the prefectural middle school. He was one of its first heads. The man with whom he shared this responsibility was Yu Zhaoshen, a former member of the Hanlin Academy who had been associated with the "Emperor's Faction" during the Sino-Japanese War and had left office in disgust over the national humiliation of the Boxer Rebellion in 1900. Yu's connections with the Ruian reformers were further cemented by the marriage of his son to a daughter of Chen Fuchen.[84] Another old friend managed the sericulture school and tutored the daotai's children. In 1903 Sun and Yu resigned as heads of the middle school, which had experienced initial problems ranging from local opposition by scholars to financial strain, staffing problems, and student discontent. Control remained within Sun's circle, however, because the new director had worked with Sun in Ruian the year before. He was succeeded in turn by Liu Shaokuan of Pingyang district, another product of the

Ruian scholar circles of the 1880's, who continued to head the middle school until at least the late 1910's.[85]

From these beginnings, gentry in the four main Wenzhou districts of Yongjia, Ruian, Luoqing, and Pingyang went on to found an unusually large number of schools (see Table 15). In addition to the widely distributed primary schools, three middle schools were established outside the prefectural capital. Sun Yirang also founded a chemistry school in 1905. A school to educate clerks was begun in Yongjia in 1906—reflecting the old reformist concern over the quality of the sub-bureaucracy. Girls' schools existed in all the major district capitals, and Chen Fuchen sponsored five more in Ruian while he was teaching in Canton during 1908.

Sun Yirang was the key to this activity, even though he was not directly involved in all projects. By 1905 his national reputation as a scholar and educator was secure. He declined an invitation to teach at Beijing University and rejected the urging of Minister Zhang Boxi to come to Beijing. Sun did, however, use his connections with Zhang (an old friend who had also belonged to the "Emperor's Faction") to strengthen his position in Wenzhou. On Zhang's recommendation, the Zhejiang governor appointed Sun to be head of a special gentry-run bureau to promote education in Wenzhou and Chuzhou that was unusual because it placed gentry in charge of encouraging education in two prefectures rather than a single district. By using this post to promote education in the two prefectures, Sun extended his network of associates into Chuzhou.[86] Other members of Sun's inner circles had their own local connections.[87] This vigorous and interconnected elite activity was thus encouraged, but not really controlled, by sympathetic officials in the higher levels of the prefectural bureaucracy, and it was reinforced by Sun's connections in Beijing.

As the schools in Wenzhou became more numerous, Sun also developed an interest in protecting his educational system from official interference. This interest was illustrated in 1906 when Sun clashed with provincial authorities after a returned student and revolutionary party member, with whom he was very slightly acquainted, was caught distributing subversive literature in a girls' school in Luoqing. When this man appealed for help, Sun used his Beijing connections to have the case dropped despite strong pressure from the Manchu lieutenant governor. Although Sun professed not to believe the charges, one account indicates that his greatest concern was to protect his Wenzhou complex from outside official harassment.[88]

Sun and his associates also dominated the functional associations that began to be established in 1906. Sun was the first president of the chamber of commerce in Ruian, and he was succeeded by a man who had supervised one of the primary schools founded in 1902. The first president of the Wenzhou chamber of commerce was a *jinshi* and a former official, who was a friend of the Ruian reformers. Later the post was occupied by Yu Zhaoshen. The first president of the Yongjia educational association was also Sun's friend, and the president in Pingyang cooperated with Sun, even though he may not have been part of the inner circle. Yu Zhaoshen headed the Yongjia district assembly in 1911, and the only member of the Ruian district assembly whose name I know was almost certainly a relative of one of the 1902 school promoters.[89]

This surge of public activity was accompanied by private, modern business ventures. Sun Yirang established a steam launch company to run between Ruian and Yongjia, and he also encouraged mining. One student who returned from Japan to Wenzhou established a bureau in Ruian to promote a canning industry in 1906, and another sought to improve mining technology. These years were generally economically expansive in Wenzhou. Between 1905 and 1908 seven small trading companies with capital of ten to twenty thousand yuan were registered with the Ministry of Agriculture, Industry, and Commerce, reflecting a continuing expansion of trade along the southeast coast.[90]

Finally, New Policy leaders were involved in maintaining local order. Banditry and occasional border unrest continued in Wenzhou, and the gentry contributed money for military affairs. A scholar who would soon be part of the prefectural educational establishment organized a militia in Pingyang during the Boxer Rebellion.[91] Ten years later the superintendent of the

Yongjia normal school led gentry from his native Luoqing in petitioning the governor to send troops to aid elite-led forces against bandits.[92] Like their late nineteenth-century predecessors, New Policies public activists were not defined by military roles, but they shared a sensitivity to social unrest.

They also had to find ways to finance their ambitious plans in an area that was developing but was considerably less prosperous than the core districts of the five northern prefectures. Sun Yirang complained of difficulty in raising money,[93] and shortages continued to plague the school system. Although it was common throughout Zhejiang for school expenditures to exceed income, the overruns in such districts as Yongjia and Pingyang were large enough to suggest real difficulties. In 1907 Yongjia school expenditures were 25,279 yuan, but income was only 19,937. Only 3,086 yuan came from the official treasury, and 3,000 of that went to the prefectural middle school. Endowments, interest, and student fees brought in another 7,161, leaving 9,568 to be raised by taxes—not to mention a 5,500 yuan deficit to be covered somehow.[94]

Sun first proposed paying for schools by adding four copper cash to the copper-silver ratio used in calculating the land tax, and he later petitioned the governor for a hundred-cash surcharge on each silver tael paid for grain tribute. When officials refused to allow the land tax to be used for gentry-run institutions, Sun and his associates turned to miscellaneous taxes and contributions. They also used temple property where they could,[95] and wealthy individuals supported a few schools.

There are only two pieces of information available about efforts to raise taxes for education. During 1903 and 1904 Yongjia gentry approved the idea of a tax on oranges, which were a local specialty exported by steamship to northern markets. A bureau was established to collect the tax that, it was estimated, would raise a few hundred yuan annually, but orange-growers instigated a riot and lodged a suit against the man in charge of collections. Unnecessary arrests by the prefect inflamed the opposition. The daotai had to intervene, but the tax was evidently not entirely abandoned.[96]

Luoqing gentry also agreed in 1906 that "great households"

should contribute the sums they saved through tax privileges acquired during the mid-nineteenth century to support district education. Sun Yirang tried to persuade the Ruian gentry to accept a similar proposal the following year, but we do not know the outcome.[97] It appears that there was considerable elite support for new education but the need for money produced frictions. Officials tried to keep New Policies gentry managers away from the land tax, and managers aroused the ire of special groups when they devised other taxes.

At least some of the New Policies leaders in Wenzhou looked upon their activities in part as an extension of the principle that local men should manage local affairs for the common good of the community.[98] The leading figures set this goal in larger perspectives that linked self-government to constitutionalism and national crisis. Sun had already set forth goals of national survival and social solidarity in *The Political Essentials of the Rites of Zhou,* and he used similar arguments to advocate the elimination of big household tax privileges in Ruian. If China were to survive in "perilous times," the "old, inequitable laws" had to change. Otherwise the country had no hope of long-term security, and discussions about preserving minor prerequisites were ridiculous.[99] Evidently not all the Ruian gentry agreed with Sun, but the kind of communal social idealism associated with the Sun family persisted into the twentieth century, and the prefectural middle school continued into the 1920's to mix ideas derived from Wenzhou's Southern Song intellectual heritage with Western theories.[100]

Sun and his friends not only dominated district and prefectural affairs, but they were also active in outside organizations. They were the area's major external spokesmen at the end of the Qing. In 1907 Sun held public positions at four different urban levels: he was chairman of the Ruian district chamber of commerce, head of the Wenzhou-Chuzhou educational bureau, president of the Zhejiang educational association in Hangzhou, and a second-class consultant to the national Ministry of Education.[101] He corresponded with the Jiangsu provincial educational association about his educational plans in Wenzhou. In addition, he was a director and a sizable investor in the Zhejiang Railway Company, and he telegraphed the Ministry of Foreign Affairs in 1907 to protest the British railway loan.[102] At least three of five Wenzhou representatives to the provincial assembly, President Chen Fuchen, Wang Lifu, and Hang Xiangzao, had been his friends or associates.[103] Other men from the same circles took part in planning the 1911 Revolution in Wenzhou, which began with a meeting of teachers and administrators of the middle and normal schools. Provincial assembly members also returned home after the revolution. Chen Fuchen, who had split with provincial revolutionaries and whose local ties had become attenuated in the past decade, failed in his bid to head the new Wenzhou government, but Wang Lifu became the head of the Ruian civil government.[104]

The momentum of the New Policy period appears to have slowed in Wenzhou during the Republic, in part perhaps because the financial base was not equal to the base in the northern cores. It is not clear how much the 1911 Revolution shook the hold of Sun's establishment, but some members of the old group or their descendants were locally active into the 1930's.[105] Wenzhou was certainly not typical of Zhejiang. Nonetheless, many characteristics of the New Policies activists there appear in the more fragmentary material on other areas. Leaders were personally interconnected, prestigious members of the elite who were consciously reformist and patriotic. They had good relations with officials, but they took initiatives outside official channels and developed institutional interests that sometimes conflicted with the interests of the bureaucracy. Despite opposition to new taxes, they had significant support in local elite society. They were vigorous, politically conscious, and aware of external affairs. In 1911 they did not remain loyal to the Qing government.

Summary: The Elite and the New Policies

The New Policies of the last Qing decade occupied a critical position between the older public activism of the nineteenth century and the institutional experiments and social movements of the republican period. Continuities in local leadership and similarities between the functions of new institutions and previous public organizations obviously point to the past heritage. New aspects lay in the institutions themselves—the schools, the functional organizations established by government order, and the assemblies—and in the ways these institutions affected both state-societal and local social relationships. The combination of existing public activism and new organization accelerated elite social mobilization at the end of the Qing and contributed to its movement in more overtly political directions.

The existence of social continuities in local leadership does not, of itself, indicate that this leadership was conservative. Chūzō Ichiko[106] has suggested that gentry were reluctant to accept changes that might undermine their status. When they were forced to accept changes because of official abolition of the examination system, however, they quickly perceived that the new schools and other new institutions could also be used to preserve their positions. They therefore pragmatically cooperated with officials to establish local self-government that benefited both sides by seemingly extending bureaucratic power while formalizing the lower gentry's local roles. The New Policies thus paved the way for the familiar end-of-dynasty pattern of autonomous control over peasants by socially conservative local oligarchies that emerged after state power fragmented.

This analysis probably explains some events in some districts, particularly in the peripheral areas; it is partially applicable everywhere. It does not, however, adequately explain the situations that developed in the economic cores. According to Marianne Bastid,[107] commercialization and intensification of agricultural production had fostered an "agrarian bourgeoisie" that was not particularly dependent upon state titles and degrees. I have argued similarly that social changes produced by commercialization and foreign trade were not confined to large cities but spread throughout the towns of the prosperous areas of Zhejiang—pushing members of the elites into new relationships and roles. At the beginning of the twentieth century, these social changes did not encourage local political fragmentation. The integrative features of late imperial polity and society were still present (although weakening), and social changes had not produced an unbridgeable gap between modern urban centers and the countryside. Moreover, since at least the Tongzhi, leading men involved in local public affairs had displayed cosmopolitan attitudes and reformist leanings. The New Policies did not reverse these situations, and heightened national consciousness intensified the outward orientation of local leadership in the cores. Class and local interests did not cause members of the elite to entrench themselves in their home areas. Leadership continuities indicate a continuation of progressive late nineteenth-century activity rather than a conservative adjustment to official reforms.

The question of the relationship of local elites to state power during the New Policies period has been the topic of considerable recent research. Whereas Ichiko based his theory on the premise of a cyclical weakening of dynastic control over local gentry societies, Philip Kuhn [108] has pioneered the view that the New Policies were part of a long-range movement toward the bureaucratic penetration of local society that reversed nineteenth-century trends toward local autonomy. Thus the Qing, in the end, initiated a series of twentieth-century attempts to extend the bureaucratic structure downward to the village level. Bringing lower gentry into district-level government gave them a new and more substantial position in local affairs, but it did not resolve the continuing competition between centralizing and autonomous forces.

This thesis makes a major contribution to understanding the intrusive aspects of bureaucratic state-building that became a major political factor in the 1900's. Like Ichiko's theories, however, it assumes that governmental state-builders were pitted against localistic members of the elite who were seeking autonomy to pursue their private social interests. It underplays the cumulative effects of expanding public management and elite social organization. Institutionalized elite participation in local affairs and selection by community consensus were already well established in practice. The New Policies did not simply pull gentry into formal contact with lower levels of the bureaucracy. They also provided a larger number of institutions through which already-mobilized members of the elite could aggressively expand their previous initiatives and redefine their positions, both at home and in relation to the nation. The resulting demands for political participation had a revolutionary impact at the end of the Qing.

Keith Schoppa[109] has argued that the organizational proliferation in the inner-core regions of Zhejiang from the New Policies period onward portended more involvement in government and politics by members of elites outside the bureaucracy. The effect was two-edged. Organizations were potential tools for enlisting cooperative elite support for government. Nevertheless, although there were more links between state and social structures than before, it was actually more difficult to integrate these energetic, organized elites under bureaucratic leadership.

By the same token, it is misleading to picture the New Policies as bringing an essentially static stratum of lower gentry (shengyuan) into formal local governmental positions. The shengyuan were not a distinct group. New Policy institutions, like the public institutions of the nineteenth century, were run by personally connected, locally sanctioned elite establishments that cut across formal status and occupational roles within the upper levels of local societies. The shengyuan, as well as higher-status gentry, had been affected by the growth of career opportunities during the Qing. Their income, status, and primary occupations were not defined simply by their possession of the lowest degree. As new social groups began to emerge at the turn of the century, changes in political power led to the social redefinition (and self-redefinition) of various members of the elite during the republican period. This process, as described by Helen Chauncey,[110] left more scope for elite initiative in producing socio-political change than the attachment of one old, low-status category to the lowest levels of the government as hypothesized by Kuhn.

Stephen MacKinnon[111] has studied the New Policies in Zhili province to the north. He has retained the idea that members of the elite used changes to entrench themselves locally, but he suggests that there was a symbiotic relationship between state and local power structures during a time of political change. Political institutions and the power they conferred were expanding at several levels at the end of the Qing. Thus it was possible for Governor-General Yuan Shikai to increase the authority of the provincial bureaucracy by implementing centralizing reforms in cooperation with local members of the elite, who thereby expanded their own power vis-à-vis other social groups in the district. Bureaucratic and non-bureaucratic supporters of the New Policies therefore cooperated more than they competed. The major divisions were between people who benefited by being part of new institutional structures and people whose existing positions were undermined by change. People outside the new establishments, including peasants and many merchants, had little political voice and often little protection. MacKinnon's analysis makes the important points that political power was not static and that the political sphere was expanding at the beginning of the twentieth century. It also provides an explanation of some of the local divisions produced by the New Policies. It does, however, appear more applicable to north China, where Qing power had not been so compromised by elite activism. Moreover, whether or not merchants were relatively powerless in Zhili, they were so interwoven with elite elements in the core areas of the south that they must have shared in the growth of elite power.

The most persuasive analyses of the impact of the New Policies relate their functioning (if not their theory) to the expansion of elite political demands. Joseph Esherick[112] has suggested that a progressive, urban elite emerged at the end of the Qing. While the upper classes retained their interest in social stability and suppressed lower-class unrest, reformers in large cities sought to develop industry, resist imperialist economic encroachment, and limit government interference in what they considered their economic and political rights. Their nationalism and liberalism brought them into conflict with the Qing government, and they used provincial assemblies to further their own political interests, which remained primarily autonomous but had become identified with the interests of the nation.

John Fincher[113] goes further in positing a broad, flourishing pluralistic democracy based on the assemblies of the late Qing and the first two years of the Republic. Assemblies and, to Fincher, the less important, new functional associations were created by the government to extend its control and enlist elite support for its modernization policies. In practice, however, Fincher argues that autocratic governmental reform created conditions under which many members of elites outside the bureaucracy could assert their interests and political claims in vigorous movements for self-government. The success of the New Policies at the peripheries of governmental power arose from the vigor of elite social groups incorporated into the electorate, and this very success created political tensions that undermined the central power that the policies were intended to conserve.

Such theories do much to define the political dynamics of the last Qing decade. It must be stressed, however, that the processes were longer and broader than the theories suggest. Nineteenth-century public expansion was crucial to twentieth-century developments, and public activity spread throughout the cores without being confined to the highest urban levels. The institutional basis for elite political assertion was not suddenly interjected by the state; it accumulated through decades of extra-bureaucratic initiative. Assemblies, in particular, only functioned for two years during the Qing. They were an avenue for elite interests, but they would not have had much impact if they had not rested on public functional institutions, and if they had not been accompanied by voluntary organizations through which elites also expressed their interests. In other words, assemblies did not mobilize the elite, but they became a high-level institutional tool of an existing social mobilization.

The New Policies were introduced from above by the state, but their functioning reflected the mobilization of society. The combination enlarged the public sphere. During the 1900's there was a second wave of social reorganization that went beyond the institutional proliferation of the reconstruction period. The rapid addition of new institutions ensured that the public sphere would not only grow quantitatively through an increasing elaboration of the old institutional structures upon which managerial power had rested. Although the social momentum of the 1890's and the changes that were beginning to occur in elite class structure indicate that the upper classes would have generated new relationships with the state in any case, the New Policies hastened the progression from organization to political mobilization.

Under these circumstances, the expanded public sphere was neither under firm state control nor totally autonomous, just as members of the elite at the end of the Qing were neither totally dependent upon the state nor separate from it. Relationships were exceedingly complex and variable, and the convergence of state and societal momentum under rapidly evolving conditions opened numerous possibilities for either cooperation or conflict. The issue in the 1900's was not so much the latitude that the state would give members of the elite to pursue autonomous, private interests (although this factor certainly figured into disputes) as the relative roles of state and societal representatives in structuring political situations and building new institutions of government.

As the decade progressed, whatever possibilities had existed for cooperation and power-sharing were obscured by state-societal conflict. Insofar as the Qing New Policies combined centrally directed state-building with modernization, they were bound to run afoul of the aspirations of elite activists in Zhejiang. The new institutions, ideologies, and contexts amplified and reformulated older aspirations. Assertive, politically aware members of the elite could not accept bureaucratic monopolies over power, nor could they tolerate the intention of the government to solidify control at the top while it directed social mobilization. The result was not localistic separatism but a new range of political tensions between mobilizing elite activists and a more interventionist bureaucratic state. Competition for national leadership emerged alongside the institutional changes of the New Policies, and politicized mobilization, not self-government per se, brought down the Qing. These state-societal struggles would provide both the epitaph and the legacy of the bureaucratic monarchy, and they dwarfed the significance of local friction produced by the New Policies.

SEVEN

Political Conflict

Railway and Constitutionalist Movements in Zhejiang

The New Policies period began with a wave of modernizing, self-strengthening reformism. It ended in irreconcilable political conflict. During the 1890's political activity had broken through the stringent boundaries imposed by the centralized bureaucratic monarchy. It would be an exaggeration to say that by 1902 members of elites in Zhejiang had become generally politicized, but the press and leading activists (who had local ties even if they were not actually engaged in affairs at home) were aware of, and disturbed by, national events. A political purpose was inherent in their conviction that governmental policies had to be changed, leadership had to be broadened, and men outside the government had to take still wider initiatives for national reasons.

In effect, the overt, organized movements of the New Policies period combined the two long-term nineteenth-century trends toward societal organization and oppositionist political expression. They derived their strength from the previous organizational development, but they also reflected current internal and external threats and pressures. The ensuing political action repeatedly brought members of the elite in the economic cores of the Yangtze basin and Guangdong province into conflict with officials. Such clashes had a logic of their own, encouraging elite activists to expand their initiatives into more explicit demands for political participation. Governmental attempts to control these initiatives produced hostile reactions, but the main political impetus came from members of the elite themselves as they reached out for new roles and power. The already shaken consensus that had conferred legitimacy upon the Qing was thus quickly eroded. In less than ten years, men who had cooperated with officials to begin new ventures accepted the need for revolution.

The politics of the 1900's was not, however, only an extension of nineteenth-century trends. Both officials and oppositionist leaders had begun to make wide use of Western political theories and institutions that suited their purposes. Their conceptions of the roles of the government and the people in political relationships were changing. The new wave of societal organization during the New Policies further increased elite capacity to mobilize. Moreover, the scope of oppositionist politics was widened by the emergence of a small number of people whose educations and careers no longer bound them closely to old structures. They contributed a new radicalism and were a major element in the revolutionary parties. Perhaps most important of all, the coincidence of an assertive bureaucratic movement for modernization and controlled social mobilization from above with equally assertive societal initiatives from outside the state structure introduced political issues that could not have arisen earlier under the centralized bureaucratic monarchy.

It has been pointed out that the leading constitutionalist publicist, Liang Qichao, saw constitutionalism as a way to strengthen the country through popular participation, not as a guarantee of individual liberties.[1] This insight also applies to the elite political activists of the 1900's, who had absorbed many of the ideas rationalized and popularized in Liang's conceptions of citizenship. Railway activists and constitutionalists wanted to enlarge the private sector, but they also maintained that the private sector had public, nationalistic purposes that justified their demands for participation in government.

This combination was not simply a rationalization of private interests: the course pursued by the politically aroused members of the elite was shaped both by economic and social changes and by the history of state-societal interaction within the unitary structure of late imperial government. In part, their political activities may be understood in terms of Western liberal principles that supported bourgeois demands for freedom to pursue private interests. Their activities also expanded old Chinese ideas of the responsibility of educated men for state affairs, however, and they pressed further along the paths followed by nineteenth-century oppositionists. The widely used concept of citizenship was a logical step beyond the earlier ideas of participatory self-strengthening and carried with it a more aggressive and more politicized sense of social power. The logical conclusion that national power could result from an upward, converging flow of autonomous initiatives proved incompatible with the centralized integration from above that was increasingly envisioned by dominant officials and members of the Manchu court in Beijing.

There was no one pattern and certainly no firm plan on either side. In this fluid and fluctuating political process, there were often no hard lines between officials and non-officials—because of overlapping careers, personal ties, similar social backgrounds, and shared commitments to national reform and self-strengthening. Prestigious social leaders were often more reluctant than less important men to break with the government. Conflicts did, however, define different interests, and old acquaintances in different structural positions within and without the bureaucracy ended up on different sides of the fence.

These politics were epitomized by the constitutionalist and railway movements and by the clashes between provincial assembly members and officials. In Zhejiang the railway issue was particularly important in mobilizing members of the elite, but similar processes were at work with local variations throughout the economically advanced regions of the Yangtze Valley and southeast coast. They enabled elite activists to develop demands for representation and other forms of political power that led to a complete break with the government. Smaller, and often

localized nationalistic protests contributed to elite mobilization. Revolutionaries in the province contributed an unsuccessful but well publicized uprising in 1907. These largely elite
struggles took place against a disequilibrating background of
floods, food shortages, inflation, rice or anti-tax riots, banditry,
and local struggles for control. These kinds of socioeconomic
problems were also beginning to impinge upon elite consciousness in new ways and would contribute to political divisions
during the Republic. For the moment, however, they mainly increased feelings of uneasiness. The great issues of the decade
were the issues that brought mobilized members of the elite
into open confrontation with the existing system of government, ultimately destroying the balances between state and
elite society that had been established under the centralized
bureaucratic monarchy.

The Zhejiang Railway and Constitutionalist Leadership

The railway issue mobilized many members of the elite in
Zhejiang. Like the post-Taiping reconstruction, the patriotic
manifestations of the 1880's and 1890's, and the early reform
endeavors after the Sino Japanese War, this mobilization rested
on an expanding social organization and a spontaneous initiative that had no single leader. Nonetheless, the most influential organizations of the decade were headed by high-level,
personally interconnected members of the elite who formed
horizontal networks similar to the networks of earlier macroregional activists. Shanghai had become the center of the new
politics in the region, but members of the Zhejiangese elite
who migrated there still retained their home ties. They now included a few modern professionals, however, and more promoters of modern industry and banking, raising again the question of the role of the bourgeoisie in the 1911 Revolution.

In the continuing debate over the bourgeoisie's revolutionary
role, there is general agreement that there was a small urban
capitalist class by the beginning of the twentieth century. The
issue is whether it was politically potent. It has been argued
that the Chinese bourgeoisie was still very weak and was timid

therefore in pressing its demands. A decade later, in the favorable international environment of the late 1910's and early 1920's, the bourgeoisie gained a somewhat firmer place on the national political stage, but 1911 came too soon for it to have much political impact.[2] The corollary is that the political leaders at the end of the Qing emerged from the gentry class. This gentry influence has been interpreted in different ways. Some historians have seen it as the conservative, racist reaction of a basically static class. Others have seen members of the gentry interacting with newly educated men and people with new kinds of wealth to form an aggressive, new political force.[3]

Other authors have argued that an emergent bourgeoisie, which is broadly defined to include professionals and intellectuals, was a basic political force during the last Qing decade. It was comparable in size to the French and English bourgeoisies of the seventeenth and eighteenth centuries. Regardless of whether bourgeois Chinese actually joined the revolutionary parties, the 1911 Revolution reflected their nationalistic and autonomous (usually termed anti-feudal by Chinese Marxists) interests.[4]

Indeed, a general surge of elite opposition to the government in the southern and central cores encompassed both the constitutionalist and the revolutionary movement. It seems difficult to call the ensuing revolution bourgeois, however—in part because such a broad range of elites were involved, but also because China did not subsequently have a general capitalist revolution. The immediate question is how an opposition strong enough to overthrow the existing political system could emerge from the changing combinations of old and new elements in elite society. Data on the officers and directors of the Zhejiang Railway Company and on the members of the Society to Prepare for Constitutional Government (yubei lixian gonghui) in Shanghai give us an idea of the composition of the macroregional elite that furnished oppositionist leaders (see Tables 20–22). Here I will only look at Zhejiangese, but the data on Jiangsu men are similar, and leading figures in the two provinces were often intimate.[5]

The merchants among the railway founders and directors included some of the richest businessmen residing in Shanghai—men like Zhou Jinbao, Li Houyou, Yan Xinhou, and Yu Xiaqing, who had made fortunes during the mid-to-late nineteenth century. Most were already involved in industry or banking. Some were also the leaders of the three most important Shanghai guilds: Ningbo (*siming gongsuo*), old-style banking, and silk. The considerable number of men from Ningbo reflected the prominence of that prefecture in the Shanghai trade. Typically, these men had purchased degrees or been awarded honorary rank, but they also enjoyed prestige based on their business success. Several were compradors, but even these men had numerous business interests that made them relatively independent of specific foreign ties. Nor did they depend upon official connections. Even though three of the founders had been connected with the China Merchants Steam Navigation Company, and Zhou Jinbiao was director of the Chinese Telegraph, only Shen Dunhe (who did not maintain a strong connection with the railway company) was intimately associated with the system of official supervision and merchant management. Because of their autonomous business activities, they were similar to modern European capitalists; some continued to pursue their interests during the Republic as members of the Zhejiang Financial Clique.[6] In the early 1900's, however, they were still, like the older gentry and merchant elite, closely tied to familial and local interests, and they still had not completely divorced their business prominence from status conferred by the government.

The gentry railway founders also demonstrate the continuing interpenetration of merchants and gentry and underline the importance of status conferred by the old regime. Some, like Vice President Liu Jinzao, came from prominent merchant families; others acquired business interests during the first decade of the twentieth century. These gentry were as prominent as the merchant directors. Most had *jinshi* degrees, all had served in the metropolitan bureaucracy, and five of nine gentry listed in Table 20 had been members of the Hanlin Academy. They were connected by ties arising from the examination sys-

TABLE 20

Founders and First Officers, Zhejiang Railway Company, 1906–1907

Name	District	Degree	Office	Business/profession	Public activities	Guild	Political activities
Fan Fen	Zhenhai			Shipping, other, Ningbo, Shanghai	Welfare, schools, Shanghai, Ningbo	SMGS, NLTH	Blockade running, Sino-French War
Fan Gongxu	Renhe	jinshi 1871	Hanlin, ed. commissioner		CC pres.; welfare; Sericult. Inst., Hangzhou		Protest closing yanliu, 1885
Hu Shandeng	Yuyao			Banks	CC, Shanghai	Qianzhuang, Shanghai	
Li Houyou	Zhenhai			Shipping, banks	CC, City Council, Shanghai		U.S. boycott, 1905
Liu Jinzao	Guian	jinshi 1894	Board sec'y, reader, Grand Secretariat	Silk	Various, Nanxun		Anti-missionary
Shen Cengtong	Jiaxing	jinshi 1886	Hanlin				Didang, 1898 Reform, Anti-Boxer
Shen Dunhe	Yin		Customs daotai, Shanghai	Insurance, silk, guandu shangban	CC, Shanghai, welfare	SMGS, NLTH pres.	
Shi Ziying	Tong-xiang			Silk, banking, CMSNC		Silk, pres., Shanghai	U.S. boycott, 1905
Sun Tinghan	Zhuji	jinshi 1891	Hanlin		Zhejiang Ed. Assoc. pres., 1909; ZLTH, pres. 1909		
Sun Yirang	Ruian	juren 1867	Board sec'y 1885; Wen-Chu ed. bur.; consultant, Xuebu 1906	Mining, steamship cos., Juian	Schools, Ruian, etc.; CC Ruian, pres.; Agr. Assoc., Ruian; Zhejiang Ed. Assoc., pres., 1906		Didang/Qingliu connections, 1898 Reform

Name	Native place	Degree	Official career	Business	Public/education	Guild	Activities
Tang Shouqian	Shanyin	jinshi 1892	Hanlin, magistrate, salt intendant	Several modern cos.; editor, *Jingshi bao* 1897	Sericult. Inst., Hangzhou, 1898; schools, Hangzhou		Didang, 1898 Reform, Anti-Boxer, U.S. Anti-Boxer, U.S. boycott 1905, YLG v.-pres., 1911 Rev.
Wang Kangnian	Qiantang	jinshi 1892	Sec'y, Grand Secretariat, 1904	Editor, *Shiwu bao, Zhongwai ribao*	Education, Hangzhou 1895–98		Anti-Boxer, 1898 Reform
Xie Lunhui	Yuyao			Banking	School, Yuyao	Qianzhuang, Shanghai	U.S. boycott, 1905
Yan Xinhou	Ciqi		Supply gov't troops, Taiping	Banking; CMSNC; various, Shanghai, Ningbo, etc.	CC pres., Shanghai; famine relief, 1880s	SMGS	Anti-Russia, 1903
Yu Xiaqing	Zhenhai			Comprador, banking, various business	CC, Shanghai	NLTH	1911 Revolution
Zhang Meiyou				nanyang gongxue			
Zhang Yuanji	Haiyan	jinshi 1892	Hanlin	Publishing, editing: *Dongfang zazhi*, Commercial Press	Education, Haiyan		Dicang, 1898 Reform, Guohui 1900, YLG
Zhou Jinbiao	Ciqi			China Teleg., banking, silk, etc., Shanghai, Ningbo	CC, Shanghai	SMGS	U.S. boycott 1905, Debt Redemp. 1909, YLG
Zhu Peizhen	Dinghai			Comprador, other business	CC, City Council v.-pres., Shanghai	SMGS	U.S. boycott 1905, 1911 Revolution

SOURCES: Sources for Table 20 are at the end of the notes for this chapter, on p. 381. Note that information on public and political activities and guild membership is less complete than for other categories because sources give poorer coverage. Career information is given through 1912.

ABBREVIATIONS: CC, Chamber of Commerce. CMSNC, China Merchants' Steam Navigation Co. NLTH, *Ningbo lu-Hu tongxiang hui*. SMGS, *siming gongsuo*. YLG, *yubei lixian gonghui*. ZLTH: *Zhejiang lu-Hu tongxiang hui*.

TABLE 21

Selected Officers and Directors, Zhejiang Railway Company, 1908–1911

Name	District	Degree	Office	Business/ profession	Public activities	Guild	Political activities
Chen Chunlan, dir. 1911	Shanyin			Comprador, oil, banks, hides			
Chen Wei v. pres. 1910	Shanyin	juren 1906[a]	Metropolitan bureaucracy	Engineer			
Chu Chengbo auditor 1910	Haiyan	jinshi 1880	Daotai				1898 Reform, Anti-Jap. demonstr. Hangzhou, 1910
Hu Huan dir. 1910–11	Hangzhou	juren		Banks, industry, Hangzhou	School		
Jiang Honglin dir. 1910	Hangzhou			Banks			
Jiang Ruzao dir. 1910	Guian	juren 1903					1898 Reform
Shen Mingqing dir. 1908–11	Jiaxing		2d class Board sec'y	Banks			
Sheng Bingwei v. pres. 1910	Zhenhai	jinshi 1880	Hanlin, ed. official		Ningbo Ed. Assoc.; schools, Ningbo, Zhenhai		
Su Debiao dir. 1909–10	Ningbo				CC, dir., Shanghai 1911	Assoc. Ningbo merchants, Shanghai	U.S. boycott, 1905
Wang Lian auditor 1910	Dinghai			Coal	School, Ningbo	Assoc. Ningbo merchants, Shanghai	1911 Revolution
Wang Xirong dir. c.1910	Hangzhou	fusheng	Board sec'y	Banks	CC v. pres., Hangzhou		Constitutional agitation 1910, Anti-Jap. demonstr. Hangzhou, 1910

Name	Native place	Degree	Official position	Business	Educational assoc.	Guild/political
Wu Zhenchun dir. 1909	Hangzhou	*jinshi* 1898	Hanlin	Educator, supt. Zhe higher school, 1907–9	Zhe Ed. Assoc. pres., 190?	
Xu Guannan dir. 1910	Tongxiang			Silk, banks		Silk
Yan Yibin dir. 1908–10	Ciqi			Diversified family business		SMGS
Yao Mulian dir. c.1910	Jiaxing			Dir. China Teleg., silk, sugar, dry goods, Shanghai, etc.		
Ye Jingkui auditor 1910	Hangzhou			Banks		
Ye Youxin dir. 1911	Zhenhai			Banks, diversified family business, Shanghai, etc.		SMGS
Zhou Xiangling auditor 1910	Huzhou					Assoc. of Huzhou Natives in Hangzhou, SGH
Zhu Fushen dir.	Haiyan	*jinshi* 1886	Censor, Ed. Com.	Banks, shipping, Manchurian land development		YLG, 1911 Revolution

SOURCES: Sources for Table 21 are at the end of the notes for this chapter, on p. 383. Note that information on public and political activities and guild membership in particular is incomplete because of fragmentary sources.

ABBREVIATIONS: CC, Chamber of Commerce. SGH, *shangxue gonghui, Hangzhou*. SMGS *siming gongsuo*. YLG, *yubei lixian gonghui*.

*Returned student.

258 *Political Conflict*

TABLE 22
Social Characteristics of Zhejiangese Members of
the Society to Prepare for Constitutional
Government, 1906

Social group	Number
Businessmen/capitalists/merchants	20
Gentry/ex-officials	21[a]
School graduates/gentry/professionals	9
Indeterminate merchant or gentry	8
TOTAL	58[b]

SOURCE: Zhejiang sheng Xinhai geming, pp. 210–22.
[a]The available sources show that at least 12 of these men had modern business interests.
[b]Zhejiangese constituted 25 percent of the total membership of 233 from all provinces. The average age of the 33 Zhejiangese members with known ages was 41. Three became members of the Zhejiang Provincial Assembly, and at least 18 became officers, directors, or political supporters of the Zhejiang railway.

tem and their experiences in office. Such ties did not guarantee cooperation, but networks derived from the bureaucracy often unified the leadership of the railway.

Subsequent company officers (Table 21) continued to fit into this general pattern. At least through 1911 almost all came from the core districts of the five northern prefectures. At least four more *jinshi*, two of them from the Hanlin Academy, became officers or directors. Many of the new men were relatives or close friends of the original promoters. Yan Xinhou's son became a director in 1908, and a member of the Ye merchant and banking family from Zhenhai was added in 1911. Liu Jinzao involved other members of the wealthy, interconnected merchant-gentry families of Nanxun town, and one of them, Jiang Ruzao, became a director. Merchant members of the board of directors often had banking interests, and some literati members had moved into professions. However, only Chen Wei, elected vice president in 1910, had received a new-style education. In general the gentry railway leaders, like the merchants, remained close to their origins in the elite of the late imperial period.

The Society to Prepare for Constitutional Government shows more clearly the political emergence of men in new professional occupations, although they still constituted a minority (Table 22). Otherwise, the social backgrounds of members of this society confirm the existence of personal connections and organizational ties between merchants and gentry and underline their mutual political and economic interests. The large number of merchant members shows that businessmen did not hold themselves aloof from issues of government and politics. The considerable overlap between society members and railway activists suggests the connections between economic enterprise and demands for political participation that appeared repeatedly during the next five years.[7] Cooperation between these men was not limited to the railway and constitutionalist organizations. Several merchants were members of the same guild. They did business with one another and joined to form other corporations. Tang Shouqian, Zhou Jinbiao, Zhu Peizhen, Fan Fen, Li Houyou, and Yan Xinhou, for instance, joined Zhang Jian in founding modern companies.[8] New Policies institutions and philanthropy in either Shanghai or Hangzhou were other arenas of cooperation. There was an indication of competition between Ningbo and Jiangnan factions within the railway company as pressures mounted in 1909–11, but mutual interests generally outweighed native place loyalties.

The railway and constitutionalist leaders were products of both the processes that were altering elite class structures during the late Qing: first, the fusion of gentry and merchants, and, later, the incipient refragmentation of the late imperial elites. They also illustrate two other major trends, which can not be pinpointed in terms of social class although they indicate social change. One was organizational growth. These leaders came from the activist, managerial segment of the macroregional elite.[9] They cooperated with one another in philanthropy, education, and New Policies institutions as well as business and politics.

The other trend was the expansion of oppositionist politics. A striking number of the leading gentry organizers of the Zhejiang and Jiangsu railways emerged from the militant patriotic movements in the bureaucracy during the 1880's and 1890's.[10] In the Zhejiang railway, President Tang Shouqian and directors

Zhang Yuanji and Shen Cengtong had been members of the "Emperor's Faction." Vice President Liu Jinzao had passed the *jinshi* examinations with Zhang Jian (an "Emperor's Faction" member). Fan Gongxu's militant record went back to the Sino-French War. The Jiangsu railway under Zhang Jian tapped this same source of disillusioned officials. The large number of Hanlin academicians in both companies is thus not surprising, because this institution had been a breeding ground for frustrated oppositionism in the nineteenth century—whether specifically connected to the "Emperor's Faction" or not.[11]

The same oppositionist background contributed to ties with railway companies in adjoining provinces. The Fujian railway president, Chen Baochen, had been a member of the militant Pure Current (*qingliu*) of the 1880's and had maintained social contacts with militant officials after being forced to retire after the Sino-French War. The honorary president of the Jiangxi railway, Chen Sanli, had also been a member of the "Emperor's Faction."[12] Thus railways in four adjacent provinces were led by men whose political positions had first been shaped in oppositionist circles within the metropolitan bureaucracy. In late 1905 railway representatives of these provinces and Anhui formed a society to coordinate company regulations and policies.[13]

It is difficult to determine just how important the nineteenth-century oppositionist heritage was below the top leaders. The provincial movement in Zhejiang (and Jiangsu) continued to absorb men who left office because of their doubts about government policy. The transfer of the oppositionist drive from the metropolitan bureaucracy to the provinces contributed to political organization in the Lower Yangtze. Such organization, in turn, offered more alternatives to the discontented and provided new potential routes back to Beijing. At the same time, new nationalistic and anti-governmental movements were forging other ties between older oppositionists and younger political figures. The inclusion of the older men postponed the break between constitutionalists and the center. Like wealthy merchants who had capital to protect, these high-status oppositionists were slow to reject the political system to which they had initially owed their social position. Instead, they wished to change it so that they would have more leverage in the capital.

On the other hand, they widened the range of political opposition within Zhejiang. Although historians have focused on Zhang Jian as the prototype of the "gentry-industrialist," there were actually many less famous "Zhang Jians" among the members of the Lower Yangtze elite. Demands for representation and autonomy were linked through them to older patriotic impulses and doubts about centralized autocracy that were embedded in Zhejiang scholarly society. This was not merely a backward pull. During a time of rapid change, such attitudes were held by men who were active in the new public spheres but not necessarily comfortable with the latest theories and Western styles espoused by radicals and younger professionals and constitutionalists. These oppositionist tracks merged in the railway and constitutionalist conflicts, and therefore more members of the elite supported the new movements than would have done so if these movements had only represented the interests of the new urban capitalists.

The flamboyant president of the Zhejiang railway, Tang Shouqian, personified the interaction of new and old oppositionist trends with the different manifestations of social change in Zhejiang.[14] Tang came from a moderately well-off Shaoxing family of farmers, traders, and scholars. His father, who had a local reputation for righteousness, filial piety, and humanitarianism, studied the classics, taught in his home village, and was active in relief and rehabilitation after the Taiping Rebellion. Thereafter, he served as a private secretary of a lineage member who was an official in Shenxi. Tang succeeded brilliantly in the examinations, becoming a *jinshi* in 1892 and entering the Hanlin Academy, but his official career was disjointed and brief. He served short terms as a magistrate in 1895 and a salt intendant in 1903. Although it has been suggested that he did very well financially in such potentially lucrative posts, little is actually known about his official service. He never remained long in office and declined appointments years before becoming involved in the railway movement. His resignations and his well-publicized solicitude for his parents' health are suggestive of late nineteenth-century eremitism. He was associated with the oppositionist "Emperor's Faction" before the Sino-Japanese War, and his tract *Words of Warning* (*Weiyan*) placed him among those early Westernizing reformers who were critical of bureaucratic autocracy.

By the late 1890's, Tang had many acquaintances in Hangzhou and Shanghai. He had worked with reformers from Wenzhou on the *Journal of Statecraft* (*Jingshi bao*) and had taught briefly at the academy founded by prominent members of the merchant-gentry elite of Nanxun town. He had also been involved in negotiating the agreement with England to keep the Boxer hostilities out of the Yangtze Valley.[15] Tang's numerous contacts and his strong reputation as a reformer lay behind his election as president of the Zhejiang Railway Company a few years later. Tang helped found several other companies; he was a vice president of the Society to Prepare for Constitutional Government and a leader of the privately sponsored movement to redeem China's foreign debt. From 1906 to 1911, however, his public image was inseparable from the image of the railway. Unlike Zhang Jian in Jiangsu, he declined a seat in the provincial assembly and devoted himself to railway affairs. Whatever his abilities as an administrator, Tang's great popularity with most of the elite in Zhejiang rested on his image as a hero battling evil officials in Beijing on behalf of the people, the province, and the country. This popularity led to his selection as the first civil governor in Zhejiang after the revolution and his appointment as minister of communications in the Nanjing provisional government headed by Sun Yat-sen.

Tang did not find a position from which he could exercise political power after the 1911 Revolution, however. He was honored and rewarded by the new government in Beijing and at least acquiesced to the nationalization of the Zhejiang railway in 1914. Even so, he evidently did not fully trust President Yuan Shikai. After he left the Nanjing government, his decision to travel to Southeast Asia to confer with overseas Chinese may have been a way to remove himself from unappealing political situations that he could not control. He died in 1916 without seeing any consummation of the great influence he had achieved in Zhejiang before 1911.

Organization for National Goals

The Zhejiang railway, its counterpart in Jiangsu, and the Society to Prepare for Constitutional Government were major products of the renewed mobilization of Lower Yangtze elites after 1900. The circumstances of their organization were affected both by the Qing New Policies and by sharpened business competition with foreigners after the Sino-Japanese War. When the railways were first founded, they were neither strictly private ventures nor oppositionist political organizations. Rather they claimed to be autonomously organized, public-spirited enterprises run by socially acknowledged provincial leaders for national purposes.

The Zhejiang railway was established by a specific group of gentry and merchants, who defended their business interests against other provincial and foreign groups, identified their goals with those of nationalistic public opinion, and sought official backing and diplomatic support.[16] Interest in railway construction dated back to 1897, when the Ningbo businessman Li Houyou and others petitioned the governor for permission to build a short line connecting Hangzhou city with its port on the Qiantang River.[17] This project never materialized, and in 1898 the prominent self-strengthening official Sheng Xuanhuai negotiated a concession giving the British and Chinese Corporation the right to finance and construct a line from Suzhou to Ningbo via Hangzhou. A British engineer made a preliminary survey in 1898, but no further action was taken. A few years later, Zhejiangese plans for a provincial railway began to take shape amid rising foreign interest in railways and mines and growing resistance to foreign investment within Zhejiang and other provinces.

In 1903 Japanese and German groups approached Zhejiangese merchants with plans for joint railway development,[18] and a Hangzhou businessman received permission to arrange a loan with a British syndicate to form a company to mine coal and iron in several prefectures.[19] These foreign incursions led to protest meetings by Chinese students in Japan and encouraged Li Houyou and his associates to revive the idea of a short line at Hangzhou. They enlisted support from Zhejiangese officials in Beijing to block other plans and began to put pressure on the Ministry of Communications to repudiate the 1898 agreement with Great Britain.[20]

Little progress in actually organizing a company was made during 1904, but there was nationalistic resistance to other foreign businesses. Backers of provincial railways in both Zhejiang and Jiangsu took part in the campaign against the concession to an American syndicate to construct a Canton-Hanzhou line in 1904–5.[21] Some were involved in opposition to the British-backed Shanghai-Nanjing railway in 1905. During the same year some were active in the boycott of American goods to protest exclusion of Chinese immigrants by the United States.[22] In Hangzhou there were protests against a new attempt to conclude a mining agreement with foreigners.[23]

Formation of the Zhejiang Railway Company was precipitated in 1905 by the news that a representative of an American corporation was trying to enlist support among Hangzhou merchants and gentry for a loan to construct a line from the provincial capital to the Jiangxi border.[24] Members of the original railway group thereupon petitioned the governor and appealed to their friends among officials in Beijing. The high-ranking gentry among the railway founders were able to secure strong backing among Zhejiangese officials. In 1905 memorials supporting establishment of the company came from such major officials as Grand Councillor Wang Wenshao, President of the Board of Punishments Ge Baohua, and board vice president Shen Jiaben. Additional backing came from middle and lower-level metropolitan literati-officials, including Sun Yirang's old friend Huang Shaoji, Zhu Xien (a censor who had received his *jinshi* degree with Zhang Jian and Liu Jinzao and came from the same district as director Zhang Yuanji), and Hanlin academician Shen Wei (who had also graduated with Zhang and Liu).[25]

On July 22 about 160 Zhejiangese, including representatives of each prefecture, metropolitan officials, and students in Japan, met in Shanghai to discuss ways to discourage foreign business, collect funds, and construct railways. During the next month Tang Shouqian and Liu Jinzao were elected president and vice president of the company, and railway supporters requested the government to repudiate the agreement with Britain. The court backed these initiatives. Tang's election as president was followed by an imperial edict appointing him to that position and awarding him fourth official rank. Then on October 27 Sheng Xuanhuai was ordered to abrogate the 1898 concession.[26] The first stockholders' meeting in the fall of 1906 authorized a railway school and a bank with prefectural branches to handle capital funds and sell stock, and it called for an investigation of coal resources.[27]

Most of the initial capital was raised from large investors, including some of the organizers and officers.[28] The involvement of very rich merchants and bankers in the railway ensured the company of its initial capital but also meant that stock would be expensive. Full shares cost one hundred yuan, and, although fractional shares were available at ten yuan, the subscribers were likely to be rich. Nonetheless, organizers made an effort to generate public support through meetings and telegrams. The Shanghai press, especially the recently founded *Shi bao* (*The Times*), whose publisher, Di Baoxian, was a director of the Jiangsu railway, helped to spread a favorable picture of both companies. Meetings of officials in Beijing and students in Tokyo, as well as meetings of gentry and merchants and "gentry and teachers" in Hangzhou, had backed the idea of a provincial railway before the company was established.[29] Broadening elite support soon affected company procedures and regulations. The Xingye Bank, which was established to handle railway company funds, set out to sell shares in every prefecture, and the first stockholders' meeting in 1906 somewhat modified the company's highly restrictive voting regulations.[30] Thus the railway company was not a tightly held corporation even at the beginning. Statements made by supporters when the railway was organized pictured it as a widely supported public enterprise. Such rhetoric foreshadowed the rationales put forth when plans were thwarted a year later.[31]

Meanwhile, a closely related group in Jiangsu laid plans for its own railway company after failing to block the British loan to build the Shanghai-Nanjing line in 1904–5. The Jiangsu Railway Company was formally organized in the spring of 1906, with the recently retired vice president of the Ministry of Commerce, Wang Qingmu, as president. Zhang Jian and the former consul to Belgium Xu Dinglin were vice presidents.[32] This company also held its first stockholders' meeting in the fall of 1906, and the two railways held ground-breaking ceremonies for a jointly constructed line from Shanghai to Hangzhou early in 1907.[33] Besides their own opposition to foreign investment in the Lower Yangtze, the Zhejiang and Jiangsu leaders were well aware of the successful movement in Hunan and Guangdong to redeem the right to construct the Canton-Hangzhou railway line.[34] Provincial railway development was very much in the air, and the companies were determined to carry out their plans without British interference.

As the railway companies were getting under way, much the same group of people began to organize for constitutional government. The Society to Prepare for Constitutional Government held its first meeting on December 16, 1906, under the presidency of the long-time foreign affairs expert Zheng Xiaoxu. Zhang Jian and Tang Shouqian were vice presidents. Jiangsu railway president Wang Qingmu and two vice presidents of the companies, Liu Jinzao and Xu Dinglin, were also members. Li Houyou, Zhang Yuanji, and Fan Fen from Zhejiang and Li Zhongjue, Yang Tingdong, and Wang Tongyu from Jiangsu were among the many other railway promoters in the society.[35]

There is little doubt that these men linked the issues of constitutional government and economic enterprise. The society's inaugural statement pictured constitutionalism as a remedy for the political gulf created by elevating superiors and debasing inferiors. Securer rights and protection from harsh punishment would enable the people below to take responsibility upon themselves instead of simply following orders. Constitutionalism would also mitigate the pursuit of personal profit that led to official corruption and merchant willingness to yield economic rights to foreigners. The society intended to promote the study and debate of the government's domestic and foreign policies and to foster industry to "develop the people's livelihood."[36] These new elite initiatives, in which nationalism and mechanisms to express public opinion appeared as two sides of the same coin, suggested an ambiguous relationship to the central government. The society took its name from a recent imperial edict that instructed the gentry and the people to prepare for the implementation of constitutional government, but its members added a critique of autocracy. The balance between established authority and nationalistic initiative was inherently delicate.

The railway companies were a practical test of whether state and societal initiatives could be combined, and initially there was cooperation between the companies and the government. The companies needed official sanction; equally important, they required governmental support to terminate the railway concession to Britain. Officials wanted to promote modernization, and such leading policy-makers as the Board of Commerce president, Zaizhen, and his father, Prince Qing, were inclined to back provincial railways to keep out foreigners. Moreover, Zhang Zhidong, who had joined forces with members of provincial elites in Guangdong and Hunan against the Chinese-American Development Corporation, had good relations with Lower Yangtze leaders.[37] Company officials even cooperated with their future adversary Sheng Xuanhuai, who had been ordered in 1903 to inform the British that the concession would be void if construction did not start within six months.

Their cordiality began to fade as the loan problem proved intractable. The British minister, Sir John Jordan, did not think that the Chinese companies could build a railway. He believed that, although Prince Qing said he "feared" public opinion, he was using it to negotiate better terms.[38] Jordan was therefore determined to stand firm in defending British interests and did not realize how committed the railway founders were to constructing the line without foreign capital. On the other hand, Sheng Xuanhuai may never have told the Zhejiangese that Britain had decisively refused to give up the 1898 concession.[39] By

1905 railway leaders were criticizing Sheng for making concessions to foreigners, and public pressure began to be applied
through meetings and petitions as it became clearer that the
British would not yield easily.[40]

Caught between the British and the provincial companies,
Chinese officials were divided and uncertain in the inconclu-
sive negotiations of 1906–7. Any hope that one or another
party might lose interest if discussions dragged on indefinitely
disappeared in the summer of 1907, when the British government insisted on serious talks. Former ambassador to England
and Vice Minister of Foreign Affairs Wang Daxie then negotiated a loan agreement without consulting provincial leaders.
Although the Ministry of Foreign Affairs worried about the
best method to conciliate the people of Jiangsu and Zhejiang,[41]
the government seems to have been unprepared for the furor
created by the edict of October 10 announcing the agreement
with Great Britain.[42]

Political Mobilization: The Anti-Loan Movement

1907 was indeed a year that officials in Zhejiang might have
wished to forget. Food shortages caused by severe flooding in
the Yangtze basin led to riots and unrest. In July the woman
revolutionary Qiu Jin led an unsuccessful rising in Shaoxing.
Then furious agitation against the railway loan erupted in the
fall. Had the last two events coincided, the government's situation might have been even more difficult. As it was, the loan
issue decisively politicized elite activists and brought the macroregional leadership into closer cooperation with other elites in
the province. Whatever chance there was for serious collaboration between social activists and the central bureaucracy
foundered in 1907 so far as the Lower Yangtze was concerned.
Thereafter, political mobilization continued through cumulative conflicts with the government.

Some accounts of the anti-loan agitation have stressed its
broad social resistance to imperialism by pointing to the participation of gentry, merchants, students, army officers, wom-
en, shopkeepers, workers, and overseas Chinese. Others have

stressed its bourgeois character.[43] In fact it was more than a narrow bourgeois struggle, but it fell short of a nationalistic union of all classes. Agitation was located mainly in the core districts of the five northern prefectures and Wenzhou, which were already centers of elite organization. Although some upper gentry and students from the southwest and south were involved, the railway question had little impact in those areas.[44] On the other hand, there are records of participation down to the level of prosperous market towns within the core districts. Members of local elites in such places often had direct ties to both the railway company[45] and activists in metropolitan centers.

Even in the core districts, there is no record of peasant involvement. In the large cities the lower classes learned of the loan issue either by word of mouth or by placards urging people to resist the danger to China.[46] Over two thousand sedan bearers in Hangzhou held a meeting at which they pooled small individual contributions to buy shares in the railway, and there is a mention of workers who contributed in the city of Ningbo. Much of the lower-class participation may, however, have come from workers at schools or businesses where students or merchants were involved in the agitation.[47] Such incidental occurrences were not widespread enough to alter the elitist character of the movement.

The elites that took part in the movement were far from monolithic. Diverse economic and political interests were activated by the railway movement. Nevertheless, the participants acted as nationalists, not as members of interest groups. Again and again, the anti-loan literature pointed to the organic unity of Zhejiang and the rest of the country, the merging of social elements into a single citizenry, the interdependence of individuals and country, and the need for joint action to galvanize the government to resist foreign encroachment.[48] Patriotism could not dispel class barriers, but it could weld different segments of the elite into an oppositional force by bringing out their mutual differences with the government. The anti-loan movement can thus be seen as a representative of the series of state-societal conflicts that culminated in the 1911 Revolution. It calls attention to the important role that people who have been called constitutionalists played in this political process, but it also suggests that this is too narrow a term. What has been called constitutionalism was one manifestation of a broad elite political mobilization arising from the factors that we have seen affecting relationships between government and elite society during the late Qing.[49]

Political methods. The loan opponents angrily confronted the government and used provocative rhetoric, but their opposition was largely non-violent. Most of the gentry and merchants, professionals, and New Policies managers involved in the dispute were reluctant to use force. The Qing government still appeared formidable, and, at least at the outset, there were hopes that it might be persuaded to listen to public opinion. Therefore loan opponents held meetings and established organizations. They sought to assure the railway companies of their support, to mobilize public opinion, to convey popular opposition to officials through telegrams and letters,[50] and to demonstrate their ability to raise large sums of capital. Similar demonstrations took place in Jiangsu. Although natives of each province supported their own railway and only rarely invested in the company of the other province, it was a single anti-loan movement. Leaders coordinated their plans, and events in both provinces received detailed coverage and support from the Shanghai press. Railway companies, schools, associations, and newspapers in still other provinces gave moral support to the Jiangsu and Zhejiang companies.[51] Metropolitan officials from the two provinces sought repudiation of the loan. New Policies institutions and voluntary associations in the provinces provided ready-made foundations for political organization. Even though most of the leaders resided in Shanghai or Hangzhou, spontaneous meetings and demonstrations soon occurred in other cities and towns.

The first reaction in Zhejiang to the loan was a meeting of a few hundred gentry and merchants in the provincial educational association offices on October 22, immediately after the railway companies received the news from the Association of Zhejiangese Natives in Beijing. The meeting established the Zhejiangese Citizen's Association to Oppose the Loan Treaty

(*Zhejiang guomin jukuan hui*), which then elected officers, drafted a statement opposing the loan, telegraphed railway companies in other provinces, requested the governor to memorialize against the loan, and sent out public announcements of a major demonstration to be held on November 25. Elite leaders in each district were requested to send two to ten representatives chosen from gentry, merchants, students, and the army.[52]

Almost constant protests followed during the next month. One hundred fifty-eight prominent gentry from all eleven prefectures signed a petition for the governor to forward to Beijing. Prefectural anti-loan associations were established. Meetings were held by numerous schools and functional associations. In Ningbo seventeen schools combined to establish one organization.[53] A week later students and teachers at the Zhejiang higher school called a joint meeting of over thirty Hangzhou schools to establish the United Association of Zhejiangese Schools to Oppose the Loan Treaty. This group, which described itself as an auxiliary of the merchant-gentry organization, held frequent meetings, established connections with schools outside Hangzhou, developed its own fund-raising apparatus, and made its own banking arrangements.[54]

Since Hangzhou was both the provincial capital and a large city, protests there were to be expected. Activities in Jiaxing give us an idea of what was going on in smaller cities and towns, although here, too, protests may have been particularly frequent because the prefecture was highly commercialized and surrounded the projected railway line. Telegrams were sent from the prefectural city to the governor, the Ministry of Agriculture, Industry and Commerce, the Ministry of Foreign Affairs and the railway company by "gentry," the chamber of commerce, "student circles," the middle school, and an individual *juren*.[55] On November 3 the superintendent of the normal school (a man active in several New Policies organizations) called a meeting of students and scholars, who elected two delegates to the forthcoming Hangzhou demonstration.[56] That afternoon the chairman of the chamber of commerce (a *shengyuan* closely related to a retired Hanlin academician who was also active in the railway movement) called another meeting, which elected three more representatives with strongly reformist or radical backgrounds.[57] On November 8 and 10 there were meetings to sell railway shares at the middle school and the normal school.[58] An anti-loan association was organized, and on November 15 a mass meeting of over twelve hundred merchants, gentry, and students was headed by essentially the same group of organizers: the president of the chamber of commerce, the principal of the middle school, and the head of a leading local bank.[59]

Outside the prefectural city, gentry in Pinghu district telegraphed the prefectural chamber of commerce. In Shimen the chamber of commerce telegraphed the Ministry of Foreign Affairs, and a meeting to protect the railway was attended by six hundred people. An anti-loan association was established in the market town of Fengjing in Jiashan district. The chamber of commerce of Japu in Haiyan telegraphed the Ministry of Agriculture, Industry and Commerce, and members of the elite in the town of Wangdian telegraphed the provincial anti-loan association.[60]

Several characteristics of the agitation in Jiaxing appeared in other parts of the province. The agitation was led by prominent managers of new schools and functional associations, and it attracted sizable numbers of students, gentry, and merchants. Meetings also brought forth less-established men like the future provincial assembly vice president Chu Fucheng, who first moved into provincial-level politics as one of the representatives elected by the Jiaxing chamber of commerce. When members of district city and market town elites demonstrated against the loan, they reacted as quickly as the leaders in larger cities. They formed their own associations and telegraphed high officials. Managers of new institutions were thus drawn into overt political activity, and new political leaders were defined. The new sphere of management was also delineated more clearly, because older kinds of public organizations were not involved in these political activities.

Zhejiangese outside the province held meetings at native place associations or guilds and helped encourage support from other provinces.[61] Students in Shanghai, in Japan, and at Beijing University held meetings.[62] These meetings were climaxed by a gathering of several thousand Zhejiangese in Shanghai under the chairmanship of railway director Zhou Jinbiao,[63] a stockholders' meeting in Shanghai a few days later,[64] and the Hangzhou meeting on November 25.

It seems quite possible that several tens of thousands of Zhejiangese attended anti-loan meetings in late October and November. The emotional level was raised by the protest suicides of an assistant engineer of the railway company and a student at the railway school, and some meetings became unruly.[65] For the most part, however, the demonstrations were orderly attempts to show the seriousness of responsible opposition and put pressure on officials to repudiate the loan. Although not altogether successful, participation in the demonstrations did much to politicize elite-run organizations in Zhejiang (see Table 23). Ad hoc anti-loan associations faded after the loan issue became less pressing, but successors were established under similar leadership in subsequent crises.[66] Both ongoing local New Policies institutions and old-style private native place associations acted as adjuncts of the oppositionist movement rather than as instruments of bureaucratic control. Many members of the elite participated in forming organizations, electing officers and representatives, and expressing opposition to the loan. The movement could not be sustained at the level of the first month, but once this segment had been activated, it remained sensitive to political issues and was quick to mobilize again.

The most tangible method of demonstrating a commitment to the railway was to purchase stock. Railway adherents sought to raise large sums of money, both to prove to officials the extent of public support and to eliminate any possible excuse for borrowing abroad.[67] Most students, as well as gentry and merchants, regarded this method as the best way to express public views forcefully but legally.[68] At the outset there was much spontaneous enthusiasm for purchasing shares. Schools in particular pledged to invest, but restaurants and businesses also held fund-raising meetings, and gentry managers in at least

TABLE 23
Sources of Telegrams, 1907 Demonstrations

Source		Number
Schools/students/educational circles		47
Corporate elite social groups		33
Gentry	12	
Merchants	3	
Gentry/merchants	8	
Merchants/students	4	
Gentry/merchants/students	6	
Native place associations		30
Chambers of commerce		24
Stockholders		17
Individuals		14
Anti-loan associations		11
Educational associations		10
Non-Zhejiangese provincial railway companies		10
Elites or institutions of provinces other than Zhejiang		6
Army/police		3
Constitutional associations, Japan		2
Southeast Asia		1
Business firm		1
TOTAL		209

SOURCE: *Jiang-Zhe tielu fengchao*, pp. 69–113, 283–356.
NOTE: Multiple telegrams are counted only once. Sources of telegrams are Zhejiangese unless otherwise specified.

Pingyang district invested educational funds in railway stock.[69] Employees of the railway decided to set aside a portion of their salaries to buy shares.[70] Suggestions poured in for money-raising schemes like lotteries, the sale of public grain, and even the payment of one month's rent in stock.[71] Some groups opened bank accounts to handle the money they raised. They also arranged for joint purchase by more than one person and set up ways for people to save until they had accumulated enough money to buy a share. Vast and uncountable sums were pledged during November 1907. The general magnitude is indicated by pledges totaling 22 million yuan made by prefectural representatives at the meeting on November 10 in Shanghai.[72] Most of these commitments were never fulfilled, but they were sincerely made by representatives at the meeting, and they reflected the kinds of promises that were being made back in Zhejiang.

After the meeting leading merchant and gentry supporters of the railway set up a more formal structure that was reminiscent of previous philanthropic fund-raising. Prominent individuals assumed at least nominal charge of the subscription drive in a given prefecture. Branches of prefectural bureaus were to be established in district cities and some important market towns. The price of stock was halved to fifty yuan for a full share and five yuan for a fractional share, and it was payable in three installments.

At least some of this structure was put into operation and functioned for several years. There are records of subscription bureaus or branches in Ningbo, Jiaxing, Huzhou, and Shaoxing prefectures, and in Fenghua district (Ningbo). Prominent men went home to urge people to buy stock, and appeals were aimed at small investors. At least some bureaus made public reports. Shanghai newspapers published the names of investors purchasing even a few shares, as they had done during earlier famine relief collections.

The fund-raising inevitably stagnated as the initial nationalistic fervor subsided, well-liked organizers were succeeded by less popular men, and doubts developed about the company's future. Branch subscription offices closed, and initial pledges were not filled. In Huzhou, for instance, less than a million of the five million yuan pledged in 1907 had been paid by the summer of 1909.[73]

Even so, some people kept up their installment payments, filled pledges, or bought new stock during the next few years. Branch bureaus were still collecting money in Jiaxing market towns in 1910.[74] Without resorting to the taxation used by some other provincial railways, the company raised enough capital to construct 150 miles of track from Hangzhou to the Jiangsu border and to begin work on the Hangzhou-Ningbo segment. By the end of 1906, it had issued shares worth five to six million yuan and had actually collected about five million yuan.[75] By 1911 it had raised 9,250,000 yuan, and 10,600,000 yuan was in hand early in 1912.[76]

The composition of the stockholders also changed because of the anti-loan movement. According to one estimate, 60 to 70 percent of the investors after late 1907 were small stockholders, although earlier capital had come mainly from large purchasers.[77] Considering the large number of claims on private capital during the first decade of the twentieth century, the record of the Zhejiang railway was fairly impressive. Its success was based on a mixture of the business expertise and the wealth of Zhejiangese merchants, the long experience of managerial elites in soliciting donations for public purposes, and the patriotic mobilization of a considerable segment of the elite populace.

Political demands. The railway supporters demonstrated against a foreign loan and for the right of the companies to raise money and build a railway without interference. They did not advance a political program as such. However, four political themes pervade the anti-loan literature: nationalism, autonomy, constitutionalism, and rebellion. The rhetorical outpouring of the first month of demonstrations is preserved in *The Railway Agitation in Jiangsu and Zhejiang* (*Jiang-Zhe tielu fengchao*), published in Shanghai in mid-December 1907. The highly repetitive phraseology and opinions that appeared in telegrams and in the editorials of Shanghai newspapers indicate that people in different places were reading the same material and absorbing similar ideas. There was a considerable elite audience ready to support the political ideas associated with the railways in the politically involved districts of Zhejiang.

Nationalistic expressions appear throughout the anti-loan literature. The anti-loan demonstrators were heirs to the militant patriotism and nationalism that had become widespread in the Lower Yangtze during the past 25 years. Language and concepts recalled the militant rhetoric of the Sino-French and Sino-Japanese wars. Older phrases found new uses in such currently popular concepts as social Darwinism, and the fears of foreign encroachment expressed by both reformers and revolutionaries during the 1900's were an integral part of the railway literature.[78] All aspects of the nationalist background contributed to the breadth of elite mobilization, and the vital contribution of the railway movement lay in its linking of nationalism to new definitions of societal autonomy and representational government. Nationalism itself took on additional connotations and ultimately strengthened and justified other, more clearly oppositionist elite demands.

Autonomous aspirations appeared in the repeated characterization of the railway as either "self-managed" (*ziban*) or "merchant-managed" (*shangban*), as opposed to "officially managed" (*guanban*), "officially supervised and merchant-managed" (*guandu shangban*), or controlled by foreigners. "Merchant management" and "self-management" were used interchangeably.[79] "Self-management," in particular, was an ambiguous term, which meant either Chinese rather than foreign management[80] or private ownership and direction rather than governmental control.[81]

The loan agitation neatly fused the issues of nationalism and autonomous initiative. Besides believing that the government was failing to protect Chinese economic rights, railway supporters also suspected that it secretly aimed to establish control over the companies. Shanghai papers ranging from moderately reformist to radical in their political affiliations charged that the Ministry of Foreign Affairs was using the loan to bring the railways under official management and supervision.[82] Old merchant suspicions of the system of "official supervision and merchant management"[83] fed into new accusations that officials hoped to use foreign support to achieve centralization and that foreigners encouraged the idea because they believed that they could control the court.[84] The remedy linked principles of societal activism, autonomous management, and representational government. Pointing out the progress already made in constructing the Shanghai-Hangzhou line, *Shi bao* observed, "If the affairs of the empire are managed only by officials, they absolutely can not succeed. If citizens capable of constitutional government manage the public affairs (literally, manage for the public benefit—*gongyi*) of their areas, how can one fear that they will not succeed?"[85]

Tang Shouqian eventually expanded this mixture of nationalism and mistrust of bureaucratic administration into a grandiose vision of a national railway system operated by private provincial companies, and he began to plan for a trunk line from Shanghai to Canton.[86] Railway self-management was sometimes linked to local self-government (*zizhi*), but the loan issue was related to national constitutional government more often than to local autonomy. The significance of the loan conflict can be seen in the movement of railway adherents from old arguments that government policy should represent public opinion to the idea that political organization was necessary to convey opinion to an authoritarian government and to assertions that success in the anti-loan struggle was vital to the future of constitutionalism.

The railway literature is filled with terms denoting public opinion.[87] After the loss of national sovereignty, adverse public opinion was the main reason given for demanding a reversal of government policy. Because assertions that officials should listen to public opinion could not actually require them to do so, some authors sought a remedy in a national assembly that would be able to supervise and check the power of administrative officials. They argued that if, for instance, there had been an assembly in 1907, foreign ministry officials responsible for the loan would have been dismissed for flouting public opinion.[88]

Even while concentrating on the loan issue, Zhejiangese behaved and argued as advocates of representational government. Stockholders elected "representatives" (*daibiao*), which were clearly distinguished from more independent "deputies" (*daili*),[89] to put their case before officials in the capital. Some people feared that a few representatives isolated in Beijing would be coerced or bribed to accept the loan,[90] but others saw the step as an opportunity for political organization. Proposals for meetings of representatives of all provinces to discuss railway and mining issues in Shanghai and suggestions for continuing organizations to keep up pressure on the government[91] anticipated methods that would be used to demand a national assembly in 1909 and 1910.

Railway supporters were acquainted with, and invoked, the liberal principles of popular rights and the rule of law to justify their positions.[92] Equally significant was their virtual abandonment of the belief that such rights could be achieved in harmony with like-minded rulers and officials. Loan opponents maintained that although members of the government said they wanted people to participate in public affairs, they still did not understand the breadth of political support for the railway companies.[93] More fundamentally, officials did not realize that they could not use the old dictatorial methods but had to listen to public opinion and be bound by law during a period of preparation for constitutional government.[94] The press asserted quite clearly that meaningful representation, participation, and rights would have to be won through struggle. The loan dispute was thus presented as the beginning of a conflict between the center and the people. It would set a precedent for the future by testing whether the public had the courage to resist the power of ministries in Beijing.[95]

Shi bao summed up the picture in an editorial that said, "In a period of preparation for constitutional government, one can not crush popular rights. . . . Now, one can not have constitutional government without establishing a national assembly, and one can not have a national assembly without respecting popular rights. If popular rights are not respected, constitutional government will not have anyone to put it into effect. Today the people and scholars of Jiangsu and Zhejiang have nobly risen up and united in a strong struggle over borrowing foreign funds for the [railway] companies." The editorial argued that the government had ignored public opinion, sought to force a foreign loan on the companies, and maneuvered to regain control of them. To provincial railway proponents, such coercion violated popular rights and made a mockery of the official plans for constitutionalism.[96]

The relatively specific issue of representational constitutional government floated amid vaguer expressions of anger, frustration, and apprehension. Warnings spoke of foreign humiliation, losing the people's hearts, and future misfortunes. Ironically echoing a phrase in the edict announcing the loan, railway adherents charged that officials were unwilling to break faith (*shixin*) with foreigners but were willing to betray their own people.[97] This rhetoric, too, arose out of the long history of oppositionist critiques of governmental domestic policy and its handling of foreign affairs. The vocabulary had been appropriated by the press to comment on the social and political crises of the late nineteenth century. During the anti-loan movement, however, the old warnings of impending disaster were less pleas for official corrective action and more suggestions that elite groups should take the initiative in curtailing bureaucratic power. The attendant accusations of governmental oppression were tied to the idea that the rights of people outside the government limited official political discretion.[98] This "oppression" included acts that reversed policy arbitrarily, ignored legal processes, flouted public opinion, and endangered popular well-being by failing to protect national sovereignty. Representational constitutional government was thus brought into the package of nationalism and autonomy. One gentry and merchant group telegraphed the censorate, "When the loan goes into effect, the people's wealth will be lost and the people's hearts will depart. How then will it be possible to establish a constitution? How will it be possible to plan for the [future] existence [of China]?"[99]

The rhetorical suggestion that faith in government was contingent upon modifying the political system to make room for societal initiatives (and to strengthen the nation) raises the question of the extent to which railway adherents were willing to carry their opposition. The anti-loan literature was not anti-Manchu, and some protesters went out of their way to declare their loyalty to the emperor.[100] Nonetheless, hostility was running high, and the possibility of violence was much on people's minds. Some of the warnings reflected elite interests in maintaining order and protecting trade.[101] Others suggested that government policy might force members of the elite into violent opposition, and the existence of revolutionary parties made these suggestions more plausible. The secretary of the Jiangsu railway alluded to rebellion in a letter to the Ministry of Foreign Affairs.[102] The Shanghai papers, including the supposedly conservative *Shen bao,* ran editorials suggesting that violent measures were needed to block the loan.[103] The constitutionalist *Shi bao* warned that, if the ministry continued to ignore the people, the revolutionary movement would grow, as "men of resolve" became frustrated and depressed.[104] Radical publications openly referred to Xu Xilin's recent assassination of the Anhui governor and to the subsequent arrests of reformers as well as radicals.[105]

Violence was briefly possible. Officials in Zhejiang warned of possible revolt, and the Grand Council cautioned Lower Yangtze officials to be prepared for gentry-led disturbances.[106] Additional troops were sent to the area, ostensibly to suppress smugglers but quite possibly also to intimidate loan opponents.[107] Neither the railway leaders nor central officials desired an open clash, however, and governors advised Beijing not to precipitate trouble by ignoring the depth of the opposition.[108]

The methods actually used by most loan opponents were not as extreme as their rhetoric. Revolutionaries urged their supporters to hold general strikes in cities, withhold tax payments, and declare provincial independence.[109] There were also rumors of plans to assassinate Wang Daxie because he had negotiated the loan.[110] Other suggestions included an anti-British boycott.[111] The non-revolutionary press also carried suggestions for tax resistance, merchants in Hangzhou considered refusing to pay the house tax, and a mass meeting in Shaoxing held out the possibility of school and merchant strikes if the government was not swayed by the more respectable method of fundraising.[112] The imported slogan of "no taxation without representation" had an appeal for merchants and gentry, who might also have been annoyed by unrelated governmental attempts to find new revenue.[113] Yet Zhejiangese generally eschewed violence in favor of meetings, fund-raising, and written expressions of outrage. As for a boycott, the economy of the Lower Yangtze was too tied up with the British trade to make that idea attractive to merchants and gentry. It has been suggested that it was the big shareholders who were willing to back down on the loan issue, but in reality it seems unlikely that the Lower Yangtze activists as a whole were ready for revolution. As matters drifted toward a choice between fighting and compromise, the appeal of compromise increased.

Compromise of the loan issue. At the summons of the Ministry of Foreign Affairs, railway stockholders elected a delegation headed by retired Grand Councillor Wang Wenshao to go to Beijing. The delegates arrived in December and held meetings with both government officials and the British and Chinese Corporation through the end of January.[114] These little-known discussions produced a new loan agreement, announced by the Ministry of Foreign Affairs on March 6, 1908.

This second agreement was unusually favorable to China.[115] The key concession to the railway companies was the provision that the loan be made to the Ministry of Posts and Communications, which would, in turn, make a separate loan to a bureau created by the two companies to construct a Shanghai-Hangzhou-Ningbo line. The foreign loan was thus divorced from control over company policy. The bureau was to employ a British engineer and to give preference to British manufacturers, but the independence of the companies as private "merchant-managed" corporations was reaffirmed.

Despite this seemingly successful resolution, the underlying issues between the central government and the railway companies remained unresolved. High officials had varied in their willingness to accommodate provincial groups. Zhang Zhidong, for instance, had argued against the loan and had warned that public opinion should be heeded, while Yuan Shikai had favored borrowing and had downplayed the importance of the provincial agitation.[116] Spokesmen for the throne, however, emphatically continued to reject the idea that public opinion should define policy. An edict on constitutional government issued shortly after the railway representatives arrived in Beijing denounced the frivolous criticism by "gentry, merchants, scholars, and people" and the constant clamor for constitutional rights. Instead of the current disarray, people and officials should harmoniously follow their proper functions. A parliament would select what was good from public opinion, but there would be limits to discussion.[117]

The gulf between this autocratic conception of constitutionalism and the views held by members of the social elite presaged further conflict. The reluctance of railway activists to use extreme methods belied the seriousness of their determination. The repeated use of the concept of citizenship by the loan opponents not only indicated their identification with the Chinese nation but also expressed a newly heightened social self-awareness. This fragile sense of cohesiveness was broadly upper class, but it appears to have fallen somewhat short of a new class-consciousness—viewed either in terms of a communality of interests or in terms of a differentiation from other social groups. Its most immediate manifestations were more extensive demands for new state-societal relationships. Its political import was different from the cosmopolitanism of the reconstruction activists who, four decades earlier, had seen local statecraft activities as alternative ways to strengthen the existing system. In effect, members of the elite were moving toward social mobilization to capture and redefine the state from the outside, if not exactly from below.

Only total victory would have been really satisfying. Instead, members of the elite remained ultimately dependent on the attitudes of high officials, who would never give in completely to public pressure. Frustration, continued dissatisfaction, and further demands to control policy were likely, and the railway companies never fully accepted the provisions of the treaty. Foreigners still had some role in the companies, and the ministry loan had centralizing implications that were only slightly better than a foreign loan. A month after the settlement a Zhejiang Railway Company stockholders' meeting resolved to solicit more capital and avoid accepting loan payments from the Ministry of Posts and Communications.[118] Compromise quickly turned into an attempted end run.

The Break with the Government, 1908–1911

The tensions inherent in the simultaneous extension of central bureaucratic power and social mobilization came to a head in the short, politically troubled reign of the infant Xuantong emperor (r. 1909–12). In the Lower Yangtze, the members of the elite who had acquired a nationalistic political consciousness over the past two decades had been decisively mobilized by the loan issue. The throne's commitment to constitutional government in 1906 had also made political organization more possible. Previously, it had been almost as illegal and dangerous to advocate limited monarchy as to call for republican revolution. From 1906, however, respectable, established members of the elite who shrank from illegal opposition had an excuse to organize in pursuit of government-backed goals. It was not surprising that they defined their roles in the new system more broadly than leading metropolitan officials and the court had envisioned. They pursued their aspirations with a vigor altogether incompatible with the governmental view that constitutional institutions could unite the country and mobilize social elites under central leadership. Officials like Yuan Shikai, who did not think that local self-government threatened bureaucratic authority but who believed it necessary to harness the railway movements, had a good appreciation of the political situation.[119]

The 1907 anti-loan agitation was the most dramatic event in Zhejiang, but the mobilization it produced fed into a cumulative process of political alienation. Nationalistic agitation, the continuing railway movement, and the constitutionalist drive for a national assembly and a responsible cabinet interacted to heighten political tensions. During these years, most of the nationalistic demonstrations were produced by local incidents. Constitutional questions mainly involved the provincial and macroregional elites, while the railway question continued to activate a broad spectrum of elites in core districts. All these issues interacted to keep social mobilization alive and to sharpen political demands. As their conviction grew that national leaders would neither share power in the capital nor allow independent initiative outside it, reformist activists were prepared to accept the revolutionary overthrow of the political system.

Nationalistic agitation. A new rash of local protests against foreign (usually Japanese) business expansion outside the treaty ports had begun in 1907, eventually leading to an attempt by the provincial assembly to place more restrictions on the sale of land to foreigners.[120] These protests continued for several years and intermingled with demonstrations against expansive missionary activities (like the Baptist Duncan Main's acquisition of a temple near Hangzhou for a hospital) or against imagined insults (like the flying of a Japanese flag at a theater in Jiaxing to advertise the coming of a Japanese troupe).[121] The major incident was an anti-Japanese riot in Hangzhou early in 1910, caused by the injury of a Chinese boy during a fight in a Japanese-owned cake shop. Merchants and gentry met in protest, and demonstrations followed.[122]

There were also meetings and organization over national foreign policy. A gathering in Jiaxing during 1910 kept alive the memory of humiliations suffered during the Boxer Rebellion, and some three thousand people attended a meeting in Hangzhou to launch the Zhejiang branch of the movement to collect private contributions to redeem China's foreign debts.[123] Railway activists played a role in the anti-Japanese demonstrations in Hangzhou and Jiaxing and in the opposition to missionary expansion in Huzhou. Tang Shouqian, along with several other railway supporters, spearheaded the debt redemption movement. Despite its quixotic impracticality, the idea of paying off the foreign debt through private donations was significant as another manifestation of the elite mobilization that was being expressed in the railway and constitutionalist movements. By the summer of 1910 the Shanghai press was warning about the new dangers posed by Russia and Japan in Manchuria. It was strongly linking issues of national preservation with constitutional government.[124]

Railways and constitutions. Just as nationalism mobilized the elite, the provincial railway and constitutionalist questions focused the political conflict. Politically aroused members of the elite mobilized rapidly to meet narrowly separated crises, despite their lack of a permanent political organization. Each new organization drew upon much the same pool of men, and continuing institutions lay behind the temporary political groups. The railway company with its fund-raising apparatus, the New Policies institutions, and the native place associations lay behind the temporary railway protection associations. The Society to Prepare for Constitutional Government was the starting point from which more overtly oppositionist constitutional groups emerged, and after 1909 the provincial assembly provided a political forum and a pool of potential political leaders in Hangzhou.

Early in August 1908, shortly after the temporary resolution of the railway loan issue, the Shanghai-based Society to Prepare for Constitutional Government cooperated with followers of Liang Qichao in the soon-to-be-banned Political Information Society (*zhengwen she*) to call a meeting in support of constitutional government. Given the overlap between the society and the railway, railway leaders were naturally involved. Tang Shouqian joined Zhang Jian and the society's president, Zheng Xiaoxu, in sending two telegrams calling for a national assembly that would meet within two years. One of the three Zhejiangese representatives who went from Shanghai to Beijing had been a leader of the 1907 agitation, and another railway activist was among the Beijing officials who supported the constitutionalist requests.[125]

The edict of August 27, 1908, establishing a nine-year schedule for the establishment of constitutional government, caused a temporary hiatus in oppositionist political activity. Meanwhile, the Zhejiang and Jiangsu railway companies pushed ahead with their construction of the Shanghai-Hangzhou line and completed it in August 1909. Despite its technical shortcomings, its relatively speedy construction was a source of provincial pride—and also produced constant friction with Britain. British representatives repeatedly complained about such matters as the railway companies' unwillingness to grant authority to the British engineer, their shoddy work, and their failure to buy English equipment.[126] In reality, loan payments were the explosive issue. Even though the situation was extremely confused, two points seem clear. First, loan payments were made by the Hong Kong and Shanghai Banking Corporation to the Ministry of Posts and Communications, but the ministry did not make all the scheduled payments to the railway companies—whose officers subsequently argued that failure to maintain the schedule voided the agreement. Second, the companies genuinely tried not to use those funds they did receive, and they returned at least part of the money to the ministry. This situation infuriated the British, who saw their claims to influence being undermined; they suspected that their money was ending up in the pockets of ministry officials. That may indeed have happened, but it is also true that ministry officials had hoped to consolidate the two loans by establishing central control over the railway. By 1910 they were probably delaying payments deliberately in order to weaken the companies, but even at the outset they may have been less than enthusiastic in forwarding funds to be used by the uncooperative provincial leaders.[127]

In the meantime, the deaths of both Empress Dowager Cixi and the Guangxu emperor in November 1908 altered the political situation in Beijing. Yuan Shikai was forced to retire at the beginning of 1909. Although Yuan had favored centralization, his departure may nonetheless have sharpened the possibilities for political conflict. Prince Chun, the regent for the infant emperor, was inclined to assert central authority with little sensitivity to public opinion, and some of the young nobles were even more determined to use centralization as a means to restore Manchu power.[128] His leadership made it more likely that positions would harden on both sides. Racial mistrust would become a factor, but the basic conflict was not Manchu-Chinese. Members of the court found allies among Chinese officials in the capital who favored bureaucratic centralization, because of their own interests and because it seemed the best way to unify, strengthen, and modernize China.

The relative political calm in Zhejiang following the edict granting constitutional government and the imperial deaths was broken in May 1909. In that month, the two men Zhejiangese leaders blamed most for the loan, Sheng Xuanhuai and Wang Daxie, were appointed vice-presidents of the Ministry of Posts and Communications. Tang Shouqian memorialized his opposition, stressing the importance of public opinion, raising the constitutionalist issue, and threatening to resign.[129] The appointments presaged nationalization plans that were not com-

pletely adopted for over a year. They also inaugurated a period
of political maneuvering between Tang Shouqian and the Zhejiang railway on one side and the Ministry of Posts and Communications and centralizers at the court on the other. This
provincial issue overshadowed constitutionalist politics within
Zhejiang, but the two conflicts unfolded together.

At first, Tang and the railway were successful. The court and
ministry officials were angry over the criticism of the appointments, but Wang Daxie resigned his post and Sheng Xuanhuai
was occupied with other duties until 1910.[130] When railway
stockholders met in July, they refused to accept either Tang's
well-publicized resignation or that of Vice-President Liu. The
victory was ephemeral, however, because ministry officials and
members of the court were determined to get rid of Tang. In August he was appointed provincial judge in distant Yunnan—a
move that only resulted in more agitation during the late summer and fall.

Elections for the provincial assembly were held during this
conflict. Perhaps in the hope of calming public opinion before
the assemblies met in October, Tang was summoned to Beijing
for an audience with the prince regent.[131] Tang delayed his departure until mid-November, when provincial assembly representatives from all parts of China were gathering in Shanghai to
discuss the immediate opening of a national assembly. Tang
stopped in Shanghai en route to the capital.[132] Then he went on
to Beijing, where he remained until the end of February 1910.

The first unsuccessful effort of provincial delegations to persuade the throne to convene a national assembly occurred during January 1910.[133] We do not know what, if any, contacts Tang
had with the provincial constitutionalist representatives. In
any case, he was fairly successful in putting forth his own case
and that of the railway. After he submitted a long memorial on
national affairs to the prince regent,[134] his appointment was
changed to that of Jiangxi educational commissioner. When he
still refused an official post, the government gave up its effort to
move him from Zhejiang. Tang remained railway president
with strong stockholder backing.[135] However, the war continued. Governmental plans for centralization had not been

abandoned, despite policy vacillations that may have reflected confused and divided governmental leadership. Leading officials in the Ministry of Posts and Communications were reportedly advocating nationalization of the Shanghai-Hangzhou-Ningbo line.[136] It is possible that they were playing a double game by encouraging British complaints, trying to keep public opinion quiescent, and planning to take over the railway companies when they were exhausted.

During the spring the provincial chamber of commerce in Hangzhou selected an eight-man delegation to join in a second petition to the throne for a national assembly. Two of the delegates were railway directors, and at least two more had joined in the 1907 agitation against the loan.[137] Tang Shouqian, for his part, resumed public political activity immediately after he left Beijing, giving speeches to promote a national assembly and raise money for the railway.[138] In June the throne again turned down provincial delegates requesting a national assembly,[139] and railway stockholders in Zhejiang resolved that Tang should continue as president and repudiate the loan agreement.[140]

Early in August still a third group of constitutionalist representatives arrived in Beijing. Shortly thereafter, on August 17, the railway company's quarrel with the government came to a crisis when Sheng Xuanhuai was ordered to take up his post as vice-president of the Ministry of Posts and Communications. Tang Shouqian responded with a biting memorial on August 22, in which he attacked Sheng Xuanhuai for corruption and accused him of harming China for the benefit of foreigners.[141] The next day Tang was dismissed from the presidency by imperial edict. A fresh wave of Zhejiangese agitation in favor of Tang overlapped the third drive for a national assembly.[142] This time the court agreed to advance the opening date to 1913, but it refused to reinstate Tang. British pressure may have had some influence, but a combination of Tang's political activities and governmental plans for railway nationalization appear to have been the main factors behind his dismissal.[143]

The railway issue kept Zhejiang in political turmoil from mid-1909 through 1910. Tang's presidency was a more narrowly provincial issue than the foreign loan had been, and the Jiangsu railway supporters were much less involved. Members of elites in other provinces did, however, recognize that government interference in Zhejiang presaged difficulties for similar enterprises elsewhere. Zhejiangese native place associations and assemblies in other provinces expressed support.[144] Zhejiangese officials in Beijing and successive governors in Hangzhou also helped the company, but they would not oppose an imperial edict directly.[145]

Within Zhejiang the demonstrations were similar to the demonstrations of 1907. Many of the old leaders reappeared.[146] Special stockholders' meetings were held in both 1909 and 1910, and mass meetings of reactivated railway protection associations were held in Hangzhou and Shanghai. There is less record of student involvement, but chambers of commerce, educational associations, and self-government organizations again held meetings and formed associations in prefectural cities, district seats, and market towns. Both the stockholders and the people attending a mass meeting in Hangzhou elected representatives to go to Beijing in the fall, where they had futile discussions with the Ministry of Posts and Communications.[147]

Large numbers of demonstrators took part. *North China Herald* reported that a crowd of ten thousand people saw Tang Shouqian off to Beijing at the Hangzhou railway station in 1909.[148] In 1910 over two thousand people were said to have attended the meeting of the Shanghai society to support the railway. Several thousand people showed up for the stockholders' meeting the next day, and 2,130 stockholders signed a telegram to the Grand Council.[149] Large crowds, variously reported as several thousands or several tens of thousands of people, turned out for meetings in Ningbo.[150] There seems little reason to doubt that Tang was a genuine hero to most members of the gentry and merchant elite of the province and that the politicization of elite-run organizations produced by the anti-loan agitation continued.[151]

New representational bodies were also pulled into the battle. At least ten (and most certainly more) members of the Zhejiang provincial assembly had actively supported the railway in 1907.[152] In 1909 eleven of thirteen representatives chosen by the railway protection association to call on the governor were newly elected members of the provincial assembly.[153] Tang's dismissal was the cause of a major clash between the assembly and the governor the following year. At the request of assembly members the governor had memorialized in favor of reinstating Tang. After this effort on behalf of members of the Zhejiangese elite brought him a rebuke from the throne, the governor refused the assembly's request that he memorialize again. The assembly thereupon suspended its sitting on October 5 and created an informal body to debate Tang's dismissal. For the next month assembly members put pressure on the governor to memorialize, while he tried to get the assembly to return to its regular business. The impasse endangered provincial finances and caused considerable controversy among assembly members. Although the governor finally agreed to memorialize again in return for the resumption of the assembly session, he never supported Tang strongly, and the incident undermined relations between the assembly and the governor's office.[154] It directly involved most assembly members in this political issue; some, like Chu Fucheng, also spoke at railway meetings.

The new National Consultative Assembly in Beijing was likewise formally brought into the picture when the provincial assembly notified it of the dispute with the governor over Tang. Since at least three of the seven Zhejiangese delegates had taken part in the anti-loan agitation,[155] the railway company was sure of a sympathetic hearing. In early January 1911 the National Consultative Assembly brought the railway situation to the attention of the throne. Nothing came of these moves. Their significance lay in drawing the barely established representational bodies, as the New Policies functional associations before them had been drawn, into political conflict with high officials and the throne. Assemblies therefore functioned as representatives of oppositionist elite interests and opinion rather than the disinterested adjuncts of dignified and harmonious decision-making that imperial spokesmen desired. Although the incident had pitted the assembly against the governor, the real quarrel was with the central government. The governor was caught between the interests of the central state

and those of societal spokesmen. Although he had little influence on either side, when forced to choose he had to cast his lot
with Beijing.[156]

Aside from electing representatives to join in the second petition to the throne in 1910, the provincial chamber of commerce sponsored the Zhejiang branch of the national Association for a National Assembly Within a Year (*guohui qicheng
hui*).[157] Plans were laid for branches throughout the province,
although I have no evidence as to whether they were actually
established. The next year Zhejiangese members of the most extremely dissatisfied of the constitutionalist parties, the Friends
of the Constitution (*xianyou hui*), included railway activists,
provincial assembly members, and members of the National
Consultative Assembly. The provincial assembly president,
Chen Fuchen, and two of his protégés organized the Zhejiang
branch.[158] Nevertheless, this activity remained secondary to the
railway mobilization.

The uproar had two opposite effects. The railway company
was weakened. Efforts to raise capital were less successful in
1909 and 1910 than in 1907. Money was particularly scarce in
1910, when the Shanghai financial crisis caused bank failures
in Zhejiang as well as Shanghai. The uncertain future of the
company, the specter of nationalization, and the departure of
Tang Shouqian worried stockholders and discouraged new investment.[159] With Tang gone, rivalries arose among remaining officers, and a prominent director was accused of transferring funds to another company in which he had interests.[160]
The Jiangsu railway, which had never been as successful at
fund-raising as its Zhejiangese counterpart, was in more serious financial trouble. It also had weaker leadership because
Zhang Jian and other originally dominant officers had transferred their attentions to the provincial assembly and the constitutional movement.

The weakness of the railway company was dwarfed, however,
by the growing political irreconcilability of governmental leadership and reformist elite activists. Zhang Zhidong's death in
the fall of 1909 had removed a voice for caution within the metropolitan bureaucracy. By mid-1910 there was little chance that

the Ministry of Posts and Communications, now dominated by centralizers like President Tang Shaoyi and Vice-President Sheng Xuanhuai, would abandon its plans for railway nationalization. Nor would the throne compromise what it considered its right to appoint and dismiss officials (including officers of major corporations) by reinstating Tang Shouqian. The court and the Grand Council reached their determination not to be dominated by public opinion at the same time that organization and pressure from public opinion leaders was seriously threatening to restrict autocratic freedom of action. The oppositionist momentum, led by highly prestigious members of the elite with the support of provincial governors and metropolitan officials, could not be easily stopped. Each effort to slow it down was defined as an act of oppression that justified further resistance. As the gap between government and the elite widened, the gap between non-violent reformist social mobilization and revolution narrowed.

The complaints of railway supporters in 1909–10 reflect the clarification of their political position since 1907. The supporters were still nationalistic, and they used some of the same hyperbolic patriotic rhetoric as two years before, but their chief concern had become the autonomy of the railway company and its implications for constitutionalism.[161] The throne, they argued, did not have the power to dismiss Tang because article 77 of the commercial code gave the board of directors power to elect and dismiss corporate presidents.[162] Merchant management was repeatedly contrasted with ministry management (*buban*) or official control (*guanzhi*).[163] Members of the elite also firmly rejected the government's contention that because railway companies were vital to national economic development, they were not the same as ordinary corporations.[164] Again the government was accused of oppression, contempt for the law, and unwillingness to recognize that the people had rights. Its behavior raised questions of the need to support the official program for constitutional government if the government acted against the popular good.[165]

An important statement of the attitude of Lower Yangtze reform activists during the summer of 1910 appeared in the editorial "On the Distinction Between Centralizing Power and Tyranny" printed by *Shi bao* four days after Tang Shouqian was dismissed from office.[166] This editorial endorsed administrative centralization within the bureaucracy by transferring authority from governors-general and other "local" officials to ministries in Beijing. This process, which had been under way since the Boxer Rebellion, suited the needs of the time. It was compatible with preparation for constitutional government as long as the government was responsive to public opinion. Such centralization did not, however, include the appropriation of the "life, property, and all the free rights" of the people. The critical distinction between a tyrannical and a constitutional government was that the former did not need to be united with the people and did not need to heed public opinion. At the end the editors sarcastically suggested that if the government achieved truly enlightened despotism, the sacrifice of a Tang Shouqian would not matter. If, however, the government was not perfect, the result would be tyranny, with unfortunate implications for constitutional government.

In the course of the year 1910, accusations of oppression or bad faith and warnings of political upheaval or national demise accompanied elite demands for a national assembly and a cabinet responsible to the legislature. The end of absolutist tyranny was deemed necessary to save the country from both renewed foreign invasion and internal disorders. Reformers were ceasing to believe that a constitution could be handed down from the throne. They were increasingly convinced that the people (i.e., elite activists) would have to take a hand in molding a workable constitutional government. Further delay would mean rebellion.[167] When the throne curtly rejected the National Consultative Assembly's impeachment of the Grand Council and expelled provincial assembly representatives from the capital in December, it only confirmed existing suspicions of governmental insincerity.

Although reform activists disagreed over the extent of their defiance, suspicion and antagonism were growing between elite leaders and the dominant policy-makers in government. The railway movement in Zhejiang had not stagnated. On the contrary, it was central to a series of issues that reflected an irreconcilable gap between the interests and attitudes of the government and the elites that were not part of it. By early June 1911 *Shi bao* could assert that the most serious "internal misfortunes" were the government's undermining of constitutionalism and the "citizens" lack of a voice in the government.[168]

By then the conflicts of the last Qing decade had greatly amplified the mutual distrust that traced back at least to the patriotic opposition of the 1880's. By 1911 a lack of faith in the government was undermining loyalty to what assertive members of the elite viewed as an oppressive system. What had begun as quarrels with individual policy-makers ended up as a general questioning of the legitimacy of the imperial system. The monarchy was rejected for a number of reasons. For many members of the elite, however, its rejection did not arise from a total abandonment of the values upon which the centralized bureaucratic monarchy rested, but it was caused by the political inability of the system to absorb large doses of outside initiative. The announcement of plans for railway nationalization in May 1911 and the appointment of a Manchu-dominated cabinet in June only capped a long process of alienation. Immediately after the outbreak of the 1911 Revolution in October, a *Shi bao* editorialist looked back on the year's events. He recalled that constitutionalists had sometimes distinguished between a peaceful "political revolution," which would transform institutions through constitutional government, and the violent "racial revolution" urged by the Revolutionary Alliance (*Tongmeng hui*). He suggested that the cabinet issue had brought together these two strands.[169] In effect, members of the elite had demanded a sweeping political revolution, which neither bureaucratic centralizers nor the court were prepared to allow. It seems likely that, if these particular incidents had not occurred, the break would simply have been precipitated in another way.

The big political battles of 1911 were not in Zhejiang, although the railway company officers and directors continued to resist governmental control. Representatives who went to Beijing in the fall of 1910 gave up their attempts to reinstate Tang

Shouqian, but they stayed until March 1911 to discuss ways of terminating the loan from the Ministry of Posts and Communications.[170] By this time representatives of the financially weaker Jiangsu railway had begun wary negotiations about governmental purchase,[171] but Zhejiangese still remained adamant about their corporate independence.

At this point the talks had a certain air of unreality. The ministry had almost certainly already agreed with Britain to cancel the loan and use the money for a line from Kaifeng to Xuzhou.[172] It would have liked to assume control of the provincial companies at the same time, but Zhejiang stockholders still nursed faint hopes of reinstating Tang, and even the more receptive Jiangsu officers would not rush into agreement. Sheng Xuanhuai complained that "southern and central scholars" liked to "listen to the words of newspapers and students."[173] The ministry strategy was to drag out talks with the Zhejiangese,[174] begin railway nationalization elsewhere, and eventually reach agreement with the wavering Jiangsu railway officers. Once the other lines were nationalized, the ministry would be in a strong position to put pressure on an isolated Zhejiangese company. Thus, although the organizations formed to support the railway continued to exist well into 1911,[175] they had no immediate battles to fight. Members of the Lower Yangtze elite had done much to define the issues. Other provinces would show that they were not alone. The ministry's strategy worked in one respect. When violent opposition to centralization broke out, it began in Sichuan, far from Zhejiang.[176]

Elite activists in the 1911 Revolution. Nevertheless, the organizational growth and political mobilization of the New Policies period was crucial to the development of the 1911 Revolution in Zhejiang. During that year influential Zhejiangese, including Assembly President Chen Fuchen, joined political parties like the Friends of the Constitution, and members of the elite gave moral support to railway demonstrations in the Middle Yangtze. Local groups also continued to be affected by national politics. Branches of the Shanghai-based Citizens' Martial Association (*guomin shangwu hui*) appeared in the northern prefectures, and chambers of commerce also organized militias. Some of these small military groups were established in response to the decision of the association of provincial assemblies at a meeting during the summer to encourage formation of physical education societies—which would, in effect, train militias to defend China against foreigners without waiting for governmental leadership. Other militias were mainly interested in local order. In neither case, however, were they primarily distinguished by their loyalty to the Qing.[177] Although the politicized elite activists of the core districts had still not taken the final step of initiating violence, there was little left to distinguish them from revolutionaries.[178] When violence began, they joined the revolution less because of their local interests than because a republic promised greater political and economic opportunity than the Qing bureaucratic monarchy—which had repeatedly disappointed their expectations—could promise.

The 1911 Revolution began with a rising of revolutionaries and soldiers at Wuchang in the middle Yangtze Basin on October 10. Within less than a month, Lower Yangtze provinces declared independence from the Qing. A provisional national government was organized in Nanjing under the Revolutionary Alliance leader, Sun Yat-sen, on January 1, 1912, and in March the emperor abdicated in favor of a republican government in Beijing headed by Yuan Shikai.

In Zhejiang as in other provinces, the 1911 Revolution was a disjointed, uneven uprising of different groups who were dissatisfied with the Qing: members of the modernized new army, constitutionalists and other elite activists, students, secret societies, and professional revolutionaries. In Hangzhou revolutionaries and the new army handled the brief fighting, but provincial assembly leaders worked out the organization of a provisional provincial government with the revolutionaries. Tang Shouqian was the first military governor. When he left at the beginning of 1912 to join Sun Yat-sen's national government, he was succeeded by the army officer Jiang Zungui, who also had the support of leading elite activists.[179] Restoration Society revolutionaries, who did not have close ties with the elite, were eliminated.

Two examples from the core areas of the Jiangnan prefectures suggest the important role of elite activists in 1911. The first military governor of Huzhou was Shen Puqin, the head of the middle school. Shen had established a girls' school, a political discussion group, and a society to study military affairs. In 1907 he had been vice president of the association in Huzhou to oppose the railway loan. Shen's assistant at the middle school headed the civil government, and a student force helped bring them to power. They were replaced in three months by people who had the support of Huzhou-born revolutionaries in Shanghai. The new head was a *juren* who had also opposed the railway loan, and another of the new officials had promoted education in his home village.[180]

In Jiaxing the military governor was the middle school superintendent. The head of the civil government was probably related to the president of the educational association, and people who had taught in the new school occupied many of the lesser posts. The chamber of commerce and the self-government association backed the provincial declaration of independence from the Qing. Contact with Hangzhou was chiefly through the progressive vice president of the Qing provincial assembly, Chu Fucheng, who was closely involved with New Policies institutions at home.[181] Despite all the local variations, the new governments in core districts were likely to include elite activists who had been caught up in the political trends of the previous decade.

The same kinds of activists also took part in organizing new governments outside core areas, but these places had not been deeply affected by the politics and the organizational changes of the last decade. As Keith Schoppa has pointed out, members of elites in such districts had less to say in the making of the revolution. They tried to maintain their local positions in the face of uncontrollable outside events and swelling disorder by fighting or negotiating with secret society leaders, bandits, small groups of local radicals, and military adventurers.[182] As the Qing collapsed, the political future seemed to be taking shape in the cores. It remained to be seen whether the organizational development and political momentum of the early 1900's could provide an adequate foundation for continued elite power in the changed political environment of the Republic.

EIGHT

Conclusion

Several factors came together in the late Qing
to alter the political structure of China. These included economic and demographic expansion, changes in the composition of social elites, the international situation, and the inadequacy of the existing imperial state structure to meet the
continuous crises of the nineteenth century. The resulting
changes in the balances of power between social leaders and the
state can be analyzed in terms of organization, mobilization,
and politicization on one side, and piecemeal restructuring followed by deliberate state-building on the other.

The initial stages of these processes stretched out over the
nineteenth century and were governed mainly by internal circumstances. A critical change occurred during the last decades
of the century, when the impact of foreign intervention became
more visible and stimulated rapid changes in state-societal
relationships. Even so, the new political issues incorporated
earlier tensions—between, for instance, the literati and the
throne and the upper bureaucracy or between social leaders
outside of government and the bureaucracy. I have argued that
the most significant politicization at the end of the Qing arose
in the most commercially developed parts of China and was
based on the protracted growth of elite social organization. The

social mobilization in areas like the five northern prefectures of Zhejiang transcended local boundaries and brought down both the Qing dynasty and the imperial state structure in the 1911 Revolution. This mobilization was so far advanced that it precluded any reconstitution of the old governmental system. Constitutionalists asked for changes in the distribution of political power that were almost as fundamental as the changes revolutionaries were demanding.

The processes involved in these events were similar to some that have been identified in European history, but differences in timing, historical context, and socioeconomic and political structures caused them to develop in different ways. There were many factors shaping state-societal relationships in the late Qing, but I will comment on four of them here: the unitary political structure, the impact of nineteenth-century crises, the final competition between state-directed and social mobilization, and the emergence of public spheres.

Late imperial Chinese political principles were integrationist. It has been suggested that during the period when state structures were replacing feudal systems in Europe, separatist principles embedded in the heritages of Christian teaching, Roman law, medieval Catholic church-state conflicts, and feudalism influenced the evolution of new state-societal relations.[1] In China Confucian teaching about authority, ritually buttressed autocracy, the long history of the imperial state, and the system of recruiting and defining members of elites through the bureaucratic examinations all encouraged unitary hierarchical views. The general idea that the polity and social order should be unified remained strong in theory even while it was being eroded in practice.

Integration did not, however, mainly rest on the intrusion of state power into society. On the contrary, it can be argued that the system was maintained over long periods because it allowed considerable social latitude and flexible adjustments between state and social power. This latitude was as important as the examination bond between state and elites in maintaining a system in which shared norms, consensus, and historical experience contributed to integration. The challenge to the kind of integration that existed under the Qing came more from societal than from state initiatives, but the continuing hold of the idea affected the rise of organization, mobilization, and conflict, and posed problems that would persist through the twentieth century.

Integration meant that the organizations that would ultimately provide the means to mobilize against the state grew up under the aegis of imperial military and political power. Initially, both autonomy and conflict were limited, but a growing gap appeared between the formal designations of political authority and the way it actually functioned.[2] The shift away from officials and toward elite leaders can be seen in other gentry-run bureaus as well as the welfare and educational institutions stressed in this study.

Another effect of integration can be seen in the pattern of opposition at the end of the Qing. Despite desires for economic independence, self-government, and political rights, the most explosive demands of politically conscious members of the elite at the end of the Qing did not arise from a defense of group interests but from the claim that their economic, political, and often local, initiatives were undertaken on behalf of the nation. The significance of late nineteenth-century interpretations of the *Rites of Zhou* lay in justifying the beginnings of this upsurge of elite initiative in terms of existing ideology. Soon afterward, a societal defense of the country would be seen as a reason for members of the elite to interfere in national policy and demand reorganization of the governmental structure.

Such unbounded, expansive societal initiative was incompatible with both the autocratic and the bureaucratic aspects of the existing state—and more threatening to the system than the competitions between local elites and the bureaucracy that were a familiar feature of late imperial politics. The growing organizational capacity of both society and government created opportunities for new political power, but this potential was not infinitely expandable. Officials and members of the elite might balance expanding roles in specific localities and situations where, as Stephen R. MacKinnon has suggested, the supply of political power increased. The exercise of such power and its pursuit produced conflict, however, when both sides took initiatives of the magnitude seen in the Lower Yangtze.

Nonetheless, such conflict did not destroy the belief that state and society should be united. At first the idea of unity slowed the growth of opposition among members of the old-regime elite, who still formed the majority of activists at the end of the Qing. Then it became part of a long-lasting twentieth-century problem of political legitimacy. Throughout the republican period, governments seeking new ways to integrate the state and society needed not only to increase the interventionist capacity of the bureaucracy but also to convince social leaders that it merited social support.

Internal and external crises had triggered the processes that undermined late imperial integration and stimulated social organization. State-making also began within the late imperial framework.[3] However, these concurrent trends developed along separate tracks, and social and governmental activism failed to merge into a single effort. Domestic and foreign crises impinged upon state-societal relationships in different ways. Internal problems surfaced in rebellions that promoted state-elite cooperation more than they undermined it. Elite and governmental interests in social order were not identical. The record in Zhejiang, for instance, shows that the failings of government as a whole, or of individual officials, fostered the view that social elites could do a better job of running local affairs harmoniously. Some people went so far as to blame the governmental structure for the unrest, not only its misguided policies or the aberrations of its officials. Nonetheless, disorder prompted members of elites to turn to the state for help at the same time that they were organizing for self-defense. The mid-century rebellions encouraged elite activism and organization, but the successful joint effort to suppress uprisings (combined with official military self-strengthening) left the state stronger against internal enemies.[4] Disorders and their aftermaths stimulated local autonomous activities, but they did not turn members of the elite against the entire political structure.

Imperialist incursions, on the other hand, aroused hostility that fed patriotic or nationalistic consciousness. Repeated in-

ability to end these threats was a major—probably the major—
factor in the breakdown of political consensus that turned
people without political authority against the power holders in
the government.[5] This development was instrumental in causing the Chinese pattern to diverge from that of state-building
in western Europe. Charles Tilly has suggested that in Europe
there was a relatively apolitical, although often violent, preliminary stage during which rulers established military and territorial control, developed bureaucracies, and enlarged revenues
needed to support a state apparatus, and a later phase of nation-
building, which involved education, the spread of participation
in the government, and the inculcation of civic loyalties.[6]

In China the coincidence of state-restructuring and nation-
building rendered the first task more difficult. The Qing government embarked upon its major phase of fiscal, military, and
administrative reorganization after 1900 at the same time that
it was trying to restructure education and mobilize energies by
means of state-led constitutionalism and self-government tied
to the bureaucracy. This would have been a large undertaking
under the best of conditions, but it was an even more risky
proposition because powerful segments of the elite in key parts
of China had enlarged their organizational capacity and become politicized, nationally conscious, and distrustful of government. Chinese society was never perfectly united, and the
erosion of ties between elites and the state meant that elite nationalistic mobilization could easily become tied to the defense of—or the extension of—group interests against government. Thus nationalism exacerbated differences and pushed
social mobilization toward revolution, not toward support of
the center, at the end of the Qing. In other words, change was
precipitated by social organization as well as by the state. Government had to react defensively against this social mobilization while seeking to enlarge its own power.

Competition between state and society at the end of the
Qing involved the opposition of interests in a centralizing bureaucratic mobilization and autonomous social initiatives. It
raised questions about the extension of political participation
and the definition of national policy in a new system that por-

tended more state intervention and more "citizen" involvement. Because of differences in timing, the ensuing conflict
was different from its European counterparts. Instead of a progression from defensive-reactive to acquisitive-proactive behavior on the part of social groups,[7] the politics of the New
Policies period simultaneously produced reactive and proactive
behavior by both the government and the social leaders. The
extension of state power produced defensive reactions, illustrated most clearly by the question of taxation. The central
government, overburdened with the expense of bureaucratic expansion and military and economic modernization while paying large foreign debts and indemnities, had to increase revenues, but its needs conflicted with the needs of provincial
governments and local elites that were also financing new programs.[8] Each group sought to increase its income or to force
other levels of government to assume expenses, and the combined extractions led to defensive protests from taxpayers.
While segments of society were reacting against state intervention, officials and the court were themselves reacting against
the initiatives of other social segments, which sought to dimin-
ish state control over national policy.

New power and new political roles were demanded by organized elites at the expense of both the autocratic monarchy and
the bureaucracy. Although officials had lost ground to elite organization, they remained unreceptive to assertive societal
efforts to accumulate political power. Many people inside and
outside the government accepted the idea that mobilizing the
energies of "citizens" would strengthen China internationally.
However, the desire of central officials to control and limit
mobilization rather than ride on top of it meant that the local
and provincial political initiatives of the New Policies period
pushed members of the elite closer to the revolutionaries. The
railway movement is a prime example of how proactive conflicts acquired a momentum of their own. It is not important
whether a member of a town chamber of commerce protesting
the British loan in 1907 was a convinced constitutionalist and
nationalist or simply interested in a return on his investment

in stock. He was part of a social mobilization headed toward political revolution.

A new wave of reorganization in the public sphere was a second legacy of the foreign crises at the end of the nineteenth century. The New Policies in Zhejiang were an outgrowth of social initiative as much as the creation of official policy, and their institutions can better be called public than quasi-bureaucratic. Local public spheres continued to develop during the Republic, when public functional associations interacted with private societies, clubs, political parties, and some bureaucratic bureaus. Many of these institutions were not inherently political, but they served as vehicles to express interests and mobilize the populace when political issues arose. When effective national government disappeared, members of local elites often ran the public spheres of their home areas as they wished. In the gradually widening cores, however, members of the elite were not isolated from national events, and nowhere were they immune from military or governmental intrusion. Public spheres became political barometers. During the Republic answers to the question whether the late Qing elite social mobilization could continue and mature into a successful bourgeois-style revolution or whether the legacy of Qing bureaucratic power could be remodeled into an effective instrument of state control were found in these arenas.

Neither the various governments claiming state power nor the local elites could operate autonomously during the republican period. Nor could either side dominate the other, despite the increased use of military force. A recurrent theme of twentieth-century politics was the unwillingness of the government to accommodate societal initiatives even though it was unable to control them. The first years of the Republic saw an extension of the conflict between centralized bureaucratic modernization, led by Yuan Shikai, and elite activism, manifested in a burgeoning democratic movement—symbolized by local assemblies that flourished until they were cut off by Yuan Shikai after 1913.[9] During the 1920's there was another wave of elite social mobilization in the cities. Then, during the Nan-

jing decade from 1927 to 1937, the Guomindang again attempted
to combine bureaucratic modernization with centralization,
the downward extension of governmental power and institutions, and social mobilization under the control of the party or
auxiliary organizations like the Youth Corps.

Although it has been argued that processes of administrative
elaboration and penetration of society continued throughout
the disorders of the republican period,[10] it is less evident that
successful state-building resulted. It is evident, however, that
the buildup of societal organization continued. The provincial
governments headed by militarists in Zhejiang may have had
better control over elites by the mid-1920's than they had
shortly after the revolution. Their authority was not secure,
however, and they did not succeed in dominating social organizations. Such organizations did not automatically serve as a
basis for bureaucratic or military control; instead, they often
made control more difficult to impose.[11] This proposition, based
on the history of Zhejiang before the Northern Expedition
brought the Nationalists to power in the Lower Yangtze, also
seems applicable to the Nanjing decade.

Nonetheless, it is evident that the elite organizations were
not adequate bases from which to reorganize the political structure of China. It soon became clear that the constitutionalists
and the republican revolutionaries who formed the 1912 Nanjing provisional government headed by Sun Yat-sen could not
gain control of the country. There was not an effective bourgeois revolution in China, for complicated reasons that range
from the diverse and uneven levels of socioeconomic development—patterns in urban-oriented cores were not replicated
throughout the country—to the unfavorable international situations—most dramatically, of course, in the 1930's when the
world depression was followed by the war with Japan. Here I
will point to three factors that relate directly to political processes illustrated in Zhejiang during the late Qing.[12]

The first involves the lack of a completely autonomous, de-
fensible power base. It was possible for social organization to
increase, for authority to shift from the bureaucracy toward the
elite, and for political opposition to develop under the cen-

tralized bureaucratic monarchy. Nevertheless, until the very end, it remained both illegal and difficult to establish independent military power, autonomous territorial enclaves, or oppositionist groups.[13] Elite power grew within this system to the point where it brought down the imperial structure, but in the long run it suffered because the elite social organizations had grown under the military and political umbrella of the Qing. Once the umbrella was gone, the bourgeois and old-regime successors of the late imperial merchant-gentry could not match the force commanded by militarists emerging from the new army or peripheral societies. Representational institutions on the liberal-democratic model were easily suppressed. The most promising political route for members of the elite was still organizational expansion to the point where wealth and influence could be translated into national political power. The economic expansion in urban and coastal areas during the favorable international conditions of the late 1910's and early 1920's offered some prospect of such a development.[14] It contributed to the opposition to warlords and imperialism that was sometimes expressed in provincialist movements, but it also fed into support for the reorganized Guomindang in the mid-1920's. There was, however, no time for the necessary long-term accretion of non-military social and economic power. Whatever chance the elite may have had was swamped by economic downturn, rising disorder, and war.

A second set of factors relates to the disappearance of a national center. After 1911 there was no legitimatized central government, and for more than a decade after 1916, there was not even much pretense of central authority. This situation vitiated the kind of proactive outreach from local organizational bases that was so important at the end of the Qing. For a time, what passed for national politics appeared split off from the localities. Although authoritarian, militarist-bureaucratic regimes could block elite expansion, they could not control members of the elite or neutralize their defensive strategies. Localistic, defensive behavior became a politically significant part of elite interaction with governmental authority. As members of elites continued to build their organizations and redefine their public involvement, they became more likely to identify with their province,[15] their district, or their town[16] than with the nominal national government, which could not inspire support and which, until the Nanjing decade, might even be too fleeting to oppose.

Third, members of the elite themselves were more politically divided during the Republic than during the late Qing. In part, this condition reflected a progressive fragmentation into new social components, but it also related to changes in the major politicizing issues. Non-military members of the elite sometimes united against warlords wielding political power, and nationalism continued to unite elites in opposition to governmental authority. This phenomenon can be seen, for instance, in the opposition to Yuan Shikai's acquiescence to Japan's Twenty-one Demands in 1915, in the May Fourth Movement, in the revolutionary phase of the Guomintang during the mid-1920's, and in the opposition to the Nanjing government's failure to resist Japan from 1931 to 1936.

Divisive social questions, however, outweighed the effect of nationalism in unifying members of the elite during the republican period. At the end of the Qing socialist ideas of economic equality and redistribution of social power—which were different from the old ideals of an equitable, harmonious agrarian society under gentry dominance—had just begun to be raised by a few radicals. Once the goal of political revolution was realized by establishing a republic, social questions rapidly acquired political import. Fear of disorder may not adequately explain core-area elite involvement in the 1911 Revolution, but it did contribute to the willingness of established elites to limit revolution in favor of authority in the years that followed. Other elites developed a concern, buttressed by anarchist, Marxist, and other socialist ideologies, for the social problems readily apparent in a poor society with large discrepancies in wealth, which was experiencing disruptive economic change and sociopolitical turmoil. The idea of peaceably achieved social justice attracted members of the new middle classes with various political affiliations. However, the willingness of some members of the elite to make common cause with peasants or workers, and particularly to use social violence as an instrument of change, involved matters of life, death, and livelihood that split the elite more dramatically than the political questions of the late Qing.[17]

Divisions within the elite did not follow class lines, although they often reflected the political or social prospects of groups or individuals. Political action was more violent than it had been during the late Qing, and mobilization became more widespread. Many members of the elite preferred to pursue affairs within their own localities without risking wider political involvement. People whose views and methods were outside the range tolerated by regimes controlling their territory were not only excluded; they also risked imprisonment or death.[18] Given the fragmentation of authority, however, they often had an option of fleeing elsewhere. Communists had a chance to establish their base areas in peripheries and to mobilize the discontent existing in peasant communities because of this political fragmentation and the further disruptions of a major war. Subsequent political trends could no longer be seen only in core areas, nor would revolutionary political demands continue to arise mainly from the interests of the elite.

As both governmental and societal organization continued to expand and adapt during the turmoil of the republican period, foundations were being laid for a new sociopolitical integration. This integration would not, however, be on the lines mapped out by the late Qing protagonists. After the revolution destroyed the monarchy, the bureaucratic-statist expansion and the elite organizational expansion cancelled each other out. To capture the divergent social and political strands traceable to the nineteenth century, another revolutionary movement was required, which would reorganize society and build up the sociopolitical organization from below. That revolution would then produce its own set of political conditions and problems, which would no longer so closely reflect the late imperial heritage.

Appendixes

APPENDIX A

Jinshi *Degree Holders from Zhejiang During the Qing*

Native place	1644–1695	1696–1745	1746–1795	1796–1850	1851–1904	Total
Hangzhou						
Renhe	47	88	103	87	59	384
Qiantang	33	87	81	84	51	336
Haining	34	35	21	15	13	118
Yuhang	12	2	6	4	4	28
Fuyang	5	2	1	5	4	17
Lin'an	4	2	2	0	0	8
Xindeng	2	1	0	3	0	6
Yuqian	1	1	1	0	1	4
Changhua	1	1	1	0	0	3
Total	139	219	216	198	132	904
Jiaxing						
Jiaxing	26	15	21	13	11	86
Xiushui	20	18	19	12	13	82
Jiashan	29	20	15	15	6	85
Pinghu	23	17	7	21	6	74
Tongxiang	16	24	9	8	8	65
Haiyan	19	32	13	10	4	78
Shimen	8	8	10	5	2	33
Total	141	134	94	84	50	503
Huzhou						
Wucheng	26	38	20	13	13	110
Guian	24	40	32	36	25	157
Deqing	15	20	17	9	6	67
Changxing	16	11	4	5	0	36
Wukang	5	1	1	0	0	7
Anji	2	1	1	2	1	7
Xiaofeng	0	0	0	0	0	0
Total	88	111	75	65	45	384
REGION TOTAL	368	464	385	347	227	1,791

Native place	1644–1695	1696–1745	1746–1795	1796–1850	1851–1904	Total
Shaoxing						
Shanyin	23	28	29	28	33	141
Guiji	19	33	26	32	30	140
Xiaoshan	10	11	16	31	21	89
Yuyao	15	7	9	14	15	60
Zhuji	8	8	0	7	11	34
Shangyu	4	9	6	5	8	32
Cheng	2	1	0	4	2	9
Xinchang	3	1	1	6	1	12
Total	84	98	87	127	121	517
Ningbo						
Yin	43	16	11	18	43	131
Ciqi	18	9	5	9	16	57
Zhenhai	0	4	4	5	16	29
Fenghua	2	1	0	1	2	6
Xiangshan	2	0	1	0	1	4
Dinghai	7	1	1	0	1	10
Total	72	31	22	33	79	237
REGION TOTAL	156	129	109	160	200	754
Jinhua						
Jinhua	1	1	1	9	7	19
Lanqi	4	6	2	4	2	18
Dongyang	2	0	3	4	3	12
Pujiang	0	2	2	4	0	8
Tangqi	0	1	0	1	0	2
Yongkang	0	2	0	2	3	7
Yiwu	5	1	1	5	3	15
Wuyi	1	1	0	1	1	4
Total	13	14	9	30	19	85
Yanzhou						
Jiande	6	5	0	2	3	16
Suian	7	4	1	0	0	12
Qun'an	6	3	2	0	0	11
Shouchang	0	1	1	0	0	2
Fenshui	0	5	0	0	0	5
Tonglu	0	1	0	1	1	3
Total	19	19	4	3	4	49
Quzhou						
Qu	3	5	2	6	3	19
Jiangshan	0	0	0	0	0	0
Longyou	3	1	0	1	2	7
Changshan	1	1	0	0	0	2
Kaihua	3	1	1	1	0	6
Total	10	8	3	8	5	34
REGION TOTAL	42	41	16	41	28	168

Native place	1644–1695	1696–1745	1746–1795	1796–1850	1851–1904	Total
Taizhou						
Linhai	4	0	1	0	3	8
Huangyan	1	3	0	4	12	20
Tiantai	1	2	2	0	3	8
Ninghai	0	0	0	0	2	2
Xianju	1	1	0	0	0	2
Taiping	0	0	1	1	0	2
Total	7	6	4	5	20	42
Wenzhou						
Yongjia	2	4	1	3	3	13
Ruian	0	0	2	3	11	16
Pingyang	0	1	0	0	0	1
Luoqing	0	1	0	0	1	2
Taishun	1	0	0	1	2	4
Yuhuan	0	0	0	1	0	1
Total	3	6	3	8	17	37
Chuzhou						
Lishui	0	0	0	0	0	0
Songyang	1	0	0	0	1	2
Jinyun	2	0	0	0	1	3
Qingtian	0	0	0	1	1	2
Qingyuan	0	0	1	0	0	1
Suichang	0	0	0	1	1	2
Xuanping	0	1	0	0	0	1
Yunhe	0	0	0	0	0	0
Jingning	0	0	0	0	0	0
Longquan	0	0	0	0	0	0
Total	3	1	1	2	4	11
REGION TOTAL	13	13	8	15	41	90
PROVINCIAL TOTAL	579	647	518	563	496	2,803

SOURCE: Fang and Du, *Zengjiao.*

NOTE: The figures presented here are lower than figures derived from gazetteers—which inflate the record by sometimes including permanent out-migrants, etc. The Fang-Du list provides a single source from which to compare districts. The totals for Hangzhou, Shaoxing, Jiaxing and Huzhou prefectures do not agree with figures in Ho, *Ladder*, but my count of the provincial total from the Fang-Du list is very close to Ho's (p. 228). My last two periods are 55 years instead of 50 years because it is more useful to have nineteenth-century breakdowns coincide with reign periods than to have five equal fifty-two-year periods. The additional five years does not alter the trends observable from the figures.

Academies in Zhejiang During the Nineteenth Century

	Founding dates[a]						
Location	Pre-Qing	SZ–YZ, 92 yrs.	QL, 60 yrs.	JQ–DG, 55 yrs.	XF–GX, 50 yrs.	Not known	Total
Hangzhou							
Renhe/Qiantang	4	3	–	2	–	1	10
Haining	1	3	–	2	2	–	8
Yuhang	–	–	1	1	–	1	3
Fuyang	–	–	–	1	–	–	1
Lin'an	–	–	1	–	–	–	1
Xindeng	–	–	–	–	–	–	0
Yuqian	–	–	1	–	1	–	2
Changhua	–	–	–	–	1	–	1
Subtotal	5	6	3	6	4	2	26
Percent[b]	20.8%	25%	12.5%	25%	17.7%		
Jiaxing							
Jiaxing/Xiushui	1	1	–	1	3	–	6
Jiashan	1	–	1	–	2	–	4
Pinghu	2	1	3	–	1	–	7
Tongxiang	–	–	1	–	2	–	3
Haiyan	–	1	1	1	1	–	4
Shimen	1	–	1	–	1	–	3
Subtotal	5	3	7	2	10	0	27
Percent	18.5%	11.7%	25.9%	7.4%	37%		
Huzhou							
Wucheng/Guian	1	–	–	1	4	–	6
Deqing	–	–	2	–	–	–	2
Changxing	1	–	–	–	1	–	2
Wukang	–	–	1	–	–	–	1
Anji	–	–	1	–	–	–	1
Xiaofeng	–	1	–	–	–	–	1
Subtotal	2	1	4	1	5	0	13
Percent	15.3%	7.6%	30.7%	7.6%	38.4%		
REGION TOTAL	12	10	14	9	19	2	66
PERCENT	18.7%	16%	21.8%	14%	29.7%		

Location	Pre-Qing	SZ–YZ	QL	JQ–DG	XF–GX	Not known	Total
Shaoxing							
Shanyin/Guiji	2	2	1	–	–	–	5
Xiaoshan	–	2	1	–	–	–	3
Yuyao	1	–	1	–	3	–	5
Zhuji	1	–	1	–	1	3	6
Shangyu	–	1	1	1	–	–	3
Cheng	2	–	1	2	2	–	7
Xinchang	1	–	1	–	1	–	3
Subtotal	7	5	7	3	7	3	32
Percent	24.1%	17.2%	24.1%	10.3%	24.1%		
Ningbo							
Yin	–	1	–	2	–	–	3
Ciqi	1	1	–	–	–	–	2
Zhenhai	1	1	2	1	3	1	9
Fenghua	2	3	1	–	1	–	7
Xiangshan	1		1	1	3	–	6
Dinghai	1	1	–	1	1	–	4
Subtotal	6	7	4	5	8	1	31
Percent	20%	23.3%	13.3%	16.6%	26.6%		
REGION TOTAL	13	12	11	8	15	4	63
PERCENT	22%	20.3%	18.6%	13.5%	25.4%		
Jinhua							
Jinhua	–	3	–	–	1	–	4
Lanqi	–	–	1	1	–	–	2
Dongyang	–		–	–	–	–	
Pujiang	4	–	–	1	–	–	5
Tangqi	–	–	–	–	1	–	1
Yongkang	1	2	1	1	–	–	5
Yiwu	–	1	1	–	–	–	2
Wuyi		1	–	–	–	–	1
Subtotal	5	7	3	3	2	0	20
Percent	25%	35%	15%	15%	10%		
Yanzhou							
Jiande	–	1	–	2	–		3
Suian	2	–	–	1	–	–	3
Qun'an	–	1	–	–	1	–	2
Shouchang	–	–	–	1	–	–	1
Fenshui	1	–	–	–	–	–	1
Tonglu	1	1	–	–	–	–	2
Subtotal	4	3	0	4	1	0	12
Percent	33.3%	25%	0%	33.3%	8.3%		
Quzhou							
Qu	–	2	1	–	–	–	3
Jiangshan	1	1	–	–	–	–	2
Longyou	–	–	3	1	1	–	5
Changshan	–	1	–	1	–	–	2
Kaihua	–	1	–	1	2	1	5
Subtotal	1	5	4	3	3	1	17
Percent	6.2%	31.2%	25%	18.7%	18.7%		
REGION TOTAL	10	15	7	10	6	1	49
PERCENT	20.8%	31.2%	14.5%	20.8%	12.5%		

		Founding dates[a]					
Location	Pre-Qing	SZ–YZ, 92 yrs.	QL, 60 yrs.	JQ–DG, 55 yrs.	XF–GX, 50 yrs.	Not known	Total
Taizhou							
Linhai	4	1	1	1	7	–	14
Huangyan	1	2	2	–	9	1	15
Tiantai	–	–	–	–	–	–	0
Ninghai	2	–	1	1	5	2	11
Xianju	1	–	1	3	1	–	6
Taiping	–	–	1	–	14	–	15
Subtotal	8	3	6	5	36	3	61
Percent	13.7%	5.1%	10.3%	8.6%	62%		
Wenzhou							
Yongjia	3	–	1	–	–	–	4
Ruian	–	1	1	1	–	–	3
Pingyang	–	1	4	–	2	–	7
Luoqing	–	1	–	2	–	–	3
Taishun	–	–	–	–	–	–	–
Yuhuan	–	–	1	–	1	–	2
Subtotal	3	3	7	3	3	0	19
Percent	15.7%	15.7%	36.8%	15.7%	15.7%		
Chuzhou							
Lishui	1	1	–	–	1	–	3
Songyang	–	–	1	–	–	–	1
Jinyun	–	–	1	1	3	3	8
Qingtian	1	1	1	1	1	1	6
Qingyuan	–	–	1	–	–	–	1
Suichang	1	–	1	1	–	–	3
Xuanping	–	–	1	–	–	–	1
Yunhe	–	–	–	1	–	–	1
Jingning	1	1	–	–	–	2	4
Longquan	1	–	2	–	–	–	3
Subtotal	5	3	8	4	5	6	31
Percent	20%	12%	32%	16%	20%		
REGION TOTAL	16	9	21	12	44	9	111
PERCENT	15.6%	8.8%	20.5%	11.7%	43.1%		
PROVINCIAL TOTAL	51	46	53	39	84	16	289
PERCENT	18.6%	16.9%	19.4%	14.2%	30.0%		

SOURCES: Zhejiang prefectural and district gazetteers.

NOTE: Because little information is available for the early to mid-Qing, I have excluded academies that appear to have been defunct before 1800. I have also excluded academies that are specifically described as lineage academies, and do not seem to have been open to others, and a few established in the late 1890's that were really modern schools. The sources underreport either because gazetteer coverage is not complete or because prefectural and even district gazetteers sometimes omit academies established at lower urban levels. There is also some minor inflation because I have tended to be inclusive when it is uncertain whether an academy continued to operate.

[a] SZ, Shunzhi (1644–61); YZ, Yongzheng (1723–35); QL, Qianlong (1736–95); JQ, Jiaqing (1796–1820); DG, Daoguang (1821–50); XF, Xianfeng (1851–61); GX, Guangxu (1875–1908). Because academies were not established after the 1890's, I have counted the Guangxu reign years only to 1900.

[b] Percentages calculated from the number of academies with known founding dates.

Main Sectors of Modern Business in Zhejiang Before 1912

Shipping

Company	Place	Date	Capital (000 yuan)	Ships	Tons
Daishengchang Merch't Ship'g Co.	Hangzhou-Suzhou-Shanghai	1892	120	25	
Zhenhai Merch't Ship'g Co.	Ningbo-Zhenhai	1900	15	1	69
Ning-Xiang Steamship Bureau	Ningbo-Xiangshan	1904	30		
Ning-Hai Merch't Steamship Co.	Ningbo-Xiangshan	1905	30	2	173
Hu-Shao Steamship Co.	Shanghai-Shaoxing	1905	300		
Yong-Rui Steamship Co.	Yongjia-Ruian	1905	12	2	
Lishe Co.	Ningbo-Zhenhai	1906	20	2	86
Yongli Merch't Steamship Co	Taizhou	1906			
Yongan Co	Ningbo-Yuyao	1907	3	1	96
Qianjiang Merch't Steamship Co.	Hangzhou	1908	20	5	
Ning-Shao Steamship Co.	Shanghai-Ningbo	1909	1,000	3	5,900
Liyong Merch't Steamship Co.	Ningbo-Yuyao	1910	20		
Xing Zhangtai Co.	Shanghai-Ningbo-Wenzhou				
Yong River Co.	Ningbo-Zhenhai			6	
Meiyi Merch't Steamship Co.	Ningbo-Yuyao			1	80
Yong-Ning Steamship Co.	Ningbo-Haimen-Wenzhou			4	
Waihai Steamship Co.	Ningbo-Haimen-Wenzhou			1	480
Tongyi Co.	Hangzhou		300		

SOURCES: Li Guoqi, *Zhongguo*, p. 336; Yan Zhongping, pp. 223–24; Tōa Dōbunkai, *Shina*, pp. 281–318.

Silk Filatures / Cotton Spinning and Weaving

Place	Date	Reels/ spindles/ looms	Capital (000 yuan)	Founders
		SILK FILATURES		
Hangzhou	1895	240 r.	424	Pang Yuanji/
Tanglou				Ding Bing
(Shaoxing)	1897	208 r.		
Xiaoshan	1897	208 r.	240	Chen Boyun/
				Lou Jinghui
Shaoxing	1901	108 r.		
Huzhou	1911	200 r.	100	
Xiaoshan	1911	336 r.		
Tangqi	1911	276 r.		
		COTTON SPINNING AND WEAVING		
Ningbo	1896	11,048 s.	450	Li Houyou
Hangzhou	1897	20,000 s.	533	Pang Yuanji/
				Ding Bing
Xiaoshan	1899	10,192 s.	450	Chen Boyun/
				Lou Jinghui
Deqing	1903	weav'g		Chen Wen
Hangzhou	1904	weav'g		Yu Huaju
Hangzhou	1904	34 l.		
Qu	1905	spin'g/weav'g		
Shaoxing	1905	weav'g		
Jinhua	1906	weav'g		
Shaoxing	1906			
Jiaxing	1906	spin'g		
Lishui	1907			Chen Tahe
Haining	1907	weav'g		Ting Yuzhang
Yiwu	1907	weav'g		
Dinghai	1907	weav'g		
Ningbo	1908			
Deqing	1908			

SOURCES: For silk, Sun Yutang, 1.2: 973, 976; 2.2: 634–40, 691, 694–96, 794, 798, 839–40, 902, 1091–95; Chen Zhen, 4.2: 181, 198; IMC, *Trade Reports*, 1898, p. 340; 1904, p. 538; 1906, p. 323; Nonggongshang bu (1910), 2.5: 8a; *Xiaoshan xianzhi gao*, 1: 39a–40a; *Deqing xian xinzhi*, 3: 16a; *Dongfang zazhi*, 4.12: *shiye* 160; Yan Zhongping, pp. 98–99; Eng, pp. 58–59; Li Guoqi, *Zhongguo*, p. 307. For cotton, Li Guoqi, *Zongguo*, p. 307; *Dongfang zazhi, passim*; Sun Yutang, 2.2: 691, 695, 794, 798, 839–40, 892, 1044.

Reference Matter

NOTES

Complete authors' names, titles, and publication data are given in the Selected Bibliography, pp. 385–408.

Chapter One

1. Major articles on the "sprouts of capitalism" have appeared in several collections, beginning with Zhongguo Renmin Daxue, *Taolun ji*, in 1957. See also, more recently, Zhongguo Renmin Daxue, *Lunwen ji*. The issues of the appearance of the bourgeoisie in the late nineteenth century and the role of the bourgeoisie in the 1911 Revolution will be considered more specifically in Chapters 2 and 8.

2. Peng, "Fazhan," pp. 43–60.

3. Estimates differ. See Perkins, p. 207; Ho, *Population*, pp. 281–82.

4. Perkins, pp. 51, 186–87; James Lee, pp. 738–41.

5. Elvin, *Pattern*, p. 306, estimates that agricultural returns per additional labor input were rapidly diminishing in the late eighteenth century. Perkins, p. 188, suggests a later date in the early twentieth century. On nineteenth-century expansion of commerce and proliferation of market towns in the Ningbo and Shanghai areas, see Shiba, "Ningpo," and Elvin, "Market Towns."

6. Bastid, *Réforme*, p. 26; Chang Chung-li, *Income*; Cole, "Shaohsing," pp. 89–98; Rankin, "Rural-Urban Continuities;" Schoppa, *Chinese Elites*, pp. 59–60; Schoppa, "Composition." On Japanese studies of rural elites' combined commercial, landholding, and usurious interests, see Grove and Esherick, pp. 412, 424.

7. See, for instance, Metzger, "Ch'ing State," pp. 19–27.

8. Mobility within the gentry is suggested in Ho, *Population;* the variety of careers pursued by gentry are studied in Chang Chung-li, *Income;* the expansion of the number of both upper- and lower-degree holders is stressed in Chang Chung-li, *Chinese Gentry.* None of these works suggests that the gentry's relations to the state were changing, and both Chang, *Income,* pp. 43–73, and Ho, *Ladder,* pp. 34–35, strongly differentiate *shengyuan* from upper-degree holders. Debates over the dividing line between upper and lower gentry are beyond the scope of this work. I include *gongsheng* among upper-degree holders.

9. Shiba, pp. 414–18; Elvin, "Market Towns," pp. 464–67; Morita, p. 266; Mann [Susan Mann Jones], "Finance," pp. 50–69; Yu, *Chunzai,* 4:2381–82.

10. On sojourning, see Skinner, "Mobility Strategies." The balance between permanent and temporary migration is not known. Barren land in Sichuan was filling up by the mid-nineteenth century, and land reclamation in Hunan had reached diminishing returns in the eighteenth century. Immigration to Yunnan reached its height in the late eighteenth and early nineteenth centuries, but Chinese migrated to Manchuria in the twentieth century. Ho, *Population,* chap. 7; James Lee, pp. 742–43; Perdue, pp. 754–57; Perkins, pp. 212, 236. There is substantial evidence for temporary, job-related mobility, and it is logical to assume that it increased with population growth, commercialization, urbanization, and industrialization.

11. Skinner, "Regional Urbanization," pp. 213, 229. On regional zonation and core-peripheral distinctions in China, see ibid., pp. 214–20. Schoppa, *Chinese Elites,* chap. 2, provides a detailed core-periphery model for Zhejiang. For a more dynamic application of core-periphery concepts in the history of European capitalism, see Wallerstein. Historians of China have often substituted urban-rural for core-peripheral distinctions. There are difficulties, however, in drawing a line between the city and the countryside. The amount and type of contact between higher and lower urban levels differed between the core and the periphery, and there were more intermediate towns in the cores.

12. Skinner, "Marketing."

13. In such respects, dependency theories of underdevelopment require modification when applied to China. For this theory, see Wilber. For evidence of the impact of the Western-centered world economy on parts of the Chinese economy since the sixteenth century, see Atwell, "Notes," and Marks, *Revolution,* chap. 5. Moulder, *Japan, China,* is a generalized first attempt to apply dependency theory to China.

14. Lillian M. Li, *Silk Trade,* pp. 96–112.

15. Bastid-Bruguière, pp. 539–71.

16. An English summary is Yang, "Administration." The classic late imperial statement on the subject is Gu, "Junxian lun" (On the centralized bureaucratic monarchy) in *Gu Tinglin,* pp. 12–17. A good

introduction to the ideas of other Ming and Song thinkers concerned with this and related topics is Xiao Gongquan, *Sixiang shi*.

17. Chang Chung-li, *Chinese Gentry*, p. 116.

18. This view of Chinese absolutism is well summarized in Ho, "Salient Aspects," pp. 9–25. A classic statement on despotism appears in Wittfogel, *Oriental Despotism*; the view is also inherent in much of the Marxist literature on the Asiatic mode of production. Hsiao, *Rural China*, focuses on problems of despotic control in what he views as a period of cyclical decline in the nineteenth century.

19. On this process in Europe, see Tilly, *National States*.

20. Theories linking the rise of European absolutism to capitalism originated in the writings of Marx and Engels. This literature is surveyed and the countertheory that absolutism protected the feudal nobility is set forth in Anderson, *Lineages*, Chap. 1.

21. A cogent statement of Qing dynastic decline appears in Michael, "Introduction."

22. Zelin, pp. 18–21.

23. Bartlett, pp. 296–308.

24. A relatively positive assessment of Chinese officialdom appears in Weber, *China*, chap. 2, but Weber nonetheless considers the bureaucracy too dependent upon extralegal income and deficient in specialization and rationality. Negative views that regard the political development of the Chinese empire (and, in part, of its bureaucracy) as less differentiated, adaptable, and autonomous than "modern" Western states are summarized in Badie and Birnbaum, *Sociology*, pp. 46–47.

25. The major study is Metzger, *Ch'ing Bureaucracy*.

26. Political implications are discussed in Moore, *Social Origins*, pp. 181–87.

27. Zelin, pp. 303–8.

28. Stepan, pp. 26–40.

29. Anderson, pp. 226–35.

30. Beattie, pp. 256, 260–63, 266; I Songgyu.

31. Grove and Esherick, p. 412; Marks, chap. 2.

32. This view is implicit in Michael, "Introduction," and Hsiao, *Rural China*; it is a major theme in Wakeman and Grant, pp. 2–4 and *passim*.

33. The vast literature on the normative use of "public" is beyond the scope of this study. It may be noted, however, that critics of autocracy during earlier dynasties such as Chen Liang, Ye Shi, Huang Zongxi, and Gu Yanwu reversed the equation of the emperor and state with public by arguing that the system had become perverted because the emperor pursued his personal, private advantage. Xiao Gongquan, 2: 154, 157, 258, 270.

34. See, for example, Xuebu zongwu si (General Affairs Office of

the Ministry of Education), *Guangxu sanshisan nianfen, diyi ci jiao-yu tongji tubiao* (First educational statistical tables, 1907). I thank William Rowe and Keith Schoppa for pointing out the routine use of the public category in water control.

35. Dennerline, "Wuxi County"; Rowe, pp. 313–15. Temples also might perform public functions. Schipper, pp. 668–69.

36. Skinner, "Introduction: Urban Development," pp. 19–21, notes that the number of local administrative units had been declining relative to the population since the Tang because the state lacked the fiscal, communicative, and control capacities to keep increasing the size of the bureaucracy. This trend would have, of course, accelerated during the Qing because of rapid population growth.

37. Lillian M. Li, "Introduction," pp. 691, 697.

38. Late nineteenth-century management and early twentieth-century self-government could be related back to Gu Yanwu's seventeenth-century proposals for giving local men a greater role in local affairs. Gu's ideas were definitely used at the end of the Qing. See Kuhn, "Local Self-Government," pp. 261–70. Newspapers, periodicals, and essays referred to Gu quite frequently. However, managerial activities were too situational to be rationalized only by seventeenth-century theories, and the theories themselves were being fashioned anew under changing circumstances.

39. Collective action might involve most of the community in a village, but not at higher urban levels. One definition of collective goods—as those which must be made available to all members of a group if possessed by some—and group action appears in Olson, *Collective Action*. His view that collective goods are provided through exchange transactions, in which individuals contribute in return for non-monetary rewards of privilege and status, requires some modification in the context of Qing public management to allow room for public action based on shared norms and definitions; his arguments that all groups (not just the state) provide collective goods and that small groups are more effective than large ones seem applicable. In the nineteenth century, concepts of state responsibility were combined with community expectations and appropriated to the elite-managed public sphere. Managers, who formed into small groups, could function effectively. For the sake of prestige and community status, they might identify their actions with what they considered the collective good of the community rather than use their positions to pursue private interests.

40. Watt, pp. 112, 158. The extent of the decline varied in different geographical areas and different spheres. Dike administrators continued to serve in Hunan. See Perdue, p. 750.

41. Reischauer and Fairbank, pp. 311–13.

42. For a negative picture of lower gentry, see Gu Yanwu's essay on

shengyuan. Gu Tinglin, 1. 22–26; also Hsiao Kung-chuan, pp. 133–37 and *passim*.

43. Watt, pp. 144–45, 164.

44. Such practices, which are often considered symptoms of decay, can be viewed positively as adjustments of the political system to changing circumstances. Loyalty was maintained by increasing the number and variety of people who had access to, and benefited from, the system.

45. Kuhn, *Rebellion*, pp. 217–18, 222; Ichiko, "Gentry," pp. 298–99; Polachek, "Gentry"; Ocko, p. 8.

46. Gu, *Rizhi lu*, 3 *shang*: 47–49.

47. Elman, *From Philosophy*, pp. 13–22; Guy, conclusion.

48. Elman, *From Philosophy*, chaps. 3–4; Whitbeck, "The Historical," pp. x–xi, 83–98, 225 n. 3.

49. Whitbeck, pp. 47, 97–98, chap 3; Jones, "Scholasticism"; Jones and Kuhn, "Dynastic decline," pp. 148–54.

50. Polachek, "Literati," pp. 68, 450–51.

51. On the Opium War *qingyi* debates, see ibid., part 2, chap. 1.

52. On institutional divisions between emperors, female regents, and the Grand Council, see Kwong.

53. Huber, pp. 32–37.

54. This framework is suggested and the evolution of *qingyi* analyzed in Rankin, "Public Opinion." Qi, "Didang," p. 36, suggests a split between members of the ruling class with and without authority.

55. The theory of *qingyi* as an oppositionist expression of frustrated literati officials without policy influence comes from Polachek, *Opium War*, chap. 2.

56. Chan, "Government," pp. 460–62.

57. Fairbank, *World Order*, chap. 1. I use the word patriotism to describe attitudes before the 1890's mainly to avoid unnecessary disputes over whether people must have a fully formed conception of a nation-state to be nationalistic. Some Chinese made this transition, but other members of the old-regime elite who took part in nationalistic movements seem to have slid easily and imperceptibly from "patriotism" into "nationalism" without rejecting old values or unambiguously transferring their loyalty from the dynasty to a Chinese nation-state.

58. See, for instance, the interpretation that the Enlightenment worked its way down from the French old-regime elite, which had absorbed new ideas, rather than coming from the bourgeoisie. Darnton, pp. 28–29.

59. On this process in Western Europe, see the articles in Tilly, *National States*.

60. On the shift to commercial taxes, see Yeh-chien Wang, *Land Taxation*, pp. 79–83; on the lost opportunity to transform the government by upgrading and seriously using the sub-bureaucracy, see Ocko,

pp. 130–35, 176–77. The problem of restructuring and bureaucratizing taxation is studied in Mann, "Commercial Taxation."

61. These points draw upon, but also diverge from, the views of the historians whose works will be more specifically discussed and cited in Chapter 6. The most important are Esherick; Fincher; Ichiko, "Political and Institutional Reform"; Ichiko, "Gentry"; Kuhn, "Self-Government"; Mann, "Commercial Taxation"; MacKinnon.

62. Tilly, Tilly, and Tilly, p. 244.

63. Ibid., p. 244–54.

Chapter Two

1. *Chinese Elites*, chap. 2, map p. 14, appendix B. A major source of data is *Zhongguo shiye zhi*. On macroregions in China, see Skinner, "Regional Urbanization," pp. 211–49.

2. Shangyu district might be included, but it appears to have been somewhat less developed in the nineteenth century than Xiaoshan and Yuyao. The core regions of Jiangnan had been established for centuries, and those of Ningbo and Shaoxing since at least the mid-Qing. Actually, each district had its own core and periphery, so the situation was complex.

3. Liu Shiji, 8.7: 328.

4. For a detailed study of Jinhua, see Li Guoqi and Zhu Hong.

5. Ibid., pp. 124–30; Lillian M. Li, *Silk Trade*, pp. 106, 110–11; Eng.

6. General geographies of Zhejiang include Zhang Qiyun, *Zhejiang*; Ge Suicheng; Lin Chuanjia; Xu Baoshan.

7. *Zhongguo shiye zhi*, J107–8. During the Qing there would have been thirteen districts. Those that divided prefectural capitals were combined after 1911.

8. See Chuan and Kraus, p. 77. Detailed figures for the early 1930's show only 18 of 75 districts with a rice surplus. Ten of these have been classified by Schoppa as inner- or outer-periphery, and only four as inner-core, i.e., a surplus generally indicated low levels of urbanization. *Zhongguo shiye zhi*, J51.

9. On acreage, see ibid., J167–68; on local specializations, see Eng, pp. 158–60.

10. Shiba, "Ningpo."

11. Skinner, "Regional Urbanization," p. 215.

12. Li Guoqi, "Min-Zhe-Tai," p. 431.

13. IMC, *Trade Reports*, 1882, p. 224; 1887, p. 246.

14. Ma, 1: 5b.

15. *Shen bao*, Dec. 22, 1874, p. 2; May 4, 1876, p. 2; Cole, "Shaohsing," p. 167.

16. Lin, pp. 251–86; Li Guoqi and Zhu Hong, pp. 119, 130, 143, 153, 164.

17. *Yongkang xianzhi*, 2: 20b; *Pujiang xianzhi gao*, 4: 59a, 66b; Kang, "New Data," p. 731.

18. Ho, *Ladder*, pp. 227, 230, 241, 247; Chang Chung-li, *Chinese Gentry*, p. 123.

19. This observation is compatible with Pan and Fei's conclusion (p. 9) that 43 percent of selected Zhejiang *jinshi* came from rural townships.

20. Cole, "Shaoxing Connection," pp. 320–21 and *passim*.

21. Wakeman, *Strangers*, pp. 181–85. For more detail, see Liu Boji, and Grimm, p. 481. My figures for Zhejiang are not comparable to the Guangdong figures because the latter include *shexue, yixue*, and lineage academies while I have tried to restrict my count to public academies. The academy structure in the two provinces was different.

22. Zhang Yin; Elman, *From Philosophy*, chap. 3.

23. For a summary of these schools, see Elman, "Ch'ing," and Liang.

24. On the Eastern Zhejiang Historical School, see *Liang*, pp. 19–24; He Bingsong; Zhang Xuecheng, 1.2: 56–57; Nivison, pp. 17, 271–79.

25. On the Yongjia and Yongkang schools see He Bingsong; Tillman; Lo; John Langlois; Hou, 4: 692–96, 740–51; Xiao, 2: 153–67; Wu, pp. 3–8.

26. See Appendix A. In the period 1851–1904 there were 200 *jinshi* from Shao-Ning and 227 from Hang-Jia-Hu compared to 160 and 347 from 1796 to 1850 and 109 and 385 from 1746 to 1795. See also *Guozhao Liang-Zhe ke ming lu*.

27. The exclusion of academies closed before the nineteenth century weights the percentages toward later periods. However, the number is small and may be compensated for by the longer timespan of the Qianlong (1736–95) and the exclusion of the transitional academies of the 1890's. Because sources are incomplete, percentages can not be interpreted literally, but the main point that more academies were established per year in the late nineteenth century than at any other time during the Qing appears valid.

28. *Shen bao*, Oct. 29, 1882, p. 2; *Xiangshan xianzhi*, 14: 35b. Grimm, p. 486, reaches similar conclusions about Guangdong academies.

29. *Nanxun zhi* (1922) 3: 1b–2a; *Wucheng xianzhi* 2: 22a–b; *Shuanglin zhenzhi*, 8: 3a.

30. *Linhai xianzhi gao*, 8: 19a–32b. For examples of market town academies in other districts, see *Zhenhai xianzhi*, 11: *xuexiao xia* 11a, 12a–b; *Haining zhouzhi gao*, 4: 12b, 4a–b (here the *jiangshe* were in effect academies); *Jiaxing xianzhi*, 5: 13a, 17b, 34b; *Wu-Qing zhenzhi*, 24: 10a–b.

31. *Daishan zhenzhi*, 8: 3b–4a; *Puyuan zhi*, 8: 14b; *Wu-Qing zhenzhi*, 24: 11b.

32. Jen, pp. 306–7, 371, 433–43, 478–91.

33. Ibid., p. 436; Li Zhufeng; Hu Fengdan Yongkang, 1b–2a; Cole, People, pp. 9–21.

34. See, for example, Shouchang xianzhi, 10: 9a–15b; Cole, People, pp. 20–21.

35. Perkins, p. 212; Ho, Population, p. 246. Official population statistics (which probably underestimate) show an even more dramatic decline to slightly over 6 million after the rebellion and a slow rise to 11.9 million by the turn of the century. Yan Zhongping, pp. 369–71. Jiangsu, Jiangxi, and Hubei also had high population losses.

36. Tan Baozhen, pp. 400–402. These estimates were by Governor Tan. Presumably, an unknown percentage of the 605,205 acres was simply unreported on the registers, but a substantial portion was probably still uncultivated.

37. Shen bao, Dec. 25, 1880; p. 1; Dec. 13, 1881, p. 1; North China Herald, July 10, 1885, pp. 39–40.

38. Li Guoqi, "You Min-Zhe," pp. 422–23. Liu Shiji, p. 275, calculates population pressure per acre of cultivated land at 1.77 in 1812 and 1.61 in 1913 using tables in Perkins, pp. 212, 236.

39. Ma, 3: 53a–57b.

40. Ho, Population, p. 243; Longyou xianzhi, 6: 43b. A similar, but less drastic, drop in land prices in districts on the Zhejiang-Anhui-Jiangxi border is recorded in Chao, "New Data," pp. 728–29.

41. Tangqi xianzhi, 3: 47b; Shen bao, Mar. 5, 1878, p. 3; Xiaoshan xianzhi gao, 4: 35a; Cole, "Shaohsing," pp. 122–24. Tenancy levels are approximate. Figures of 60–70 percent for Zhejiang and 50 percent for Quzhou are given in Li Guoqi, "Shijiu shiji," p. 149. Tenancy may not have revived uniformly throughout the province. On changes in tenancy relations in Jiangnan, see Liu Yao, pp. 115–20 and passim.

42. Zong, 2: 3a, 5b, 22a.

43. Ibid., 9: 10a; Shen bao, Aug. 4, 1882, p. 2; Sept. 21, 1879, p. 1; Yuhang xianzhi, 2: hukou, n.p.; Lin'an xianzhi, 2: hukou 3b; Ho, Population, p. 157. In Lin'an there were 12,200 natives and 34,300 immigrants in 1900.

44. Shen bao, Sept. 4, 1878, p. 1; Sept. 21, 1879, p. 1; Sun Yutang, 2.2: 1173.

45. Zong, 9: 10a; Shen bao, Oct. 7, 1878, p. 1.

46. Shen bao, Jan. 11, 1879, p. 2; Jan. 15, 1879, p. 1.

47. For example, the Zhuji gazetteer records 102,000 males and 40,000 females in 1917. Even if overstated, a sex imbalance existed. Zhuji xianzhi, 16: 18a; Deqing xian xinzhi, 4: 1a; see also Li Guoqi, "Shijiu shiji," pp. 144–45.

48. Zong, 9: 1a; Shen bao, Feb. 27, 1877, p. 2; June 22, 1877, p. 2; Aug. 4, 1877, p. 2.

49. Incidents were frequently reported in Shen bao. See, for example, Nov. 23, 1876, p. 2; Sept. 4, 1878, p. 1; Sept. 21, 1879, p. 1;

Feb. 20, 1881, p. 5; Nov. 14, 1881, p. 1; Apr. 9, 1882, p. 2; Apr. 10, 1882, p. 2; May 28, 1882, p. 2; June 5, 1882, p. 2; June 20, 1882, p. 2; June 2, 1883, p. 2.

50. *Shen bao*, Jan. 23, 1873, p. 2; July 21, 1873, p. 2; Aug. 5, 1873, p. 1; Dec. 25, 1874, p. 2; Jan. 8, 1875, p. 2; Jan. 11, 1875, p. 1; May 4, 1876, p. 2; June 10, 1876, p. 2; July 20, 1876, p. 2; Aug. 2/, 1878, p. 2; Sept. 3, 1878, p. 1; Feb. 6, 1882, p. 2; Jan. 27, 1883, p. 2.

51. On Huang's rising, see *Shen bao*, 1881–83 *passim*, especially Sept. 9, 1881, p. 1; Sept. 14, 1881, p. 1; Nov. 28, 1881, p. 1; Aug. 16, 1883, p. 1; Tan Baozhen, pp. 469–79, 481–83; Liu Bingzhang, 2: 3a, 12b–17b, 20b. On a similar profusion of guns in adjoining Wenzhou, see *Shen bao*, Nov. 4, 1882, p. 2.

52. *Shouchang xianzhi*, 10: 9a–15b.

53. Zong, 6: 4a; *Shen bao*, Jan. 26, 1875, p. 2; Oct. 16, 1876, p. 2; Oct. 31, 1876, p. 2; Sept. 4, 1878, p. 1; *Jingning xianzhi* (1873), 6: 12a–b and chap. 6; Tao, p. 19. On the general decline of militia after the Taiping period, see Chang Chung-li, *Income*, p. 70. In Xuanping (Chuzhou) self-defense units were led by men from dominant klu groups and organized in ancestral halls. Despite this integration into local social structures, the gazetteer has no record of militia between the Taiping Rebellion and 1898. *Xuanping xianzhi*, 7: 4a–5b. On banditry in peripheral parts of Shaoxing, see Cole, "Shaohsing," p. 167.

54. Lillian M. Li, *Silk Trade*, pp. 119–22.

55. Jen, pp. 422, 489.

56. Huzhou and Jiaxing are generally credited with populations of about 100,000 during the early twentieth century. See *Zhongguo nianjian*, p. 9; *Shen bao nianjian*, p. D9. One set of figures for Hangzhou is 254,000 in 1884, 426,000 in 1911, and 817,000 in 1928; and for Ningbo, 215,000 in 1855, 436,000 in 1912, and 730,000 in 1930. Li Guoqi, *Zhongguo*, pp. 438–40; see also IMC, *Trade Reports*, 1879, p. 124.

57. Li Guoqi, *Zhongguo*, pp. 442–46, IMC, *Silk*, pp. 79–80; Liu Shiji, 8.7: 335; Yü-fa Chang (Zhang Yufa), "Regional Modernization," p. 11.

58. On mercantile contributions, see Ma, 4: 23b–24b; 5: 26a–28a; the section below entitled "The Zhejiangese merchants in Shanghai." Ma says Zhejiang natives contributed 1,266,159 taels for supplies. Much of this sum had to come from merchants in Shanghai. On refugee contacts, see Liu Shiji, p. 330; Chapter 3 below.

59. Trade appears to have helped Lanqi in the southwest to recover, but this was an exception. Li Guoqi and Zhu Hong, p. 130; Li Yingjue, p. 319.

60. The standard work on *lijin* is Luo, *Zhongguo lijin shi*. See also Li Yingjue; *Zhejiang tongzhi lijin mengao*. It must be assumed that *lijin* statistics are variably reported and underestimate production and

collections by perhaps 25 percent. Other problems include: (1) *lijin* on different commodities was collected at different rates in different monetary units and by different methods, (2) the ease of avoiding stations varied from place to place, (3) the burden on trade varied. In some places, like Ningbo, strong guilds could negotiate lump payments, whereas elsewhere they could not limit collections. In other places, like Jiaxing before 1897, substations proliferated out of proportion to the volume of trade, thereby increasing the likelihood of multiple collections. Various geographical patterns reflected developmental levels and trading patterns. Stations were spread evenly about Jiaxing, but in Huzhou they were found mainly around the prefectural city and in the five main market towns of Wucheng/Guian. All but one of the Ningbo stations lay in a large circle about Ningbo city. In Shaoxing they were found in all districts. Most stations in the southeast were in prefectural cities or other ports. All four Jinhua stations were in Lanqi. A few stations were located in the tea-producing areas of Quzhou and Yanzhou, mainly in a limited number of prefectural or district cities. With these reservations, *lijin* statistics can provide a rough measure of commercial activity, but they are less reliable indicators of the tax burden on trade.

61. Eng, pp. 24–25.

62. E-tu Zen Sun, "Sericulture," p. 107.

63. Ibid., p. 98; Faure, "Rural Economy," p. 410.

64. Lillian M. Li, *Silk Trade,* pp. 78 (table 11), 86–88 (table 16); Liang-lin Hsiao, pp. 102–3.

65. Something like one-third of China's silk exports in these years must have come from Huzhou and about 60 percent from all of northern Zhejiang. An impressionistic newspaper report in 1873 confirms the importance of Huzhou silk, although the figures are approximate. It states that Huzhou exported twenty thousand yuan (about fifteen thousand H. K. taels) annually, or over half the total value of silk exports at that time. *Shen bao,* July 5, 1873, p. 1.

66. Hangzhou figures averaged from IMC, *Trade Reports,* 1910, p. 507. An unknown part of this amount was shipped abroad via Shanghai, so it would also appear in the Shanghai re-export figure. The export drop of the 1880's began with a bad harvest in 1881. Business was then unsettled by Hu Guangyong's effort to corner the silk market in 1881–82 and his bankruptcy in 1883; it was hurt further by the Sino-French War.

67. *Shimen xianzhi,* 11: 4a.

68. IMC, *Trade Reports,* 1887, pp. 222–23.

69. Ibid., 1893, p. 281; Tōa Dōbunkai, *Shina,* pp. 409, 418, 447; Peng, *Zhongguo,* 2: 236.

70. Chao, *Development,* p. 130.

71. IMC, *Trade Reports,* 1887, p. 281.

72. Ibid., 1898, p. 340; 1900, p. 272; 1910, p. 521; Li Guoqi, "Min-Zhe-Tai," p. 434. Note that cotton cultivation in Shao-Ning increased after foreign trade developed and that cotton spinning there was not as important a household handicraft as in the older cotton-producing regions northeast of Hangzhou. In parts of eastern, central, and southwest Zhejiang, household weaving began with imported yarn, or spinning and weaving began together. Therefore, the impact of yarn imports was less socially unsettling than in some other areas like the Canton Delta.

73. IMC, *Trade Reports*, 1880, p. 157; 1894, p. 315.

74. IMC, *Trade Reports*, 1894, p. 314; Sun Yutang, 2.2: 714; Yü-fa Chang, "Regional Modernization," p. 7.

75. Jones, "Finance," pp. 52–55; Jones, "Ningpo," pp. 78–83; Shiba, p. 436 and *passim*; *Shanghai yanjiu ziliao xuji*, pp. 291–94.

76. IMC, *Trade Reports*, 1890, p. 254; 1900, p. 356; 1910, p. 517.

77. Ibid., 1879, p. 115.

78. When the Maritime Customs began keeping statistics on junk trade in 1905, Ningbo's imports and exports increased by 50 percent. Hangzhou had been a treaty port for only a few years in 1900. By 1910 the total value of trade going through its Maritime Customs was over 20 million taels, but by then Ningbo's was over 35 million.

79. These figures from IMC, *Trade Reports* summary tables may reflect inconsistencies in the annual data. Trade volume of some items in the 1880's may be overstated relative to the 1890's, but the general trends still hold up.

80. Increases in steamship tonnage after 1900 indicate more activity, although, if trade values are adjusted for the approximate doubling of prices between the 1880's and the 1890's (Nankai price index), real values of trade increased only slightly.

81. In contrast to most miscellaneous items, foreign demand for hats did not recover after dropping sharply in the 1890's (Table 10).

82. The major work on industrial modernization in Zhejiang is Li Guoqi, *Zhongguo*.

83. *Zhongguo nianjian*, p. 1435.

84. Sun Yutang, 2.2: 654.

85. Ibid., 2.2: 724; *Dongfang zazhi*, 2.5: *shiye* 91; 3.6: *shiye* 138; 3.8: *shiye* 174; 4.2: *shiye* 52; 5.5: *shiye* 100; *Qu xianzhi*, 6: 34a–36a; Li Yingjue, pp. 319–21.

86. Telegraphs, for instance, were merchant-managed and not government-managed companies. Yü-fa Chang, "Modernization of China," p. 25. The Hangzhou mills received government loans (Sun Yutang, 2.2: 1044), but such loans were sometimes unreliable because hard-pressed officials might demand early repayment (ibid., 2.2: 1045).

87. Ibid., 1.2: 976, 993; 2.2: 1065.

88. For examples of Shanghai merchant investment, see ibid., 2.2: 1091–95; Nonggongshang bu, 2.5: 3a.

89. These are reported in Sun Yutang, 2.2: 880–90, 906; 1.2, 2.2 passim; Nonggongshang bu; IMC, Trade Reports; Dongfang zazhi, vols. 1–5, shiye sections.

90. IMC, Trade Reports, 1910, pp. 504, 530. On the attempt to preserve the China Merchants Steam Navigation Co. monopoly, see Wang Jingyu, pp. 44–45.

91. Xie Bin, p. 238.

92. Dongfang zazhi, 6.4: jishi 22; Great Britain, Foreign Office, 371/1019/09.

93. See also Schoppa, Chinese Elites, pp. 24–25. Information compiled from North China Herald, Sept. 25, 1908, pp. 715–16; May 13, 1910, p. 317; June 10, 1910, pp. 617–18; July 15, 1910, p. 138; Sept. 9, 1911, p. 660; Shi bao, Dec. 1, 1909, p. 5; Apr. 23, 1909, p. 5; IMC, Trade Reports, 1909, p. 466; Great Britain, Foreign Office, 228/180/2016 (Hangzhou Intelligence Report, Dec. 1910). An example of dislocation was the rise in price of mulberry leaves in Jiaxing because the railway could deliver locally grown leaves to Hangzhou without wilting. Poor peasants had to throw away silkworms because they could not afford to feed them. North China Herald, June 10, 1910, pp. 617–18.

94. Of 54 factories and manufacturing companies, 20 were located in Hangzhou city, 12 in Ningbo city, and 4 in Xiaoshan district. No other city had more than 2, and there were only 6 in the southern prefectures. These incomplete figures give an idea of distribution. Dongfang zazhi; Nonggongshang bu; Sun Yutang.

95. Wu-Qing zhenzhi, 21: 1b–2a.

96. Shen bao, Sept. 17, 1874, p. 3.

97. IMC, Trade Reports, 1891, p. 271; 1879, p. 138.

98. Zhejiang difang yinhang zonghang, 2: 164. My sources on qianzhuang are Shanghai qianzhuang shiliao; McElderry; Jones, "Finance."

99. Zhongguo shiye shi, 9: 34–68; Zhejiang difang yinhang zonghang, 2: 164; Li Guoqi, "Min-Zhe-Tai," pp. 438–40. Of the 72 banks that were established during the Qing and were still operating in the 1930's, 33 were founded between 1900 and 1911. Although one would expect fewer nineteenth-century banks to have survived, it does seem that more appeared after 1900 in response to increased business activity.

100. Shanghai qianzhuang shiliao, pp. 731–47.

101. Shen bao, Nov. 2, 1874, p. 2; Feb. 23, 1881, p. 2; Shi bao, Apr. 6, 1910, p. 3; Apr. 11, 1910, p. 3; Apr. 17, 1910, p. 3; June 23, 1910, p. 3; June 28, 1910, p. 3; July 5, 1910, p. 3. Several panics are outlined in McElderry, chaps. 4–5; on the 1910 crisis, see Bergère, Crise.

102. Zhejiangese were also among the leaders of the modern banking that developed during the 1900's. For names, see Jones, "Ningpo," p. 90, and Negishi, pp. 114–15, 153. On the Zhejiangese modern banks, see Li Guoqi, "Min-Zhe-Tai," p. 439.

103. General works on Chinese guilds and native place associations: Ho, *Zhongguo;* Golas; Hamilton. Superior descriptions of guilds in a single city are found in Negishi, and in Rowe, chaps. 7–9.

104. Negishi, pp. 7–10, 32–35, 73–86, 110–14; *Shanghai yanjiu ziliao,* pp. 145–49, 299; *Shanghai yanjiu ziliao xuji,* pp. 392–404; Jones, "Ningpo," p. 77.

105. Tōa Dōbunkai, *Shina,* pp. 739–40. This source records nineteen associations in Hangzhou during the early Republic. Four were Shao-Ning *huiguan,* one was for Jinhua men, and several were for natives of Anhui or other provinces. On Ningbo, see Shiba, pp. 416–18.

106. Available data on distribution of native place associations are sub-statistical. Information in this paragraph is from Shiba, p. 417; Cole, "Shaohsing," pp. 15–16; Tōa Dōbunkai, *Shina; Deqing xian xinzhi,* 3: 15a; *Fuyang xianzhi,* 11: 4a–b; *Nanxun zhi,* 2: 15b–16a; *Qu xianzhi,* 4: 50a–b, *Shuanglin zhenzhi,* 8: 2a–b; *Shouchang xianzhi,* 4: 13b–14a; *Wu-Qing zhenzhi,* 9: 28a; *Xindeng xianzhi,* 5: 9a; *Yongjia xianzhi* 35: 15a–b.

107. *Deqing xian xinzhi,* 3: 15a–b; *Nanxun zhi,* 1922, 2: 16a; *Puyuan zhi,* 7: 5b–6a; *Shuanglin zhenzhi,* 8: 2b. There were eight guilds in the town of Wu in the 1930's, but the founding dates are not given. *Wu-Qing zhenzhi,* 9: 27b–28a.

108. Shiba, p. 417.

109. Ibid., p. 416.

110. Tōa Dōbunkai, *Shina;* Eng, p. 157; Lillian M. Li, *Silk Trade,* pp. 154–62, Li Guoqi and Zhu Hong, p. 161.

111. Sources for the Li family are *Zhenhai xianzhi,* 27: 12b–13a; 19: 33b; *Hangzhou fuzhi,* 17: 10a, 11a; *Shanghai qianzhuang shiliao,* pp. 734–37, *Nonggongshang hu* (1909), 2.5: 38; *Quanguo yinhang nianjian,* p. 625; Great Britain, Foreign Office, 228/2524/1915; Zhang Yufa, *Qingji,* p. 368; Zhang Cunwu, pp. 48, 158; *Shanghai shi zizhi zhi,* 1.1b; Sun Yutang, 2.2: 1091–95; *North China Herald,* Apr. 1, 1910, p. 39; *Dongfang zazhi,* 3.3: shiye 85; 3.12: shiye 237; 4.4: shiye 82.

112. Sun Yutang, 2: 945, 953; Eng, p. 106; *Shanghai yanjiu ziliao xuji,* pp. 290, 294; Negishi, pp. 52–56, 74; Leong, pp. 30, 47, and passim.

113. See, for example, the biography of Qin Zuze in Negishi, pp. 118–19.

114. On the Fangs, see Jones, "Ningpo," pp. 84–85; *Shanghai qianzhuang shiliao,* pp. 730–34; *Zhenhai xianzhi,* 19: 36b, 37b, 39b, 41a, 43a; 26: 31b–32b; 27: 13a–15a; Negishi, pp. 58, 142–46.

115. Basic biographical material on Dai Siyuan: *Zhenhai xianzhi,* 27: 41a–b. On Ye Chengzhong: *Zhenhai xianzhi,* 27: 40a–b; *Shanghai qianzhuang shiliao,* pp. 743–44; Ho, *Ladder,* pp. 308–10. On Liu Yong: Zhang Xiaoruo, *Zhang Jizi, wenlu,* 14: 1a–2b; *Nanxun zhi,* 1922, 21: 18a–19a; Chang Chung-li, *Income,* p. 159.

116. On Zhejiang compradors in Shanghai, see Hao; Negishi, pp. 156–64; Jones, "Ningpo," pp. 90–93; Sun Yutang, 2.2: 965; Fujii, p. 29.

117. Yen-p'ing Hao makes it clear that compradors specializing in foreign trade also established independent domestic businesses and that they competed with foreigners even though working for them. They were an important, but not always the major, source of private capital for modern industry. Hao, chap. 3, pp. 184–95. For a different view, see Zhang Guohui.

118. Yu Xiaqing won a reputation in Shanghai in 1898 by leading resistance to French claims to land long occupied by the Ningbo guild cemetery in order to build a school, a hospital, and a slaughterhouse. Jones, "Ningpo," pp. 86–87.

119. *Nanxun zhi,* 1922, 21: 2b–4a, 10a–12b, 14b, 23a, 24b; 30: 21b; *Shimen xianzhi,* 11: 4a; Negishi, pp. 112, 116–17.

120. Chiang Monlin, p. 31.

121. *Shanghai xian xuzhi,* 2: 51a–b. *Shanghai shi zizhi zhi,* 1.1b; Elvin, "Administration," p. 249. One of the first two vice-presidents was Zhou Jinbiao, and the first president of the south city chamber of commerce was the comprador Wang Zhen (Yiting). Other Zhejiangese officers of the chamber of commerce included Li Houyou, Xie Lunhui, Zhu Peichen, Shen Dunhe, Yu Xiaqing, and Hu Shandeng. Zhu Peizhen, Li Houyou, and Wang Zhen were members of the Shanghai City Council.

122. Sun Yutang, 2.2: 1091–95; Jones, "Ningpo," p. 87.

123. *Nanxun zhi,* 1922, 35: 13a–27a.

124. Yan Xinhou managed a salt monopoly (Sun Yutang 2.2: 927–30); Zhang Songxian reorganized the Zhejiang salt administration (Zhang Xiaoruo, *wenlu,* 13: 11a–b); Liu Yong managed salt and tea monopolies in Yanzhou (*Nanxun zhi,* 21: 18b); Dong Bingyu contributed 100,000 silver ounces (*Ciqi xianzhi,* 33: 12a); Hu Guangyong procured supplies and made contributions (Zhang Xiaoruo, *wenlu,* 14: 1b, and Stanley, chaps. 1–2.

125. Stanley, chaps. 3–4; Feuerwerker, p. 21.

126. On official supervision and merchant management, see Feuerwerker, chap. 1 and *passim.* On merchant reservations about the system, see Chan, "Government," pp. 434–37. On Chinese investment in foreign firms in Shanghai, see Eng, p. 74.

127. The next three paragraphs are written in light of the analysis in Wang Jingyu, "Chinese bourgeoisie."

Chapter Three

1. *Shen bao,* Aug. 28, 1879, p. 2; see Elvin, "Market Towns," for adjacent Jiangsu.

2. Ma, 1: 47a–49a; 3: 4a–7b; 4: 9a–13a; 6: 4a–10b.

3. Cole, "Shaohsing," pp. 100, 102; Perdue, pp. 759, 761–63.
4. Elvin, "Market Towns," pp. 470–72; *Haining zhouzhi gao*, 2: *shuili* 22b.
5. Yu, *Chunzai*, 4: pp. 2381–82, 2638.
6. *Haining zhouzhi gao*, 2: *shuili* 22b, 6: *xuetang* 2a, 5b, 13a; Zong, 1: 2a, 2: 7a, 3: 3b, 4: 5b; 5: 4b; *Wucheng xianzhi*, 2: 14b, 19b; 4: 2b, 3b; *Hangzhou fuzhi*, 53: 17b, 19a–b, 36b; Ding Lizhong, 1: 25a, 2: 4b, 27a, and chap. 2 *passim*.
7. The public relief home in Pujiang allegedly dated back to the Yuan. *Pujiang xianzhi gao*, 12: 16a. Some common terminological variants are *peiyuan tang: Linhai xianzhi gao* 5: 26a; *jishan tang: Shangyu xianzhi*, 35: 17b; *zhongshan ju: Jingning xianzhi*, 1873, 2: 6b. As usual, terminology is no sure guide. Some *yangji yuan* were re-organized in the Tongzhi (1862–74). Some *shantang* predated the Taiping Rebellion and do not seem to have been particularly active in the late nineteenth century. Core-peripheral distinctions were often the governing factor.
8. For example, *Ciqi xianzhi*, 5: 25a for a Daoguang (1821–50) founding, and *Yuyao xianzhi*, 13: 2a, for Qianlong (1736–95).
9. *Nanxun zhi*, 1922, 25: 8a; 34: 9a.
10. *Tongxiang xianzhi*, 4: *jianzhi zhong* 13a–14a; Yan Chen, *Tongqi*, pp. 59a–61a. See also Ding Lizhong, 1; 24b, 27a; *Hangzhou fuzhi*, 73: 4b, *Wucheng xianzhi*, 2: 14a–b, *Guian xianzhi*, 18: 16b, for united welfare agencies in Hangzhou and Huzhou. See *Shuanglin zhenzhi*, 32: 8b–9a, *Nanxun zhi*, 1922, 25: 7a; *Wu-Qing zhenzhi*, 24: 10a–b; *Qu xianzhi*, 20: 21a; *Longyou xianzhi*, 19: 24a; *Tangqi zhi*, 14: 3a, for other relief and reconstruction bureaus.
11. *Nanxun zhi*, 1922, 25: 7a; *Tongxiang xianzhi*, 4: *jianzhi zhong* 13a–b; *Jiashan xianzhi*, 4: 2a; Zong, 3: 6a–7b.
12. *Wu-Qing zhenzhi*, 24: 10a–b; *Pinghu xianzhi*, 3: 38a; *Kaihua xianzhi*, 3: *jianzhi si* 8b.
13. *Shuanglin zhenzhi*, 32: 8b–9a.
14. *Nanxun zhi*, 1922, 34: 8b; *Tongxiang xianzhi*, 4: *jianzhi zhong* 14a.
15. *Yuyao xianzhi*, 13: 4a; *Dinghai tingzhi*, 22: 18b; *Dinghai xianzhi*, 4: 18b; *Daishan zhenzhi*, 9: 6b; *Shangyu xianzhi*, 35: 18a.
16. *Wu-Qing zhenzhi*, 24: 10a–b; *Tongxiang xianzhi*, 4: *jianzhi zhong* 14b.
17. *Linhai xianzhi gao*, 5: 26a. See also *Shangyu xianzhi*, 35: 18a; *Yuyao xianzhi*, 13: 4b; *Jingning xianzhi*, 1873, 2: 6b, 9b. Other functions included free medicine, free coffins, and disposal of wastepaper with characters written on it.
18. *Shen bao*, Feb. 25, 1881, p. 2; Mar. 8, 1877, p. 2; Feb. 1, 1883, p. 3; Yu, *Chunzai*, 4: 2770; Ding Lizhong, 2: 22a; 3: 9b, 23b.
19. *Shen bao*, Dec. 2, 1879, p. 1. The managerial board of the foundling home in the peripheral district of Songyang (Chuzhou) had

48 members in the republican period. *Songyang xianzhi,* 2: 7a. For embezzlement and intimidation by a manager in the 43d *du* (outside of
Hangzhou city), see *Shen bao,* Nov. 29, 1881, p. 2; Dec. 4, 1881,
pp. 1–2. For embezzlement in Wenzhou, see ibid., May 8, 1882, p. 2;
June 4, 1882, p. 3.

20. *Shen bao,* Feb. 25, 1881, p. 2, states that the Zhejiang provincial judge sent a communication between equals (*zhaohui*) to the gentry manager of the Hangzhou welfare association. The managers at
that time included Ding Bing and other prominent, though not high-
ranking, men.

21. *Kaihua xianzhi,* 3: *jianzhi wu* 6b; Tang Zhaoxi, 3: 9a.

22. Some examples involving foundling homes are *Tongxiang xianzhi,* chaps. 4–7; *Nanxun zhi,* 1922, 3: 1b; 21: 8b–9a, 10b–11a, 18a–
19a, 22b; 34: 4b, 10b; *Haining zhouzhi gao,* 6: *xuezheng* 2a; supplement: 4b–5a, 6a; *Linghu zhenzhi,* 2: 3a, 6b, 8a; 3: 1b; *Jiande xianzhi,*
5: 32b, 42a; 6: 18a–b, 27b; *Pingyang xianzhi,* 21: 1a; 39: 1a–b, 5b–6a;
Songyang xianzhi, 2: 6b; 9: 54a, 73b, 98a; *Fenghua xianzhi,* 3: 16b,
20a; 11: 28a; 21: 16a. This generalization does not hold up in Longyou.
Longyou xianzhi, 5: 7a.

23. Ding Lizhong, 2: 10a; *Tongxiang xianzhi,* 4: *shantang* 2b;
Haining Banhai Zhangshi zongpu, 39: 81b. Writers did not always follow this terminology, and some areas had their own local terms, for
example, *zhengying,* sometimes used in Ningbo. *Yin xianzhi,* 2: 16b.

24. Ocko, pp. 52–54, 98.

25. *Fenghua xianzhi,* 3: 20b–23b; *Yanyuan xiangzhi,* 1: 11a–b.
See also *Tongxiang xianzhi,* 4: *shantang* 2a–b; *Wu-Qing zhenzhi,* 23:
6a; 29: 24a; *Haining zhouzhi gao,* 6: *xuezheng* 1a–6a. For lineage
foundling homes, see *Yanyuan xiangzhi,* 1: 11b; *Fenghua xianzhi,* 3:
24a; *Zhuji xianzhi,* 3: 13a.

26. Sheng Langxi, *Zhongguo,* gives general information on academies. Academy headship was a prestigious position that could pay
quite well. The head of the Longyou academy (with 60 students in
southwest Zhejiang) received 160 yuan out of annual expenses of
about 800 yuan. *Longyou xianzhi,* 27: 7a, 9b.

27. Sources do not identify Zhejiang academies as officially or privately founded. Taga, pp. 249–50, credits non-officials with founding
125 of 187 academies. Most of the additional 51 academies listed in
Appendix A were located outside administrative centers and presumably most were privately founded. Charitable schools were even more
likely to be established outside administrative centers and were run by
the local elite—sometimes in conjunction with welfare institutions
(*Zhenhai xianzhi,* 11: *xuexiao xia* 15a). They were not a major public activity in Zhejiang, where families and lineages supported much
education. Taga, pp. 241–43, calls most Jiangsu academies officially
founded. On Jiangxi and Guangdong, see Grimm, pp. 479, 481.

28. Grimm, p. 439.

29. *Jiaxing xianzhi,* 5: 3a; *Wu-Qing zhenzhi,* 24: 10a–b; *Pinghu xianzhi,* 3: 38a. For other examples of linkages, see Zong, 2: 7a; 3: 3b; *Shuanglin zhenzhi,* 20: 57b–58b; *Nanxun zhi,* 1922, 21: 22b; *Jiashan xianzhi,* 5: 11b, 12b, 17a–b, 34b; *Pingyang xianzhi,* 39: 6a; *Kaihua xianzhi,* 3: *jianzhi si* 8b.

30. *Jiashan xianzhi,* 5: 34b.

31. The Longyou academy cost 4,800 yuan about 1890 (*Longyou xianzhi,* 27: 8b); Nanxun town academy cost about 4,000 yuan about 1870 (Zong, 3: 8a). See also *Dinghai tingzhi,* 22: 18b; *Daishan zhenzhi,* 8: 2b.

32. Yu, *Chunzai,* 4: 2298, 2770. In a similar range, see *Shangyu xianzhi,* 35: 18a–19a; *Zhenhai xianzhi,* 11: 8a.

33. Zong, 3: 8a.

34. Ibid., 3: 6b–7a. The bureau admitted to a total income of about 50,000 yuan for 1864–68.

35. *Haining zhouzhi gao,* 6: *xuezheng* 2a–b, 5a. Copper cash–dollar ratios from Faure, "Rural Economy," p. 429. See also *Tongxiang xianzhi,* 4: *shantang* 2a.

36. *Minhu ribao,* June 11, 1909, p. 197; July 29, 1909, p. 529; Aug. 5, 1909, p. 587. By comparison, Shaoxing middle schools had 16,119 yuan and all Shanyin/Guiji lower schools had 62,405 yuan in 1909. *Xuebu zongwu si* (1910), Zhejiang: 18

37. *Shi bao,* Nov. 28, 1910, p. 3.

38. For example, *Shuanglin zhenzhi,* 8: 3a; *Jiaxing fuzhi,* 8: 32a; *Yuyao xianzhi,* 13: 5a; *Fenghua xianzhi,* 3: 16b, 17b; *Suichang xianzhi, waibian* 4: 1a–3a; *Jinhua xianzhi,* 4: 12b; *Lanqi xianzhi,* 3: *xuegong* 48b–50a.

39. *Yuyao Liucang zhi,* 15: 3a; *Shen bao,* Oct. 19, 1882, p. 2.

40. *Qingtian xianzhi,* 2: 29a.

41. For example, *Shen bao* reported an undignified squabble between Ningbo prefect Zong Yuanhan and a wealthy Ningbo native over just how much the latter had promised to contribute to a fund that Zong was raising for relief, water control, granaries, and gazetteer revision. *Shen bao,* Jan. 8, 1879, p. 2; Mar. 18, 1879, p. 2.

42. *Zhenhai xianzhi,* 11: 8a.

43. *Yongkang xianzhi,* 2: 21a; 3: 8a–11a; Sun Yiyan, *Sunxue zhai wenchao,* 2: 12b; Ma, 3: 37a. For other examples, see *Haining zhouzhi gao,* 4: *xuexiao shang* 11a; *Ciqi xianzhi,* 5: 8a–24b.

44. *Xiaoshan xianzhi gao,* 10 *xia:* 2b; *Xiangshan xianzhi,* 14: 33a; *Lanqi xianzhi,* 3: *zhengshu* 14b; *Deqing xian xinzhi,* 1: 24a. Women are identified by the surname of their natal family and described as the wife (or mother) of so-and-so.

45. For example, see *Lanqi xianzhi,* 3: *chengshu* 14b, 3: *xuetang* 7b; *Xinchang xianzhi,* 5: 25b, 26b; *Daishan zhenzhi,* 8: 1b; *Cheng xianzhi,* 5: 41a; *Xiangshan xianzhi,* 14: 36b, 16: 34b, 28: 38a; *Shuanglin zhenzhi,* 5: 10a; *Deqing xian xinzhi,* 1: 17b.

46. *Xiangshan xianzhi*, 26: 16b; also Ying Baoshi, see *Yongkang xianzhi*, 2: 38a.

47. *Nanxun zhi*, 1922, 21: 18a; 34: 4b, 10b.

48. See the biography of Wu Shanqing in *Shaoxing xianzhi ziliao, diyi ji, renwu:* 197a–b. See also the biography of Bao Chengxian in ibid., *renwu:* 176a–b, and the biography of Zhang Chengming in *Haining zhouzhi gao*, 31: *yixing* 17b.

49. *Pinghu xianzhi*, 4: 22b.

50. *Yanyuan xiangzhi*, 1: 11a.

51. *Longyou xianzhi*, 30: 38a–40b, 42a–43b; 31: 2a–b. Probably similar methods were used in Kaihua. *Kaihua xianzhi*, 3: *jianshu si* 8b.

52. The welfare association of Ciqi with land in Yin and Zhenhai was an exception (*Ciqi xianzhi*, 5: 25a), but a prefectural institution might have land in several districts. *Yongjia xianzhi*, 35: 5a–9b.

53. *Suichang xianzhi, waibian*, 4: 1a–30a.

54. List compiled from all gazetteers in the bibliography; the Yongjia and Fenghua foundling homes had over 2,000 *mou*. *Yongjia xianzhi*, 3: 5a–9b; *Fenghua xianzhi*, 3: 16b–17b.

55. *Yuyao xianzhi*, 13: 7a. Similarly, endowments for charitable ferries (later used to support a bridge) in Longyou were 1,196 *mou*. *Longyou xianzhi*, 31: 19b.

56. *Linhai xianzhi gao*, 5: 27b; *Longyou xianzhi*, 27: 7a.

57. The detailed information for the academy at Longyou is internally inconsistent, but it indicates that the academy could not depend entirely on rents, despite an endowment of 519 *mou*. Estimated operating expenses in the 1890's were 800 yuan annually. Theoretically the endowment income was about 208 *shi* of rice (figured at one *shi* rent per 2½ *mou*). This would have given an income of 656 yuan at the average Shanghai rice price for the period 1890–94 or 992 yuan at the average Shanghai rice price for the period 1895–99. (Presumably rice prices and, therefore, income, were lower in southwest Zhejiang.) Managers claimed that they were able to collect less than one-half the rent due until 1898–99, when they allegedly collected 1,200–1,300 yuan with official help. Clerical corruption subsequently cut actual collections again. *Longyou xianzhi*, 27: 7a, 8b–10a, 30b. Shanghai rice prices are taken from Faure, "Rural Economy," p. 425.

58. *Longyou xianzhi*, 27: 33b–34a. Similarly, the foundling home in Tangqi town (Hangzhou) switched to *lijin* after the Taiping Rebellion because it was not receiving any rents from its endowment. *Hangzhou fuzhi*, 7: 36a–b.

59. One can not tell how much income was derived from urban and how much from rural rents. For examples of institutions with urban property in not-very-commercialized districts, see *Daishan xianzhi*, 8: 1b; *Jinhua xianzhi*, 4: 12b.

60. For example, see *Haining zhouzhi gao*, 6: *xuezheng* 4a; *Jiaxing xianzhi*, 5: 34b; *Longyou xianzhi*, 27: 7a; *Jinhua xianzhi*, 4: 12b. The

data are insufficient to say whether investment in pawnshops occurred mainly in the north and southwest. These areas shared the experience of Taiping destruction despite differences in ecology and commercial levels.

61. *Haining zhouzhi gao*, 6: *xuezheng* 2a–b; 4: *xuexiao* 11a–12a; *Cheng xianzhi*, 2: 14a. See also *Tongxiang xianzhi*, 4: *shantang* 2a; *Xinchang xianzhi*, 1: 61b.

62. *Daishan xianzhi*, 8: 2b; *Yongjia xianzhi*, 35: 9a; *Lishui xianzhi*, 4: 16a; *Linhai xianzhi gao*, 5: 22b; *Taizhou fuzhi*, 57: 4b; *Pujiang xianzhi gao*, 4: 65a; *Qu xianzhi*, 3: 33b; *Lanqi xianzhi*, 3: *chengshu* 15b; *Kaihua xianzhi*, 3: *jianzhi er* 3a.

63. *Lishui xianzhi*, 4: 16a; *Taizhou fuzhi*, 57: 4b. For continued use in the twentieth century, see *Shi bao*, Nov. 28, 1910, p. 3.

64. *Jinhua xianzhi*, 4: 12a–b; *Lanqi xianzhi*, 3: *chengshu* 16a–b, 50a; *Qu xianzhi*, 20: 22a.

65. Yu, *Chunzai*, 4: 2299.

66. Luo, pp. 254–55. For examples of different calculations, see Zong, 3: 6b–7a; *Tongxiang xianzhi*, 4: *shantang* 2a; *Wu-Qing zhenzhi*, 24: 10a–b; *Shuanglin zhenzhi*, 8: 3a; *Deqing xian xinzhi*, 3: 8b.

67. Zong, 3: 6b–8a; *Tongxiang xianzhi*, 4: *shantang* 1b–2a; *Wu-Qing zhenzhi*, 24: 10a–b; *Puyuan zhi*, 8: 2a.

68. *Haining zhouzhi gao*, 6: *xuezheng* 2a–b, 13a; *Hangzhou fuzhi*, 73: 37b, 41b; *Tangqi zhi*, 18: 23a.

69. *Nanxun zhi*, 1922, 2: 16a–b; 25: 6b–7a; 34: 8b; 35: 5a. Future activities of the men recorded on these pages are set forth in chaps. 2, 3, 25, 35, and the biography section of the gazetteer. The linkage between silk *lijin* and charity is clarified in Zong, 11: 2b.

70. Polachek, "Gentry," pp. 244–45. Suggestions of connections between *lijin* collectors and local philanthropists outside the three northern prefectures: in Shangyu a *lijin* official founded a charitable school that received support from *lijin* revenues (*Shangyu xianzhi*, 37: 13a); in 1888 a *lijin* deputy in Ninghai established a charitable school supported by the cattle tax.

71. Ch'ü, p. 161.

72. Under-reporting of subdistrict-level institutions is dramatized by comparing the list of charitable institutions in the *Yuyao xianzhi* with that for the subdistrict in *Yuyao Liucang zhi*. The district gazetteer (13: 5a) lists only one of the thirty-five institutions in the latter (16: 6b–9a).

73. For example, the Fengshan charitable estate of the Xu lineage in Yuyao, established in the Guangxu (1875–1908) with a large endowment of 1,220 *mou*, provided for bridge repairs, road maintenance, and charity. *Yuyao xianzhi*, 13: 8b. A *gongsheng* by purchase in Taiping district founded a granary for the lineage poor. *Taiping xianzhi*, 2: *cangchu*, 4a. Lineages established charitable graveyards and burial societies (*Fenghua xianzhi*, 3: 25b; *Xiaoshan xianzhi gao*, 7: 35a–

37b; *Haining Banhai Zhangshi zongpu*, 41: 7a), foundling homes (*Yanyuan xiangzhi*, 1: 11b), academies (*Pujiang xianzhi gao*, 4: 67b, 72a; *Xianju xianzhi*, 6: 33a; *Yin xianzhi*, 9: 28b, 38b), and charitable schools (27 lineage charitable schools are listed in *Yin xianzhi*, 9: 28b–48b. Evidence for lineage-supported facilities in single-lineage villages (or villages dominated by a strong lineage) is clear in *Xiaoshan xianzhi gao*, 10 *xia:* 6a–11a, and is almost as definite in *Yuyao Liucang zhi*, 15: 8a, 9b; 16: 1a, 8b. These facilities might be maintained even though there was no formal charitable estate. For a description of highly developed lineage functions in Wuxi, Jiangsu, see Dennerline, "Wuxi County."

74. These were likely to be relatively small miscellaneous institutions, but wealthy philanthropists might also sponsor independent institutions to perform currently fashionable welfare functions already performed by the main welfare agency.

75. For a comparable suggestion about Jiangsu, see Ocko, p. 126.

76. Chen Xunci, p. 23; Ding Lizhong, 1: 6b, 9a–10b and *passim;* *Hangzhou fuzhi*, 53: 17b, 19b, 35b; 73: 9b. The scholarly side of Ding's career is emphasized in Hummel, 2: 726–27.

77. *Pingyang xianzhi*, 39: 1a–5a. Militia organization may have been more important in expanding gentry functions in some other provinces than in Zhejiang. Kuhn, *Rebellion;* Polachek, "Gentry," pp. 244–45.

78. For example, see *Xiaofeng xianzhi*, 3: 71a, 72a; 6: 8b–9a, for Wang Jingyi; *Wucheng xianzhi*, 2: 19a, and *Wuxing Niushi xizhi jiapu, shiyishi:* 28a and *chuanwen:* 27a, for Niu Fujie; Shen Bingying, *Chunxing caotang ji*, introduction by Shen Bingying.

79. *Haining Banhai Zhangshi zongpu*, 39: 78a, 79a–80b.

80. *Fuyang xianzhi*, 15: 1b–3a; 11: 1a–4a; 13: 1a–2a. Schoppa, *Chinese Elites*, p. 18, characterizes Fuyang as outer-core in the mid-Republic, but that designation appears to reflect development during the twentieth century. For Taiping destruction in Fuyang, see Jen, p. 488.

81. For an example of this overlap, see *Cheng xianzhi*, 46: 40a.

82. *Shen bao*, Nov. 23, 1877, p. 2. The term *zhishang* (directing merchant) was also used in the late nineteenth and early twentieth centuries, but from contexts it is unclear whether it included merchants managing public institutions as well as those running officially sponsored business enterprises.

83. For example, see *Nanxun zhi*, 1922, 34: 10b; *Taiping xianzhi*, 2: *shuyuan* 59a; *Xindeng xianzhi*, 12: 3b. See also Rankin, "Rural-Urban Continuities," p. 103.

84. *Nanxun zhi*, 1922, 34: 3a–4b; 27: 2b, 7a, 23a; 21: 10b–11a, 18a–20a; supplement: 16a, 18a–b. *Gongsheng* were commonly found among managers down to the *zhen* level in the economic cores. For other examples of *jinshi* and *juren*, see *Jiashan xianzhi*, 19: 77a;

Zhenhai xianzhi, 27: 27a, 28a–b; and information on managerial establishments in text below.

85. Bao Ruchao; see *Jiande xianzhi,* 5: 33a, 6: 27b, 10: 25a, 14: 72a.

86. *Qu xianzhi,* 3: 33b, 23: 61a; *Kaihua xianzhi,* 3: *Jianzhi* 4: 7b; 9: *renwu ba* 23b; *Jingning xianzhi* (1873), 2: 7a; (1933), 11: 3a (several *gongsheng* by purchase were also involved); *Songyang xianzhi,* 2: 6b; 8: 23b; 9: 54a, 73b, 98a. In Longyou out of forty-five men who became regular *gongsheng* after 1850 at least eight were active in local institutions before 1900. Only three men had higher degrees. For names, see sources in n. 96.

87. *Meili beizhi,* 2: 3b, 22a; 5: 32b, 42a; 6: 18a–b, 27b; *Pingyang xianzhi,* 39: 12a; *Longyou xianzhi,* 19: 16b–21a.

88. *Wu-Qing zhenzhi,* 23: 6a; 29: 23b–24a, 25a–b; Rankin, "Rural-Urban Continuities," p. 72; *Longyou xianzhi,* 19: 22b. See also *Xindeng xianzhi,* 15: 4/a; *Xincheng zhenzhi,* 12: 9b

89. *Qu xianzhi,* 3: 36b; 23: 63b; *Fuyang xianzhi,* 11: 4a; *Kaihua xianzhi,* 3: *jianzhi er* 3a; *Yongjia xianzhi,* 3: 36a, 42a, 49a.

90. *Qu xianzhi,* 20: 18a. Gazetteers from Hangzhou, Ningbo, Wenzhou, and other major cities do not give adequate information. On Shanghai in the 1900's, see Elvin, "Administration," p. 249. For an earlier example, see Jing, introduction: 7. On Hankow, see Rowe, pp. 245–46.

91. For a similar conclusion about Jiangsu, see Ocko, p. 137.

92. *Longyou xianzhi,* 31: 2a, 32. 1a.

93. *Pingyang xianzhi,* 39: 16a–17b. A comparison of the names of men who organized militias during the rebellion *and continued military careers thereafter* with the names of later local activists shows no overlap.

94. Evidence on this point is not clear, and local situations varied. Yan Chen oversaw the foundling homes that he encouraged at lower urban levels in Tongxiang district. *Tongxiang xianzhi,* 6: 9a.

95. For a diagram of sub-district administration in Jiangsu, see Ocko, p. 138. For ward and sector directors in Shanghai, see Elvin, "Administration," p. 256; Yu, *Chunzai,* 4: 2381–82, 2638; *Shen bao,* Feb. 26, 1880, p. 3; Tang Zhaoxi, 1: 13a; *Longyou xianzhi,* 30: 38a–39b. Sub-district divisions were not uniform in Zhejiang.

96. *Longyou xianzhi,* 30: 43b (dike repairs); 31: 2a, 6a, 30b (bridge); 5: 9a–b and 30: 25a (school); 30: 37b (granary); 32: 1a, 24a (foundling home); 27: 7a, 20b, 33b (academy). Also see biographies, 19: 16b–25b.

97. See *Longyou xianzhi,* 27: 33b, in comparison with lists cited in note 96; biographies of Xu Fu (19: 24a) and Lin Chenlin (19: 22b).

98. Gazetteers are the basic source for determining the existence of local managerial establishments. *Wenji* (literary collections) are the chief supplementary source. The data are fragmentary and non-uniform at best. The minimum criterion is identification of a few people active in several local public institutions. Supplementary data

establishing their social connection (sometimes obtainable by checking all relevant gazetteer chapters) are needed for some degree of certainty. Other particularly good examples are found in the *Jiashan xianzhi* and *Shuanglin zhenzhi*. There is also substantial evidence in the gazetteers of Deqing, Shuanglin, Linghu, Hangzhou, Haining, Linan, Jiaxing, Jiashan, Puyuan, Xinchang, Ciqi, and Pingyang.

99. On Lu, see Hummel, 1: 545–47; Shou, "Qianyuan." The *jinshi* were Shen Bingying (Shen Bingying, introduction), Zhou Xuejun (*Wucheng xianzhi*, 9: 23a), Niu Fujie (*Wuxing Niushi xizhi jiapu, jiushi* 9a, *shishi* 12a–15a, *shiyishi* 22a–33b, *xinfa* 8a–23a).

100. The relatives were Niu Fuhai (a *juren* killed in 1862) and *jinshi* Zhou Xueyuan. *Wucheng xianzhi*, 18: 28b–29a.

101. Zong, 1: 2a; 2: 7a; 3: 3b–4a, 16a; 4: 2a–b, 5b, 7a, 10a; 5: 4b; *Wucheng xianzhi*, 2: 19a; *Guian xianzhi*, 3: 7b, 9: 2b; *Wuxing Niushi xizhi jiapu, chuanwen* 22a; *Huzhou fuzhi*, 18: 8b; Lu, pp. 34, 37, 50, 59, 115. Zong Yuanhan was noted as an exemplary local official who served most of his career in Zhejiang. Zhao Erxun, *liechuan:* 239.

102. See also Chapter 2; Rankin, "Rural-Urban Continuities," pp. 75–80. On the Jiangs, see *Nanxun zhi*, 1922, 21: 3b–4a, 10a–11a, 12a–b; Zhang Xiaoruo, *wenlu*, 14: 10b–11b. On the Lius, see *Nanxun zhi*, 21: 18a–19a; 46: 47a; Zhang Xiaoruo, *wenlu*, 14: 1a–b; Chang Chung-li, *Income*, p. 159. On the Zhous, see *Nanxun zhi*, 1922, 21: 19b, 20b–21a, 25b–26b; 27: 27b. On the Zhangs, see *Nanxun zhi*, 3: 5a; 21: 13b–14a; 27: 8a, 33a; Zhang Xiaoruo, *wenlu* 13: 17a; Chang Chung-li, *Income*, p. 160. On the Pangs, see *Nanxun zhi*, 21: 22a–b; 27: 27b; 35: 1a, 22b; Nonggongshang bu (1909), 2.5: 12a, 25a–b.

103. *Nanxun zhi*, 1922, 2: 16b; 3: 2a; 21: 8b–9a, 15b–17b, 19b, 23a; 34: 1a, 4b, 8b, 10b, 11b; 35: 5a, 6a, 25a–b.

104. Ibid., 2: 4a, 7b–8b; 3: 4a, 5a; 34: 31b; 35: 1a, 4a, 6a, 8b, 9a.

105. Yan Chen, *Tongqi*, 57b, 59a–b, 60b, 65a, 78a; *Tongxiang xianzhi*, 6: 4a. One of Yan's in-laws was the *jinshi* Shen Bingcheng, who wrote an introduction for the 1881 Guian gazetteer. This connection linked Yan to the Huzhou prefectural reconstruction establishment.

106. Yan recorded his local activities in the gazetteer he edited: *Tongxiang xianzhi*, chaps. 4, 5, 6, 7. Also see *Wu-Qing zhenzhi*, 29: 25b–26b; 38: 12b–13b, 72b; *Puyuan zhi*, 8: 4b. Yan Chen, *Tongqi*, gives more attention to the social and literary side of his life.

107. Yan Chen, *Tongqi*, p. 61a.

108. *Wu-Qing zhenzhi*, 14: 11a–12b; 29: 19b, 25a–b, 28a, 29b–30a, 33a–b, 34b–35a; *Tongxiang xianzhi*, 14: 15a, 15: *yixing*, 6a–b, 10a–b, 22a.

109. *Wu-Qing zhenzhi*, 23: 6a, 11a, 16a, 19b; 24: 10a–b; 29: 23b–24a; *Tongxiang xianzhi*, 7: *juanxu* 13a. Yan Chen's successor was Shen Shandeng, a *jinshi* and a Hanlin scholar. He was also granary manager.

110. *Wu-Qing zhenzhi*, 6: 7b, 8b, 9b; 9: 21b, 27b, 29a, 31a; 21: 21a; 23: 9b; 24: 12b.

111. *Tongxiang xianzhi*, 15: *yixing* 25b. Yu Yue wrote Shen's tombstone inscription. Yu, *Chunzai*, 4: 2386.

112. For biographical information on the Sun family, see Sun Yiyan, *Sunxue zhai wenchao*, 3: 12a; 6: 9a–13a; Zhu, pp. 1–3; Sun Yirang, *Zhouqing*, 1: 1a, 14a, 16a–19a, 28a–b. For degree holders in Wenzhou, see *Oufeng zazhi huikan*, 2.3: 1a–17b.

113. Sun Yiyan, *Sunxue zhai wenchao*, 2: 23a–b, 27a, 45b; Sun Yiyan, *Sunxue zhai xu wenchao*, 3: 18a, 23a; Liu Zhufeng; Sun Yirang, *Zhouqing*, 1: 3a.

114. On Sun Qiangming, see *Oufeng zazhi huikan*, 2.3: 7b; *Pingyang xianzhi*, 39: 12b. On Sun Yiyan's patronage, see, for example, *Pingyang xianzhi*, 39: 3a; *Oufeng zazhi*, 10: *wenyuan neibian* 1b.

115. *Oufeng zazhi huikan*, 2.3: 5b–16b.

116. *Pingyang xianzhi*, 39: 12b; *Luqiao zhilüe*, 1: 42b.

117. For basic biographical sources on Sun Yirang, see Zhu, *Sun Yirang*; Hummel, 2: 677–79. On Chen Fuchen, see Chen Mi, *Chen*. On Chen Qiu, see Lloyd Eastman, "Reformism," pp. 699–700; Chen Mi, "Dong-Ou"; *Oufeng zazhi*, 1.11: *wenyuan neibian* 7a–9a; On Song Heng, see *Pingyang xianzhi*, 39: 12a–14a; 92: 17b.

118. This influence was thus similar to the informal local dominance long exercised by certain lineages, families, etc., but it was specifically connected with, and to a considerable extent exercised through, ongoing public institutions.

119. Yan Chen, *Mohuayin*, 8: 3b, 9: 4a. See also Yan's comment that if no men capable of "seeking [solutions to the problems of] the times" (*jiushi*) came forth, "the [opportunity to set right the] times would be lost" (*shishi*) and it would not be possible to have such necessary institutions as foundling homes. *Tongxiang xianzhi*, 4: *jianzhi* 3b.

120. *Jiashan xianzhi*, 24: 44; *Haining zhouzhi gao*, 2: *shuili* 23a.

121. Elman, *From Philosophy*, pp. 443–47.

122. *Hangzhou fuzhi*, 16: 12a–16a, especially the names of teachers on 14a–15b. Several early teachers, including Sun Xingyan, Wang Jiaxi, Chen Bin, Yao Wentian, and Chen Wenshu, had essays in He Changling, *Huangzhao*. See Zhang Yin, pp. 1–3.

123. Yu, 4: 2340, 2421, 2424, 2525, 2535. One of the people praised for statecraft was the Zhenhai merchant Li Chengfu. Yu had essays on governance, feudalism, and other statecraft subjects in Sheng Kang, 10: 3b–5b; 12: 32a–33a. He also wrote an introduction to Ge Shijun, *Huangzhao*.

124. Zhang Yin, p. 3; Chen Dongyuan, p. 11. The Shanghai Gujing Jingshe, Longmen Academy of Shanghai, and Nanjing Academy in Jiangyin were all modeled on the Hangzhou Gujing Jingshe.

125. Lu, pp. 34–38, 59, 110–15, 307–8.

126. *Linhai xianzhi gao*, 20: 50a–b; Chen Mi, *Chen*, 11b, 14b, 15a, 19b, 21b. The 311 titles in the academy library listed in *Longyou*

xianzhi, 27: 13b–20a, include works on mathematics, geography, water control, and military affairs.

127. For an example of corruption in the chief academy at Jiaxing, see *Shen bao,* Apr. 28, 1882, p. 2.

128. *Shen bao,* Feb. 18, 1879, p. 2. Entrance exams were open to *jiansheng* as well as *juren* and *gongsheng.* The courses of study were classics, history, historical records, mathematics, geography, and poetry and essays. Huang Yizhou, a famous Zhenhai scholar who had been at the Gujing Jingshe, was one of the teachers.

129. *Haining zhouzhi gao,* 4: *xuexiao shang* 14b; 31: *yixing* 17b. One of the founders, Zhang Baohua, was a friend of Yu Yue and the scholar Wang Guowei.

130. For example, both Sun Yiyan and the young Li Ciming worked there. Ma, 5: 50b; Ding Lizhong, 2: 3b; Zhang Dechang, p. 17.

131. Sun Yiyan, *Sunxue zhai wenchao,* 2: 17a–18a. Gu Yanwu's *Rizhi lu* had been reprinted in 1795 and 1834 (Hummel, 1: 124). Lu Xinyuan's studio was named for Gu Yanwu (Hummel, 2: 915). In an introduction to Lu Xinyuan, *Yigu tang ji,* Yu Yue called the book a statecraft collection in the spirit of Gu Yanwu.

132. Sun was following the pattern of the *Song-Yuan xuean* (Compilation of Song and Yuan dynasty scholarship) begun by Huang Zongxi and finished by Quan Zuwang in the eighteenth century. That manuscript was finally purchased in 1846 by Feng Yunhao, a bibliophile from Ciqi, who had it printed. Feng was active in district affairs before the Taiping Rebellion and helped plan and finance defense during the rebellion. His descendants continued to be active in local education and welfare.

133. Chen Liang; Hu Fengdan, *Jinhua,* chaps. 126–35.

134. On Zhang Lüxiang, see Su Dunyuan, *Zhang.* As a disciple of Liu Zongzhou of Shaoxing, Zhang took part in the seventeenth-century movement away from the teachings of Wang Yangming toward those of Zhu Xi. He permanently withdrew from office during the late Ming factional fighting and was a part of the eremitic scholarly circles in Zhejiang during the early Qing. Zhang cultivated in himself, and also wrote about, a simple personal and social morality grounded in the Confucian "five relationships" and the observance of proper formalities. He advocated "dwelling in seriousness" and "investigating principles to the utmost" as the paths to human understanding. He also practiced managerial farming, and his best known work was the *Shenshi nongshu* (Agricultural treatise of the Shen family). In addition to reprinting his works, Yan Chen succeeded in having him canonized, and he gives Zhang a large place in the 1882 Tongxiang gazetteer. *Tongxiang xianzhi,* 13: *renwu shang,* 17a–21a, 28b–49a.

135. Hummel, 2: 915; Tang Zhen, *Qianshu.*

136. Sun Yiyan, *Yongjia,* introduction by Li Chunxi.

137. *Pingyang xianzhi,* 39: 12b.

138. Here I stress only social morality, but scholars might well go one step further and emphasize personal moral self-cultivation as a foundation for both community morality and good government. For example, see Yu Yue, "Shuo zhi, xia" (On governance, part two), in Sheng Kang, 10: 5b; Sun Yiyan, *Sunxue zhai wenchao*, 2: 18a, 42a; see also Yan Chen's approving portrait of Zhang Lüxiang, *Tongxiang xianzhi*, 12: 29a, 31a.

139. *Kaihua xianzhi*, 11: *yiwu* 5a–6a.

140. Views on foundling homes are compiled from *Tongxiang xianzhi*, 4: *jianzhi zhong* 3a–4a; *Xincheng zhenzhi*, 18: 8a; *Pingyang xianzhi*, 92: 29a; Sun Yiyan, *Sunxue zhai xu wenchao*, 3: 18a–20a; *Shen bao*, Aug. 14, 1881, p. 1; Dec. 9, 1882, p. 3. On restoration attacks on unorthodox social customs, see Ocko, pp. 39–51. A long list of examples in Pingyang appears in Tang Zhaoxi, 3: 20b–28a and chap. 3 *passim*.

141. *Deqing xianzhi*, 10: 7b–8a.

142. On the shortcomings of elite-sponsored charitable and community schools in educating the poor, see Woodside.

143. *Tongxiang xianzhi*, 4: *jianzhi zhong* 3a; *Shen bao*, Sept. 20, 1878, p. 1 (English trans. in *North China Daily News*, Oct. 17, 1878, p. 375).

144. See n. 85 for Deqing academy. Such ideal formulations did not mean that gentry were not also critical of actual academy shortcomings (for example, Lu, p. 328). For Gu Yanwu's idea of community contentment as a basis for a strong country, see Hou, 5: 252. The *Shen bao* article cited in n. 90 does not mention Gu Yanwu, but it contrasts administration in antiquity by numerous "low" officials (drawn from the local populace) who were close to the people with government by a smaller number of high officials responsible for large territories after the demise of "feudalism." This picture suggests Gu's famous dictum, "When low officials are numerous the age is prosperous, but when high officials are numerous the age declines." (Gu Yanwu, *Rizhi lu*, 8: 10a.) The article makes a characteristic call for comparisons of ancient and modern times to decide how to handle contemporary issues, even though "feudalism" in the old sense could not be revived. The idea of upward movement does not appear in this article, but it is associated with discussions of education, examinations, and recruitment of talent for government. Similar ideas were afloat in the seventeenth century, suggesting an upper-gentry perception of a special role in maintaining the empire and the ruler. (Hou, 5: 249–50.) They were compatible with, and could be linked to, either "autonomous" interests or a unified vertical state structure. For example, Dai Wang criticized Gu Yanwu's proposals on local officials and suggested that each district select a man annually for examination in the capital. The most successful candidates would become metropolitan officials, those in

the second category would become assistant magistrates in prefectures near their own, and those in the third would be bookkeepers and guards in their own districts. Central and local officials would thus have the same origins in home-district selections for national examination. Sheng Kang, 24: 7a–b.

145. Sun Yiyan, *Sunxue zhai wenchao,* 2: 1a–b.

146. Yan's efforts from 1875 to 1881 are set forth in documents written by him and collected in *Tongxiang xianzhi,* chap. 6. Their purpose was to make the official reduction of grain tribute and curbs on non-statutory excess charges effective in Tongxiang. Yan's solutions eventually focused on a system in which taxpayers deposited their own payments without the intervention of clerks and on fixed ratios to convert payments in copper cash to taxes levied in silver. The documents also provide excellent examples of the difficulty of eradicating corruption in tax collection, the official suspicions of upper elite-sponsored voluntary collection, and the disarray of records in the post-Taiping period.

147. *Tongxiang xianzhi,* 6: 3a, 5a.

148. Ibid., 6: 4a.

149. In 1880 collection boxes for taxpayers to deposit their own taxes had been established, and the silver-copper conversion ratio for taxpaying had been fixed. Boxes were set up at only three locations, however, and the system applied only to the first date for tax payment in the spring, which was used primarily by the great households. Lesser households did not have to pay money until the second payment date after the cocoons were harvested in the summer, but at that time the *dibao* and runners were free, in effect, to manipulate the silver-copper ratio to get back what they had lost through the abolition of excess charges. Yan wanted the number of collection points increased, the collection date determined by the date the cocoons went on the market, and the fixed ratio to apply to the summer collection. Ibid., 6: 8a–9a.

150. This interpretation is compatible with the view of Takahashi Kōsuke that after the Taiping Rebellion large gentry landowners advocated tax reduction to recement their common interests with small taxpaying landowners—and hence prevent the fusion of anti-rent and anti-tax sentiment. See Grove and Esherick, pp. 417–18. Unresolved problems include the extent to which tax reduction actually occurred and the extent to which it solidified the interests of landowners and bound them to the state.

151. *Haining zhouzhi gao,* 6: xuezheng 3a–4b.

152. *Shen bao,* Dec. 27, 1880, p. 1; Dec. 8, 1882, p. 2; Ding Lizhong, 3: 9b; *Yuyao xianzhi,* 3: 5a, *Xincheng zhenzhi,* 12: 9b. The Hangzhou bureau lasted only six years.

153. *Shen bao,* June 12, 1883, p. 1.

154. *Tongxiang xianzhi,* 6: 5a–b, 6b, 7a.

155. *Qu xianzhi,* 12: 21a; *Pingyang xianzhi,* 26: 16b, 17a; 27: 3a; Yu, *Chunzai,* 4: 2553.

156. *Jiashan xianzhi,* 23: 41b.

157. *Longyou xianzhi,* 10: 19a–23a. On the rapid rotation of magistrates, see Weiss, pp. 16–18.

158. See *North China Herald,* Oct. 7, 1885, p. 411, for Guangdong. On Jiangsu, see Faure, "Disturbances," p. 396 and chap. 3 *passim.*

159. *Tongxiang xianzhi,* 6: 10a. Yan Chen entitled the gazetteer chapter devoted to his efforts "Xinzheng" (Renewal of government). He also used this term in poetry (Yan Chen, *Mohuayuan,* 7: 7b). The connotations seem to be similar to those associated with the term restoration, but Yan envisioned considerable extrabureaucratic initiative. *Xinzheng* was also used in *Shen bao* articles on such matters in Zhejiang as administrative restructuring, municipal maintenance, and the control of undesirable customs. One article used the term in sarcastic criticism. See *Shen bao,* June 19, 1877, p. 2; Sept. 23, 1879, p. 2; Feb. 23, 1880, p. 2; Mar. 8, 1880, p. 1; Apr. 30, 1882, p. 2.

160. The fullest discussion of "feudalism" in traditional Chinese theory is Min, *Chungguk,* pp. 170–173. See also Yang, pp. 1–21; Kuhn, "Self-Government," pp. 262–68. Members of the Yongjia and Yongkang schools and seventeenth-century thinkers such as Gu Yanwu, Huang Zongxi, and Yan Yuan are commonly cited as examples of "feudal" thinkers. Feng Guifen is usually considered the chief adapter of "feudalism" to the post-Taiping period. Among the Zhejiangese, Yu Yue (Sheng Kang, 12: 32–33), Dai Wang (ibid., 24: 7a–9b), and Yang Xiangji of Xiushui (Jiaxing) wrote specifically on this topic, and it more generally related to the sociopolitical writing of the day. Although some degree of local control over local affairs within a unified system was the essence of "feudal" demands, the idea also extended to such issues as the irresponsible use of monarchical power, the use of law, and the literati role in the metropolitan bureaucracy.

161. *Shen bao,* Dec. 18, 1878, p. 2; *Pinghu xianzhi,* 4: 22b, *Jiashan xianzhi,* 5: 14a.

162. *Shen bao,* May 20, 1875, p. 3; June 1, 1875, p. 3.

163. *Shen bao,* Aug. 3, 1875, p. 3; June 14, 1878, p. 2; *Loqing xianzhi,* 8: 115a.

164. *Pinghu xianzhi,* 4: 22b; also *Cheng xianzhi,* 2: 14b; Ding Lizhong, 2: 27a.

165. *Shen bao,* Sept. 6, 1878, p. 1. Whether or not the term for self-government came from Japan, it was circulating by the late 1870's (and was not introduced in 1897 by Huang Zunxian as suggested by Kuhn, "Self-Government," p. 270). It was a logical extension of other applications of "self" to local affairs and seems to have been cut loose from its original meaning of individual moral self-governance or self-cultivation.

166. Cai Zhaocheng, in *Shuanglin zhenzhi*, 20: 58b.

167. *Longyou xianzhi*, 27: 34a, 43a; *Shen bao*, Sept. 18, 1878, p. 2; *Tongxiang xianzhi*, 4: *jianzhi zhong shantang* 15a; Ding Lizhong, 2: 27a; *Nanxun zhi*, 1922, 34: 5b. This problem probably encouraged the elite to avoid the land tax in financing public institutions, but officials probably also did not want to share that revenue.

168. On weaknesses in local governmental structure that enhanced the power of the sub-bureaucracy and on the theoretical "feudalistic" expression of demands for a larger gentry role in local administration, see Kuhn, "Self-government," pp. 262–64.

169. See Zong Yuanhan's regulations for village granaries in Ningbo prefecture, *Shen bao*, June 14, 1878, p. 2.

170. Zong, 1: 27a; Ma, 1: 11a, 48b; *Longyou xianzhi*, 27: 6a; *Shen bao*, Mar. 20, 1877, p. 1.

171. *Hangzhou fuzhi*, 54: 7a; *Longyou xianzhi*, 27: 35b. On Ding Richang's distrust of gentry, see Ocko, pp. 140, 143.

172. Zong, 3: 6b–8a, 10b–11a. See *Haining zhouzhi gao*, 6: *xuezheng* 2a, and *Deqing xian xinzhi*, 3: 14b, for similar descriptions of the silk *lijin* surcharge as a levy on local goods.

173. *Longyou xianzhi*, 27: 34b–36a, 43a. The use of "rights" is a new touch.

174. These comments appear in an account of a shrine erected in Hangzhou to commemorate the Wenzhou dead and in an account of the Gold Coin Rebellion. Sun Yiyan, *Sunxue zhai wenchao*, 2: 42a, 47a–b. Sun was bitter over the death of his eldest son, who was killed fighting at home while Yiyan was away in office.

175. *Pingyang xianzhi*, 92: 9b–10a.

176. *Tongxiang xianzhi*, 6: 9b.

177. Ibid., 6: 5a.

178. *Shen bao* ran frequent articles on the murder case, for example, Feb. 9, 1876, p. 1; Feb. 11, 1876, p. 1; Mar. 20, 1877, p. 1. On merchant boats, see ibid., Nov. 2, 1875, p. 2; June 30, 1876, p. 3. On Jiaxing *lijin*, see ibid., Aug. 31, 1876, pp. 2–3.

179. Ibid., Mar. 18, 1879, p. 2; Mar. 15, 1879, p. 3.

180. Ibid., Nov. 22, 1879, p. 1.

181. *Tongxiang xianzhi*, 12: 29a, 31a. The quote is attributed to Confucius.

182. *Wu-Qing zhenzhi*, 29: 25b; Kwong, pp. 39–40. Yan had been part of several social literary societies with fellow Zhejiangese, and he had made and retained friendships with prominent officials. Yan Chen, *Tongqi*, 18a–28a.

183. Lu was dismissed for financial irregularities in Fuzhou two years after his second retirement. He could never return to office, but shortly before his death he had an audience with the emperor, who honored him with second-class rank. Lu named the garden in which he resided *Qianyuan* (Secreted garden, or Garden of retirement), and

one of his *hao* was Qianyuan Laoren (Old man of the garden of retirement; Hummel, 1: 545). Such names had eremitic implications.

184. For many years Yu was bitter about his dismissal, but eventually he preferred the life of Lower Yangtze academic circles. Zeng Zhaoxu, pp 4–5, 8–9.

185. Mote, "Eremitism"; Schneider, *Madman.*

186. For a similar turning to the local level under the different circumstances of the late Ming, see Dennerline, *Loyalists*, pp. 201–5. Yan Chen's poems suggest he believed he was serving his country in retirement. In a poem to his brother written about the time he left office, he contrasted his cares as a literati official, through which he repaid the favor bestowed upon him by the country (*baoguo*), with his brother's concentration on family economic affairs. Later poems juxtapose or link activities that served the country with those that benefited the family at home. Yan Chen, *Mohuayin*, 7: 7b; 9: 9a–b.

187. Sun Yiyan, *Sunxue zhai wenchao*, 5: 12a–14a. This account shows Zhang using the standard eremitic props, including a lute. Zhang offers the lower level, which he chose, as an alternative course for the upright man. Sun Yiyan himself is an ambiguous case. Even while he was an official, he had definite reservations about the way government functioned, and he chose to retire at 60 *sui* to live fifteen more years in Wenzhou. Sun Yirang, who held a metropolitan post for just one year in the mid-1880's (Zhu, p. 53), definitely rejected an official career. Song Heng, *Song Pingzi*, p. 60.

188. Yan Chen speaks of restoration (*zhongxing*) in his poems (Yan Chen, *Mohuayin*, 9: 4b, 5b, 6a). Restoration appears to have been a general concept applied differently in different cases.

189. A similar observation is made by Ocko, pp. 143–44.

190. This view defines restoration in terms of internal reform currents in the early and mid-nineteenth century. Restoration failed in its aim of reviving state power more because events stimulated societal organization beyond official control than because (as suggested by Mary Wright) conservative Confucianism was unadaptable to the modern world. Wright, *Last Stand*, introduction and p. 312. See also Cohen, *Discovering*, pp. 24–25, 79.

Chapter Four

1. For networks in Chinese society, see Lapidus, p. 42 and *passim.* On external careers, see Skinner, "Mobility Strategies," pp. 335, 354, and *passim.*

2. *Hangzhou fuzhi*, 16: 12b; Yu, *Chunzai*, 4: 2298, 2386, 2420–21, 2418–21, 2423–24, 2953–56; Ding Lizhong, 2: 13b; 3: 7a and *passim*; Yan Chen, *Tongqi*, 69a; Zeng Zhaoxu, pp. 6–9, 20–21, 23; Zhu, p. 3; Sun Yutang, 2.2: 695; *Zhejiang shengli tushuguan guankan*, 1: 7–8 (Oct. 1932).

3. Men from Shaoxing and Ningbo were also part of this establishment, but the lack of gazetteers for the districts containing prefectural cities makes it hard to establish relationships. The Dinghai classicist Huang Yizhou, for instance, was intimate with scholars in Hangzhou. (Huang had been at the Gujing Jingshe and contributed to the *Xuantang leibian* compiled in 1900 by Ding Lizhong in memory of his father, Ding Bing.) See also the list of scholars at the Gujing Jingshe divided according to native place in *Hangzhou fuzhi*, 16: 14b–15a. Hu Fengdan is an example of a scholar from a locally active, prominent kin group in a peripheral district who knew many men in Beijing and Hangzhou. Hu Fengdan, *Yongkang*, 5a, 11b, 15a.

4. *Puyuan zhi*, 8: 4b; *Xincheng zhenzhi*, 13: 10a. For similar examples, see *Daishan zhenzhi*, 8: 3b–4a; *Wu-Qing zhenzhi*, 24: 11b; *Shuanglin zhenzhi*, 8: 3a. Such interchange was not inevitable; for example, two of three heads of the Longyou district academy were local *gongsheng* (*Longyou xianzhi*, 5: 8b–9a).

5. Out of 35 gazetteers that give a useful amount of information, 15 show that one or more local public leaders held these posts. They seem to have been the most frequently held posts, but the data are incomplete.

6. A quick check of gazetteers indicates that this was the general practice throughout China, although provinces with few scholars, like Gansu and Shenxi, might draw on a combined pool. The practice appears to have become established during the Ming, but during that dynasty local educational officials were sometimes districtmen.

7. For example, see *Linhai xianzhi*, 20: 50a–b.

8. *Jiashan xianzhi*, 23: 41b; Yu, *Chunzai*, 4: 2709–10. See also *Shaoxing xianzhi ziliao, renwu:* 157a.

9. *Wucheng xianzhi*, 12: 15a; Zong, 4: 2a–b; *Yuhuan tingzhi*, 2: 21b.

10. *Pinghu xianzhi*, 4: 22a; *Tongxiang xianzhi*, 4: *shantang* 2a. Longyou managers followed the model of the Huzhou foundling home. *Longyou xianzhi*, 32: 12a.

11. Chen Dongyuan, p. 18; *Shanghai xianzhi*, 9: 33b–37a; *Shanghai xian xuzhi*, 9: 10b–16b.

12. Chen Dongyuan, p. 20; *Shanghai xian xuzhi*, 9: 17b–18a; Hummel, 2: 838.

13. Ying, a *juren* from a major, publicly active lineage in Yongkang, had studied the English language and Western technology during the 1850's. During the Taiping Rebellion he was employed by Li Hongzhang and Zeng Guofan to aid refugees in Shanghai, deal with the British anti-Taiping army, and supply troops. He later held specialized posts in Shanghai, including the positions of customs daotai and director of the Shanghai arsenal. Yao Zhenchang, "Ying." Shen was a compiler of the 1881 Guian district gazetteer, a friend of leading Hu-

zhou prefectural reconstruction managers, and an in-law of Yan Chen. *Shanghai xian xuzhi,* 15: 3a; *Guian xianzhi,* frontis; Yan Chen, *Tongqi,* 65a.

14. *Shanghai xian xuzhi,* 9: 16a.

15. *Shanghai xianzhi,* 9: 34b; *Shanghai xian xuzhi,* 9: 13a. The latter source misidentifies Sun Qiangming's native place as Suian rather than Ruian.

16. *Wu-Qing zhenzhi,* 29: 33a–b. Shen Baoyue stayed with this man when a refugee in Shanghai during the Taiping Rebellion.

17. Jing Yuanshan was the son of a merchant who had managed and contributed to welfare in Shanghai and at home (*Shangyu xianzhi,* 14: 1a–2a). Yuanshan followed in his father's footsteps but acquired Western technical skills that gained him jobs in official self-strengthening enterprises. He was one of the merchants who sought to transform the officially supervised Shanghai textile company into a private corporation (Wang Jingyu, p. 43). He also established the Jingzheng Academy in Shanghai in 1893, which was merged into the better-known Nanyang Public Institute in 1897 (*Shanghai xian xuzhi,* 11: 8a, 11a), and he founded the first Chinese-run girls' school in Shanghai in 1898 (ibid., 11: 11a).

18. The editor Qian Zheng was a son-in-law of Wang Tao and went to Hong Kong to examine newspapers there. Wang contributed to *Shen bao* after he moved to Shanghai in 1884. Hummel, 2: 838; Britton, p. 64.

19. *Shen bao* started listing distribution outside Shanghai in 1880. There are few data on circulation; Britton, p. 68, estimates it at fifteen thousand for 1895. The inclusion of an editorial in the 1881 Tongxiang gazetteer compiled by Yan Chen indicates that the managerial elite might read the paper. *Tongxiang xianzhi,* 16: *shihuo zhi shang* 24a–25a.

20. *Shen bao* guan, 3: 27.

21. *Shen bao* devoted less space to Lower Yangtze local news as it began to be sold throughout the country. Inauguration of the Tianjin-Shanghai telegraph line in 1882 and its extension to Beijing in 1884 encouraged a more national focus.

22. Human-interest stories might feature women, and women are mentioned fairly often in local news articles. The paper would be a good source for late nineteenth-century women's history.

23. *Shen bao,* Feb. 11, 1875, p. 3; Sept. 18, 1878, p. 3; Feb. 26, 1880, p. 3; Nov. 17, 1880, p. 2; Mar. 5, 1880, p. 3.

24. *Shen bao,* Aug. 14, 1881, p. 1; Dec. 9, 1882, p. 3.

25. *Shanghai xinwen shiye shiliao jiyao,* p. 246.

26. For example, in the spring of 1878, tinfoil beaters in Hangzhou were thrown out of work because of diminished demand for their products in Shenxi, Shanxi, and Henan. *Shen bao,* Jan. 16, 1888, p. 2.

27. *North China Daily News*, Jan. 28, 1878; *Shen bao*, Dec. 4, 1878, p. 3.

28. *North China Daily News*, Mar. 25, 1878, p. 275; *Shen bao*, May 21, 1878, p. 2.

29. *North China Daily News*, July 16, 1878, p. 55; memorial of Zuo Zongtang, *Guangxu zhao Donghua lu*, p. 68. The banker was Hu Guangzhong.

30. The Guoyu and Puyu agencies. *Shanghai xian xuzhi*, 2: 21a, 22a.

31. *Shen bao*, May 24, 1879, pp. 3–4. These were not the only agencies accepting donations in these cities (*Shen bao*, Aug. 10, 1879, p. 3; Sept. 17, 1879, p. 4). A fifth bureau at Zhenjiang, Jiangsu, appears to have been less important.

32. Jing, 2: 41a–42a.

33. Rough accountings published in *Shen bao* reported that the 1878 collections consisted of 393,000 taels as of December (Dec. 4, 1878, p. 3). Collections for the first half of 1879 *only* were 161,000 taels (Sept. 11, 1879, p. 3). 339,000 taels had been collected in 1880 as of November (Nov. 23, 1880, p. 3).

34. *North China Daily News*, July 12, 1878, p. 43; *Shen bao*, May 17, 1878, p. 3; July 25, 1878, p. 4; June 13, 1879, p. 3; July 4, 1879, p. 2; July 20, 1879, p. 1; Aug. 10, 1879, p. 3; Sept. 3, 1879, p. 1; Sept. 9, 1879, p. 3; Sept. 13, 1879, p. 4. *Shen bao* articles mention organized local collecting in Huzhou, Jiaxing, and Shaoxing cities; the district cities of Pinghu and Xiaoshan; and the towns of Chenze, Nanxun, Shuanglin, Linghu, Wu-Qing, and Xinde.

35. *Shen bao*, Aug. 2, 1879, p. 1; Aug. 24, 1879, p. 3; Oct. 23, 1879, p. 3; Jing, 2: 15a.

36. *Shen bao*, July 20, 1879, p. 1.

37. *Shen bao*, July 21, 1879, p. 3; Sept. 4, 1879, p. 3; Sept. 8, 1879, p. 3. These men were Pan Minbao, Jin Fuceng, and Yan Zuolin. Many of their letters and reports were published in *Shen bao*; see, for example, Feb. 21, 1879, p. 3; Sept. 17, 1879, p. 3. For a biography of Jin, see Jing, 3: 11b–12a. These famine relief activists and prominent welfare activists were likely to know each other. Jin, for instance, had met Ding Bing while searching for his father's corpse after the Taiping Rebellion.

38. *Shen bao*, Aug. 15, 1881, p. 1. The author uses southeast, not south, for all coastal provinces from Jiangsu through Guangdong.

39. Jing, 2: 42a; 3: 10a.

40. *Shen bao*, Aug. 16, 1881, p. 1.

41. Ibid., Aug. 14, 1879, p. 3. See also Nov. 7, 1879, p. 3.

42. Ibid., Aug. 15, 1881, p. 1.

43. Jing, 3: 9a–10b. Jing makes the point that, although by this time Jin Fuceng had joined the Yellow River Conservancy, he was managing voluntary, not official, relief in the flooded areas in Shandong in 1883.

44. See comment in *North China Herald*, June 15, 1889, p. 729. The paper says that Chinese would give donations for relief to foreign-run agencies, but not to officials. It seems more probable, however, that the preference was for elite-managed committees—in this case a Sino-Western one. See also *North China Herald*, Apr. 20, 1889, p. 485, for resistance of the Hangzhou tea guild to the governor's demand for famine contributions.

45. *Shen bao*, Nov. 7, 1879, p. 3; Nov. 8, 1879, p. 3; Nov. 29, 1879, p. 2; Dec. 21, 1879, p. 3.

46. Ibid., Nov. 23, 1882, p. 3; Dec. 2, 1882, pp. 3–4; Dec. 6, 1882, pp. 3–4; Dec. 16, 1882, p. 4.

47. Ibid., Aug. 16, 1883, p. 4; Dec. 7, 1883, p. 4; Dec. 9, 1883, p. 4; Dec. 10, 1883, pp. 4–5.

48. *North China Herald*, Sept. 15, 1888, p. 304; Mar. 15, 1889, p. 310; Apr. 25, 1890, pp. 499–500.

49. *Shen bao*, Apr. 30, 1883, p. 1; Ding Zhongli, 2: 23b; *North China Herald*, Apr. 3, 1890, p. 404.

50. *Shen bao*, Dec. 7, 1883, p. 4. The involvement of the Shanghai telegraph bureau explains why telegraph bureaus in Ningbo, Shaoxing, and Langqi were collection points in 1883 (*Shen bao*, Dec. 10, 1883, p. 5). By the end of 1887 the silk guild had published 1,350 collection reports in *Shen bao* (Dec. 7, 1883, p. 4).

51. Elite managers in Tianjin had been heavily involved in famine relief since 1878. *Shen bao*, Dec. 10, 1883, p. 4, lists collections from twenty-two localities in Jiangsu, ten in Zhejiang, and one or a few in Fujian, Guangdong, Guangxi, Anhui, Jiangxi, Hunan, Hubei, Sichuan, Henan, Shanxi, Yunnan, and Guizhou. See also *North China Herald*, Apr. 25, 1883, p. 500.

52. *Yapian zhanzheng*, 4: 374–433, reprints excerpts from gazetteers of Dinghai, Zhenhai, Yin, Ciqi, Pinghu, Yuyao, and Haining about the Opium War. See also 4: 386, 399, 403, 417–19. *Ciqi xianzhi*, 33: 5b, states that a merchant established a militia. *Xiangshan xianzhi*, 25: 33b, relates that a local man raised funds to repair city embankments.

53. *Yapian zhanzheng*, 4: 431–32. For social unrest in Guangdong, see Wakeman, *Strangers*, pp. 61–71.

54. Yu, *Chunzai*, 4: 2709–10.

55. *Shen bao*, Sept. 15, 1874, pp. 2, 3; Nov. 2, 1874, pp. 2, 3.

56. Ibid., Sept. 17, 1874, p. 4.

57. Ibid., Oct. 6, 1875, p. 1.

58. Ibid., Nov. 12, 1880, p. 1; Nov. 25, 1880, p. 1; Nov. 27, 1880, p. 1; Dec. 2, 1880, p. 2; Dec. 17, 1880, p. 2.

59. Ibid., Feb. 2, 1882, p. 2.

60. Ibid., Dec. 21, 1880, p. 1.

61. Ibid., Dec. 18, 1880, p. 1. During the winter of 1880–81 *Shen bao* carried editorials urging preparations against Russia.

62. On the militant opposition during the Sino-French War, see Eastman, "Ch'ing-i," and William Ayers, chap. 4. For an alternative interpretation emphasizing political aspects, see Rankin, "Public Opinion." (See pp. 461, 478–79, for Zhejiangese militants.) For a definition of "literati officials" within the metropolitan bureaucracy and for a history of *qingyi* in the 1830's and 1840's, see Polachek, *Opium War.*

63. Xue, especially pp. 36, 67–69, 113–16, 131, 135–36, 183.

64. Ibid., p. 45; *Dinghai tingzhi*, introduction, p. 3; *North China Herald*, Apr. 8, 1885, p. 408.

65. *North China Herald*, Aug. 22, 1884, p. 203.

66. Xue, p. 67.

67. *North China Herald*, Oct. 15, 1884, p. 420; Nov. 5, 1884, p. 499.

68. Ibid., June 19, 1885, p. 702.

69. Ibid., June 12, 1885, p. 671.

70. *Zhenhai xianzhi*, 27: 45a, 45b; *Dinghai tingzhi*, introduction, p. 3; Chen Qiu, "An Introduction to a Record to Requite the Country" (*Baoguo lu*), in "Zhilu cungao," 2.2: 9b.

71. *Zhenhai xianzhi*, 27: 44a. Sun Yiyan, retired in Ruian, was among those who presented plans. Aying, *Zhong-Fa*, pp. 438–40.

72. Liu Bingzhang, 3: 16b, 8a–18b; 4: 17b–18a; Aying, *Zhong-Fa*, p. 308. The figure of three hundred thousand is from Governor Liu Bingzhang. The account in Aying says that over 60 battalions of Zhejiang troops were supported by one hundred thousand (yuan?) from salt, tea, silk, and cotton taxes, three to four hundred thousand from silk, tea, Western medicine, and salt firms, banks, and pawnshops in Ningbo, and two hundred thousand from contributions raised in Ningbo prefecture.

73. *Zhenhai xianzhi*, 27: 41b.

74. For example, the tea exporter Yuan Zaixing. Ibid., 27: 49a–b.

75. Chen Qiu, *Jiushi*; Chen Qiu, *Jingshi*; Tang Zhen (Tang Shouqian), *Weiyan*; Song Heng, *Liuzhai* (also excerpted in Song Heng, *Song Pingzi*, pp. 14–33). Aspects of Tang's and Chen's writings are studied in Eastman, "Reformism," pp. 702–3. Tang Zhen changed his *ming* to Shouqian after the publication of *Weiyan*. This new name referred to the seventeenth-century tract *Qianshu* (Writings in retirement) by the Ming political critic Tang Zhen. (The names of the two Tangs were pronounced similarly but written with different characters, and *Weiyan* was immediately compared to *Qianshu*). He will be called Tang Shouqian in descriptions of his subsequent political activities.

76. Rankin, "Public Opinion," pp. 472–76. On territorial awareness as an element in nationalism, see Bastid, "Party," pp. 5–6.

77. *Shen bao*, June 25, 1883, p. 1; July 5, 1883, p. 1.

78. For example, see ibid., Dec. 27, 1883, p. 1.

79. Ibid., Jan. 9, 1884, p. 2; Jan. 20, 1884, p. 1; Jan. 25, 1884, p. 1.

80. Edict of June 28, 1884, in *Guangxu zhao Donghua lu*, p. 1676.

81. *Shen bao,* June 6, 1883, p. 1.
82. Yu, "Zijiang." This undated essay could have been written at any time from the mid-1880's through the mid-1890's; the ideas were current by the mid-1880's.
83. Chen Qiu, *Jingshi,* p. 222.
84. Song Heng, *Liuzhai,* in *Song Pingzi,* pp. 16–22. Song's use of the Confucian-Legalist dichotomy was atypical. His views probably reflected continuing antipathy in Wenzhou to the Zhu Xi school of Neo-Confucianism, that went back to disputes in the Southern Song.
85. Song Heng, *Song Pingzi,* p. 45. Song did not attack the Manchus, but some of his writings had an anti-steppe-barbarian caste.
86. See description in Chen Qiu, "Zhilu cungao," 2.2: 25a–27a. Unfavorable rumors about this society circulating in Beijing caused the founders to disband it in 1890. Although the group was probably not political, Tao Qian was not a neutral role model, since he was noted for his rejection of official service and his bucolic eremitism to protest the overthrow of the dynasty he had served.
87. *Shaoxing xianzhi ziliao, renwu:* 146b; Zhou, *Tizhai xuji,* 1. 13a, 14b. Dates for this society differ, but the early 1880's given by the draft Shaoxing gazetteer seems most plausible. The post Sino-Japanese War date in *Tizhai xuji,* 1: 7a, is impossible because one major member was dead by then. Zhang Lüxiang could be claimed by Shaoxing natives because he had studied their under I in Zongzhou. Zhou Yunliang used terms like "dwelling in seriousness" and "knowing difficulty and fear," which were key elements in Zhang's thought. Cai Yuanpei, in an introduction to *Tizhai xuji* (introduction, 1a), called this society proto-socialist, but it would seem more accurate to relate the members' ideas to Confucian social theory.
88. That this type of social concern could also lead to ideas closer to European social philosophies is indicated by a later essay by Zhou Yunliang. Here he expresses hopes that a revitalized China might pioneer a better society, in which natural science would be used to benefit mankind rather than build military machines as people did in the West. If the Chinese developed their understanding and their will to resist foreign encroachment, they might move on to investigate the causes of poverty, develop a free and equal government, and equalize the differences between rich and poor, labor and leisure. Ibid., 2: 26a, 32b.
89. Chen Qiu, "Zhilu cungao," 2.2: 9b–10b. This tract, *Baoguo lu* (A record to requite the country) was first written when Chen tried to establish a militia during the Sino-French War, it was published under a new title when he was given authority to raise a militia in 1894.
90. Connections made by Zhou Yunliang between education, the alleviation of poverty, and the development of people's spirit for defense appear in Zhou, *Tizhai xuji,* 2: 34b. In the seventeenth century

Gu Yanwu had made similar connections in his essay *Junxian lun* (On the centralized bureaucratic monarchy) between the overcentralization of power, popular poverty, and national weakness. See Gu, *Gu Tinglin*, pp. 12–13.

91. For example, Chen Qiu, *Jingshi*, p. 222.

92. Zhou Yunliang, *Tizhai xuji*, 2: 15b–16a.

93. For Chen Qiu's proposals on local administration, see *Jingshi*, p. 220. A more general advocacy of opinion expression and administrative improvement appears in ibid., pp. 218–19. Tang Zhen [Tang Shouqian], *Weiyuan*, 1: 4b–10b, 4: 29b.

94. Chen Qiu, "Zhilu cungao," 2.2: 10a. Yu Yue endorsed feudalism on the different ground that it was superior in defending the country. Yu, "Fengjian."

95. Literati officials in Beijing often combined in *qingyi* movements against the new men, as epitomized by protégés of Li Hongzhang. Outside the capital, people in all the groups might be acquainted and might share the feeling that they were powerless and "unrepresented."

96. *Shen bao*, Dec. 7, 1883, p. 1.

97. Chen Qiu in *Zhiping sanyi* (Three principles of order and peace), written in 1883, sought the basis for a new political system in the role attributed to the clans of antiquity (*zongfa*) and hoped to produce a harmonious world order by extending feudalism. Feng Guifen also drew on the concept of the *zongfa*, but the two men reached their ideas independently. Onogawa, pp. 27–28. For Wang Tao's use of the concept of "feudalism" to limit autocracy, see Cohen, *Between Tradition*, p. 43. K. C. Liu has pointed to the desire of the literati to mitigate autocracy throughout the nineteenth century. Kwang-ching Liu, pp. 177–78.

98. Kwang-ching Liu, pp. 25–27, surveys the early interest in Western political institutions and points to a shift after the Sino-French War. Onogawa distinguishes between the *yangwu* of the late 1880's, which had a military (especially naval) focus, and the beginnings of fundamental reformism (*bianfa*), which focused on political institutions. She also points to an equation of Western government with the *Rites of Zhou* and suggests that reformism after the Sino-Japanese War emerged from the twin streams of "reviving antiquity and *Zhouli*" and "changing to the new and Western studies."

99. *Shen bao*, Apr. 23, 1882, p. 1. For an example of an editorial by Wang Tao criticizing autocracy in the late 1870's, and for Wang's ideas on parliaments, see Cohen, *Between Tradition*, pp. 215–16, 220–31. Wang later wrote editorials for *Shen bao* and was one of the sources of representational ideas that were spread by that paper.

100. Rankin, "Public Opinion," p. 467.

101. Chen Qiu suggested provincial assemblies to the Shandong

governor in 1890 (Onogawa, p. 28). In *Jingshi*, pp. 219–20, he advocated a national body of 36 officials from the censorate and the six boards and also called for district assemblies. *Jiushi*, p. 228, proposed assemblies of degree holders in departments and districts, and called for increasing the number of metropolitan and provincial officials who could memorialize the throne. Tang Zhen, *Weiyuan*, 1: 6a–b, called for a two-chamber national assembly—the upper body to be composed of board presidents and vice presidents and Hanlin scholars of fourth rank or above; the lower body to be drawn from metropolitan officials below the fourth rank.

102. *Shen bao*, May 1, 1887, p. 1.
103. *North China Herald*, Dec. 28, 1894, p. 1046; Jan. 11, 1895, pp. 39, 54.
104. Ibid., Aug. 24, 1894, p. 387.
105. Ibid., June 21, 1894, p. 944; *Nanxun zhi*, 1922, 2: 4a.
106. *North China Herald*, Mar. 22, 1895, p. 421; May 10, 1895, p. 685; Jan. 31, 1896, p. 164
107. Ibid., Mar. 1, 1895, p. 307; Jan. 11, 1895, p. 39.
108. *Shanghai xinwen shiye*, p. 253; *North China Herald*, Aug. 23, 1895, p. 313. Chinese newspapers, including *Shen bao*, reported victories instead of defeats. *North China Herald*, Jan. 1, 1895, p. 88.
109. Some of these works are listed in Aying, *Zhong-Ri*, pp. 16–29.
110. For examples of newspapers and pamphlets in Ningbo, Jiaxing, and Wenzhou, see *North China Herald*, Aug. 10, 1894, p. 223; Mar. 15, 1895, p. 386; Aug. 23, 1895, p. 313; Sept. 20, 1895, p. 479.
111. There were strong similarities between the *qingyi* literature of the Sino-French and Sino-Japanese wars, but in the 1890's the old phrases were attached to expanded concepts of reform and accompanied by more assertive political action. Rankin, "Public Opinion," pp. 472–75.
112. Editorial of July 15, 1895, in Aying, *Zhong-Ri*, p. 55.
113. Ibid., pp. 491–93.
114. Ibid., pp. 493–94.
115. Ibid., pp. 527–31.

Chapter Five

1. Esherick, chap. 3, introduced the concept of an urban reformist elite. Lewis, pp. 41–45, describes a self-strengthening reformism in Hunan that challenged basic Confucian precepts.
2. *North China Herald*, Oct. 4, 1895, p. 563.
3. See the list of investments of thirteen Shanghai merchants in Sun Yutang, 2.2: 1091–95. Yan Xinhou, Pang Yuanji, and Lou Jinghui were, for instance, major investors in the mills and filatures of Ningbo, Hangzhou, and Xiaoshan.
4. *North China Herald*, Dec. 13, 1895, p. 964; Sept. 17, 1897,

p. 523. The *North China Herald* contrasted oversubscription of shares in the Hangzhou Electric Light Company with difficulties in raising capital in Suzhou. The paper specifically mentions share offerings in Hangzhou and Shanghai. It seems probable that shares of Shao-Ning companies, at least, were also sold in Ningbo.

5. Xu Heyong, p. 180.

6. On these papers, see Chen Mi, "Dong-Ou," p. 11; Chen Mi, *Chen*, pp. 25a—b; Song Heng, *Song Pingzi*, pp. 51—55; Xu Heyong, p. 180; Shen Yuwu, p. 168; *North China Herald*, May 1, 1899, p. 764; *Hangzhou baihua bao*, no. 1, *gaobai* 1a—b. The date of 1895 for *Hangzhou baihua bao* given in Hong Shiyun, *Zhejiang xinwen shi* (A history of Zhejiangese newspapers) cited in Xu Heyong, p. 180, appears to be too early.

7. *Shaoxing xianzhi ziliao, renwu:* 163b; Cole, "Shaohsing," pp. 190—91; Jing, 2: 48a—49b. The *Chinese Progress* (*Shiwu bao*) masthead listed bookstores, schools, two telegraph bureaus, one salt *lijin* bureau, and various people as distributors in Zhejiang cities. The *Hangzhou Vernacular Journal* listed individuals, two old-style banks, one rice firm, one paper firm, and one academy in Shangyu.

8. Wang Ermin, 24.2: 17; *Hangzhou fuzhi*, 17: 9a—b; Wang Yinian, p. 64.

9. *Hangzhou baihua bao*, 3: *Zhong wai xinwen* 2b—3a, 4a.

10. *North China Herald*, May 7, 1897, p. 815.

11. Jing, 2: 55b, 60b; *Yuyao Liucang zhi*, 15: 8a, 9b; 16: 1a.

12. *Cheng xianzhi*, 16: 44a.

13. *Nanxun zhi*, 1922, 3: 4a; *Zhulin bayu zhi*, 4: 3a; 6: 37a; *Qu xianzhi*, 3: 24a; *Shaoxing xianzhi ziliao, renwu:* 163b, 176a.

14. Hu Sijing, 4.3: 24a—29a, gives figures on financing reform projects in the provinces during the 1898 period. Zhejiang with an expenditure of 700,000 taels ranks sixth. The 600,000 (86 percent) contributed by "gentry, merchants, and people" was by far the highest percentage of non-official investment. However inaccurate, these figures suggest high levels of elite activity in Zhejiang.

15. Schoppa, *Chinese Elites*, chap. 7, suggests that this trend gradually began to reverse during the first decades of the Republic as elite activities spread outward to less developed adjacent districts.

16. *Shiwu bao*, 46: 9a—b; *Hangzhou fuzhi*, 17: 2a, 3a.

17. *Wuxu bianfa*, 4: 555—56.

18. These men were Yun Zuyi and Ren Daoyung. *North China Herald*, Jan. 23, 1899, p. 105; Zhang Jinglu, Lin Song, and Li Songnian, pp. 218, 236.

19. Sun Yutang, 2.2: 695. Ding's involvement is plausible because of his prestige, although he was by then almost fully retired.

20. Wang Yinian, pp. 66, 69; *North China Herald*, Dec. 11, 1896, p. 999; *Hangzhou fuzhi*, 17: 2b—3b, 16a. The administration of the Qiushi Academy was stable, although it went through several reorga-

nizations to become the provincial college. The Hanlin academician Lu Maodong was head from 1897 to 1905, except during 1904 when his place was taken by Tao Baolian of Xiushui—a future constitutionalist and the son of Liang-Jiang Governor-General Tao Mo.

21. *Hangzhou fuzhi*, 17: 9a; *Dongfang zazhi*, 1.10: *shiye* 180; Nonggongshang bu, 2.4: 7b; *Da Qing (Guangxu) shilu*, 3: 1858; Eastman, *Throne*, p. 192.

22. Cole, "Shaohsing," pp. 191–92.

23. *Shaoxing xianzhi ziliao, renwu:* 163b–164a, 176a; Cole, "Shaohsing," pp. 142–45, 190–92; *North China Herald,* Mar. 8, 1894, p. 360. The examples of Xu Shulan and other early reform activists indicate that cultural barriers to Western-inspired reforms were not as strong as has often been assumed.

24. *Oufeng zazhi huikan*, 2.5: *wenyuan neibian* 5a–b.

25. Chen Mi, *Chen*, 11a; *Oufeng zazhi*, 1.11: *wenyuan neibian* 8b. It is not clear whether this hospital was influenced by Western (missionary!) practices. There was also a strong tradition of medical study in Wenzhou, traceable probably to the Song. Chen Fuchen's brother was a doctor, and Chen Qiu had studied medicine.

26. Zhu, p. 69; *Zhejiang chao,* 4: 182.

27. Xu Heyong, pp. 186–97. *Oufeng zazhi*, 1.11: *wenyuan neibian* 9a; Chen Mi, *Dong-Ou*, p. 12; *Zhejiang chao,* 4: 180, 182; *Pingyang xianzhi*, 39: 14b–15a.

28. *Oufeng zazhi*, 1.11: *wenyuan neibian* 9a.

29. Jing, 2: 48a–63b, 3: 66a–69b.

30. The friend, Luo Zhenyu, was a co-founder of the agricultural society established by Wang Kangnian in Shanghai. Zhang Yufa, *Lixian*, p. 199.

31. Jing, 2: 54a–65b. The ambiguous modernity of this Shanghai group is underlined by their discussion of whether to offer prayers for rain during the current drought. Although some members scorned prayer as superstitious, others accepted its usefulness as a matter of course. That particular issue was resolved when it rained during the debate. Thereupon everyone happily agreed to make a thanks-offering.

32. Neither the Shangyu nor the Yuyao district gazetteer gives the names of school founders. The sub-district *Yuyao Liucang zhi*, 15: 1b–15b, shows that three of thirteen men mobilized by Jing in 1898 sponsored educational change in that part of the district during 1902. It seems likely that others were active elsewhere where their names were not recorded.

33. See masthead of *Shiwu bao*, no. 51. The cities were Hangzhou, Jiaxing, Xiushui, Huzhou, Ningbo, Shaoxing, Zhuji, Yongjia, Ruian, Huangyan, Lanqi. The Ruian outlet was the school founded by Sun Yirang.

34. *Hangzhou baihua bao*, nos. 10, 12, 14: mastheads. These places were Hangzhou, Huzhou, Nanxun, Jiaxing, Haining, Shaoxing,

Shangyu, Cheng, Xinchang, Zuji. This paper was also sold in a few major cities in other provinces.

35. Sun Yirang, *Zhouqing*, 2: 11a. The newspaper might have been the *Hangzhou baihua bao*, which carried an article on that school (14: 1a).

36. *Hangzhou baihua bao*, 3: *Zhong wai xinwen* 2b–3b.

37. Chen Mi, *Chen*, pp. 25a–b. The Shaoxing men were Tong Xueqi and Hu Daonan. For Tong, see *Xinchang xianzhi*, 6: 10b; 9: 43b; for Hu, see *Shaoxing xianzhi ziliao, renwu:* 182a.

38. Wang Yinian, pp. 58, 71, 88; Zhang Yufa, *Lixian*, p. 200.

39. *Hangzhou baihua bao*, *Zhong wai xinwen* 3a–b.

40. Wang Ermin provides a very incomplete list, but he does indicate the large number in Shanghai.

41. For Liang's political thought, see Hao Chang, especially pp. 99–120, 155, and chap. 8. Chang suggests a much sharper break with statecraft orientations than I do.

42. Jing, 2: 48a, 49b, 53a.

43. Ibid., 2: 53b, 54b.

44. The most comprehensive study of Sun Yirang's thought is Wang Gengsheng, *Zhouqing*. Several short articles appear in *Zhejiang xuebao*. In English, Chang Ch'i-yun, "Chou-li," is based on Sun's larger study *Zhouli zhengyi* (The true principles of the *Rites of Zhou*). Sun wrote the shorter *Political Essentials of the Rites of Zhou* after *The True Principles* had enjoyed a vogue among pro-reform metropolitan officials following the Boxer Rebellion. It was intended in part to refute the idea that Zhou institutions were simply like Western ones. Wang Gengsheng, 1: 229a.

45. Sun Yirang, *Zhouli zhengyao*, 1: 4a–5a, 18b.

46. Ibid., 1: 20a–21b. The quote from Gu Yanwu was his well-known precept that society declined when there were many high officials and few low ones, but it flourished when high officials were few and low ones numerous.

47. Ibid., 1: 32a–36a.

48. Ibid., 1: 24a–26a. See also Sun Yirang, *Zhouqing* 1: 26b, and Cao, p. 9.

49. Sun Yirang, *Zhouli zhengyao*, 2: 2b–4a; *Pingyang xianzhi*, 39: 15b has a laudatory biography of a scholar who continued survey work while slowly dying after being attacked by dogs.

50. Ibid., 2: 4b–9b.

51. Ibid., 2: 33a–b, 32a–36b; for Chen Qiu's views, see Chen Qiu, *Jingshi*, p. 222.

52. For the general events of the 1898 Reform Movement, see the documentary collection *Wuxu bianfa*, and Tang Zhijun, *Wuxu bianfa shi*. For a recent reevaluation, see Kwong. On reformist aspects of the "Emperor's Faction," see Rankin, "Public Opinion," pp. 470–71, and Schrecker.

53. Wang Kangnian broke with Liang and Kang. Liang and Sun Yirang respected one another but had no close contact.
54. Zhang Yufa, *Lixian*, pp. 179–84, 186–88.
55. *Wuxu bianfa*, 4: 403–4.
56. *Oufeng zazhi*, 11: *wenyuan neibian* 8a.
57. Wang Yinian, p. 58; *Zhenhai xinzhi heigao, xia:* 14b.
58. Qian, *Wen Yunge*, pp. 43, 45–50, tells of oppositionist literati meetings in Shanghai.
59. *North China Herald*, Jan. 30, 1899, p. 169. See Table 12 for examples of schools established in 1899 or 1900. The Qiushi Academy in Hangzhou remained open, as did the Chinese and Western School in Shaoxing and the major new school in Ningbo. In Ruian the school founded by Chen Qiu closed, but the one established by Sun Yirang continued. The crucial factors seem to have been reasonably solid funding, and the backing of a prestigious member of either the local elite or officials (or both).
60. Ibid., Apr. 18, 1900, p. 675.
61. Ibid., Mar. 20, 1899, p. 469; May 1, 1899, p. 764; May 29, 1899, p. 949; July 3, 1899, p. 15; Dec. 27, 1899, p. 1267.
62. Ibid., July 11, 1900, pp. 62–63; July 18, 1900, p. 122.
63. Xu Heyong, pp. 187–97; *North China Herald*, July 11, 1900, pp. 62–63; July 18, 1900, p. 122; July 25, 1900, pp. 178, 197–98; Sept. 12, 1900, p. 57; *Qu xianzhi*, 9: 36a–38a.
64. For example, Ningbo merchants organized their own guard force. See *North China Herald*, July 18, 1900, p. 145; *Yihe tuan*, 3: 325–62, for official telegrams about keeping the peace in the Yangtze Valley and protecting Chinese (as well as foreign) merchants and property.
65. *Shaoxing xianzhi ziliao*, pp. 156a–157a.
66. *Shen bao*, July 1, 1900, in *Yihe tuan*, 4: 172.
67. *Zhong wai ribao*, Jan. 15, 1900, Dec. 8, 1900, in *Yihe tuan*, 4: 179–81, 226–28.
68. *Zhong wai ribao*, July 14, 1900, July 21, 1900, in *Yihe tuan*, 4: 189–92. The editorialist also called for troops to put down rebels, and for diplomatic negotiations, military reinforcement, the management of government finances, the encouragement of human talent, the collection of funds to aid suffering people, and the establishment of more granaries.
69. Gasster, pp. 192–93.
70. Li Bingheng was considered the main Chinese culprit. *Shen bao*, July 1, 1900, Aug. 19, 1900, in *Yihe tuan*, 4: 171–74.
71. Guo Tingyi, 2: 1080; Zhao Erxun, *liezhuan:* 1432.
72. *North China Herald*, Jan. 17, 1900, p. 82; Mar. 21, 1900, p. 489; Apr. 11, 1900, p. 639; Apr. 18, 1900, p. 687; May 9, 1900, p. 286.
73. Ibid., Mar. 7, 1900, p. 393; Mar. 28, 1900, pp. 545–56.
74. Hummel, 2: 945–48; *North China Herald*, Aug. 15, 1900,

p. 334. Xu Jingzheng was from Jiaxing, and Yuan Chang came from peripheral Tonglu (Jinhua) but was well known in Hangzhou scholarly circles.

75. These men included Wang Kangnian, Ye Han, Zhang Yuanji, Song Heng, and Zhang Binglin. Zhang Yufa, *Lixian*, pp. 257–61; Zhonghua minguo kaiguo, 1.10: 336–39; Feng, pp. 47–48.

76. Xinchao she, pp. 1–3.

77. For members, see Rankin, *Revolutionaries*, p. 141. However, the date 1903 given for the *Hangzhou Vernacular Journal* should be 1901.

78. Su Yuanlei, introduction: 2, 4, 8; 53–54. See also Song Heng, *Song Pingzi*, pp. 41–54; Yao Zong, p. 8.

79. Chen Mi, *Chen*, p. 24b.

80. Rankin, *Revolutionaries*, p. 142.

81. On these men, see *Zhulin bayu zhi*, foreword: 1a–b; 4: 1a–4b; 6: 35a–37a, 39a–40a; Rankin, *Revolutionaries*, p. 161; *Jiang-Zhe tielu fengchao*, pp. 83, 136; *Dongfang zazhi*, 4.7: *jiaoyu* 172; *Shi bao*, July 12, 1910, p. 3; *Xinhai geming huiyi lu*, 7: 152.

Chapter Six

1. Governmental reforms are surveyed in Ichiko, "Political and Institutional Reform," pp. 375–415. On education, see also Cameron, pp. 71–73, and Franke. On commercial laws and agencies, see Chan, *Merchants*, chaps. 8–10.

2. Zhu, p. 86; Song Heng, *Song Pingzi*, p. 61.

3. The gazetteer data are incomplete, but evidence of increases in local forces or the extension of police to lower administrative levels after 1911 can be found in some republican gazetteers. For example, see *Puyuan zhi*, 7: 1b, 4a–5a; *Zhenhai xinzhi beigao, shang:* 9a; *Qu xianzhi*, 9: 10a, 14a–16a.

4. Agricultural associations or sericulture schools were established before 1900 in Hangzhou (1898), Zhulin market (1899), Haining (1898), Qu (1898), and Ruian (1896). Others were founded in Jiaxing, in Qing town (1910), and in Songyang before 1911. *Hangzhou fuzhi*, 17: 9a; *Zhulin bayu zhi*, 6: 37a; *Qu xianzhi*, 3: 30b; *Zhejiang chao*, 4: 182; *Shi bao*, Apr. 24, 1910, p. 3; *Wu-Qing zhenzhi*, 9: 29a; *Songyang xianzhi*, 2: 5b. This is not a complete record.

5. The most comprehensive, but not complete, listing of chambers of commerce is *Zhongguo nianjian*, pp. 503–4. See also Nonggongshang bu, (1909), 2.4; (1910), 2.5, and Tōa Dōbunkai, *Shina*, 13: 770–92. The Haining chamber of commerce was not formed until 1912, although there was one in the chief market town of Xiashi in 1907. On educational associations, see Xuebu (1907), pp. 543–44; Xuebu (1910), *Zhejiang*: 1–2. For a brief summary of New Policies organizations, see Schoppa, *Chinese Elites*, pp. 35–39.

6. *Shi bao*, May 13, 1910, p. 3.

7. The 1914 governmental regulations theoretically required that four-fifths of chamber members be guild members (Schoppa, *Chinese Elites*, p. 35). This percentage was presumably not always attained, and earlier membership was even more varied.

8. *Shi bao*, Nov. 2, 1910, p. 3.

9. *Dongfang zazhi*, 3.11: *neiwu* 239; 5.2: *neiwu* 142; 5.4: *neiwu* 267. In Laipu town, in the Huzhou border-district of Changxing, "gentry" established a defense and public benefit society to study self-government and improve agriculture and trade. It elected managers who were to cooperate with village managers, heads, and guards. Ibid., 5.3: *neiwu* 212.

10. Ibid., 4.10: *neiwu* 509; 5.4: *neiwu* 267.

11. Ibid., 4.10: *neiwu* 509.

12. Ibid., 3.11: *neiwu* 239.

13. Ibid., 4.10: *neiwu* 509.

14. For example, *Shi bao*, May 18, 1910, p. 3. The Cheng self-government study office set up a "home for virtuous widows" that cared for both men and women. This was too radical for some people in the local elite-community, and they persuaded the governor to forbid it.

15. *Dongfang zazhi*, 4.10: *neiwu* 509.

16. *Zhongguo nianjian*, p. 29.

17. *Wu-Qing zhenzhi*, 23: 6a; *Minli bao*, July 3, 1911, p. 4.

18. *Shi bao*, Apr. 16, 1911, p. 3; Schoppa, "Self-Government," p. 508.

19. For example, one local source says 300 schools were established in one Zhuji township before 1911 (Schoppa, *Chinese Elites*, p. 254), but the Ministry of Education lists only 101 for the entire district in 1909, Xuebu (1910), *Zhejiang*: 8.

20. Districts in Table 15 were selected to give fairly systematic coverage of the educational range of the 78 districts, but some details are not recorded. The table does not fully show the strong educational activity in Jinhua (half its districts ranked in the top third), and it does not fully show the rapid slippage of Chuzhou districts from intermediate to lower ranks between 1907 and 1909. The number of students in core Huzhou districts were rapidly increasing by 1909 after a slow start. Most of the core Jiaxing districts (which had vigorous managerial histories), however, were bunched slightly above median rank.

21. *Hangzhou fuzhi*, 17: 5a. In 1907 there were 26 primary schools in the city, 3 in the suburbs, and 3 in rural townships. After a strong effort by the district educational association, there were 36 in the city and 20 in rural townships in 1910.

22. For example, *Cheng xianzhi*, 6: 20b–23a; *Xinchang xianzhi*, 5: 62a–65a; *Xiaoshan xianzhi gao*, 10 *xia*: 5b–8a.

23. *Pingyang xianzhi*, 11: 1a–15a.

24. *Cheng xianzhi*, 6: 20b–23a. Examples of similar diffusion:

Xiaoshan xianzhi gao, 10 *xia*: 4b–11a; *Linhai xianzhi*, 8: 38a–40b; *Xiangshan xianzhi*, 14: 38a–42b; *Yuyao Liucang zhi*, 15: 1a–15b; *Xindeng xianzhi*, 12: 28b–39b. For an example of concentration in and near the administrative center, see *Songyang xianzhi*, 5: 2a–19a.

25. *Songyang xianzhi*, 9: 55b, 72b; *Xuanping xianzhi*, 4: 48a; 6: 4a.

26. *Dongfang zazhi*, 3.1: *jiaoyu* 27; *Oufeng zazhi huikan*, 2.5: *wenyuan neibian* 5a, 6a.

27. For example, see *Shaoxing xianzhi ziliao, renwu*: 197a–b; *Zhenhai xinzhi beigao, shang*: 47a, *xia*: 5a.

28. *Shi bao*, Aug. 14, 1910, p. 5.

29. Xuebu (1907), pp. 37–38; Xuebu (1910), *gesheng* 10–11.

30. Zhuang, p. 13. Other evidences of independent elite initiative were two-level primary schools and middle schools outside prefectural cities, neither of which were called for in the government plans. Middle schools in district cities declined between 1907 and 1910, but by 1910 Zhejiang and Guangdong were the provinces with the highest number of two-level primaries. Xuebu (1907), pp. 35, 548–54; Xuebu (1910), *gesheng* 8–9.

31. The pattern in Guizhou is also similar, although presumably for different reasons.

32. Xuebu (1910), *gesheng*: 10–13, 15–16.

33. For example, see *Haining zhouzhi gao*, 6: *xuezheng* 4b; *Nanxun zhi*, 1922, 34: 31b; *Wu-Qing zhenzhi*, 23: 13a; *Cheng xianzhi*, 2: 14b; *Qu xianzhi*, 3: 34b.

34. *Dongfang zazhi*, 1.8: *shiye* 131.

35. For example, *Minhu ribao*, July 29, 1909, p. 529.

36. See Chapter 2; the best sources are *Dongfang zazhi* and Nong-gongshang bu.

37. *Zhejiang chao*, 3: 195–96, lists the following papers sold in Hangzhou in 1903: *Zhong wai ribao* (500 copies), *Su bao* (50 copies), *Xinwen bao* (230–40 copies), *Shen bao* (500–550 copies), *Hangzhou baihua bao* (700–800 copies), *Xinmin congbao* (200 copies), *Yishu huibian* (250 copies). For the new Zhejiang journals, see *Dongfang zazhi*, 5.1: *jiaoyu* 44; *Minhu ribao*, Aug. 9, 1909, p. 606; *Dongfang zazhi*, 5.6: *jiaoyu* 149; *Shi bao*, June 30, 1910, p. 3. The *Shaoxing baihua bao* became the *Shaoxing gongbao*.

38. *Dongfang zazhi*, 4.7: *jiaoyu* 180; 5.6: *jiaoyu* 149.

39. Ibid., 5.3: *jiaoyu* 94. Atypically, this journal was established by an official determined to promote education in a peripheral district.

40. *Dongfang zazhi*, 5.4: *neiwu* 264, 265; *Minhu ribao*, Aug. 11, 1909, p. 620; *Shi bao*, July 15, 1910, p. 3. Some anti-opium associations appear to have been essentially voluntary organizations (although the edict prohibiting opium in 1906 provided the legal basis), whereas others were officially established elite-run bureaus. For an example of the latter, see *Minhu ribao*, Aug. 9, 1909, p. 606.

41. *Dongfang zazhi*, 5.4: *neiwu* 264; Li Guoqi, *Zhongguo*, pp. 583–

84, gives a list based on gazetteers of Hangzhou prefecture and Deqing, Pingyang, and Qingtian districts.

42. Cole, "Shaohsing," pp. 175–85, gives examples of lectures against geomancy, litigiousness, vendettas, lewd plays, and footbinding, and for hard work, thrift, and frugality.

43. Wang Ermin, 24.2: 20; 24.3: 16, 19. On the Commercial Educational Association, see *Dongfang zazhi*, 6.6: *jishi* 164–65; *Minhu ribao*, May 24, 1909, p. 73; Zhejiang sheng xinhai geming, pp. 7–13. On the Improvement Association, see *Dongfang zazhi*, 3.12: *neiwu* 278. The principles of this association included both patriotism and reverence for Confucius. On the Shaoxing organization, see *Minli bao*, Nov. 15, 1910, p. 4.

44. *Shi bao*, Sept. 28, 1910, p. 5.

45. This is a major thesis in Schoppa, *Chinese Elites*, where it is approached through organization theory, but the process is not traced back before the last few years of the Qing.

46. *Dongfang zazhi*, 4.9: *jiaoyu* 221.

47. Rawski, p. 161.

48. On local divisions introduced by the New Policies, see Prazniak, pp. 224–37, 245; MacKinnon, chap. 5.

49. These are collected in *Xinhai geming*, 3: 438–64. Riots in Tongxiang, Ciqi, Shouyang, and Deqing are summarized in Prazniak, pp. 165–72.

50. *Dongfang zazhi*, 7.6: *Zhongguo dashi ji* 48–49.

51. *Shi bao*, June 24, 1910, p. 3.

52. Prazniak, "Community and Protest," is the major study of reactive violence during the New Policies. Esherick also points to reactive violence and spontaneous risings among the urban poor of Changsha (pp. 117–42) and to spontaneous rural unrest that pitted gentry-controlled militias against peasant-supported secret societies (pp. 63–64). Rhoads similarly points to peasant hostility to the New Policies (pp. 76–77, 175–79), which he sees as a class reaction against reforms that were beneficial to the gentry. The growth of reactive violence during the New Policies period has been widely documented. In my view, this violence did not express lower-class ambitions to reach out for more power but demonstrated the desire of threatened groups to protect themselves from painful change.

53. Schoppa, *Chinese Elites*, pp. 72, 109, 126–27, 140–41.

54. *Longyou xianzhi*, 10: 9b; 19: 21b.

55. *Dongfang zazhi*, 1.10: *shiye* 180; Nonggongshang bu (1909), 2.4: 7b, *Minhu ribao*, June 11, 1909, p. 197; June 28, 1909, p. 312.

56. *Minhu ribao*, June 28, 1909, p. 312.

57. Ibid., July 29, 1909, p. 529.

58. Gazetteers almost never give the full membership of functional associations, but some list presidents and vice presidents. Names can be garnered from such sources as *Dongfang zazhi* and other con-

temporary periodicals, Nonggongshang bu, newspapers, and memoirs. Aside from the miscellaneous character of the information, the varying use of *ming* and *zi* for given names creates difficulties of identification.

59. For example, Zhan Xi and Zheng Yongqi of Qu were *juren* (*Qu xianzhi*, 3: 26b, 28b, 29b, 30b; 6: 32b; 13: 16b–17a); Pan Zhenlin of Changhua was a *sui gongsheng* (*Changhua xianzhi*, 9: 14a, 22a); Ding Zhongli of Dinghai was a *juren*, (*Dinghai xianzhi*, 8: 6b, 7b; 9: 1b); Zhang Fubao of Yin was a *juren* (Tahara, p. 453).

60. *Xiangshan xianzhi*, 13: 35a; *Suian xianzhi*, 5: 19a.

61. Wang Yuesong (*jinshi*) in Yongjia and Sun Yirang (*juren*) in Juian (Nonggongshang bu [1909], 2.4: 30, 42); Ding Zhongli (*juren*) in Dinghai (Ibid. [1908], 2.4: 41b); Gao Zhensheng (*jinshi*) in Qu (*Qu xianzhi*, 3: 30b; 24: 23b); Cai Song (*juren*) in Shuanglin town (*Shuanglin zhenzhi*, 8: 4a). Cai organized the chamber of commerce but declined the first presidency because he was then an educational official in Xiaoshan. Later he became president.

62. Keith Schoppa, "Self-Government," pp. 506–8, 512.

63. *Wu-Qing zhenzhi*, 9: 18a, 21b, 27b, 29a; 24: 12b. The Shen family presence in Qing public affairs continued into the 1930's.

64. *Zhenhai xinzhi beigao, xia:* renwu 3a.

65. *Xinchang xianzhi*, 1: 61b–63a, 68a–b; 2: 26a; 5: 30b, 62a; 9: 54a.

66. *Qu xianzhi*, 3: 26b, 29b, 30b; 13: 16b, 38a–b, 40b; Lü, p. 115. See similar data on the Pans and the Lius in *Jingning xianzhi*, 1933, 2: 24b; 4: 9a–b; 8: 6b, 20a–24b; 11: 6b, 19b, 20a.

67. For example, Wang Zhangxiao, in *Qu xianzhi*, 3: 26b; 23: 60a; Wu Qing of Xiashi town, in *Haining zhouzhi gao*, 4: *xuexiao xia* 8a, 14a; *Xinhai geming huiyi lu*, 4: 171–73.

68. *Haining zhouzhi gao*, 4: *xuexiao xia* 11a, 19a, 27b, 28a.

69. *Jiande xianzhi*, 10: 27b; 11: 2a, 12b, 72a; *Songyang xianzhi*, 9: 72b. See also *Xuanping xianzhi*, 6: 4a, 9a.

70. Schoppa, *Chinese Elites*, p. 114, makes this observation. It is consistent with the frequency with which *gongsheng* were managers in peripheral districts during the nineteenth century.

71. For examples of men active at two urban levels, see Wang Yugun in *Xiangshan xianzhi*, 14: 37a, 40a; 26: 15b; Gao Baoquan in *Xincheng zhenzhi*, 5: 5a, 13b; 11: 5a, and Nonggongshang bu [1909], 2.4: 41b; Cai Chengrui in *Jiande xianzhi*, 11: 1b, 2a; *Longyou xianzhi*, 10: 10a; 27: 33b. On Xia, see *Puyuan zhi*, 8: 4b, 6a, 8a–b.

72. *Qu xianzhi*, 23: 60b, 63b; 33: 39a.

73. *Wu-Qing zhenzhi*, 9: 21b; 27: 31b; *Haining zhouzhi gao*, 4: *xuexiao xia* 1a–15b; 41: 6a–b.

74. Meetings of the provincial assembly are reported in *Shi bao*, for example, Nov. 11, 1910, p. 5; Nov. 13, 1910, p. 5; Dec. 13, 1910, p. 5, and Oct.–Dec. 1910, *passim*. An account of the inaugural meeting, a

summary of topics discussed during the first session, and reports on committee membership and attendance appear in Zhejiang sheng xinhai geming, pp. 164–89. See also Geng, pp. 59–66.

75. The 37 upper-degree holders consisted of 4 *jinshi*, 18 *juren*, and 15 *gongsheng*. Major general works on provincial assemblies and the constitutional movement are Zhang Yufa, *Lixian*; Zhang Pengyuan, *Lixian*; Fincher, *Democracy*. The list of provincial assembly members used appears in *Dongfang zazhi*, 6.10: supplement 14–16. A more comprehensive list, including substitutes for men who resigned, appears in Zhejiang sheng xinhai geming, pp. 190–97. Biographical data was compiled from gazetteers and various biographical lists and dictionaries—the most useful of which was Tahara, *Shimmatsu*. Schoppa, *Chinese Elites*, p. 160, arrived at similar figures on degree-holding and occupational backgrounds of members. The larger number of officials in his table includes post-1911 careers, and he does not have data on local management. These data compare with Esherick, pp. 99–102, and Rhoads, pp. 158–61.

76. Of those who held official posts, five had been metropolitan or provincial officials. Three had been local educational officials in Zhejiang, and two had held new-style positions in Hangzhou.

77. Schoppa, *Chinese Elites*, p. 172, reaches a similar conclusion about members of republican assemblies.

78. *Jiang-Zhe tielu fengchao*, 40, 114; Zhang Pengyuan, p. 273; Zhang Yufa, p. 483, *Shi bao*, Dec. 11, 1911, p 2; Nagai, p. 5; Tahara, p. 696.

79. *Puyuan zhi*, 8: 7a.

80. Ibid., 8: 5a.

81. *Haining zhouzhi gao*, supplement: 5b 6a

82. Tong, 1: 29a–b, *passim*; *Pingyang xianzhi*, 39: 14b–15a.

83. Chen Qiu published a textbook in 1903 using a script he devised for the Wenzhou dialect; he planned to use the book at the School for New Writing in the Wenzhou Dialect (*xinzi Ouwen xuetang*). Chen Qiu, *Xinzi*. Information on schools and societies in Ruian is from *Zhejiang chao* 4: 177–83. For other information in this section, see Chen Mi, "Dong-Ou," pp. 12–18; *Oufeng zazhi huikan* 1.5: *wenyuan neibian* 5a, 6a; 2.5: *wenyuan neibian* 6b–7a; Tong, chaps. 1, 3; Liu Shaokuan, *Houzhuang*; *Pingyang xianzhi*, chap. 11; *Dongfang zazhi*, sections on education and industry, vols. 1–4; Sun Yirang, *Zhouqing*, 2: 5a, 11a–19a, 40a–43b; *Nonggongshang bu*, (1909), 2.4: *passim*; (1910), 2.4: *passim*.

84. *Oufeng zazhi huikan*, 2.5: *wenyuan neibian* 6b–7a.

85. Huang, 4: 44a; Liu Shaokuan, *Houzhuang*, 2: 3a.

86. For example, Sun was behind the establishment of the Office to Promote Education in Jingning, and an acquaintance was the first president of the Songyang office. *Jingning xianzhi* (1933), 4: 9a; *Songyang xianzhi*, 9: 72b.

87. For example, Liu Shaokuan had marriage ties with a member of the executive council of one of the main Pingyang market towns. Liu Shaokuan, *Houzhuang*, 3: 18a–b.

88. Liu Shaokuan, "Zhouyuan"; Rankin, *Revolutionaries*, pp. 159–61. Huang Shaoji was one of the officials Sun contacted—another example of old scholarly ties.

89. *Shi bao*, Oct. 9, 1911, p. 2. They had similar *ming*.

90. *Dongfang zazhi*, 2.2: *shiye* 23; 3.3: *shiye* 86; 3.5: *jiaotong* 134; 3.10: *shiye* 202.

91. *Shi bao*, Mar. 8, 1910, p. 3; *Pingyang xianzhi*, 39: 15.

92. *Shi bao*, Mar. 1, 1910, p. 3; *Xinhai geming huiyi lu*, 4: 183.

93. Sun Yirang, *Zhouqing*, 2: 11a–b, 17a.

94. Xuebu (1907), pp. 563–64, 571–72.

95. Sun Yirang, *Zhouqing*, 2: 12a–b, 41b.

96. Tong, 3: 89a–90a.

97. Sun Yirang, *Zhouqing*, 2: 40a.

98. Tong, 3: 89b.

99. Sun Yirang, *Zhouqing*, 1: 12b, 26b; 2: 42a–b.

100. Chow, pp. 83–84. In 1920 middle school students established a Yongjia New Study Society, which sought a basis for educational and social reform by reinterpreting the ideas of the Southern Song Yongjia School in light of John Dewey's pragmatism.

101. Zhu, pp. 90, 98; Wang Yinian, p. 150; Nonggongshang bu (1909), 2.4: 42b.

102. Sun Yirang, *Zhouqing*, 2: 5a; *Jiang-Zhe tielu fengchao*, p. 353; Fujii, p. 29.

103. *Dongfang zazhi*, 6.10: supplement on assembly members.

104. *Xinhai geming huiyi lu*, 4: 183–86; Rankin, *Revolutionaries*, pp. 220–21; *Shi bao*, Dec. 1, 1911, p. 3; Nov. 24, 1912, p. 4. Liu Shaokuan was one of the people who were planning revolution. Yu Zhaoshen was among Chen Fuchen's supporters.

105. Huang, 4: 44a. *Oufeng zazhi*, 1: frontice. Members of the Wenzhou Society (*oufeng she*) of the 1930's included Liu Shaokuan, Wang Lifu, Shi Zhicheng, and descendants of Sun Yirang and Chen Fuchen. At least one of these men was an executive of the Ruian district government.

106. Ichiko, "Political and Institutional Reform," p. 414; Ichiko, "Gentry," p. 308. A similar picture of initial gentry resistance to the educational reform sponsored by Zhang Zhidong in Hubei appears in Bays, pp. 114–15.

107. Bastid, "Context," pp. 125–26.

108. Kuhn, "Self-Government," pp. 276–78.

109. Schoppa, *Chinese Elites*, pp. 6–9.

110. Chauncey, "Education."

111. MacKinnon, pp. 10–11, conclusion.

112. Esherick, pp. 58–65, 95–105, 215, 250–51.

113. Fincher, pp. 20, 23–28, 88, 124–26, 155, 160, 184–85, 192, 219.

Chapter Seven

1. Hao Chang, p. 202.

2. This view of the weakness of the Chinese bourgeoisie in the early twentieth century appears in Bergère, "Role." For the role of the bourgeoisie during the Republic, see Bergère, "Chinese Bourgeoisie." The second article explores the relationships of the emerging bourgeoisie to the old-style elite, as does Bastid Bruguière, "Context," pp. 555–71, 601–2.

3. The strongest statement of the first view is in Ichiko, "Gentry." The second is summarized in Chang P'eng-yuan, "Provincial Assemblies," p. 20. For a third perspective, see Eshcrick, pp. 102–5.

4. Zhang Kaiyan, "1911 Revolution." Many Chinese Marxist studies have focused on the progressive role of the bourgeoisie at the end of the Qing. The important aspects of this work are summarized in Du and Zhou, "Summary," and Zhang Kaiyan, "Xinhai geming."

5. It has been suggested by Fujii Masao (p. 29) that fewer wealthy merchants were involved in the Jiangsu railway. However, its directors included such wealthy Shanghai merchants as Gu Xingyi and Wang Zhen as well as the president of the Shanghai City Council, Li Zhongjue (Pingshu). The company also included *jinshi* and Hanlin scholars. Directors were also members of New Policies institutions and of such political groups as the "Emperor's Faction," the Society to Prepare for Constitutional Government, and the constitutionalist parties of the Xuantong reign (1909–12). The Jiangsu provincial assembly president Zhang Jian and both vice presidents were railway activists. Sources are similar to those for Tables 20 and 21, noted on pp. 381–84.

6. Yu Xiaqing, Yao Mulian, Xie Lunhui. Negishi, pp. 59–60.

7. The small number of members who were elected to the provincial assembly may reinforce the idea that local activism was more important than external careers in the choice of assembly members.

8. Nonggongshang bu (1909), 2.5: 8b, 18a.

9. There were, for instance, no members of the wealthy Fang merchant family on the railway board, but there were members of the publicly active Li and Ye families from the same district.

10. Rankin, "Public Opinion," p. 472; see also Table 20.

11. See Polachek, *Opium War*, chap. 2.

12. *Dongfang zazhi*, 5.8: tiaocha 33–35; Rankin, "Public Opinion," p. 472.

13. Great Britain, Foreign Office, 228/1631/1986 ("Hangzhou Intelligence Report," December Quarter, 1905).

14. See references for Tang Shouqian in sources for Table 20, listed on pp. 381–83. Also see Chen Mi, *Chen*, 25a–b; Guo, 2: 907; *Hangzhou fuzhi*, 17: 8b; *Nanxun zhi*, 1922, 3: 2a; *Shanghai xianzhi*, 11: 6a.

Tang was unpopular with the revolutionaries because he advised the governor to execute the revolutionary heroine Qiu Jin in 1907, but contemporary materials leave little doubt about his popularity among students as well as gentry and merchants.

15. Guo, 2: 907.

16. I am indebted to the large amount of previous research on the 1907 loan controversy. Min, pp. 364–414, and I have independently reached many similar conclusions, but I did not see an English translation in time to use the article for this book. Another detailed treatment is En-han Lee, "Gentry-Merchants." Other important articles in English are E-tu Zen Sun, "Railway," and Chi, "Railway." The best source for social aspects is Fujii Masao, and Nagai Kazumi is another useful Japanese source. Zhao Jinyu, "Su-Hang-Yong," is the main Chinese article, but Qi Longwei, "Lun Qingmo," considers the movements in Zhejiang and other provinces. Brief accounts of the railway appear in broader works like Xie Bin, *Tiedao*, and Zhang Xincheng, *Jiaotong. Jiang-Zhe tielu fengchao* is an outstanding documentary source for the 1907 agitation. For official documents, see Chen Yi and *Haifang dang*. The British side is preserved in the Foreign Office archives.

17. E-tu Zen Sun, "Railway," p. 138.

18. Great Britain, Foreign Office, 228/1561/2094, 228/1552 (King to Satow, Jan. 16, 1904).

19. This man was the very wealthy Gao Eryi. *Dongfang zazhi*, 2.9: *shiye* 166; Great Britain, Foreign Office, 37/28/6699; *Guomin ri ribao*, Oct. 13, 1903, pp. 407–8; Oct. 16, 1903, p. 414; *Zhejiang chao*, 8: 117–18, 125–29, 141, *Su bao*, p. 204.

20. Wang Yinian, p. 144; *Zhejiang chao*, 2: 113–14.

21. Li En-han, "Zhong-Mei"; Great Britain, Foreign Office, 371/26/305 (enclosure in Satow to Lansdowne, Nov. 25, 1905).

22. Fujii, p. 23; Zhang Cunwu, *passim*, in conjunction with names in *Jiang-Zhe tielu fengchao*; see Tables 20–21. Most participation was in Shanghai, although there was some briefer response in Zhejiang cities. IMC, *Trade Reports*, 1905, pp. 310, 312, 332.

23. Great Britain, Foreign Office, 371/28/6699 (1906); *Dongfang zazhi*, 2.9: *shiye* 166.

24. United States Department of State, General Records (Record Group 59), Diplomatic Correspondence, Decimal File, Consular Letters, Hangzhou, vol. 1, Cloud, June 15, 1905; Consular Letters, Shanghai, vol. 52, Aug. 15, 1905; *Dongfang zazhi*, 2.11: *jiaotong* 105–17.

25. *Dongfang zazhi*, 3.1: *jiaotong* 25–27; Wang Yinian, p. 146; *Jiang-Zhe tielu fengchao*, pp. 8–11.

26. Wang Yinian, p. 146; *Dongfang zazhi*, 2.11: *jiaotong* 151; *North China Herald*, July 28, 1905, p. 213. The railway's regulations are in *Dongfang zazhi*, 3.3: *jiaotong* 76–85.

27. *Dongfang zazhi*, 3.11: *jiaotong* 225.

28. Fujii, p. 23; *Shi bao,* Mar. 26, 1911, p. 6.

29. *North China Herald,* Nov. 24, 1905, p. 417; July 28, 1905, p. 213; Great Britain, Foreign Office, 228/2521, 371/1213 (Smith to Satow, Nov. 15, 1905). The meeting of gentry and teachers in Hangzhou also protested the leasing of mining rights to foreigners.

30. *Dongfang zazhi,* 3.11: *jiaotong* 225.

31. *Jiang-Zhe tielu fengchao,* pp. 9–11; *Dongfang zazhi,* 2.11: *jiaotong* 151.

32. *Dongfang zazhi,* 3.9: *jiaotong* 175.

33. Ibid., 3.11: *jiaotong* 225–26; 4.3: *jiaotong* 67.

34. See Bays, chap. 8.

35. Zhang Yufa, *Lixian,* p. 367; Zhejiang sheng xinhai geming, pp. 210–22.

36. Zhejiang sheng xinhai geming, pp. 203–4.

37. En-han Lee, p. 238. These relationships may have stemmed from Zhang's old associations with militant reformist bureaucratic factions as well as his more recent nationalistic stands.

38. Great Britain, Foreign Office, 371/213 (Jordan to Grey, Oct. 4, 1906; Carnegie telegram, Sept. 10, 1906).

39. En-han Lee, p. 236.

40. Ibid., p. 243; *Dongfang zazhi,* 2.3: *zazu* 19.

41. *Jiang-Zhe tielu fengchao,* pp. 36–38.

42. Ibid., p. 35; *Dongfang zazhi,* 4.10: *zazu* 24.

43. Nagai Kazumi, p. 25, stresses broad participation. Fujii Masao, p. 30, calls the railway a bourgeois movement, and Zhao Jinyu, pp. 51, 55, 60, stresses the role of students as well as capitalists in a patriotic movement. On women, see Rankin, "Elite Reformism."

44. A count by prefecture of telegrams from local organizations and social groupings in *Jiang-Zhe tielu fengchao:* Hangzhou 24, Ningbo 13, Jiaxing 11, Shaoxing 10, Wenzhou 6, Huzhou 6, only one or two from the other five prefectures.

45. *Jiang-Zhe tielu fengchao,* pp. 88, 93, 336, 338, 401; *Yuyao Liucang zhi,* supplement: 1a. Merchants from Nanxun (Liu Jinzao's home town) telegraphed support. Director Xie Lunhui attracted support from his powerful lineage in a town in Yuyao. A man who founded schools in Xiashi, Haining (and would head the merchant corps there in 1911) was a chief examiner of the railway. *Xinhai geming huiyi lu,* 4: 170–72; *Haining zhouzhi gao,* 4.1: *xuexiao xia* 8a, 14a–b.

46. *North China Herald,* Apr. 3, 1908, p. 13.

47. Zhao Jinyu, p. 54; *Jiang-Zhe tielu fengchao,* pp. 349, 371.

48. *Jiang-Zhe tielu fengchao,* pp. 200–202.

49. The works of Zhang Pengyuan and Zhang Yufa established constitutionalism as a serious subject of research. Zhang Kaiyuan, "Xinhai geming," p. 2132, calls attention to increasing research on the constitutionalists by historians in the Peoples' Republic of China since 1978. Geng Yunzhi, "The Bourgeois Constitutionalists," is a

good example. I differ from them in seeing constitutionalism as one manifestation of the political demands for participation that arose from a broader social mobilization and in seeing this mobilization as central to the 1911 Revolution. I also define the participants as a cohort of politicized activists drawn from old and new elites rather than trying to classify them as bourgeois, gentry, or some other segment of the upper class.

50. Of 277 telegrams collected in *Jiang-Zhe tielu fengchao*, 155 (52 percent) were sent to ministries, high officials, or the censorate in Beijing, 27 went to governors-general or governors, and 109 (39 percent) to railway companies, native place associations, or New Policies functional associations.

51. *Jiang-Zhe tielu fengchao*, pp. 89–90, 349, 353, 359; *Dongfang zazhi*, 4.11: *zazu* 27; Great Britain, Foreign Office, 317/79/08 (excerpts from the Hanzhou press in "Hankow Consul-General's Report, Dec. 14, 1907).

52. *Jiang-Zhe tielu fengchao*, pp. 73, 113–14, 122, 135; Zhejiang sheng xinhai geming, pp. 228–30.

53. *Jiang-Zhe tielu fengchao*, pp. 39–42, 124–25, 127, 358, 362, 373.

54. Ibid., pp. 133–34, 331, 368–69, 388–92, 414–15.

55. Ibid., pp. 92–93, 313–15, 349.

56. Ibid., p. 135. On superintendent Tao Huifu, see *Shi bao*, Apr. 25, 1910, p. 3; Apr. 28, 1910, p. 3; *Minxu ribao*, Oct. 28, 1909, p. 199.

57. *Jiang-Zhe tielu fengchao*, pp. 135–36. On Gao, see ibid., p. 39; *Nonggongshang bu* (1909), 2.4: 41b; (1910), 2.4: 3a; *Shi bao*, Nov. 1, 1910, p. 3; *Xincheng zhenzhi*, 5: 5a; 11: 5a, 8a; 13: 10a; 21: 13b. The men elected were Ao Jiaxiong (see Chap. 5), Zhu Jianxi (see Chap. 5 and *Shi bao*, July 12, 1910, p. 3), and Chu Fucheng. Chu taught at the middle school and headed another school. He became president of the chamber of commerce in 1910, president of the opium suppression bureau, and a member of the prefectural agricultural association. He was also a member of the provincial educational association in Hangzhou and a vice president of the provincial assembly. He had joined the *Tongmeng hui* while studying in Japan and kept in sporadic touch with the revolutionaries. In 1911 he was a key link between the provincial assembly and the revolutionaries, and he headed the new provincial civil government. He was imprisoned for two years after the Second Revolution as a supporter of Sun Yat-sen. During the 1930's he was a director of several firms in Shanghai. He went to Zhongjing during the Japanese war and subsequently remained in China. Fan Yinnan, p. 406; *Zhuanji wenxue*, 4.6: 31 (Dec. 1964); 16.6: 37–38 (June 1970); *Zhejiang yuekan*, 1.7: 10–11; 2.3: 11; *Zhejiang Xinhai geming huiyi lu*, pp. 133–49.

58. *Jiang-Zhe tielu fengchao*, pp. 373, 423.

59. Ibid., p. 406; *North China Herald*, Nov. 22, 1907, p. 484.

60. *Jiang-Zhe tielu fengchao*, pp. 86, 93, 351, 355, 377, 406.

61. Ibid., pp. 83, 85, 307–8, 349, 362, 384, 398.
62. Ibid., pp. 362–64, 374–75.
63. Ibid., pp. 126, 384–85; *North China Herald,* Nov. 15, 1907, p. 407; *Zhonghua minguo kaiguo,* 1.14: 668–69.
64. *Dongfang zazhi,* 4.11: *zazu* 27.
65. Ibid., 4.10: *zazu* 24; 4.11: *zazu* 27.
66. The Hangzhou association was still active in April 1908 (ibid., 5.4: *zazu* 11). Thereafter I have no record until 1909.
67. *Jiang-Zhe tielu fengchao,* pp. 144, 398.
68. Ibid., pp. 142–43, 151–52.
69. *Pingyang xianzhi,* 11: 22b. Wang Lifu, who managed education in Pingyang, knew Sun Yirang (*Jiang-Zhe tielu fengchao,* p. 353), thus connecting district educational circles to the railway leadership.
70. Ibid., p. 425.
71. Ibid., pp. 322–24.
72. Ibid., p. 385; *North China Herald,* Nov. 15, 1907, p. 407; *Zhejiang sheng xinhai geming,* pp. 287–88.
73. Information in the above three paragraphs compiled from *Jiang-Zhe tielu fengchao,* pp. 200–202, 399, 407, 420; *Shi bao,* Mar. 12, 1910, p. 6; *North China Herald,* Oct. 7, 1910, p. 803; *Minhu ribao,* June 8, 1909, p. 176; June 9, 1909, p. 183; July 10, 1909, p. 396; *Zhonghua minguo kaiguo,* 1.14: 670; *Yuyao Liucang zhi,* supplement: 1a–b.
74. *Shi bao,* Mar. 2, 1910, p. 6, divides money collected by bureaus in Jiaxing into new subscriptions and payments on past subscriptions.
75. Great Britain, Foreign Office, 228/2522 (Smith to Jordan, Dec. 18, 1906); *Jiang-Zhe tielu fengchao,* p. 70.
76. Qi Longwei, "Lun Qingmo," pp. 42–43; Xie Bin, p. 238. The 1911 paid-in capital of 9,250,000 *yuan* compares with ca. 4,500,000, Jiangsu railway; 16,450,000, Sichuan; 15,130,000, Guangtong; 1,400,000, Hunan; and 200,000, Anhui. More miles of track were constructed by the Zhejiang company than by any other provincial railway company before the revolution.
77. *Shi bao,* Mar. 26, 1911, p. 6.
78. The rhetoric of the railway movement deserves a separate study. Emotional nationalism was expressed by phrases like "existence and demise" (*cunwang; Jiang-Zhe tielu fengchao,* pp. 80, 332) and "loss of country" (*wangguo;* ibid., p. 421). The life-and-death analogy was reinforced by the constant use of the metaphoric "lifelines" (*mingmai;* ibid., pp. 74, 108) for the railway. To cut off or snatch away so organic a part of the nation would be a step toward the occupation of the country and the exploitation of all Chinese by foreigners, which would eventually lead to national and racial death (ibid., pp. 110–11, 203). The people were repeatedly called "citizens" (*guomin*), with connotations of active and responsible involvement in national affairs. Old phrases like "the multitude's resolve will act as a wall" (*zhongzhi*

cheng cheng; ibid., p. 85) were also used to imply that societal mobilization was the best defense against imperialism. In contrast, officials—particularly Wang Daxue and Sheng Xuanhuai—were accused of "toadying to foreigners" (*meiwai;* ibid., p. 336), "misleading the country" (*wuguo;* ibid., p. 85), selling the country or the railway (*maiguo, mailu;* ibid., pp. 90, 336), thievery, etc. One of the more colorful phrases was "*yin hu zuo chang*" (ibid., p. 451), likening Wang or other officials to ghosts of men devoured by tigers (i.e., the foreigners) who then urge the beasts to eat others. The level of both metaphoric exaggeration and invective in the press was high, and extremist rhetoric was certainly not limited to the more radical papers. On the patriotic rhetoric of the Sino-French and Sino-Japanese wars, see Rankin, "Public Opinion," pp. 472–76. Some of the older phrases had been appropriated by social Darwinism in the 1890's and then further popularized by Liang Qichao and other journalists. By the 1900's, the concepts of sovereignty (*zhuquan; Jiang-Zhe tielu fengchao,* p. 91) and economic (railway) rights (ibid., 80) were part of the vocabulary of the activist public, but older phrases like "national essence" (*guoti*) and the sentimental "homeland" (*sangzi;* ibid., p. 79) were also used.

79. Ibid., pp. 80, 155–57, 160; *Minhu ribao,* July 11, 1909, p. 404.

80. *Dongfang zazhi,* 4.10: *jiaotong* 206; 2.5: *shiye* 50.

81. For example, see *Jiang-Zhe tielu fengchao,* p. 80. This letter from Huzhou stockholders speaks of having collected funds to "self-manage." The frequent references to having received an edict to "self-manage" have connotations of autonomy, although it is almost impossible to separate these connotations from nationalistic ones because the term allowed a double meaning. See, for example, ibid., p. 74.

82. Ibid., pp. 155, 159, 169, 195, 450.

83. Chan, "Government," pp. 426–27.

84. *Jiang-Zhe tielu fengchao,* pp. 196, 380.

85. Ibid., p. 474.

86. *Shi bao,* Apr. 26, 1910, p. 1; *North China Herald,* Apr. 22, 1910, p. 205.

87. The terms include *qingyi,* "sentiments of the people or multitudes" (*minqing, zhongqing*), and *gonglun* or *yulun.*

88. *Jiang-Zhe tielu fengchao,* pp. 155–56.

89. Ibid., p. 478.

90. Ibid., pp. 176, 476; *Dongfang zazhi,* 4.11: *sheshuo* 209.

91. *Jiang-Zhe tielu fengchao,* pp. 181, 183, 302.

92. Ibid., pp. 158, 171.   93. Ibid., p. 476.

94. Ibid., p. 471.   95. Ibid., pp. 177, 183, 446, 469.

96. Ibid., pp. 158–59. References to constitutionalism are also found in telegrams and letters from chambers of commerce, gentry, merchants, students, etc., ibid., pp. 87, 326, 347. Emigré constitutionalists in Japan also used the railway agitation to argue for a national assembly. Ibid., p. 340.

97. Ibid., pp. 74, 77.
99. Ibid., p. 88.
101. Ibid., pp. 336, 348.
102. Ibid., p. 292. The author was Yang Tingdong of Jiangsu, who became a constitutionalist leader. His reference was to Xunzi's dictum that the people are like water, which can support or overturn a boat.
103. Ibid., pp. 188, 215, 446.
104. Ibid., p. 164.
105. Ibid., p. 99. This reference to Xu Xilin is in "A Warning to Wang Daxie," author unknown.
106. *North China Herald*, Nov. 15, 1907, p. 408; *Jiang-Zhe tielu fengchao*, pp. 55–56, 239.
107. Zhao Jinyu, p. 58.
108. *Haifang dang*, 5.2: 549.
109. *Zhonghua minguo kaiguo*, 1.14: 671–73; 2.4: 134.
110. *Jiang-Zhe tielu fengchao*, pp. 78, 98–99, 136–37.
111. Great Britain, Foreign Office, 371/79/08; *North China Herald*, Jan. 17, 1908, p. 139.
112. *Jiang-Zhe tielu fengchao*, pp. 79, 126, 273.
113. Ibid., p. 466.
114. *Dongfang zazhi*, 11.4: zazu 27–28, 4.12: zazu 29, 5.1: jiao-tong 37; Great Britain, Foreign Office, 371/79/08 (Jordan to Grey, Feb. 3, 1908), *North China Herald*, Jan. 3, 1908, pp. 21–22; Jan. 10, 1908, pp. 71, 73; Jan. 31, 1908, p. 247.
115. Chinese text: *Haifang dang*, 5.2: 582–92; English text: *North China Herald*, Mar. 20, 1908, p. 686.
116. *North China Herald*, Jan. 24, 1908, p. 219; *Jiang-Zhe tielu fengchao*, p. 495.
117. *Guangxu zhao Donghua lu*, pp. 5805–6.
118. *Dongfang zazhi*, 5.4: zazu 11.
119. *Da Qing Dezong shilu*, 575: 5628.
120. *Dongfang zazhi*, 4.1: shangwu 29–30, 4.9: shangwu 100, 4.11: shangwu 173.
121. *Hangzhou fuzhi*, 174: 18a–b; *Minxu ribao*, Oct. 21, 1909, p. 141; Oct. 28, 1909, p. 199. Another Jiaxing issue with nationalistic, economic, and public aspects was the attempt of a cocoon firm to avoid an educational tax on the grounds of Japanese ownership. *Shi bao*, June 27, 1910, p. 3.
122. Ibid., Apr. 2, 1910, p. 3; Apr. 6, 1910, p. 3; June 15, 1910, p. 3; June 18, 1910, p. 5; June 25, 1910, p. 3; July 8, 1910, p. 3. *Hangzhou fuzhi*, 174: 24a–27a; *Dongfang zazhi*, 6: Zhongguo dashi ji, 44–48.
123. *Shi bao*, Aug. 22, 1910, p. 3; Jan. 25, 1910, p. 3.
124. *Shi bao*, Aug. 14, 1910, p. 1; Sept. 14, 1910, p. 1; Sept. 25, 1910, p. 1; Dec. 16, 1910, p. 1; Dec. 26, 1910, p. 1; Dec. 31, 1910, p. 1. Railway vice president Liu Jinzao had also been involved in demon-

98. Ibid., pp. 83, 84, 335, 338.
100. Ibid., pp. 213, 298, 334.

strations against missionary land purchases in Huzhou in 1907. United States Department of State, Record Group 59, Central Files (1906–29), Numerical File, no. 7751, enclosures in report of Shanghai Consul-General Rodgers, June 17, 1907.

125. On Cai Rulin and Zhu Fushen, see Zhang Yufa, *Lixian*, pp. 384–85; Guo Tingyi, 2: 1310–11.

126. *Haifang dang*, 5.2: 631–722; Great Britain, Foreign Office, 371/1823/08, 371/1019/09, and 1908–9 files, *passim*.

127. *North China Herald*, Mar. 20, 1909, p. 706; June 5, 1909, p. 582; June 12, 1909, p. 609; July 17, 1909, p. 147; Great Britain, Foreign Office, 371/1019/09; *Shi bao*, May 2, 1910, p. 3; *Dongfang zazhi*, 6.4: *jishi* 32; *Haifang dang*, 5.2: 825. The complex arrangements for loan transfers could have been easily manipulated. The Hong Kong and Shanghai Banking Corporation made payments through the director of the Shanghai-Nanjing Railway to the Bank of Communications. The Bank of Communications sent funds to the Shanghai-Ningbo Railway—a financial entity created solely for the purposes of the loan—which divided them, sending one-third to the Jiangsu Railway and two-thirds to the Zhejiang Railway.

128. MacKinnon, p. 209.

129. *Minhu ribao*, May 19, 1909, p. 37.

130. *North China Herald*, May 29, 1909, p. 501; June 5, 1909, p. 536.

131. Ibid., Oct. 16, 1909, p. 120.

132. Ibid., Nov. 13, 1909, p. 365.

133. Zhang Yufa, *Lixian*, pp. 393–98.

134. *Dongfang zazhi*, 7.3: *zoudu* 36–48; *North China Herald*, Dec. 11, 1909, p. 605; Dec. 18, 1909, p. 642.

135. *Dongfang zazhi*, 6.13: *jishi* 648; 7.1: 3d *jizai* 7.

136. *North China Herald*, Jan. 21, 1910, p. 145.

137. *Shi bao*, Apr. 16, 1910, p. 3. The directors were Jiang Honglin and Wang Xirang. The others were He Langxian of Shanyin and Tao Zaikuan of Guiji, who was also a member of the Hangzhou Chamber of Commerce.

138. Ibid., Apr. 25, 1910, p. 1; Apr. 26, 1910, p. 1.

139. Zhang Yufa, *Lixian*, pp. 402–10.

140. *Dongfang zazhi*, 7.6: 3d *jizai* 144–48; *Shi bao*, June 12, 1910, p. 5; July 1, 1910, p. 5.

141. *Dongfang zazhi*, 7.8: *dashi ji* 108–11.

142. On this third request, see Zhang Yufa, *Lixian*, pp. 437–42.

143. Zhao Jinyu, p. 59, says Tang's dismissal signaled the decision to nationalize.

144. *Minhu ribao*, June 28, 1909, p. 312; July 1, 1909, p. 334; July 8, 1909, p. 382; July 11, 1909, p. 397.

145. Ibid., June 30, 1909, p. 325; *North China Herald*, Oct. 28,

1910, p. 279; July 7, 1910, p. 43; *Dongfang zazhi*, 7.9: 2d *jizai* 68–70, 7.11: *dashi ji* 94.

146. See, for example, the names in the accounts of the Hangzhou meeting July 8, 1909 (*Minhu ribao*, July 7, 1909, p. 402) and in the accounts of the July stockholders meeting (*Dongfang zazhi*, 6.7: *jishi* 192).

147. *Minhu ribao*, July 4, 1909, p. 355; July 5, 1909, pp. 361, 375; July 7, 1909, p. 376; July 10, 1909, p. 397; July 11, 1909, p. 423; July 15, 1909, p. 430; July 16, 1909, p. 436; *Dongfang zazhi*, 6.7: *jishi* 192, 6.9: *jishi* 277, 6.10: *jishi* 315–17, 6.13: *jishi* 468, 7.9: 1st *jizai* 67–70; *Shi bao*, Aug. 31, 1910, p. 2; Sept. 1, 1910, p. 3; Sept. 14, 1910, p. 3; Sept. 25, 1910, p. 3; Oct. 4, 1910, pp. 1, 3; Oct. 5, 1910, p. 3, Oct. 10, 1910, p. 3; Oct. 21, 1910, p. 5; Nov. 21, 1910, p. 5; Nov. 27, 1910, p. 5; Nov. 29, 1910, p. 5; Nov. 30, 1910, p. 5; *Minli bao*, Nov. 17, 1910, p. 4; Nov. 22, 1910, pp. 3, 4; Dec. 4, 1910, p. 4; Dec. 7, 1910, p. 4; *North China Herald*, Sept. 2, 1910, p. 555; Sept. 9, 1910, p. 612; Sept. 23, 1910, p. 722, Oct. 7, 1910, p. 27, Despite this dismally long list, available documentation for 1909 and 1910 is not nearly as full as it is for the month of 1907, as covered by *Jiang-Zhe tielu fengchao*, so quantitative comparisons are risky. Chu Fucheng was one of the representatives sent to Beijing.

148. *North China Herald*, Nov 13, 1909, p. 365.

149. *Shi bao*, Sept 11, 1910, p. 4; Sept. 12, 1910, p. 4; *North China Herald*, Sept. 16, 1910, p. 673.

150. *Shi bao*, Sept. 25, 1910, p. 3; *North China Herald*, Sept. 9, 1910, p. 612; Sept. 16, 1910, p. 762.

151. An account of Tang's struggles, *Zhe-lu fengchao Tang Shouqian* (Tang Shouqian of the Zhejiang Railway agitation), appeared in Shanghai in October 1910. *Minli bao*, Oct. 22, 1910, p. 5.

152. Chen Shixia, Chu Fucheng, Ding Lizhong, Cai Huanwen, Cai Rulin, Wang Xubin, Wang Lifu, Wang Zuo, Ye Gaoshu, Yu Zonglian.

153. *Dongfang zazhi*, 6.10: *jishi* 315–17.

154. *Shi bao*, Oct. 16, 1910, p. 5; Oct. 22, 1910, pp. 3, 5; Oct. 23, 1910, p. 5; Oct. 26, 1910, p. 3; Oct. 27, 1910, p. 3; Nov. 11, 1910, p. 4; *Minli bao*, Nov. 15, 1910, p. 4; Nov. 30, 1910, p. 3.

155. See the membership list in Zhang Yufa, *Lixian*, pp. 430–31; *Minli bao*, Oct. 22, 1910, p. 4. They were Wang Tingyang, Wang Zuo, Tao Baolin.

156. Edict dated Oct. 13, 1909; an English translation is enclosed in United States Department of State, RG 59, Numerical file, 1518/335, Fletcher to Knox, Nov. 16, 1909. It enjoins assemblies not to exhibit selfish interests or over-confidence that would upset the proper order of things. They should not engage in untrammeled discussion nor exceed the limits of their power. On political divisions in the National Consultative Assembly, see Zhang Yufa, *Lixian*, pp. 457–62. Geng Yunzhi, p. 89, makes the similar point that the struggles of as-

semblies with governors were basically struggles against the Qing court. The court backed the governors while public opinion supported the assemblies.

157. *Shi bao*, Apr. 16, 1910, p. 3; Zhang Yufa, *Lixian*, pp. 399–400.

158. Zhang Yufa, *Lixian*, pp. 482–83, 485. These men were Shao Xi, Chen Jingdi, Hu Zhonghan, Liu Shaoquan, and Cai Rulin. Chen Fuchen's associates were Ma Xulin and Tang Erhe.

159. For the view that Tang was essential to attract investment, see *Shi bao*, Sept. 12, 1910, p. 1.

160. Ibid., Mar. 28, 1911, p. 2; Mar. 29, 1911, p. 3; Apr. 15, 1911, p. 3. Lending between companies and organizations with interlocking management did occur; it probably reflected capital shortages and standard business practices as well as (sometimes) corruption. The Jiangsu Railway Company lent the Shanghai City Council eight thousand yuan when Li Zhongjue was a railway director and president of the council. Elvin, "Gentry," p. 152.

161. *Minhu ribao*, July 10, 1909, p. 394; *Dongfang zazhi*, 7.1: *dashi ji* 96. En-han Lee, pp. 267–68, suggests a shift from anti-imperialism to anti-Manchuism after 1908 as the result of centralization policies.

162. *Dongfang zazhi*, 7.9: 2d *jizai* 67; *Shi bao*, Aug. 26, 1910, p. 1.

163. *Shi bao*, Sept. 5, 1910, p. 3; *Dongfang zazhi*, 7.9: 2d *jizai* 67; *Minxu ribao*, Oct. 11, 1909, p. 67.

164. For example, *Shi bao*, Nov. 6, 1910, p. 5. The argument that railways were a special case was set forth in an edict of Sept. 24, 1910. See the stockholders' petition in *Dongfang zazhi*, 7.9: 2d *jizai* 69–70.

165. Ibid., 7.1: *dashi ji* 96, 7.9: 2d *jizai* 68; *Shi bao*, Aug. 26, 1910, p. 1; Sept. 11, 1910, p. 4; Oct. 9, 1910, p. 1.

166. *Shi bao*, Aug. 27, 1910, p. 1. The editorial of the previous day had opposed Tang's dismissal.

167. See especially the *Shi bao* editorials of June 11, 1910, July 1, 1910, July 7, 1910, July 14, 1910, Nov. 8, 1910, Nov. 16, 1910, Nov. 21, 1910, Dec. 22, 1910.

168. Ibid., June 12, 1911, p. 1.

169. Ibid., Oct. 16, 1911, p. 1.

170. Ibid., Dec. 28, 1910, p. 4; Mar. 28, 1911, p. 4; *Minli bao*, Oct. 21, 1910, p. 3.

171. Great Britain, Foreign Office, 371/991/10; *North China Herald*, Feb. 17, 1911, p. 372; *Shi bao*, Feb. 17, 1911, p. 4.

172. Great Britain, Foreign Office, 371/8638/11; *North China Herald*, Mar. 10, 1911, p. 579. Chinese documents on negotiations with Britain appear in *Haifang dang*, 5.2: 801–980. These show the ministry's intent to control the railway. For a statement of the situation in the spring of 1911, see ibid., 5.2: 947–49.

173. Ibid., 5.2: 953.

174. *North China Herald*, Feb. 12, 1910, p. 511; *Shi bao*, Apr. 15, 1911, p. 3; June 22, 1911, p. 4.

175. *Shi bao,* May 5, 1911, p. 5.

176. The history of the Zhejiang Railway after the 1911 Revolution was more checkered. It did not succeed in raising enough capital to extend the line to Ningbo, and financial difficulties were a major cause of the overwhelming support for nationalization among stockholders in 1914. The changed political situation was also a factor, for the company was no longer a symbol of resistance to autocracy. The original railway leaders had also been diverted to other projects, and bickering among company officers had increased. *Shi bao,* and *North China Herald,* are sources for the railway during the 1912–14 period. See also Schoppa, *Chinese Elites,* p. 64.

177. For examples of this organization, see *Shi bao,* July 2, 1911, p. 3; July 20, 1911, p. 3; *Minli bao,* July 21, 1911, p. 4; Aug. 14, 1911, p. 4; Aug. 29, 1911, p. 4.

178. For example, across the border in Jiangsu young members of banking circles in Wuxi turned against Manchus in 1911 in anger over "false constitutionalism" and railway nationalization. Yangzhou shifan xueyuan lishi xi, p. 164.

179. For the 1911 Revolution in Zhejiang, see Rankin, *Revolutionaries,* pp. 215–26, and Schoppa, *Chinese Elites,* chap. 10. Assembly president Chen Fuchen and vice presidents Chu Fucheng and Chen Shixia all helped organize the new government.

180. *Xinhai geming huiyi lu,* 4: 167–69; *Xinhai geming,* 7: 133, 152–53; *Jiang-Zhe tielu fengchao,* pp. 39, 403; *Dongfang zazhi,* 3.4: neiwu 106, 3.5: jiaoyu 99, 4.4: jiaoyu 172, 5.6: jiaoyu 140.

181. *Jindai shi ziliao,* 2: 27–28; *North China Herald,* Nov. 11, 1911, pp. 359, 440; Nov. 18, 1911, p. 637; *Dongfang zazhi,* 4.2: jiaoyu 33; *Shi bao,* Nov. 21, 1911, p. 3.

182. Schoppa, *Chinese Elites,* pp. 241–42. Schoppa points out that Ichiko's analysis of the gentry may hold up for peripheral areas, but historians like Mary Wright, who have considered the gentry to be a more progressive force, may be right about the cores.

Sources for Table 20, p. 254.

Basic sources for names are reports of stockholders meetings in *Dongfang zazhi, Shi bao,* and *Minhu ribao.* Fujii Masao, pp. 28–30, gives biographical information on some people. Names of prominent petitioners in 1905 are reported in *North China Herald,* July 28, 1905, p. 213, and Great Britain, Foreign Office, 371/1213. There are some complete biographies, but most information for Tables 20 and 21 is from incidental sources as listed below.

Fan Fen: Fujii, p. 29; *Dongfang zazhi,* 3.11: jiaotong 226; 4.12: shiye 200, 7.6: *Zhongguo dashi ji* 147; *Shi bao,* Mar. 24, 1911, p. 5; Mar. 29, 1911, p. 3; *Zhenhai xinzhi beigao, xia:* 5a.

Fan Gongxu: Fujii, p. 29; Tahara, p. 271; Rankin, "Public Opinion," p. 466; *Dongfang zazhi,* 1.10: shiye 180; *Hangzhou fuzhi,* 17: 9a;

Minhu ribao, June 11, 1909, p. 197; June 28, 1909, p. 312; Nonggongshang bu, 1909, 2.5: 7b; Great Britain, Foreign Office, 371/1213, 228/1594/2016, 228/2522/1894.

Hu Shandeng: Negishi, pp. 114–15.

Li Houyou: *Jiang-Zhe tielu fengchao*, pp. 76, 351; Zhao Jinyu, pp. 52, 56; E-tu Zen Sun, "Railway," p. 138; Fujii, p. 29; Jones, "Ningpo," p. 90; Elvin, "Gentry," pp. 55, 218; Zhang Yufa, *Lixian*, p. 368; Nonggongshang bu (1909), 2.5: 38; *Shi bao*, Apr. 23, 1910, p. 3; *Dongfang zazhi*, 3.3: *shiye* 85; 3.12: *shiye* 237; 4.4: *shiye* 82.

Liu Jinzao: Qi Longwei, "Lun Qingmo," p. 46; Tahara, p. 682; *Nanxun zhi*, 27: 2b; Nonggongshang bu (1910), 2.5: 8b; *Dongfang zazhi*, 3.1: *jiaotong* 25; Great Britain, Foreign Office, 228/1760/1929, 228/1801/2016.

Shen Cengtong: Zhang Yufa, *Lixian*, p. 180; Rankin, "Public Opinion," p. 479; Great Britain, Foreign Office, 228/2521/1894.

Shen Dunhe: Nonggongshang bu (1909), 2.5: 106; *North China Herald*, July 28, 1905, p. 203; May 6, 1910, p. 336; *Shi bao*, Nov. 25, 1910, p. 4; Chi, p. 92.

Shi Zhiying: Fujii, p. 29; *North China Herald*, 76: 213.

Sun Tinghan: Wang Yinian, p. 146; *Dongfang zazhi*, 4.7: *jiaotong* 163; 6.11: *jishi* 356; 7.6: *Zhongguo dashi ji* 146.

Sun Yirang: Fujii, p. 29; *Jiang-Zhe tielu fengchao*, p. 353; sources cited in Chap. 3, notes 112–17 and Chap. 6, notes 82–103.

Tang Shouqian: Eastman, "Reformism," p. 699; Song Cikuei; *Shaoxing xianzhi ziliao, tianluo zhi*: 38a–b, *renwu*: 192a–193a; Wang Yinian, pp. 55, 69; Nonggongshang bu (1909), 2.5: 8b.

Wang Kangnian: Wang Yinian, *passim*.

Xie Lunhui: Fujii, p. 29; Negishi, pp. 59, 112–13; *Shanghai qianzhuang shiliao*, p. 193; Great Britain, Foreign Office, 228/2524/1915; Zhang Cunwu, p. 48; *Minhu ribao*, July 15, 1909, p. 430.

Yan Xinhou: Chang Chung-li, *Income*, p. 158; Zhang Cunwu, pp. 157, 211; Elvin, "Gentry," pp. 42–43; *North China Herald*, July 28, 1905, p. 213; Great Britain, Foreign Office, 228/1505; Nonggongshang bu (1909), 2.5: 9a, 18a; Chen Zhen, 2.2: 927–30.

Yu Xiaqing: Fujii, p. 29; Negishi, pp. 56, 59; Jones, "Ningpo," pp. 90, 91, 402; *North China Herald*, July 28, 1905, p. 213; Apr. 15, 1911, p. 164; *Dongfang zazhi*, 3.1: *jiaoyu* 27.

Zhang Meiyou: *North China Herald*, July 28, 1905, p. 213.

Zhang Yuanji: Boorman, 1: 108–10; Wang Yinian, pp. 144, 146; Rankin, *Revolutionaries*, p. 62; Rankin, "Public Opinion," p. 479; *Jiang-Zhe tielu fengchao*, pp. 132, 385; Zhang Pengyuan, *Lixian*, p. 59; Zhao Jinyu, p. 56; Tang Zhijun, *Wuxu bianfa renwu*, 1: 94–96; *Dongfang zazhi*, 3.11: *jiaoyu* 372–73; 4.12: *zazu* 29; Great Britain, Foreign Office, 228/2523/1915; *Shi bao*, June 22, 1910, p. 3; Mar. 29, 1911, p. 3.

Zhou Jinbiao: Zhang Yufa, *Lixian*, pp. 101, 368; Zhang Cunwu, p. 260; *Jiang-Zhe tielu fengchao*, p. 385; Nonggongshang bu (1909),

2.4: 38b; 2.5: 18a; *Dongfang zazhi,* 5.4: *zazu* 11; Great Britain, Foreign Office, 228/2525/1915.

Zhu Peizhen: Elvin, "Gentry," pp. 245, 253; Zhang Cunwu, p. 88; Chen Zhen, 2.2: 964; *Hangzhou fuzhi,* 17: 25a, 27a; *North China Herald,* Mar. 25, 1910, p. 684; May 6, 1910, p. 336; *Dongfang zazhi,* 3.6: *shangwu* 55; Great Britain, Foreign Office, 228/2525/1915.

Sources for Table 21, p. 256.

Chen Chunlan: *Shi bao,* Mar. 29, 1911, p. 3; *Shanghai qianzhuang shiliao,* pp. 193, 754, 764; Li Quanshi and Zhao Weiren, p. 13.

Chen Wei: *Dongfang zazhi,* 7.1: 3d *jizai* 1; *North China Herald,* Aug. 2, 1907, p. 264; *Zhuanji wenxue,* 13.4: 12; Fang Zhaoying, p. 35; Fan, p. 282.

Chu Chengbo: *Jiang-Zhe tielu fengchao,* p. 73; *Dongfang zazhi,* 7.6: *Zhongguo dashi ji* 148; *Hangzhou fuzhi,* 111: 37b; Zhang Jingliu, p. 241; *Shi bao,* Nov. 28, 1910, p. 3, Aug. 4, 1911, p. 4.

Hu Huan: *Jiang-Zhe tielu fengchao,* p. 39; *Dongfang zazhi,* 1.11: *jiaoyu* 264; Great Britain, Foreign Office, 228/1634/1986.

Jiang Honglin: Fujii, p. 29; *Shi bao,* Apr. 1, 1910, p. 3; June 22, 1910, p. 3.

Jiang Ruzao: *Jiang-Zhe tielu fengchao,* p. 39; *Dongfang zazhi,* 7.6: *Zhongguo dashi ji* 147; Zhang Jinglu, p. 242; *Nanxun zhi,* 1922, 21: 4a–b; 27: 8a.

Shen Mingqing: Tahara, p. 189; *Dongfang zazhi,* 6.7: *jishi* 195; 7.6: *Zhongguo dashi ji* 147; *Jiang-Zhe tielu fengchao,* p. 39; *Shi bao,* Aug. 7, 1911, p. 3.

Sheng Bingwei: *Dongfang zazhi,* 7.1: 3d *jizai* 7; *Jiang-Zhe tielu fengchao,* pp. 39, 78, 373; *Shi bao,* Feb. 15, 1911, p. 3; *Zhenhai xianzhi,* 9: 28b, 34a, 35a.

Su Debiao: *Shi bao,* Feb. 17, 1911, p. 5; Apr. 11, 1911, p. 5; *Minhu ribao,* July 15, 1909, p. 430.

Wang Lian: *Jiang-Zhe tielu fengchao,* p 399; Rankin, *Revolutionaries,* p. 120; *Xinhai geming,* 7: 152–53; *Dongfang zazhi,* 3.9: *jiaoyu* 235; 7.6: *Zhongguo dashi ji* 144–45.

Wang Xirong: Fujii, p. 29; Tahara, p. 64; *Shi bao,* Mar. 27, 1910, p. 3; Apr. 5, 1910, p. 3; Oct. 4, 1910, p. 3; Nov. 25, 1910, p. 3.

Wu Zhenzhun: *Jiang-Zhe tielu fengchao,* pp. 39, 368; *Minxu ribao,* Oct. 13, 1909, p. 80; Fan, p. 83; *Hangzhou fuzhi,* 111: 39a.

Xu Guannan: Fujii, p. 29; Chen Zhen, 2.2: 958; *Dongfang zazhi,* 7.6: *Zhongguo dashi ji* 147.

Yan Yibin: Fujii, p. 29; *Dongfang zazhi,* 6.7: *jishi* 195; 7.6: 3d *jizai* 147; *Shi bao,* Mar. 24, 1911, p. 5.

Yao Mulian: Fujii, p. 29; Negishi, pp. 59–60; Chen Zhen, 2.2: 958; *Shi bao,* Feb. 12, 1910, p. 6.

Ye Jingkui: *Dongfang zazhi,* 7.6: *Zhongguo dashi ji* 147; Fujii, p. 29.

Ye Youxin: *Shanghai qianzhuang shiliao*, p. 743; Chen Zhen, 2.2: 954–56; Ho, *Ladder*, pp. 308–10; *Shi bao*, Mar. 29, 1911, p. 3.

Zhou Xiangling: *Dongfang zazhi*, 7.6: *Zhongguo dashi ji* 144–45; *Minhu ribao*, p. 402; *Shi bao*, Sept. 12, 1910, p. 4; July 31, 1911, p. 3.

Zhu Fushen: *Dongfang zazhi*, 7.11: 2d *jizai* 96; Fujii, p. 29, Tahara, p. 97.

Chapter Eight

1. Badie and Birnbaum, pp. 79–81, 92.
2. For this observation, see Rowe, p. 335.
3. Mann, "Commercial Taxation," chap. 1. See also Kuhn, "Local Taxation," pp. 120–31.
4. The thesis that the rise of regional armies undermined dynastic control is set forth in Spector, *Li Hung-chang*. A critique of this thesis is summarized in Kwang-ching Liu, pp. 111–13.
5. For the beginnings of this process, see Polachek, *Opium War*.
6. Tilly, pp. 6, 633, and *passim*.
7. Tilly, Tilly, and Tilly, pp. 249–50, 253–57.
8. Mann, "Commercial Taxation," chap. 5; Fincher, pp. 161–68, 192.
9. Ernest Young, pp. 225–28. Also see Fincher, pp. 219–67. Fincher recognizes the upward thrust of elite activism to provincial and national levels, but he explains it narrowly in terms of the impact of the assemblies (p. 260).
10. For an interpretation of this process and the difficulties it encountered, see Kuhn, "Self-Government," pp. 280–98. Duara, pp. 158–60, 336, and *passim*, discusses aspects of penetration and its limitations in an area of north China.
11. See Schoppa, *Chinese Elites*.
12. Some of these and other issues relating to the politics of the republican period are discussed in Rankin, Fairbank, and Feuerwerker, "Introduction."
13. This statement applies to much of China, but it does not take into account peripheral areas like the Kiangxi Highlands or areas of endemic unrest like parts of Guangdong where social conditions fostered illegal, semi-militarized organizations.
14. On this period, see Bergère, "Chinese Bourgeoisie," pp. 745–62.
15. Schoppa, *Chinese Elites*, pp. 12, 84, 169–74.
16. Chauncey, chaps. 3–4.
17. Dirlik and Krebs, pp. 145–47, point out that the willingness to use violence and endorse social conflict, as opposed to the support of a slow transition to greater equality, marked a major political dividing line.
18. Some of these questions are considered in Bush, "Industry and Politics."

SELECTED BIBLIOGRAPHY

Anderson, Perry. *Lineages of the Absolutist State.* London, 1979.

Anji xiunzhi (Gazetteer of Anji district). 1873.

Atwell, William. "Notes on Silver, Foreign Trade, and the Late Ming Economy," *Ch'ing-shih wen-t'i,* 3.8: 1–33 (Dec. 1977).

Ayers, William. *Chang Chih-tung and Educational Reform in China.* Cambridge, Mass., 1971.

Aying, pseud. [Qian Xingcun], ed. *Jiawu Zhong-Ri zhanzheng wenxue ji* (A collection of writings to study the Sino-Japanese War, 1894–95). Shanghai, 1958.

———. *Zhong-Fa zhanzheng wenxue ji* (A collection of writings to study the Sino-French War). Shanghai, 1957.

Badie, Bertrand, and Pierre Birnbaum. *The Sociology of the State.* Trans. by Arthur Goldhammer. Chicago, 1983.

Bartlett, Beatrice S. "The Vermilion Brush: The Grand Council Communications System and Central-Government Decision-Making in Mid-Ch'ing China." Ph.D. diss., Yale Univ., 1980.

Bastid, Marianne. *Aspects de la réforme de l'enseignement en Chine au debut de XXᵉ siècle, d'après des écrits de Zhang Jian.* Paris, 1971.

———. "The Party of the Emperor and Chinese Nationalism Before the Sino-Japanese War." Paper presented at the annual meeting, Association for Asian Studies, Boston, 1974.

———. "The Social Context of Reform," in Paul Cohen and John Schrecker, eds., *Reform in Nineteenth-Century China* (Cambridge, Mass., 1976), pp. 117–27.

Bastid-Bruguière, Marianne. "Currents of Social Change," in John K. Fairbank and Kwang-ching Liu, eds., *The Cambridge History of*

China, vol. 11, *Late Ch'ing, 1800–1911, Part 2* (Cambridge, Eng., 1980), pp. 536–602.

Bays, Daniel H. *China Enters the Twentieth Century: Chang Chih-tung and the Issues of a New Age, 1895–1909.* Ann Arbor, Mich., 1978.

Beattie, Hilary H. "The Alternative to Resistance: The Case of T'ung-ch'eng, Anhwei," in Jonathan Spence and John E. Wills, Jr., eds., *From Ming to Ch'ing* (New Haven, Conn., 1979), pp. 239–320.

Bergère, Marie-Claire. "The Chinese Bourgeoisie, 1911–37," in John K. Fairbank, ed., *The Cambridge History of China*, vol. 12, *Republican China, 1912–1949, Part 1* (Cambridge, Eng., 1983), pp. 722–827.

——. "The Role of the Bourgeoisie," in Mary C. Wright, ed., *China in Revolution: The First Phase, 1900–1913* (New Haven, Conn., 1968), pp. 229–96.

——. *Une crise financière à Shanghai à la fin de l'ancien régime.* Paris, 1964.

Boorman, Howard L. *Biographical Dictionary of Republican China.* 4 vols. New York, 1968.

Britton, Roswell S. *The Chinese Periodical Press, 1800–1912.* Shanghai, 1933.

Bush, Richard. "Industry and Politics in Kuomintang China." Ph.D. diss., Columbia Univ., 1978.

Cameron, Meribeth. *The Reform Movement in China, 1898–1912.* New York, 1963.

Cao Yuanbi. "Shu Sunshi *Zhouli zhengyi* hou" (After reading Mr. Sun's *The true principles of the Rites of Zhou*). *Zhejiang xuebao* (Journal of Zhejiang studies), 1.1: 9–10 (Sept. 1947).

Chan, Wellington. "Government, Merchants, and Industry to 1911," in John K. Fairbank and Kwang-ching Liu, eds., *The Cambridge History of China*, vol. 11, *Late Ch'ing, 1800–1911, Part 2* (Cambridge, Eng., 1980), pp. 416–62.

——. *Merchants, Mandarins, and Modern Enterprise in Late Ch'ing China.* Cambridge, Mass., 1977.

Chang, Ch'i-yun (Zhang Qiyun). "The Political Thought and Institutions of Ancient China: An Interpretation of the 'Chou Li.'" *Chinese Culture*, 1.2: 6–14 (Oct. 1957).

Chang Chung-li. *The Chinese Gentry.* Seattle, 1955.

——. *The Income of the Chinese Gentry.* Seattle, 1962.

Chang, Hao. *Liang Ch'i-ch'ao and Intellectual Transition in China, 1890–1907.* Cambridge, Mass., 1971.

Chang, P'eng-yuan (Zhang Pengyuan). "Provincial Assemblies: The Emergence of Political Participation, 1909–1914," *Chinese Studies in History*, 17.3: 3–28 (Spring 1984).

Chang, Yü-fa (Zhang Yufa). "Modernization of China, 1860–1916: Regional Comparisons." Paper presented at the annual meeting of the Association for Asian Studies, Los Angeles, 1979.

———. "Regional Modernization in China: Regional Comparisons," *Chinese Republican Studies Newsletter*, 5.1: 5–12 (Oct. 1979).

Changhua xianzhi (Gazetteer of Changhua district). 1924.

Changshan xianzhi (Gazetteer of Changshan district). 1886.

Changxing xianzhi (Gazetteer of Changxing district). 1892.

Chao, Kang. *The Development of Cotton Textile Production in China*. Cambridge, Mass., 1977.

———. "New Data on Land Ownership Patterns in Ming-Ch'ing China—A Research Note," *Journal of Asian Studies*, 40.4: 719–34 (Aug. 1981).

Chauncey, Helen. "Education and Social Mobilization: Tradition and Radical Transformation in Central China." Ph.D. diss., Stanford Univ., 1982.

Chen Dongyuan. "Qingdai shuyuan fengqi zhi bianqian" (Changes in practices at academies during the Qing period), *Xuefeng* (Scholarly trends), 3.5: 15–20 (1933).

Chen Liang. *Longchuan wenji* (Collected writings of Chen Liang). 1869.

Chen Mi. *Chen Jieshi xiansheng nianpu* (A chronological biography of Chen Fuchen). Ruian, 1934.

———. "Dong-Ou san xiansheng nianbiao (Chronological biographies of three Wenzhou scholars), *Zhejiang shengli tushuguan guankan* (Journal of the Zhejiang Provincial Library), 4.1: 1–21 (Feb. 1935).

Chen Qiu. *Jingshi boyi* (Extensive discussions of statecraft), abridged in *Wuxu bianfa* (The 1898 Reform Movement) (Shanghai, 1953), 1. 217–24.

———. *Jiushi yaoyi* (Important proposals to save the times), abridged in *Wuxu bianfa* (The 1898 Reform Movement) (Shanghai, 1953), 1: 224–29.

———. *Xinzi Ouwen qi yinduo* (Seven phonetic systems for the new writing in the Wenzhou dialect). 1903. Reprint, Beijing, 1958.

———. "Zhilu cungao" (Manuscripts of Chen Qiu), *Oufeng zazhi huikan* (Collection from the Wenzhou miscellany), 2.2: 1a–36b (1935).

Chen Xunci. "Ding Song xiansheng yu Zhejiang wenxian" (Ding Bing and Zhejiangese documents), *Zhejiang shengli tushuguan guankan* (Bulletin of the Zhejiang Provincial Library), 1.7–8: 1–36 (Oct. 1932).

Chen Yi et al., comps. *Guizheng jiyao* (Important documents on railway administration). *Chubian* (First collection). Beijing, 1907. *Cibian* (Second collection). Beijing, 1910.

Chen Zhen, ed. *Zhongguo jindai gongye ziliao* (Materials on modern industry in China). 4 vols. Beijing, 1961.

Cheng xianzhi (Gazetteer of Cheng district). 1934.

Chi, Madeline. "The Shanghai-Hangchow-Ningpo Railway Loan: A Case Study of the Rights Recovery Movement," *Modern Asian Studies*, 7: 85–106 (1973).

Chiang Monlin. *Tides from the West: A Chinese Autobiography.* New Haven, Conn., 1947.

Chow Tse-tseng. *Research Guide to the May Fourth Movement.* Cambridge, Mass., 1963.

Ch'ü T'ung-tsu. *Local Government in China under the Ch'ing.* Cambridge, Mass., 1962.

Chuan, Han-sheng, and Richard A. Kraus. *Mid-Ch'ing Rice Markets and Trade.* Cambridge, Mass., 1975.

Chuzhou fuzhi (Gazetteer of Chuzhou prefecture). 1877.

Ciqi xianzhi (Gazetteer of Ciqi district). 1899.

Cohen, Paul. *Between Tradition and Modernity: Wang T'ao and Reform in Late Ch'ing China.* Cambridge, Mass., 1974.

———. *Discovering History in China: American Historical Writing on the Recent Chinese Past.* New York, 1984.

Cohen, Paul, and John Schrecker, eds. *Reform in Nineteenth-Century China.* Cambridge, Mass., 1976.

Cole, James H. *The People Versus the Taipings: Bao Lisheng's "Righteous Army of Dongan."* Berkeley, Calif., 1981.

———. "Shaohsing: Studies in Ch'ing Social History." Ph.D. diss., Stanford Univ., 1975.

———. "The Shaoxing Connection: A Vertical Administrative Clique in Late Qing China," *Modern China,* 6.3: 317–26 (July 1980).

Da Qing Dezong jing (Guangxu) huangdi shilu (Veritable records of the Qing dynasty, Guangxu reign). 1937–38. 8 vols. Reprint, Taibei, 1970.

Daishan zhenzhi (Gazetteer of Daishan town). 1919.

Darnton, Robert. "The Rise of the Writer," *The New York Review of Books,* May 31, 1979, pp. 26–29.

Dennerline, Jerry. *The Chia-ting Loyalists: Confucian Leadership and Social Change in Seventeenth Century China.* New Haven, Conn., 1981, pp. 19–70.

———. "The New Hua Charitable Estate and Local-Level Leadership in Wuxi County at the End of the Qing," in *Select Papers from the Center for Far Eastern Studies, No. 4* (Chicago, 1980).

Deqing xian xinzhi (New gazetteer of Deqing district). 1923.

Ding Lizhong, comp. "Ding Bing nianpu," in Ding Lizhong, *Xuantang leibian* (Classified compilation from Xuan Studio). Hangzhou, 1900.

"Ding Song xiansheng bainian jinian ji" (A collection to commemorate Ding Bing's one-hundredth anniversary). *Wenlan xuebao* (Wenlan journal of studies), 2: 3–4 (Dec. 1936).

Dinghai tingzhi (Gazetteer of Dinghai sub-prefecture). 1884.

Dinghai xianzhi (Gazetteer of Dinghai district). 1924.

Dirlik, Arif, and Edward S. Krebs. "Socialism and Anarchism in Early Republican China," *Modern China,* 7.1: 117–52 (Apr. 1981).

Dongfang zazhi (The Eastern Miscellany). Shanghai, 1904–12.

Du Xuncheng and Zhou Yuangao. "Summary of Studies of the Bourgeoisie Since 1949," *Chinese Studies in History*, 16.3–4: 104–37 (Spring–Summer 1983).

Duara, Prasenjit. "Power in Rural Society: North China Villages, 1900–1940." Ph.D. diss., Harvard Univ., 1983.

Eastman, Lloyd. "Ch'ing-i and Chinese Policy Formation During the Nineteenth Century," *Journal of Asian Studies*, 24.4: 595 611 (Aug. 1965).

———. "Political Reformism in China Before the Sino-Japanese War," *Journal of Asian Studies*, 27.4: 695–710 (Aug. 1968).

———. *Throne and Mandarins, China's Search for a Policy During the Sino-French Controversy, 1880–1885*. Cambridge, Mass., 1967.

Elman, Benjamin. "Ch'ing Dynasty 'Schools' of Scholarship," *Ch'ing-shih wen-t'i*, 4.6: 1–44 (Dec. 1981).

———. *From Philosophy to Philology: Intellectual and Social Aspects of Change in Late Imperial China*. Cambridge, Mass., 1984.

Elvin, Mark. "The Administration of Shanghai," in Mark Elvin and G. William Skinner, eds., *The Chinese City between Two Worlds* (Stanford, Calif., 1974), pp. 239–62.

———. "The Gentry Democracy in Shanghai, 1905–1914." Ph.D. diss., Cambridge Univ., 1967.

———. "Market Towns and Waterways. The County of Shang-hai from 1480 to 1910," in G. William Skinner, ed., *The City in Late Imperial China* (Stanford, Calif., 1977), pp. 441–74.

———. *The Pattern of the Chinese Past*. Stanford, Calif., 1973.

Eng, Robert. "Imperialism and the Chinese Economy: The Canton and Shanghai Silk Industry, 1861–1932." Ph.D. diss., Univ. California, Berkeley, 1978.

Esherick, Joseph. *Reform and Revolution in China: The 1911 Revolution in Hunan and Hupeh*. Berkeley, Calif., 1976.

Fairbank, John K., ed. *The Cambridge History of China*, vol. 10, *Late Ch'ing, 1800–1911, Part 1*. Cambridge, Eng., 1978.

———, ed. *The Chinese World Order*. Cambridge, Mass., 1968.

Fairbank, John K., and Kwang-ching Liu, eds. *The Cambridge History of China*, vol. 11, *Late Ch'ing, 1800–1911, Part 2*. Cambridge, Eng., 1980.

Fan Yinnan. *Dangdai Zhongguo mingren lu* (Who's who in contemporary China). Shanghai, 1931.

Fang Zhaoying. *Qingmo Minchu yangxuesheng tilu chuji* (A preliminary summary of Chinese students abroad during the late Qing and early Republic). Taibei, 1962.

Fang Zhaoying and Du Lianzhe. *Zengjiao Qingchao jinshi timing beilu* (Revised records of the names of Qing dynasty *jinshi*-degree holders presented to the throne). Harvard-Yenching Index Series, no. 19. Beijing, 1941.

Faure, David. "Local Political Disturbances in Kiangsu Province, China, 1870–1911." Ph.D. diss., Princeton Univ., 1975.

————. "The Rural Economy of Kiangsu Province, 1870–1911," *The Journal of the Institute of Chinese Studies of the Chinese University of Hong Kong*, 9.2: 365–472 (1978).

Feng Ziyou. *Zhongguo keming yundong ershiliu nian zuzhi shi* (Twenty-six years organizational history of the Chinese revolutionary movement). Shanghai, 1948.

Fenghua xianzhi (Gazetteer of Fenghua district). 1908.

Fenshui xianzhi (Gazetteer of Fenshui district). 1906.

Feuerwerker, Albert. *China's Early Industrialization, Sheng Hsuan-huai (1844–1916) and Mandarin Enterprise.* Cambridge, Mass., 1958.

Fincher, John. *Chinese Democracy: The Self-Government Movement in Local, Provincial, and National Politics, 1905–1914.* Canberra, 1983.

Franke, Wolfgang. *The Reform and Abolition of the Traditional Chinese Examination System.* Cambridge, Mass., 1960.

Fujii Masao. "Shimmatsu Kō-Setsu ni okeru tetsuro mondai to burujoa seiryoku no ichi sokumen" (The late Qing railway question in Jiangsu and Zhejiang, and one aspect of the power of the bourgeoisie), *Rekishigaku kenkyū* (Historical research), 5: 22–30 (1955).

Fuyang xianzhi (Gazetteer of Fuyang district). 1906.

Gasster, Michael. *Chinese Intellectuals and the Revolution of 1911.* Seattle, 1969.

Ge Gongzhen. *Zhongguo baoxue shi* (A history of Chinese newspapers). Beijing, 1955.

Ge Shijun, comp. *Huangzhao jingshi wen xubian* (A supplementary collection of Qing dynasty essays on statecraft). Shanghai, 1888.

Ge Suicheng. *Zhejiang* (Zhejiang). Shanghai, 1939.

Geng Yunzhi. "The Bourgeois Constitutionalists and the Provincial Councils at the End of the Qing," *Chinese Studies in History*, 17.4: 49–111 (Summer 1984).

Golas, Peter J. "Early Ch'ing Guilds," in G. William Skinner, ed., *The City in Late Imperial China* (Stanford, Calif., 1977), pp. 555–80.

Great Britain, Foreign Office. Archives. Public Records Office, London.

Grimm, Tilemann. "Academies and Urban Systems in Kwangtung." in G. William Skinner, ed., *The City in Late Imperial China* (Stanford, Calif., 1977), pp. 475–98.

Grove, Linda, and Joseph Esherick. "From Feudalism to Capitalism: Japanese Scholarship on the Transformation of Rural Society," *Modern China*, 6.4: 397–438 (Oct. 1980).

Gu Yanwu. *Gu Tinglin shiwen ji* (Poetry and essays of Gu Yanwu). Beijing, 1959.

————. *Rizhi lu* (A record of daily learning). Comp. by Huang Rucheng. Shanghai, 1935.

Guangxu zhao Donghua lu (The Donghua records of the Guangxu reign period). Comp. by Zhu Shoupeng. 1909. Reprint, Beijing, 1958.

Guian xianzhi (Gazetteer of Guian district). 1881.

Guo Tingyi. *Jindai Zhongguo shishi rizhi* (Chronology of modern Chinese history). 2 vols. Taibei, 1963.

Guomin ri ribao (The China national gazette). 1903. Reprint, Taibei, 1965.

Guozhao Liang-Zhe ke ming lu (A record of successful provincial examination candidates in Zhejiang during the Qing). 1851 and 1858.

Guy, Kent. "The Scholar and the State in Late Imperial China: The Politics of the Ssu-k'u ch'üan-shu Project." Ph.D. diss., Harvard Univ., 1981.

Haifang dang (Records of coastal defense). Vol. 5, parts 1–2, *Tielu* (Railways). Comp. by Zhongyang yanjiu yuan jindai shi yanjiu suo (Institute of Modern History Academia Sinica). Taibei, 1957.

Haining Banhai Zhangshi zongpu (Genealogy of the Zhang lineage of Banhai, Haining). 1919.

Haining zhouzhi gao (Draft gazetteer of Haining department). 1922.

Haining Zhushi zongpu (Genealogy of the Zhu lineage of Haining). 1884.

Haiyan xianzhi (Gazetteer of Haiyan district). 1876.

Hamilton, Gary G. "Regional Associations and the Chinese City: A Comparative Perspective," *Comparative Studies in History and Society*, 21.3: 346–61 (July 1979).

Hangzhou baihua bao (The Hangzhou vernacular journal). 1901.

Hangzhou fuzhi (Gazetteer of Hangzhou prefecture). 1922.

Hao, Yen-p'ing. *The Comprador in Nineteenth-Century China: Bridge Between East and West*. Cambridge, Mass., 1970.

He Bingsong. *Zhedong xuepai suyuan* (An inquiry into the origins of the Eastern Zhejiang School). Shanghai, 1932.

He Changling, comp. *Huangzhao jingshi wenbian* (Qing dynasty essays on statecraft). 1826.

Ho, Ping-ti (He Bingdi). *The Ladder of Success in Imperial China*. New York, 1962.

———. "Salient Aspects of China's Heritage," in Ping-ti Ho and Tang Tsou, eds., *China in Crisis*, vol. 1, *China's Heritage and the Communist Political System, Book 1* (Chicago, 1968), pp. 1–92.

———. *Studies on the Population of China, 1368–1953*. Cambridge, Mass., 1959.

———. *Zhongguo huiguan shilun* (A historical survey of landsmanshaften in China). Taibei, 1966.

Hong Huanchun. *Zhejiang difang zhi kaolu* (An investigatory record of Zhejiangese local gazetteers). Beijing, 1958.

Hou Wailu. *Zhongguo sixiang tongshi* (A comprehensive survey of Chinese thought). 5 vols. Beijing, 1957–63.

Hsiao, Kung-chuan (Xiao Gongquan). *Rural China: Imperial Control in the Nineteenth Century*. Seattle, 1960.

Hsiao, Liang-lin. *China's Foreign Trade Statistics, 1864–1949.* Cambridge, Mass., 1974.
Hu Fengdan. *Jinhua congshu* (A Jinhua collection). 1869–74.
———. *Yongkang Hushi ba liezhuan* (Biographies of eight martyrs of the Hus of Yongkang). 1865.
Hu Sijing. *Tuilu quanji* (Complete works from the hut of retirement). 1913. 6 vols. Reprint, Taibei, 1970.
Huang Qinglan. *Ouhai guan zheng lu* (Records of administration in the Wenzhou circuit). 1921.
Huangyan xianzhi (Gazetteer of Huangyan district). 1877.
Huber, Thomas M. *The Revolutionary Origins of Modern Japan.* Stanford, Calif., 1981.
Hummel, Arthur W., ed. *Eminent Chinese of the Ch'ing Period.* 2 vols. Washington, D.C., 1943–44.
Huzhou fuzhi (Gazetteer of Huzhou prefecture). 1874.
I Songgyu. "Shantung in the Shun-chih Reign: The Establishment of Local Control and the Gentry Response," trans. by Joshua A. Fogel, *Ch'ing-shih wen-t'i,* 4.4: 1–34 (Dec. 1980); 4.5: 1–31 (June 1981).
Ichiko, Chūzō. "Political and Institutional Reform, 1901–1911," in John K. Fairbank and Kwang-ching Liu, eds., *The Cambridge History of China,* vol. 11, *Late Ch'ing, 1800–1911, Part 2* (Cambridge, Eng., 1980), pp. 375–415.
———. "The Role of the Gentry: An Hypothesis," in Mary C. Wright, ed., *China in Revolution: The First Phase, 1900–1913* (New Haven, Conn., 1968), pp. 297–318.
IMC (Imperial Maritime Customs), Inspectorate General of Customs. *Reports of Trade at the Treaty Ports.* Shanghai, 1878–81.
———. *Trade Reports and Returns.* Shanghai, 1882–1911.
———. *Silk.* Shanghai, 1881.
Jen Yu-wen. *The Taiping Revolutionary Movement.* New Haven, Conn., 1973.
Jiande xianzhi (Gazetteer of Jiande district). 1919.
Jiangshan xianzhi (Gazetteer of Jiangshan district). 1873.
Jiang-Zhe tielu fengchao (The railway agitation in Jiangsu and Zhejiang). Ed. by Mobei (pseud.). 1907. Reprint, Taibei, 1968.
Jiashan xianzhi (Gazetteer of Jiashan district). 1894.
Jiaxing fuzhi (Gazetteer of Jiaxing prefecture). 1878.
Jiaxing xianzhi (Gazetteer of Jiaxing district). 1906.
Jindai shi ziliao (Materials on modern Chinese history). Beijing, 1954–.
Jing Yuanshan. *Juyi chuji* (Dwelling in leisure, first collection). 3 vols. Shanghai, 1902.
Jingning xianzhi (Gazetteer of Jingning district). 1873.
Jingning xianzhi (Gazetteer of Jingning district). 1933.
Jinhua xianzhi (Gazetteer of Jinhua district). 1894.
Jinyun xianzhi (Gazetteer on Jinyun district). 1884.

Jones, Susan Mann. "Finance in Ningpo: The 'Ch'ien-chuang,' 1750–1850," in W. E. Willmott, ed., *Economic Organization in Chinese Society* (Stanford, Calif., 1972), pp. 47–78.

———. "The Ningpo Pang and Financial Power at Shanghai," in Mark Elvin and G. William Skinner, eds., *The Chinese City Between Two Worlds* (Stanford, Calif., 1974), pp. 73–96.

———. "Scholasticism and Politics in Late Eighteenth Century China," *Ch'ing-shih wen-t'i*, 3.4: 28–49 (Dec. 1975).

Jones, Susan Mann, and Philip A. Kuhn. "Dynastic Decline and the Roots of Rebellion," in John K. Fairbank, ed., *The Cambridge History of China*, vol. 10, *Late Ch'ing, Part 1* (Cambridge, Eng., 1978), pp. 107–62.

Kaihua xianzhi (Gazetteer of Kaihua district). 1898.

Kobayashi Kazumi. "Chūgoku hanshokumin chika no keizai katei to minshū no tatakai: rikin megutte, jūkyūseiki kōhan" (The economic process of China's semi-colonization and popular struggle — with reference to the *lijin* tax in the second half of the nineteenth century), *Reikishigaku kenkyū* (Historical research), 369: 1–18 (Feb. 1971).

Kuhn, Philip A. "Local Self-Government Under the Republic," in Frederic Wakeman, Jr., and Carolyn Grant, eds., *Conflict and Control in Late Imperial China* (Berkeley, Calif., 1975), pp. 257–98.

———. "Local Taxation and Finance in Republican China," in *Select Papers from the Center for Far Eastern Studies, No. 3.* (Chicago, 1979), pp. 100–136.

———. *Rebellion and Its Enemies in Late Imperial China: Militarization and Social Structure, 1796–1864.* Cambridge, Mass., 1975.

Kwong, Luke S. K. *A Mosaic of the One Hundred Days: Personalities, Politics, and Ideas of 1898.* Cambridge, Mass., 1984.

Langlois, John. "Political Thought in Chin-hua Under Mongol Rule," in John Langlois, ed., *China under Mongol Rule* (Princeton, 1981), pp. 137–85.

Lanqi xianzhi (Gazetteer of Lanqi district). 1889.

Lapidus, Ira. "Hierarchies and Networks: A Comparison of Chinese and Islamic Societies," in Frederic Wakeman, Jr., and Carolyn Grant, eds., *Conflict and Control in Late Imperial China* (Berkeley, Calif., 1975), pp. 26–42.

Lee, En-han (Li Enhan). "The Chekiang Gentry-Merchants vs. the Peking Court Officials: China's Struggle for Recovery of the British Soochow-Hangchow-Ningpo Railway Concession, 1905–1911," *Zongyang yanjiu yuan jindai shi yanjiu suo jikan* (Bulletin of the Institute of Modern History, Academia Sinica), 3.1: 223–68 (July 1972).

Lee, James. "Food Supply and Population Growth in Southwest China, 1250–1850," *Journal of Asian Studies*, 41.4: 711–46 (Aug. 1982).

Leong Yuen Sang. "Regional Rivalry in Mid-Nineteenth-Century

Shanghai: Cantonese vs. Ningpo men," *Ch'ing-shih wen-t'i*, 4.8: 29–50 (Dec. 1982).

Lewis, Charlton M. *Prologue to the Chinese Revolution: The Transformation of Ideas and Institutions in Hunan Province, 1891–1907.* Cambridge, Mass., 1976.

Li Enhan (Lee, En-han). "Zong-Mei shouhui Yue-Han tielu quan jiaoshe: Wan-Qing shouhui tielu liquan yundong de yanjiu, zhiyi (The Sino-American negotiations for the recovery of the Canton-Hanzhou railway rights: research on the late Qing movement for the recovery of railway rights, part one), *Zhongyang yanjiu yuan jindai shi yanjiu suo jikan* (Bulletin of the Institute of Modern History, Academia Sinica), 1.1: 149–215 (Aug. 1969).

Li Guoqi. "Min-Zhe-Tai diqu Qingji Minchu jingji jindaihua chutan" (Economic modernization in the area of Fujian, Zhejiang, and Taiwan during the late Qing and early Republic), *Lishi xuebao* (Bulletin of historical research), 4: 425–41 (1976).

———. "Qingmo Minchu Min-Zhe diqu renkou liudong yu dushihua de yanjin, 1860–1916" (Population trends in Fujian and Zhejiang at the end of the Qing and the beginning of the Republic and the progressive urbanization, 1860–1916), *Lishi xuebao* (Bulletin of historical research), 5: 489–522 (Apr. 1977).

———. "Shijiu shiji Min-Zhe diqu suo chengxian de chuantong shehui qingzhuang" (Traditional social forms displayed in the Fujian and Zhejiang region during the nineteenth century), *Lishi xuebao* (Bulletin of historical research), 6: 138–82 (May 1978).

———. "You Min-Zhe quyu yanjiu kan Qingdai jiejue renkou yali de zhongyao fangfa—zaipei jingji zuowu" (An important method of solving population pressure in the Qing dynasty from the perspective of research on the Fujian-Zhejiang region—cultivation of commercial crops), *Shihuo yuekan* (Agricultural commodities monthly), 4.10: 421–44 (1975).

———. *Zhongguo xiandaihua de quyu yanjiu: Min-Zhe-Tai diqu, 1860–1916* (Regional research on China's modernization: the Fujian-Zhejiang-Taiwan region, 1860–1916). Taibei, 1982.

Li Guoqi and Zhu Hong. "Qingdai Jinhua fu de shizhen jiegou ji qi yanbian" (The structure of markets and towns in Jinhua prefecture and their progressive changes during the Qing), *Lishi xuebao* (Bulletin of historical research), 7: 113–87 (May 1979).

Li, Lillian M. *China's Silk Trade: Traditional Industry in the Modern World, 1842–1937.* Cambridge, Mass., 1981.

———. "Introduction: Food, Famine, and the Chinese State," *Journal of Asian Studies*, 41.4: 687–710 (Aug. 1982).

Li Quanshi and Zhao Weiren. *Shanghai zhi qianzhuang* (The old-style banks of Shanghai). Shanghai, 1930.

Li Yingjue. *Zhezhi bianlan* (A convenient guide to Zhejiang). 1896.

Liang Qichao. "Jindai xuefeng zhi dili de fenbu" (Geographical distribution of currents of scholarship in modern times), *Qinghua xuebao* (Tsing-hua journal of studies), 1.1: 2–37 (June 1942).

Lin Chuanjia. *Da Zhonghua Zhejiang sheng dili zhi* (A geography of Zhejiang province, China). Hangzhou, 1918.

Lin'an xianzhi (Gazetteer of Lin'an district). 1910.

Linghu zhenzhi (Gazetteer of Linghu town). 1893.

Linhai xianzhi gao (Draft gazetteer of Linhai district). 1935.

Lishui xianzhi (Gazetteer of Lishui district). 1926.

Liu Bingzhang. *Liu Wenzhuanggong zouyi* (Memorials of Liu Bingzhang). 1908.

Liu Boji. *Guangdong shuyuan zhidu* (The system of academies in Guangdong). Taibei, 1958.

Liu Guangjing (Liu Kwang-ching). "Wan-Qing difang guan zishu zhi shimi jiazhi" (The historical value of late Qing officials' personal notes), in *Zhongyang yanjiu yuan chengli wushi zhounian jinian lunwen ji*. (A collection of essays to commemorate the fiftieth anniversary of Academia Sinica) (Taibei, 1978), pp. 333–64.

Liu, Kwang-ching (Liu Guangjing). "Nineteenth-Century China: The Disintegration of the Old Order and the Impact of the West," in Ho Ping-ti and Tang Tsou, eds., *China in Crisis*, vol. 1: *China's Heritage and the Communist Political System*, Book 1 (Chicago, 1968), pp. 93–178.

Liu Shaokuan. *Houzhuang wenchao* (The writings of Liu Shaokuan). Wenzhou, 1919.

———. "Zhouyuan biji" (Written records of Zhou garden). *Oufeng zazhi* (The Wenzhou miscellany), 10: 19a–20b (Oct. 1934).

Liu Shiji. "Ming Qing shidai Jiangnan tiqu de zhuanye shizhen" (Specialized market towns in Jiangnan during the Ming and Qing periods), *Shihuo yuekan* (Agricultural commodities monthly), 8.6: 274–91; 8.7: 326–37 (1978).

Liu Yao. "Taiping Tianguo shibai hou Jiangnan nongcun bianhua de zai tantao" (Further discussion of post-Taiping changes in the rural economy of Jiangnan). *Lishi yanjiu* (Historical research), 3: 105–20 (1982).

Liu Zhufeng. "Qianfei jilüe" (A brief account of the Gold Coin rebels). *Oufeng zazhi* (The Wenzhou miscellany), 8: 2a–b; 9: 3a–4a; 10: 5b–7b; 11: 8a–10b (Aug.–Nov. 1934).

Lo, Winston Wan. *The Life and Thought of Yeh Shih*. Gainesville, Fla., 1974.

Longquan xianzhi (Gazetteer of Longquan district). 1878.

Longyou xianzhi (Gazetteer of Longyou district). 1925.

Loqing xianzhi (Gazetteer of Loqing district). 1912. Reprint, Taibei, 1976.

Lu Xinyuan. *Yigu tang ji* (Collection from the Hall of Righteous Regard). 1874. Reprint, Taibei, 1970.

Lü Gongwang. "Xinhai geming Zhejiang guangfu jishi" (An account of the 1911 Revolution in Zhejiang), *Jindai shi ziliao* (Materials on modern history), 1: 104–17 (1954).

Luo Yudong. *Zhongguo lijin shi* (A history of *lijin* in China). Shanghai, 1936.

Luqiao zhilüe (Draft Gazetteer of Luqiao). 1935.

Ma Xinyi. *Ma Duanmingong zouyi* (Memorials of Ma Xinyi). 1894. Reprint, Taibei, 1975(?).

MacKinnon, Stephen R. *Power and Politics in Late Imperial China: Yuan Shikai in Beijing and Tianjin, 1901–1908.* Berkeley, Calif., 1980.

Mann, Susan (Susan Mann Jones). "Commercial Taxation in China, 1750–1950." Stanford, Calif., forthcoming.

Marks, Robert B. *Rural Revolution in South China: Peasants and the Making of History in Haifeng County, 1570–1930.* Madison, Wis., 1984.

McElderry, Andrea Lee. *Shanghai Old-Style Banks (ch'ien-chuang), 1800–1935.* Ann Arbor, Mich., 1976.

Meili beizhi (Gazetteer prepared for Mei (Wangdian) town). 1922.

Metzger, Thomas A. *The Internal Organization of the Ch'ing Bureaucracy: Legal, Normative, and Communicative Aspects.* Cambridge, Mass., 1973.

———. "The Organizational Capacities of the Ch'ing State in the Field of Commerce: The Liang-Huai Salt Monopoly, 1740–1840," in W. E. Willmott, ed., *Economic Organization in Chinese Society* (Stanford, Calif., 1972), pp. 9–46.

Michael, Franz. "Introduction," in Stanley Spector, *Li Hung-chang and the Huai Army: A Study in Nineteenth-Century Chinese Regionalism* (Seattle, 1964), pp. xxii–xliii.

Min Tu-ki. *Chungguk kŭndae sa yŏn'gu* (Studies in Modern Chinese History). Seoul, 1973.

Minhu ribao (The people's cry). Shanghai, 1909.

Minli bao (The people's stand). Shanghai, 1910–11.

Minxu ribao (The people's sigh). Shanghai, 1909.

Moore, Barrington, Jr. *Social Origins of Dictatorship and Democracy: Lord and Peasant in the Making of the Modern World.* Boston, 1966.

Morita Akira. *Shindai suiri shi kenkyū* (Research on the history of water control under the Qing dynasty). Tokyo, 1974.

Mote, Frederick W. "Confucian Eremitism in the Yuan Period," in Arthur F. Wright, ed., *The Confucian Persuasion* (Stanford, Calif., 1960), pp. 202–40.

Moulder, Frances. *Japan, China, and the Modern World Economy.* Cambridge, Eng., 1977.
Nagai Kazumi. "Kō-Setsu roji to Shimmatsu no minshū" (Railway affairs in Jiangsu and Zhejiang and the masses during the late Qing), *Shinshu Daigaku kiyō* (Journal of Shinshu University), Bunrigakubu (Faculty of Liberal Arts and Sciences), 7: 1–26 (1957).
Nanxun zhi (Gazetteer of Nanxun town). 1858.
Nanxun zhi (Gazetteer of Nanxun town). 1922.
Negishi Tadashi. *Shanhai no girudo* (The guilds of Shanghai). Tokyo, 1951.
Ninghai xianzhi (Gazetteer of Ninghai district). 1892.
Nivison, David S. *The Life and Thought of Chang Hsueh-ch'eng, 1738–1801.* Stanford, Calif., 1966.
Nonggongshang bu (Ministry of Agriculture, Industry, and Commerce). *Nonggongshang bu tongji biao* (Statistical tables of the Ministry of Agriculture, Industry, and Commerce). *Diyi ci* (First collection). Beijing, 1909. *Dier ci* (Second collection). Beijing, 1910.
North China Daily News. Shanghai, 1878–90.
North China Herald and Supreme Court and Consular Gazette. Shanghai, 1880–1911.
Ocko, Jonathan. *Bureaucratic Reform in Provincial China: Ting Jih-ch'ang in Restoration Kiangsu, 1867–1870.* Cambridge, Mass., 1983.
Olson, Mancur. *The Theory of Collective Action: Public Goods and the Theory of Groups.* Cambridge, Mass., 1965.
Onogawa Hidemi. "Qingmo bianfa lun de xingcheng" (The materialization of discussions of reform during the late Qing), *Dalu zazhi* (The continent magazine), 38.7: 25–37 (Apr. 15, 1969).
Oufeng zazhi (The Wenzhou miscellany). Ruian, 1934–35.
Oufeng zazhi huikan (Compilation from the Wenzhou miscellany). Ruian, 1935.
Pan Guangdan. *Ming Qing liangdai Jiaxing de wangzu* (Famous lineages in Jiaxing during the Ming and Qing). Shanghai, 1947.
Pan Guangdan and Fei Xiaotong. "Keju yu shehui liudong" (The examination system and social mobility), *Shehui kexue* (Social science), 4.1: 1–27 (Oct. 1947).
Peng Zeyi. "Qingdai qianqi shougongye de fazhan" (The development of the handicraft industry during the early Qing), *Zhongguo shi yanjiu* (Research in Chinese history), 1: 43–60 (1981).
———. *Zhongguo jindai shougongye shi ziliao, 1840–1949* (Materials on the history of the modern handicraft industry in China, 1840–1949). 4 vols. Beijing, 1957.
Perdue, Peter. "Official Goals and Local Interests: Water Control in the Dongting Lake Region during the Ming and Qing Periods," *Journal of Asian Studies,* 41.4: 747–66 (Aug. 1982).

Perkins, Dwight H. _Agricultural Development in China, 1368–1968._ Chicago, 1969.

Pinghu xianzhi (Gazetteer of Pinghu district). 1886.

Pingyang xianzhi (Gazetteer of Pingyang district). 1925.

Polachek, James. "Gentry Hegemony: Soochow in the T'ung-chih Restoration," in Frederic Wakeman, Jr., and Carolyn Grant, eds., _Conflict and Control in Late Imperial China_ (Berkeley, Calif., 1975), pp. 211–56.

———. _The Inner Opium War._ Cambridge, Mass., forthcoming.

———. "Literati Groups and Literati Politics in Early Nineteenth-Century China." Ph.D. diss., Univ. of California, Berkeley, 1976.

Prazniak, Roxann. "Community and Protest in Rural China: Tax Resistance and County-Village Politics on the Eve of the 1911 Revolution." Ph.D. diss., Univ. of California, Davis, 1981.

Pujiang xianzhi gao (Draft Gazetteer of Pujiang district). 1905.

Puyuan zhi (Gazetteer of Puyuan). 1927.

Qi Longwei. "Didang yu Wuxu bianfa" (The Emperor's Party and the 1898 Reform Movement), _Xin jianshe_ (New construction), 9: 35–42, 66 (1963).

———. "Lun Qingmo de tielu fengchao" (On the railway agitation at the end of the Qing), _Lishi yanjiu_ (Historical research), 2: 33–60 (1964).

Qian Osun. _Wen Yunge xiansheng nianpu_ (A chronological biography of Wen Tingshi), in _Wen Tingshi quanji_ (Complete works of Wen Tingshi). Reprint, Taibei, 1969.

Qingtian xianzhi (Gazetteer of Qingtian district). 1876.

Qingyuan xianzhi (Gazetteer of Qingyuan district). 1877.

Qu xianzhi (Gazetteer of Qu district). 1929.

Quanguo yinhang nianjian (National banking yearbook). Shanghai, 1934.

Rankin, Mary Backus. _Early Chinese Revolutionaries: Radical Intellectuals in Shanghai and Zhejiang, 1902–1911._ Cambridge, Mass., 1971.

———. "Elite Reformism and the Chinese Women's Movement: Evidence from the Kiangsu and Chekiang Railway Demonstrations, 1907," _Ch'ing-shi wen-t'i_, 3.2: 29–42 (Dec. 1974).

———. "Local Reform Currents in Cheking before 1900," in Paul Cohen and John Schrecker, eds., _Reform in Nineteenth-Century China_ (Cambridge, Mass., 1976), pp. 221–30.

———. "Public Opinion and Political Power: _Qingyi_ in Late Nineteenth-Century China," _Journal of Asian Studies_, 41.3: 453–84 (May 1982).

———. "Rural-Urban Continuities: Leading Families of Two Chekiang Market Towns," _Ch'ing-shih wen-t'i_, 3.7: 67–104 (Nov. 1977).

Rankin, Mary Backus, John K. Fairbank, and Albert Feuerwerker. "Introduction," in John K. Fairbank and Albert Feuerwerker, eds.,

The Cambridge History of China, vol. 13, Republican China, 1912–1949, Part 2. Cambridge, Eng., forthcoming.

Rawski, Evelyn. Education and Popular Literacy in Ch'ing China. Ann Arbor, Mich., 1979.

Reischauer, Edwin O., and John K. Fairbank. East Asia, The Great Tradition. Boston, 1956.

Rhoads, Edward. China's Republican Revolution: The Case of Kwangtung, 1895–1913. Cambridge, Mass., 1975.

Rowe, William T. Hankow: Commerce and Society in a Chinese City. Stanford, Calif., 1984.

Schipper, Kristofer M. "Neighborhood Cult Associations in Traditional Taiwan," in G. William Skinner, ed., The City in Late Imperial China (Stanford, Calif., 1977), pp. 651–76.

Schneider, Laurence A. A Madman of Ch'u: The Chinese Myth of Loyalty and Dissent. Berkeley, Calif., 1980.

Schoppa, R. Keith. Chinese Elites and Political Change: Zhejiang Province in the Early Twentieth Century. Cambridge, Mass., 1982.

———. "The Composition and Functions of the Local Elite in Szechwan, 1851–1874," Ch'ing-shih wen-t'i, 2.10: 7–23 (Nov. 1973).

———. "Local Self-Government in Zhejiang, 1909–1927," Modern China, 2.4: 503–30 (Oct. 1976).

Schrecker, John. "The Reform Movement of 1898 and the Ch'ing-i Reform as Opposition," in Paul Cohen and John Schrecker, eds., Reform in Nineteenth-Century China (Cambridge, Mass., 1976), pp 289–305.

Shanghai qianzhuang shiliao (Historical materials on Shanghai old-style banks). Ed. by Zhongguo renmin yinhang, Shanghai shi fenhang (Shanghai branch of the Chinese Peoples' Bank). Shanghai, 1961.

Shanghai shi zizhi zhi (Self-government gazetteer of Shanghai city). Shanghai, 1915.

Shanghai xian xuzhi (A continuation of the gazetteer of Shanghai district). 1918.

Shanghai xianzhi (Gazetteer of Shanghai district). 1871.

Shanghai xinwen shiye shiliao jiyao (A compilation of historical materials on the Shanghai newspaper business). 1941. Reprint, Taibei, 1977.

Shanghai yanjiu ziliao (Materials for research on Shanghai). Ed. by Shanghai tongshe (Shanghai history office). Shanghai, 1936–39.

Shanghai yanjiu ziliao xuji (A continuation of the collection of materials for research on Shanghai). Ed. by Shanghai tongshe (Shanghai history office). Shanghai, 1939.

Shangyu xianzhi (Gazetteer of Shangyu district). 1898.

Shaoxing xianzhi ziliao, diyi ji (Materials for a gazetteer of Shaoxing district, first collection). 1937–39.

Shen bao (The Shun-pao daily news). Shanghai, 1874–84, 1887.
Shen bao guan (*Shen bao* office). *Zuijin zhi wushi nian* (The most recent fifty years). Shanghai, 1923.
Shen bao nianjian (The *Shen bao* yearbook). Shanghai, 1933.
Shen Bingying. *Chunxing caotang ji* (Collection from the Spring Stars Thatched Hall). 1889.
Shen Yuwu. "Shijiu shiji mo Zhejiang de weixin sichao" (Currents of reformist thought in Zhejiang at the end of the nineteenth century), *Hangzhou daxue xuebao* (Journal of Hangzhou University), 1–2: 166–74 (May 1979).
Sheng Kang, comp. *Huangzhao jingshi wen xubian* (A supplementary collection of Qing dynasty essays on statecraft). 1897.
Sheng Langxi. *Zhongguo shuyuan zhidu* (The system of academies in China). Shanghai, 1934.
Sheng Xuanhuai. *Yuzhai cungao* (Collected works of Sheng Xuanhuai). 1939. Reprint, Taipei, 1974.
Shi bao (The Times). Shanghai, 1910–12.
Shiba, Yoshinobu. "Ningpo and its Hinterland," in G. William Skinner, ed., *The City in Late Imperial China* (Stanford, Calif., 1977), pp. 391–440.
Shimen xianzhi (Gazetteer of Shimen district). 1879.
Shiwu bao (The Chinese progress). 1896–98. Reprint, Taibei, 1967.
Shou Shenting. "*Qianyuan yu Pisong lou cangshu*" (The Garden of Retirement and the Pisong Library), *Zhejiang yuekan* (Zhejiang monthly), 1.8: 20–21 (May 1969).
Shouchang xianzhi (Gazetteer of Shouchang district). 1930.
Shuanglin zhenzhi (Gazetteer of Shuanglin town). 1917.
Skinner, G. William. "Cities and the Hierarchy of Local Systems," in G. William Skinner, ed., *The City in Late Imperial China* (Stanford, Calif., 1977), pp. 275–352.
———. "Introduction: Urban and Rural in Chinese Society," in G. William Skinner, ed., *The City in Late Imperial China* (Stanford, Calif., 1977), pp. 253–74.
———. "Introduction: Urban Development in Imperial China," in G. William Skinner, ed., *The City in Late Imperial China* (Stanford, Calif., 1977), pp. 3–32.
———. "Marketing and Social Structure in Rural China," *Journal of Asian Studies*, 24.1: 3–43 (Nov. 1964); 24.2: 195–228 (Feb. 1965).
———. "Mobility Strategies in Late Imperial China," in Carol A. Smith, ed., *Regional Analysis*, vol. 1, *Economic Systems* (New York, 1976), pp. 327–61.
———. "Regional Urbanization in Nineteenth-Century China," in G. William Skinner, ed., *The City in Late Imperial China* (Stanford, Calif., 1977), pp. 211–49.
———, ed. *The City in Late Imperial China*. Stanford, Calif., 1977.

Song Cikuei. "Tang Shouqian zhuan" (Biography of Tang Shouqian), *Guoshi guan guankan* (Bulletin of the National Institute of History), 1.2: 80–82 (Mar. 1948).

Song Heng. *Liuzhai beiyi* (Humble proposals from Liuzhai), in Huang Qun, ed., *Jingxiang lou congshu* (A collection from the Jingxiang studio) (Yongjia, 1929), vol. 1, chap. 10. Also excerpted in Song Heng, *Song Pingzi wenchao* (Shanghai, 1947), pp. 14–33.

———. *Song Pingzi wenchao* (The writings of Song Heng). Shanghai, 1947.

Songyang xianzhi (Gazetteer of Songyang district). 1926.

Spector, Stanley. *Li Hung-chang and the Huai Army: A Study in Nineteenth-Century Chinese Regionalism.* Seattle, 1964.

Stanley, John C. *Late Ch'ing Finance: Hu Kuang-yung as an Innovator.* Cambridge, Mass., 1961.

Stepan, Alfred. *The State and Society: Peru in Comparative Perspective.* Princeton, 1978.

Su bao (The Jiangsu journal). 1903. Reprint, Taibei, 1968.

Su Dunyuan. *Zhang Yangyuan xiansheng nianpu* (A chronological biography of Zhang Lüxiang). Hangzhou, 1864.

Su Yuanlei. *Song Pingzi pingzhuan* (A critical biography of Song Heng). Shanghai, 1947.

Suian xianzhi (Gazetteer of Suian district). 1930.

Suichang xianzhi (Gazetteer of Suichang district). 1896.

Sun, E-tu Zen. "Sericulture and Silk Textile Production in Ch'ing China," in W. E. Willmott, *Economic Organization in Chinese Society* (Stanford, Calif., 1972), pp. 79–108.

———. "The Shanghai-Hangchou-Ningpo Railway Loan of 1908," *The Far Eastern Quarterly*, 10.2: 136–50 (Feb. 1951).

Sun Yirang. *Zhouli zhengyao* (The political essentials of the Rites of Zhou). 1906.

———. *Zhouli zhengyi* (The true principles of the Rites of Zhou). 1905. Reprint, Taibei, 1959(?).

———. *Zhouqing yiwen* (Posthumous works of Sun Yirang). Ruian, 1926.

Sun Yiyan. *Sunxue zhai wenchao* (Literary collection from the Studio of Humble Study). 1864–73.

———. *Sunxue zhai xu wenchao* (Supplementary literary collection from the Studio of Humble Study). c. 1873.

———. *Yongjia congshu* (A collection of writings from Yongjia). Ruian, 1877.

Sun Yutang. *Zhongguo jindai gongye shi ziliao* (Materials on the history of Chinese modern industry), vol. 1, pt. 2 (*1840–1895*); vol. 2, pt. 2 (*1895–1914*). Beijing, 1957.

Taga Akigoro. *Kinsei higashi Ajia kyōiku shi kenkyū* (Research on the history of education in modern East Asia). Tokyo, 1970.

Tahara Tennan [Tahara Teijirō]. *Shimmatsu minsho Chūgoku kanshu jimmeiku* (Biographies of officials and gentry of the late Qing and early Republic). Beijing, 1918.

Taiping xianzhi (Gazetteer of Taiping district). 1894.

Taizhou fuzhi (Gazetteer of Taizhou prefecture). 1936.

Tan Baozhen, et al., eds. *Tan Wenqingong (Zonglin) zougao* (Draft memorials of Tan Zhonglin). Taibei, 1969.

Tang Zhaoxi. *Chushan caopu* (Draft records from the mountains). 1884.

Tang Zhen. *Qianshu* (Writings in retirement). Preface dated 1703. Reprint, Beijing, 1963.

Tang Zhen [Tang Shouqian]. *Weiyan* (Words of warning). Shanghai, 1896.

Tang Zhijun. *Wuxu bianfa renwu zhuan gao* (Draft biographies of persons in the 1898 Reform Movement). 2 vols. Beijing, 1961.

———. *Wuxu bianfa shi luncong* (Collected essays on the 1898 Reform Movement). Hong Kong, 1961.

Tangqi xianzhi (Gazetteer of Tangqi district). 1931.

Tangqi zhi (Gazetteer of Tangqi town). 1890.

Tao Chengzhang. "Zhean jilüe" (A brief account of the revolts in Zhejiang), in *Xinhai geming* (The 1911 Revolution), ed. by Zhongguo shixue hui (Chinese Historical Association) (Shanghai, 1957), 3: 3–111.

Tillman, Hoyt C. *Utilitarian Confucianism: Ch'en Liang's Challenge to Chu Hsi*. Cambridge, Mass., 1982.

Tilly, Charles, ed. *The Formation of National States in Western Europe*. Princeton, 1975.

Tilly, Charles, Louise Tilly, and Richard Tilly. *The Rebellious Century, 1830–1930*. Cambridge, Mass., 1975.

Tōa Dōbunkai (East Asian Language Association). *Chūgoku nenkan* (China yearbook). 1911. Reprint, Taibei, 1973.

———. *Shina shōbetsu zenshi* (Complete gazetteer of China by provinces), vol. 13, *Sekko-shō* (Zhejiang). Tokyo, 1919.

Tong Feiyong. *Tong Wen-Chu gong yishu* (Posthumous writings of Wenzhou-Chuzhou Daotai Tong). N.p., n.d.

Tongxiang xianzhi (Gazetteer of Tongxiang district). 1881.

United States Department of State. General Records (Record Group 59). Diplomatic Correspondence: Decimal File, 1901–5.

———. General Records. Central Files (1906–29). Numerical File, 1906–12.

Wakeman, Frederic, Jr. *Strangers at the Gate: Social Disorder in South China, 1839–1861*. Berkeley, Calif., 1966.

———. "The Price of Autonomy: Intellectuals in Ming and Ch'ing Politics," *Daedalus*, 102.2: 35–70 (Spring 1972).

Wakeman, Frederic, Jr., and Carolyn Grant, eds. *Conflict and Control in Late Imperial China*. Berkeley, Calif., 1975.

Wallerstein, Immanuel. *The Modern World-System*. New York, 1976.

Wang Ermin. "Qingji xuehui huibiao" (A classified list of study societies of the late Qing), *Dalu zazhi* (The continent magazine), 24.2: 14–20 (Jan. 31, 1962); 24.3: 16–23 (Feb. 15, 1962).

Wang Gengsheng. *Zhouqing xue ji* (A record of Sun Yirang's studies). 2 vols. Taibei, 1972.

Wang Jingyu. "Birth of the Chinese Bourgeoisic." *Chinese Studies in History*, 17.4: 3–25 (Summer 1984).

Wang, Yeh-chien. *Land Taxation in Imperial China, 1750–1911.* Cambridge, Mass., 1973.

———. "The Secular Trend of Prices during the Ch'ing Period (1644–1911)," *The Journal of the Institute of Chinese Studies of the Chinese University of Hong Kong*, 5.2: 347–72 (Dec. 1972).

Wang Yinian. *Wang Rangqing (Kangnian) xiansheng zhuanji, yiwen* (Biography and posthumous works of Mr. Wang Rangqing (Kangnian). Reprint, Taibei, 1966.

Watt, John R. *The District Magistrate in Late Imperial China.* New York, 1972.

Weber, Max. *The Religion of China.* Glencoe, Ill., 1951.

Wei Songtang. *Zhejiang jingji jilüe* (An outline of the Zhejiang economy). 1929.

Weiss, Robert. "Flexibility in Provincial Government on the Eve of the Taiping Rebellion," *Ch'ing-shih wen-t'i*, 4.3: 1–42 (June 1980).

Whitbeck, Judith. "The Historical Vision of Kung Tzu-chen, 1792–1841." Ph.D. diss., Univ. of California, Berkeley, 1980.

Wilber, C. K., ed. *The Political Economy of Development and Underdevelopment.* New York, 1973.

Willmott, W. E., ed. *Economic Organization in Chinese Society.* Stanford, Calif., 1972.

Wittfogel, Karl A. *Oriental Despotism: A Comparative Study of Total Power.* New Haven, Conn., 1957.

Woodside, Alexander. "Some Mid-Qing Theorists of Popular Schools," *Modern China*, 9.1: 3–36 (Jan 1983).

Wright, Mary C. *The Last Stand of Chinese Conservatism: The T'ung-chih Restoration, 1862–1874.* Stanford, Calif., 1957.

———, ed. *China in Revolution: The First Phase, 1900–1913.* New Haven, Conn., 1968.

Wu Kang. "Nan Song Xiangxue yu Zhexue" (The Hunan school and the Zhejiang school of the Southern Song), *Xueshu jikan* (Academic review quarterly), 4.2: 1–9 (1955).

Wu-Qing zhenzhi (Gazetteer of Wu and Qing towns). 1936.

Wucheng xianzhi (Gazetteer of Wucheng district). 1881.

Wuxing Niushi xizhi jiapu (Genealogy of the families of the western branch of the Niu lineage of Wuxing). 1931.

Wuxu bianfa (The 1898 Reform Movement). Ed. by Zhongguo shixue hui (Chinese Historical Association). 4 vols. Shanghai, 1953.

Xiangshan xianzhi (Gazetteer of Xiangshan district). 1926.

Xianju xianzhi (Gazetteer of Xianju district). 1894.
Xiao Gongquan (Hsiao Kung-chuan). *Zhongguo zhengzhi sixiang shi* (A history of Chinese political thought). 2 vols. Nanjing, 1947.
Xiaofeng xianzhi (Gazetteer of Xiaofeng district). 1877.
Xiaoshan xianzhi gao (Draft Gazetteer of Xiaoshan district). 1935.
Xie Bin. *Zhongguo tiedao shi* (A history of Chinese railways). Shanghai, 1929.
Xie Zhengguang. "Tongzhi nianjian de Jinling shuju" (The Jinling printing office during the Tongzhi reign), *Dalu zazhi* (The continent magazine), 36.1–2: 46–55 (July 1968).
Xinchang xianzhi (Gazetteer of Xinchang district). 1918.
Xinchao she (New Tide Society), ed. *Cai Jiemin xiansheng yanxing lu* (A record of the words and deeds of Cai Yuanpei). Beijing, 1920.
Xincheng zhenzhi (Gazetteer of Xincheng town). 1916.
Xindeng xianzhi (Gazetteer of Xindeng district). 1922.
Xinhai geming (The 1911 Revolution). Ed. by Zhongguo shixue hui (Chinese Historical Association). 8 vols. Shanghai, 1957.
Xinhai geming huiyi lu (Recorded recollections of the 1911 Revolution). Ed. by Zhongguo renmin zhengzhi xieshang huiyi quanguo weiyuanhui, wenshi ziliao yanjiu weiyuan hui (Committee on written historical materials of the National Committee of the Chinese Peoples' Political Consultative Conference). 5 vols. Beijing, 1961–63.
Xu Baoshan. *Zhejiang sheng* (Zhejiang province). Shanghai, 1933.
Xu Heyong, et al. *Zhejiang jindai shi* (A modern history of Zhejiang). Hangzhou, 1982.
Xuanping xianzhi (Gazetteer of Xuanping district). 1878.
Xuanping xianzhi (Gazetteer of Xuanping district). 1934.
Xue Fucheng. *Zhedong choufang lu* (An account of defense planning in eastern Zhejiang). 1886. Reprint, Taibei, 1973.
Xuebu zongwu si (General Affairs Office of the Ministry of Education). *Disan ci jiaoyu tongji tubiao* (Third educational statistical tables). Beijing, 1910.
———. *Guangxu sanshisan nianfen, diyi ci jiaoyu tongji tubiao* (First educational statistical tables, 1907). Reprint, Taibei, 1973.
Yan Chen. *Mohuayin guan shichao* (Collected poetry from the Mohuayin Hall). n.d.
———. *Tongqi dasou zibian nianpu* (Autobiography of the old man of Tongqi). 1888.
Yan Zhongping et al., eds. *Zhongguo jindai jingji shi tongji ziliao xuanji* (A compilation of statistics on China's modern economic history). Shanghai, 1955.
Yang, Lien-sheng. "Ming Local Administration," in Charles Hucker, ed., *Chinese Government in Ming Times* (New York, 1969), pp. 1–21.

Yangzhou shifan xueyuan lishi xi (Yangzhou Teachers College, Department of History), ed. *Xinhai geming Jiangsu diqu shiliao* (Historical materials on the 1911 Revolution in localities of Jiangsu). Nanjing, 1972.

Yanyuan xiangzhi (Gazetteer of Yanyuan rural township). 1916.

Yanzhou fuzhi (Gazetteer of Yanzhou prefecture). 1883.

Yao Zhenchang. "Xianxian Ying Baoshi xiansheng de zhengji" (The governmental accomplishments of the former worthy Ying Baoshi), *Zhejiang yuekan*, 12.5: 26–27 (1980).

Yao Zong. "Xinhai gemin Zhejiang shibu" (Supplementary history of the 1911 Revolution in Zhejiang), *Zhejiang yuekan*, 1.5: 8–9 (Dec. 31, 1968).

Yapian zhanzheng (The Opium War). Ed. by Zhongguo shixue hui (Chinese Historical Association). Shanghai, 1957.

Yihe tuan (The Boxers). Ed. by Zhongguo shixue hui (Chinese Historical Association). 4 vols. Shanghai, 1957.

Yin xianzhi (Gazetteer of Yin district). 1876.

Yongjia xianzhi (Gazetteer of Yongjia district). 1882.

Yongkang xianzhi (Gazetteer of Yongkang district). 1892.

Young, Ernest. "Politics in the Aftermath of Revolution: The Era of Yuan Shih-k'ai, 1912–1916," in John K. Fairbank, ed., *The Cambridge History of China*, vol. 12, *Republican China, 1912–1949*, Part 1 (Cambridge, Eng., 1983), pp. 209–58.

Yu Yue. *Chunzai tang quanshu* (Complete works from the Chunzai Hall). 1899. 8 vols. Reprint, Taibei, 1968.

———. "Zijiang lun" (On self-strengthening), in Zhonghua minguo kaiguo wushi nian wenxian bianzuan weiyuan hui (Committee on the Compilation of Documents on the Fiftieth Anniversary of the Founding of the Chinese Republic), comp., *Zhonghua minguo kaiguo wushi nian wenxian* (Documents on the fiftieth anniversary of the founding of the Chinese Republic) (Taibei, 1964), 1.7: 587–88.

———. "Fengjian junxian shuo" (On "feudalism" and the centralized bureaucratic monarchy), in Sheng Kang, comp., *Huangchao jingshi wen xubian* (A supplementary collection of Qing dynasty essays on statecraft) (1897), 12: 32a–33a.

Yuhang xianzhi (Gazetteer of Yuhang district). 1919.

Yuhuan tingzhi (Gazetteer of Yuhuan sub-prefecture). 1879.

Yuyao Liucang zhi (Gazetteer of Liucang, Yuyao). 1920.

Yuyao xianzhi (Gazetteer of Yuyao district). 1899. Reprint, Taibei, 1974.

Zelin, Madeline. *The Magistrate's Tael: Rationalizing Fiscal Reform in Eighteenth-Century China.* Berkeley, Calif., 1984.

Zeng Kunhua. *Zhongguo tielu shi* (A history of Chinese railways). Beijing, 1924.

Zeng Zhaoxu. *Yu Quyuan xueji* (A study of Yu Yue). Taibei, 1971.

Zhang Cunwu. *Guangxu sanshiyi nian Zhong-Mei gongyue fengchao* (The 1905 agitation over the Sino-American workers immigration agreement). Taibei, 1966.

Zhang Dechang. *Qingji yige jingguan de shenghuo* (The life of a metropolitan official at the end of the Qing dynasty). Hong Kong, 1970.

Zhang Guohui. "Shijiu shiji houban qi Zhongguo qianzhuang de maibanhua" (The compradorization of *qianzhuang* during the latter half of the nineteenth century), *Lishi yanjiu* (Historical research), 6: 85–98 (1963).

Zhang Jinglu, Lin Song, and Li Songnian. "Wuxu bianfa qianhou baokan zuozhe zihao biming lu (A record of alternate names and pen names of authors in newspapers and journals during the 1898 Reform Movement), *Wenshi* (Literary history), 4: 213–48 (June 1965).

Zhang, Kaiyuan. "The 1911 Revolution and the Jiang-Zhe Bourgeoisie," *Studies in Chinese History*, 18.3–4 (Spring–Summer 1985), pp. 83–133.

———. "Xinhai geming yanjiu de sanshi nian" (Thirty years of research on the 1911 Revolution), in Zhonghua shuju, ed., *Jinian Xinhai geming qishi zhounian xueshu taolun hui lunwen ji* (A collection of essays from the symposium to commemorate the seventieth anniversary of the 1911 Revolution). Beijing, 1983.

Zhang Pengyuan (Chang P'eng-yuan). *Lixian pai yu Xinhai geming* (The constitutionalists and the 1911 Revolution). Taibei, 1969.

Zhang Qiyun (Chang Ch'i-yun). *Zhejiang sheng shidi jiyao* (A historical geography of Zhejiang province). Shanghai, 1925.

Zhang Xiaoruo. *Nantong Zhang Jizhi xiansheng zhuanji* (A biography of Mr Zhang Jian of Nantong). Shanghai, 1931.

———. *Zhang Jizi jiulu* (Nine records of Zhang Jian). Shanghai, 1935.

Zhang Xincheng. *Zhongguo xiandai jiaotong shi* (A history of modern communications in China). Shanghai, 1931.

Zhang Xuecheng. *Zhangshi yishu* (The posthumous works of Mr Zhang). 8 vols. Reprint, Shanghai, 1936.

Zhang Yin. "Gujing Jingshe chugao" (A preliminary draft on the Gujing Jingshe), *Wenlan xuebao* (Wenlan journal of studies), 2.1: 1–47 (Mar. 1936).

Zhang Yufa (Chang Yü-fa). *Qingji de lixian tuanti* (Constitutionalists of the Qing period). Taibei, 1971.

Zhao Erxun. *Qing shigao* (Draft history of the Qing dynasty). 1927. 2 vols. Reprint, Hong Kong, 1960.

Zhao Jinyu. "Su-Hang-Yong tielu jiekuan he Jiang-Zhe renmin de jukuan yundong" (The Suzhou-Hangzhou-Ningbo Railway loan and the anti-loan movement in Jiangsu and Zhejiang), *Lishi yanjiu* (Historical research), 9: 51–60 (1959).

Zhejiang chao (Tides of Zhejiang). Tokyo, 1903–4.

Zhejiang difang yinhang zonghang (The Central Office of the Land

Bank of Zhejiang). *Zhejiang jingji tongji* (Economic statistics for Zhejiang). Hangzhou, 1941.
Zhejiang shengli tushuguan guankan (Journal of the Zhejiang Provincial Library). Hangzhou, 1931–35.
Zhejiang sheng xinhai geming shi yanjiu hui (Society to study the history of the 1911 Revolution in Zhejiang province), ed. *Xinhai geming Zhejiang shiliao xuanji* (A compilation of Zhejiang historical materials on the 1911 Revolution). Hangzhou, 1982.
Zhejiang tongzhi lijin mengao (Draft section on *lijin* for the comprehensive gazetteer of Zhejiang). Comp. by Gu Jiaxiang. 1919.
Zhejiang Xinhai geming huiyi lu (Recorded recollections of the 1911 Revolution in Zhejiang). Ed. by Zhongguo renmin zhengzhi xieshang huiyi, Zhejiang sheng weiyuan hui, wenshi ziliao yanjiu weiyuan hui (The Committee on Written Historical Materials of the Zhejiang Provincial Committee of the Chinese Peoples' Political Consultative Conference). Hangzhou, 1982.
Zhejiang xuebao (Journal of Zhejiang studies). Hangzhou, 1947–48.
Zhejiang yuekan (Zhejiang monthly). Taibei, 1969–83.
Zhenhai xianzhi (Gazetteer of Zhenhai district). 1931.
Zhenhui xinzhi beiguo (A prepared draft for a new gazetteer of Zhen hai district). 1924.
Zhongguo nianjian, diyi hui (The China yearbook, first edition) Shanghai, 1924.
Zhongguo Renmin Daxue, Lishi jiaoyan shi (Chinese People's University, History Department), ed. *Zhongguo zibenzhuyi mengya wenti taolun ji* (Collected articles on the question of capitalist sprouts in China). 2 vols. Beijing, 1957.
———. *Zhongguo zibenzhuyi mengya wenti lunwen ji* (Collected essays on the question of capitalist sprouts in China). Shanghai, 1983.
Zhongguo shiye zhi (Gazetteer of Chinese Industry), vol. 2, *Zhejiang sheng* (Zhejiang province). Comp. by Shiye bu guoji maoyi ju (Office for International Trade of the Ministry of Industry). Shanghai, 1933.
Zhonghua minguo kaiguo wushi nian wenxian bianzuan weiyuan hui (Committee on the Compilation of Documents on the Fiftieth Anniversary of the Founding of the Chinese Republic), comp. *Zhonghua minguo kaiguo wushi nian wenxian* (Documents on the fiftieth anniversary of the founding of the Chinese Republic). Vol. 1, pt. 7, *Qingting zhi kaige yu fandong* (Reform and reaction at the Qing court). Taibei, 1964. Vol. 1, pt. 14, *Zhongguo Tongmeng hui* (The Chinese Revolutionary Alliance). Vol. 6. Taibei, 1966.
Zhou Yunliang. *Tizhai xuji* (Supplementary collection of the posthumous writings of Chou Yunliang). Changsha, 1935.
———. *Tizhai yiji* (Posthumous writings of Zhou Yunliang). Changsha, 1935.

Zhu Fangbu. *Sun Yirang nianpu* (Chronological biography of Sun Yirang). Shanghai, 1934.

Zhuang Jifa. "Qingji xuetang jingfei de laiyuan" (The origins of school expenditures at the end of the Qing), *Dalu zazhi* (The continent magazine), 57.2: 9–23 (Aug. 15, 1978).

Zhuanji wenxue (Biographical literature). Taibei, 1963–.

Zhuji xianzhi (Gazetteer of Zhuji district). 1908.

Zhulin Bayu zhi (Gazetteer of Bayu, Zhulin village). 1932.

Zong Yuanhan. *Yiqing guan wenguo ji* (Illustrious collection from the Yiqing guan). 1877.

CHARACTER LIST

The large number of Chinese names and phrases in the text makes it necessary to restrict this list to those that are most pertinent and are not easily available elsewhere. I have excluded a few very common terms, all place names, names of well-known figures from earlier periods of Chinese history, and all names of persons and books listed in the indexes to Arthur W. Hummel, ed., *Eminent Chinese of the Ch'ing Period*. For names and terms in the Notes, the reader is referred to the sources cited. The reader should of course convert the pinyin romanization used in this book to Wade-Giles before consulting Hummel.

Anding 安定
Ao Jiaxiong 敖嘉熊
Baoguo hui 保國會
Bao Zhe hui 保浙會
baoying ju 保嬰局
Bianzhi wenhui 辨志文會
binxing 賓興
buban 部辦
Cai Rulin 蔡汝霖
Chen Chunlan 陳春瀾

Chen Fuchen 陳黻宸
Chen Qiu 陳虬
Chen Sanli 陳三立
Chen Wei 陳威
Chu Chengbo 褚成博
Chu Fucheng 褚輔成
Chucai 儲才
cun 村
cunwang 存亡
dahu 大戶

Dai Siyuan 戴嗣源
daibiao 代表
daili 代理
dibao 地保
Di Baoxian 狄葆賢
Dong 董
du 都
Fan Fen 樊棻
Fan Gongxu 樊恭煦
Fang 方
Faxue xiehui 法學協會
fengjian 封建
Fu Jian 符堅
Gailiang hui 改良會
Gezhi 格致
gongju 公舉
gonglun 公論
gongshi 公事
gongyi 公議
gongyi ju (she) 公益局（社）
guandu shangban 官督商辦
Guangzhi hui 廣智會
Gujing jingshe 詁經精舍
Guohui qicheng
    hui 國會期成會
Guomin shangwu
    hui 國民商務會
Guoyu 果育
Hai-Chang gongsuo 海昌公所
hang 行
Hang bao 杭報
Hang Xiangzao 項湘藻
Hangzhou baihua
    bao 杭州白話報
hequn 合羣
Hu bao 滬報
Hu Guangyong 胡光庸
Hu Huan 胡煥
Hu Shandeng 胡善登

Huang (Wang)
    Jinman 黃（王）金滿
Huang Tili 黃體立
Jiading tucheng lu 嘉定屠城錄
Jian Dashi 簡大獅
Jiang Honglin 蔣鴻林
Jiang Ruzao 蔣汝藻
Jiang Tang 蔣堂
Jiang-Zhe tielu
    fengchao 江浙鐵路風潮
Jiang Zungui 蔣尊簋
Jiaowu taolun hui 教務討論會
jiaoyu hui 教育會
jieying suo 接嬰所
Jing Yuanshan 經元善
jingshi 經世
Jingshi bao 經世報
Jingshi boyi 經世博議
jiushi 救世（救時）
Jiushi yaoyi 救時要議
junxian 郡縣
kemin 客民
lejuan 樂捐
li 里
li 禮
Li Chengfu 李承輔
Li Houyou 李厚祐
Li Jia 李嘉
Li Lian 李濂
Li Mi 李谷
Li Yuan 李源
Li Zhongjue 李鍾鈺
Liao Shoufeng 廖壽豐
lijia 里甲
lijin 釐金
liren 里人
Liu Jinzao 劉錦藻
Liu Shaokuan 劉紹寬
Liu Yong 劉鏞

Liuzhai beiyi 六齋卑議
Longmen 龍門
Lou Jinghui 樓景暉
Mengxue bao 蒙學報
minben 民本
Minhu ribao 民呼日報
minjuan min(shen)ban
　　民捐民（紳）辦
minqing 民情
minzhu 民主
Mo Bingyuan 莫炳垣
nanmin 難民
Ning-Shao lunchuan
　　gongsi 甯紹輪船公司
nonghui 農會
Nongxue bao 農學報
paijuan 派捐
Pang Gongzhao 龐公照
Pang Yuanji 龐元濟
Pinghu baihua bao 平湖白話報
Puyu tang 普育堂
Qian shu 潛書
Qian Zheng 錢徵
Qiangxue hui 強學會
qianzhuang 錢莊
Qin 秦
Qingliu 清流
qingyi 清議
Qiushi 求是
Qiu shu 訄書
Qiuyi 求益
Qiuzhi she 求志社
Quan Zhe ribao 全浙日報
Quanxue bao 勸學報
quanxue suo 勸學所
qun 羣
rencai 人才
shan 善
shanchang 善長

shangban 商辦
Shanghai xinwen 上海新聞
shanghui 商會
Shangxue gonghui 商學公會
shanhou ju 善後局
shantang 善堂
Shen bao 申報
Shen Baoyue 沈寶樾
Shen Bingcheng 沈秉成
Shen Cengtong 沈曾桐
Shen Dunhe 沈敦和
Shen Mingqing 沈銘清
Shen Puqin 沈譜琴
Shen Shanbao 沈善保
shendong 紳董
Sheng Bingwei 盛炳緯
shexue 社學
Shi bao 時報
Shi Ziying 施子英
shidafu 士大夫
shifan yanjiu hui 師範研究會
shishi 失時
Shiwu bao 時務報
shixin 失心
Siming 四明
siye gongsuo 絲業公所
Song Heng 宋衡
Su Debiao 蘇德鏢
sui gongsheng 歲貢生
Sun Qiangming 孫鏘鳴
Sun Tinghan 孫廷翰
Sun Yizhong 孫翼中
Taigu 太古
Tang Shaoyi 唐紹儀
Tang Shouqian
　　(Zhen) 湯壽潛（震）
Tang Zhen 唐甄
Taohua yuanji 桃花源記
Tong Feiyong 童非蓉

tongbao 同胞
tongshan tang 同善堂
tu 圖
tumin 土民
Wang Daxie 王大燮
Wang Lian 王廉
Wang Lifu 王理孚
Wang Qingmu 王清穆
Wang Tongyu 王同愈
Wang Wenshao 王文韶
Wang Xirong 王錫榮
Weiyan 危言
Wenlange 文瀾閣
Wu Zhenchun 吳震春
Wubei xueshe 武備學社
Xia Xinming 夏辛銘
xiang 鄉
Xianyou hui 憲友會
xiaohu 小戶
Xie Lunhui 謝綸輝
xiezhen gongsuo 協賑公所
Xin'an 新安
Xingye 興業
xinzheng 新政
Xinwen bao 新聞報
Xu 徐
Xu Dinglin 許鼎霖
Xu Guannan 徐冠南
Xu Shou 徐壽
Xu Shulan 徐樹蘭
Xu Youlan 徐友蘭
Xuejia gongshe 學稼公社
xuemin zhi zheng 血民之政
yahang 牙行
Yan Chen 嚴辰
Yan Xinhou 嚴信厚
Yan Yibin 嚴義彬
Yang Tingdong 楊廷棟
Yangzheng 養正

yangji yuan 養濟院
yangwu 洋務
yanlu 言路
Yanshuo hui 演說會
Yao Mulian 姚慕蓮
Ye Chengzhong 葉成忠
Ye Han 葉瀚
Ye Jingkui 葉景葵
Ye Youxin 葉又新
Ying 應
yinhang 銀行
yixue 義學
yizhen 義賑
Yong bao 甬報
Yongjia congshu 永嘉叢書
Yongjia xuean 永嘉學案
Yu Xiaqing 虞洽卿
Yu Zhaoshen 余朝紳
Yuan Zutang 阮祖棠
Yubei lixian
　　gonghui 預備立憲公會
yulun 輿論
yuying tang (ju) 育嬰堂（局）
Zhang Boxi 張百熙
Zhang Zhenkui 張振夔
Zhe hui 浙會
Zhejiang guomin jukuan
　　hui 浙江國民拒款會
Zhejiang ribao 浙江日報
zhen 鎮
zhen ju 賑局
Zheng Xiaoxu 鄭孝胥
Zheng Yongxi 鄭永禧
Zhengwen she 政聞社
Zhengzhi yanjiu
　　she 政治研究社
zhixue hui 志學會
Zhongguo gonghui 中國公會
Zhongguo yihui 中國議會

Zhou Changfu 周昌福

Zhou Jinbiao 周晉鑣

Zhou Xiangling 周湘舲

Zhou Yunliang 周蘊良

Zhouli zhengyao 周禮政要

Zhu Fushen 朱福詵

Zhu Gui 朱貴

Zhu Peizhen 朱佩珍

Zhu Xien 朱錫恩

ziban 自辦

zili 自立

zizheng yuan 資政院

zizhi 自治

zizhi shiwu suo 自治事務所

zizhi yanjiu suo 自治研究所

zizhu 自助

Zong Yuanhan 宗源瀚

zuo 作

INDEX

Library of Congress Cataloging-in-Publication Data

Rankin, Mary Backus.
  Elite activism and political transformation in China.

  Bibliography: p.
  Includes index.
  1. Elites—China—Chekiang Province—History—
19th century. 2. Social mobility—China—Chekiang
Province—History—19th century. 3. China—Politics
and government—19th century. I. Title.
HN740.C44R36 1986   305.5'2'0951   86-5875
ISBN 0-8047-1321-9 (alk. paper)